A SIAMESE PRINCE AND ATTENDANT

THE STRAITS OF MALACCA, INDO-CHINA, AND CHINA;

OR,

TEN YEARS' TRAVELS, ADVENTURES, AND RESIDENCE ABROAD.

By J. THOMSON, F.R.G.S.,
AUTHOR OF 'ILLUSTRATIONS OF CHINA AND ITS PEOPLE.'

ILLUSTRATED WITH UPWARD OF SIXTY WOOD ENGRAVINGS BY J. D. COOPER, FROM THE AUTHOR'S OWN SKETCHES AND PHOTOGRAPHS.

NEW YORK:
HARPER & BROTHERS, PUBLISHERS,
FRANKLIN SQUARE.
1875.

PREFACE.

THE accompanying recollections of my travels are addressed to those readers—I believe there must be many—who feel an interest in the remote regions over which my journeys extended, and in that great section of the human family which peoples the vast area of China—a section which, through the agency of steam and telegraphy, is being brought day by day into closer relationship with ourselves.

I have endeavoured to impart to the reader some share in the pleasure which I myself experienced in my wanderings; but, at the same time, it has been my care so to hold the mirror up to his gaze, that it may present to him, if not always an agreeable, yet at least a faithful, impression of China and its inhabitants; and of the latter, not only as I found them at home on their native soil, but also as we see them in our own colonial possessions, and in other lands to which emigration has carried them.

Since the days of the great Venetian traveller, perhaps no epoch in the history of that quarter of the globe has been more full of interest than the present. At last the light of civilisation seems indeed to have dawned in the distant East; with its early rays gilding the little island-kingdom of Japan, and already penetrating to the edges of the great Chinese continent, where the gloom of ages still broods over the cities, a dark cloud that lifts but slowly, and yields unwillingly to the daylight that now floods the shore, but which soon, perhaps, may be rent and dissipated in the thunders of now impending war.

Certain it seems that China cannot much longer lie undisturbed *in statu quo.* Her deeply reverenced policy of inactivity and stagnation has brought floods, famine, pestilence, and civil wars in its train; it cannot sink the toiling masses to yet lower depths of misery, or stay the clamours of multitudes wailing for sustenance while the rivers run riot over their fertile plains, and the roads have been converted into watercourses. The rulers meantime, with a blind pride, are arming a beggarly soldiery to fight for nothing that is worth defending, and Japan—in the vindication of her own rights, and in the interests of humanity—has planted a small but disciplined army on what is really an integral portion of the Chinese soil.

To these few words let me add that, with a view to supply not merely a pleasant readable book, but information as complete as it is trustworthy, I have in the latter part of the present work reproduced and amplified some passages which I had already given to the world in my 'Illustrations of China and its People,' passages which I have thought to be of some importance, but yet which could not reach the great body of general readers in my larger and more costly work.

J. T.

BRIXTON: *Nov.* 1874.

CONTENTS.

CHAPTER I.

CHAPTER II.

CHAPTER III.

CHAPTER IV.

CHAPTER V.

CHAPTER VI.

CHAPTER VII.

CHAPTER VIII.

CHAPTER IX.

CHAPTER X.

CHAPTER XI.

CHAPTER XII.

CHAPTER XIII.

CHAPTER XIV.

APPENDIX.

LIST OF ILLUSTRATIONS.

FULL-PAGE ENGRAVINGS.

ENGRAVINGS IN TEXT.

MAPS.

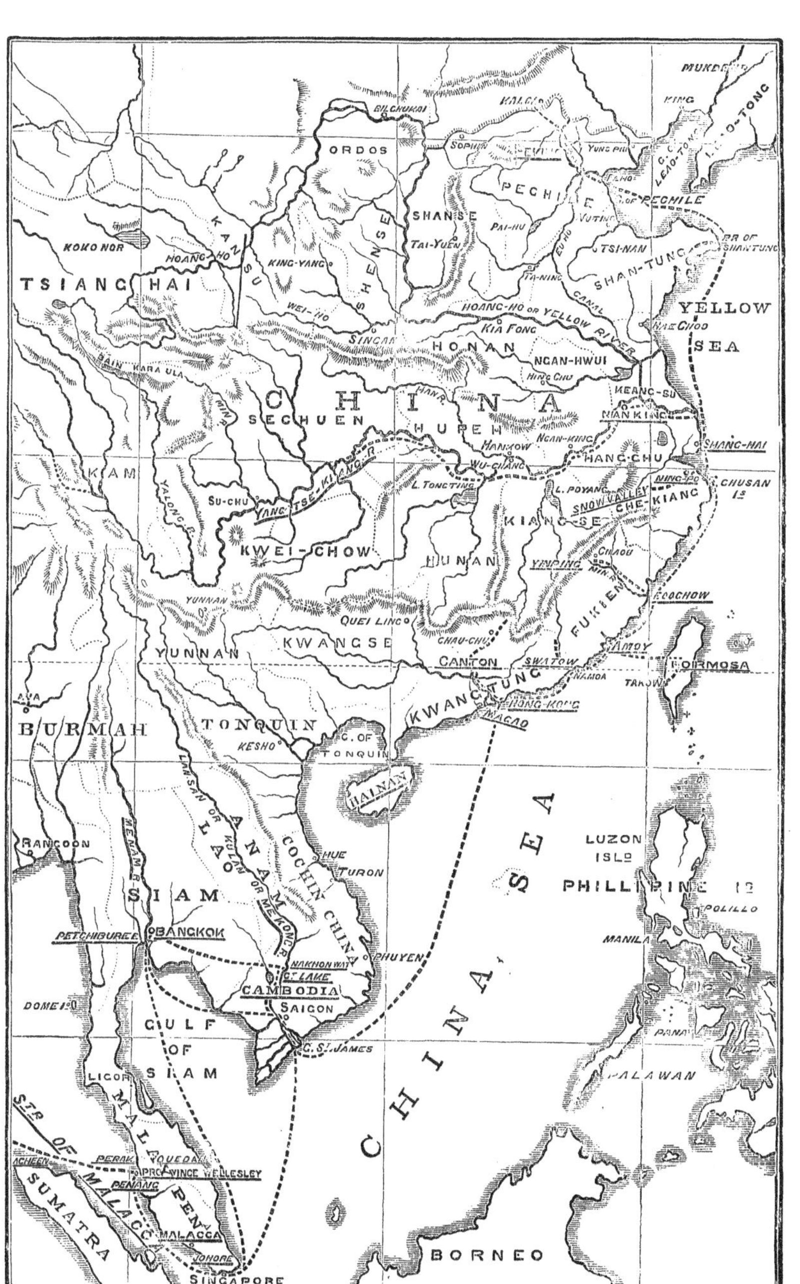

SKETCH-MAP SHOWING THE AUTHOR'S ROUTE.

THE STRAITS OF MALACCA, INDO-CHINA AND CHINA.

CHAPTER I.

The Straits of Malacca—The Dutch Operations at Acheen, in Sumatra—Penang; its Hills, Foliage, Flowers, and Fruit—The Klings, Malays, and Chinese of Penang — Occupations of the Chinese — The Chinaman abroad—A Descendant of the early Portuguese—Hospitality—A Snake at a Ball.

In 1862 the Suez Canal was yet unfinished, and estimated by many a more than doubtful undertaking. The joining of the two seas by a navigable channel, cut through a vast desert of shifting sand, people set down as the fond scheme of a visionary enthusiast; and so when I first quitted England I had to leave M. de Lesseps still carving out his fame in the sands of Egypt, and to follow the old route overland. But I need not pause to detail my experiences over one of the beaten tracks of modern tourists; nor can I even venture to describe Galle, with its hills and palms, and its cinnamon groves, as this part of Ceylon is on the highway to India, and therefore already well known. Had health permitted me, on first returning to England in 1865, it was my intention to have penetrated to the centre of the island, in order to explore its ancient Hindoo or Buddhist stone buildings, and to compare them with the magnificent remains of the cities, temples, and palaces I had just visited in the heart of Cambodia. This project I was unable to carry out, so that my experiences in Ceylon are confined to the narrow limits of Galle harbour and to the adjacent hills—such indeed as fall to the lot of all who travel by the steamers of the Peninsular and Oriental line. I must therefore invite my reader to accompany me still further eastward, to the Malayan Islands and the mainland of Indo-China, where I spent some years of my life, before I can hope to introduce him to people or places with which he may be still unfamiliar.

A voyage to a distant land, even under the most favourable circumstances, has always seemed to me long and tedious. Weary of watching the expanse of placid sea, and the fun and flirtation carried on beneath the white awning of one of the finest steamers afloat, the words 'Land on the starboard bow!' fell gratefully on the ears of the outward-bound passengers. Novels were thrown down, and games of cards, chess, and quoits abandoned; while a dozen telescopes and field-glasses scanned a faint and disappointing line on the southern horizon; that is Acheen Head, and (it may be only in fancy) the breeze off the land comes laden with a tropic perfume from the rich Sumatran coast. Acheen is the point where the Dutch, with their ponderous and sluggish movements, have struck a new blow at the power of the Malays. They have left the wound open and lacerated, but will no doubt return to lop off a fresh slice of territory at a more convenient season.

That Dutch rule in Java has been productive of mutual benefit to the island and to Holland—more especially to the latter—no one will be inclined to dispute;

nor need we doubt that the same desirable result will follow the occupation of the recently subdued provinces which are being added, slowly but surely, to the Dutch dominions in the Malayan islands. At the same time, unless our treaty rights in these regions are carefully guarded, our peaceful and profitable trading relations with those islands may suffer, as they have done, more than once, during the earlier period of our intercourse with the native states in this quarter of the globe. One would imagine too, that Acheen was a most important point to fall into the hands of a foreign power, standing as it does at the north-western extremity of Sumatra, and forming, so to speak, one of the pillars of the western gate of the Straits of Malacca. I therefore doubt whether any power, more formidable and less friendly than the Dutch, would have been permitted or encouraged to annex this territory.

Steaming eastward through the Straits, we are soon within view of Penang: a very small, but at the same time, important and productive island, and the first British possession we reach in the Straits.

A strikingly picturesque place is Penang, with its belt of bright yellow sand and its crown of luxuriant tropical vegetation; forming, too, a sort of sanitorium for our settlements in this quarter, and having a rich alluvial plain which, not many years ago, was an impenetrable jungle, but now is a perfect garden of cultivation. The shaded paths on the wooded hills, which rise over 2,000 feet above the sea, lead to the most charming retreats in the world; to bungalows nestling among rocks and foliage, and to cascades where clear cool water falls into natural basins of granite beneath. There residents may bathe beneath canopies of palms and tree-ferns; while, so balmy is the climate amid these hill-dwellings, that the lightest costumes may be at all times worn.

Many of the lower spurs of the Penang hills, and the valleys which divide them, have been cleared, and planted with cocoa, areca palms, nutmegs, and a great variety of fruit-trees; small patches of the siri vine and sugar-cane are also to be found. In such places there is a deeper and richer soil than on the plains below, while on the summit of the highest hill the temperature is low enough to allow the cultivation of European vegetables and flowers. On ascending the hill to the government bungalow, nothing amid the profusion and variety of palms, flowering shrubs, or tangled jungle, so much impressed me as the stately beauty of the tree-ferns, growing to perfection about 1,600 feet above the plain. This tree-fern rears its bare, finely-marked stem from 15 to 20 feet high above the underwood, and then curling its delicate fronds upward, outward, and in graceful arches, spreads a leafy canopy of the most tender green foliage, which it drops in a multitude of quivering points at a distance of eight or ten feet round the parent stalk.

It will hardly be credited, by those who have never visited a hill country in the tropics, that soon after sunrise the noise of awakening beetles and tree-loving insects is so great as to drown the bellowing of a bull, or the roar of a tiger a few paces off. The sound resembles most nearly the metallic whirr of a hundred Bradford looms. One beetle in particular, known to the natives as the 'trumpeter,' busies himself all day long in producing a booming noise with his wings. I have cautiously approached a tree on which I knew a number of these trumpeter-beetles to have settled, when suddenly the sound stopped, the alarm was spread from tree to tree, and there was a lull in the forest music, which only recommenced when I had returned to the beaten track. One of the most curious insects to be found on the hills so closely resembles the small branch of a shrub, that once, when following a narrow path, I picked up what I thought was a dried twig, but which wriggled and twisted in my hands, and when dropped at last, disappeared in the underwood with wonderful celerity, and a curious jerking motion. Its legs shot out from the stem just like smaller branches, but I searched in vain for this animated plant, which possibly was within eyeshot all the while. I have also seen the leaf insect on the Penang hills, which in its mimicry so imitates the leaf of a plant as to most effectually protect it from harm. The twig and the leaf insect belong to the order *Orthoptera.* The former resembled, most of its kind, the *Bacteria Sarmentosa,* although it seemed to me to be longer, more slender, and of a darker colour. Dried twig insects are species of *Phasma,* and the leaf insect is, I believe, the *Phyllium siccifolium.* Butterflies and moths in every variety and hue are also to be found in abundance, fluttering among the trees and flowering shrubs in the sunshine, where the forest opens. They vary in dimensions from a fraction of an inch to 10 inches or 12 inches across the wings, which is the size attained by the Atlas moth, 'Saturnia Atlas.' Flowers and flowering shrubs or trees are by no means abundant, nor are their hues so attractive, in any part of the island, as to come up to one's preconceived ideas respecting the wild luxuriance of tropical colouring in which scene-painters revel when depicting an Eastern forest or jungle. It is in the gardens of the foreign residents, on the hot plain, that we meet with the greatest variety of indigenous flowers, glowing, most of them, with the brilliant primary colours which seem to me to characterise the flora of tropic regions. I should single out red and yellow as predominating, while all those secondary or mixed colours (excepting green) which exhibit so many tender touches of nature in our home gardens, are conspicuous by their absence from these sunny climes.

Perhaps our men of science might be able to assign a cause for this, and to tell us whether the heat of the oriental sun develops in flowering plants a craving for the absorption of certain colours of the solar spectrum, and for the reflection of others; whether, indeed, the elective affinities of plants in this way are affected by temperature. Can we, in the same way, account for the brilliant plumage of tropical birds, in which homogeneous red, yellow, and blue, are very conspicuous, and also for the liking which uncultured eastern races show for the reds, blues, and yellows. Even in China we find red a token of rejoicing (the bridal costume), while over India and China, and all Buddhist countries, the sacred priestly robes are yellow; and with a number of the races of India and Indo-China the yellow golden skin is esteemed the highest attribute of female beauty. In China, again, blue betokens slight mourning, and white or the absence of colour the deepest sorrow. Be that as it may, I believe that the flowers of our European gardens and woods, can boast a greater variety and delicacy of colouring than those to be found in any tropical lands

I ever visited. The hues are not only much more varied, but in temperate latitudes Dame Nature seems to exhaust her resources in producing an infinite diversity of tints, blended together with such marvellous delicacy and beauty, as to appeal to the tenderest feelings of the most cultured races of mankind.

The foliage of the island of Penang, like that of the majority of the islands of the Malayan Archipelago, is dense and luxuriant, and remarkable more for its variety of form than for its different shades of green. The growth of grasses and jungle in this region is so rapid as to entail the constant labour of the husbandman to prevent their overrunning his oldest clearings. I have seen a sugar-field on Province Wellesley, which had been abandoned for little over twelve months, completely overspread with jungle; and were Penang forsaken by the British to-morrow, or rather by its Chinese cultivators, it would relapse in an incredibly short space of time, into the impenetrable jungle island which Captain Light found when he landed there in 1786. An amusing story is still told of the plan hit upon by Captain Light, to get this jungle growth in part cleared away. He loaded his guns, so the tale goes, with silver coins, and fired them into the thick bush, that the Malays might be tempted to make clearings in their search after the dollars.[1]

The rapidity with which plants will grow in Penang is truly surprising. I have myself watched young stems of the bamboo shoot up over a quarter of an inch in a single night, so that their growth is all but visible to the naked eye. The trailing vines and jungle

[1] *Our Tropical Possessions in Malayan India.* Cameron.

foliage hang over the rocks in long festoons, and creep along the yellow beach to crown old Neptune with a thousand evergreen wreaths.

Many of these plants will thrive without a grain of soil. Orchids, of course, feed on air, but I have seen forest trees rooted on a bare rock, and flourishing there as vigorously as if planted in some rich alluvial earth.

Many of the woods found on the Penang hills are exceedingly hard and durable; their specific gravity is great, as they will readily sink in water. Woods of this sort are used by the Malays and Chinese in making anchors for their praus and junks, while the bamboo and ratan furnish material for ropes, or not unfrequently ready-made cordage.

There are about a hundred different sorts of fruit grown in Penang, but the Durian and Mangosteen are by far the most famous among, them and may indeed be considered the two most delicious fruits of Malayan India. The pine-apple, custard-apple, mango and pomegranate, and some of the other varieties, are also too well known to require description here. Of the Pisang or plantain—probably the most useful and widely distributed of all tropical fruits—there are over thirty kinds, of which, the Pisang-mas, or golden plantain, so named from its colour, though one of the smallest, is nevertheless most deservedly prized.

During the ten months I spent in Penang and Province Wellesley, I was chiefly engaged in photography—a congenial, profitable, and instructive occupation, enabling me to gratify my taste for travel and to fill my portfolio, as I wandered over Penang settlement and the mainland hard by, with an attractive series of characteristic scenes and types, which were in constant demand among the resident European population. I trained two Madras men, or boys as they were called here, to act as my printers and assistants, the Chinese having, at that time, refused to lend themselves to such

MALAYS SELLING DURIANS.

devilry as taking likenesses of objects without the touch of human hands. Moreover they, as 'Orang puti' or 'White men,' shrunk from having their fingers and much-prized long nails stained black, like those of the blackest of 'Orang etam' or black men. My

Klings, on the other hand, were of the colour of a well-sunned nitrate of silver stain all over; and had they, who even pride themselves on their fairness of skin, objected to the discoloration of their fingers, I should have had no difficulty in obtaining negroes of an ivory black in this small island, as a wonderful mixture of races is to be found, and 'phases of faith' as multiform as the nationalities are diverse.

Besides the English residents, who comprise the government officials, professional men, and merchants, there are descendants of the early Portuguese voyagers, Chinese, Malays, Parsees, Arabs, Armenians, Klings, Bengalees, and negroes from Africa. Besides these, the European merchants comprise men of different nationalities. On landing from the steamer it is difficult to discover that one is actually on a Malayan island. We meet one or two Malays squatted beneath the trees selling sugar-cane or 'Penang lawyers' (a polished cane with a large heavy, egg-shaped root), but there are also a host of Klings in charge of boats and gharries (cabs). Dark, sharp and active are these Klings, without a trace of calf on their straight limbs, and yet able to run for a whole day alongside their diminutive ponies without showing a token of fatigue. These men oil themselves all over till they look like varnished bronze, and this oiling may account for their suppleness. All of them speak Malay, and some know a little English. I remember one, who, in his eagerness for a hire offered to drive me to the devil for a dollar. From his appearance I declined the offer, almost fancying myself in the presence of his sable majesty, or his washerman, already.

At Georgetown, on the north-west, opposite the

mainland, there is a Kling bazaar where all sorts of foreign commodities are sold, and at prices which rarely exceed the sums they can be bought for, in the countries where they are manufactured. There are also a number of grog-shops and lodging-houses. The town contains, besides, a large Chinese population, made up of merchants, shopkeepers, and handicraftsmen, immigrants

MALAY BOY.

from the island of Hainan, Kwangtung, and from the several districts of the Fukien province. These men are the most successful traders and patient toilers in the East. We could not do without them in our Malayan possessions, and yet they are difficult members of society to manage. To convey some idea of their usefulness, I need only say, that they can make anything required by a European; and in trade they are indispensable to us, as they have established connections in almost all the islands to which our foreign commodities are carried. Their agents reside in Sumatra, Borneo, and on the Indo-Chinese mainland, collecting produce by barter with the natives, to whom they are not unfrequently related by social, as well as by commercial ties. In this way much of the produce shipped from Penang to England and other foreign countries, passes through the hands of Chinese middle-men.

Then again, the European merchant at almost all the Eastern ports finds it indispensable to have in his employment a Chinese comprador, or treasurer, who not only pays for produce, and receives and collects moneys on behalf of the firm, but is also responsible for the weight and purity of the silver in which payments have been made. Under him he has assistants called schroffs, trained to detect spurious coin, and who display in this matter a keenness of perception which is puzzling to a European; for the schroff sees readily at a single glance, and picks out from among the heap of dollars, some doubtful coin which he himself, however expert, would have failed to discover. But as we shall see hereafter, some of these schroffs have received their education at the hands of the counterfeit coiners and doctors of dollars in China. The comprador hires the labourers who load and discharge ships, and also with the aid of his staff frequently acts as broker in buying and selling for the firm. He is also useful in discovering the standing of Chinese firms, and in procuring for his employer office and domestic servants, for whose good conduct he will hold himself personally responsible. He has seldom any trouble on this score, as the men he has about him and employs are of his own clan, and are most loyal to their chief. I have no doubt, however, that this loyalty is as often due to the dread influence of the congsees, or secret societies to which comprador and men belong, as to the strong ties of kindred which are also esteemed by the Chinese.

It will be conceded, then, that the comprador must be a man endowed with an undoubted capacity for business. He is indeed, in his way, the model trader of the East, and to such men as he, we owe much of our commercial success in these islands. He is, as a rule, thoroughly to be relied upon. He lives temperately, and at all times has his trading wits about him. Yet he never appears other than a leisure-loving, fat, prosperous personage, who, as Mr. Wallace truly remarks, 'grows richer and fatter every year.'

A walk through the streets of George Town will disclose still further the important position which Chinese labour occupies in Penang. There we find carpenters, blacksmiths, tailors, and indeed artisans of every kind, busily plying their handicrafts in open shops, or beneath the shade of wayside trees. All over the island, too, Chinese are scattered as planters, squatters, and tillers of the soil; some of them, who have long been settled in the place, and who have wedded native wives, dwell in large and elegant houses environed with fruit and flower-gardens, while their humble toiling brethren live in rude huts, built of bamboo and palm leaves, in the centre of their small vegetable gardens or pepper plantations; and to outward appearance the latter are the most patient, industrious.

and contented cultivators to be met with on the surface of the earth. But they are not without ambition, as we shall see by-and-by. The Chinaman out of his own country, enjoying the security and prosperity which a more liberal administration confers, seems to develop into something like a new being. No longer chained to the soil by the iron fetters of a despotic government,

CHINESE COOLIE.

he finds wide scope for his energies, and high rewards for his industry. But the love of combinations, of the guilds and unions in which all Chinamen delight, tempts them too far. They first combine among themselves to get as much out of each other as they possibly can, and when practicable to monopolise trade and rule the markets; and then, feeling the strength of their own organisation, the societies set up laws for the rule and protection of their members, and in defiance of the local government. The congsee, or guild, thus drifts from a purely commercial into a semi-mercantile semi-political league, and more than once has menaced the power of petty states, by making efforts to throw off the yoke which rested so lightly on its shoulders. The disturbances at Perak are the latest development of this tendency, and we have had many previous instances of the same insubordination in Penang, and elsewhere. Nor are these the only dangers: the feuds of the immigrants are imported with them, and break out again as soon as they have set foot on foreign soil. Thus, in Penang not long ago there were two Chinese societies, known as, if I remember aright, the Hilum and Hokien congsees, that is the Hainan and Fukien societies. The members of the one were all men from the island of Hainan in Kwangtung, and the others men from the Fukien province. The two provinces are said, at an early period in Chinese history, to have formed independent states, and the dialects spoken are still so widely different, that natives of Kwangtung are looked upon by the lower orders in the Fukien country as foreigners. I was present on one occasion in Penang at a village which, on the previous night, had been sacked and burned by the members of an opposing clan, and it required strong measures on the part of the government to put down these faction fights.

This is the sort of village warfare which, as we shall see when we reach the 'Flowery Land,' the imperial government in the south of China has at times been either unable or unwilling to suppress. In the neighbourhood of Swatow, for example, the village clans were brought into subjection to the authorities only about three years ago, by a process of wholesale slaughter, recalling the summary dealings in 1663 (Javanese era), when the Chinese attempted to overthrow the power of the Dutch government in Java. A Javanese native historian says of the Chinese:[1] 'Their hearts swell as they grow richer, and quarrels ensue.' It has therefore always been a difficult matter in these islands to deal with the Chinese immigrants. Sir Stamford Raffles found it so during the period of his enlightened administration; and the recent disturbances, which I propose to notice in another chapter, only confirm his remark that 'The ascendancy of the Chinese requires to be cautiously guarded against and restrained.'[2]

This is a question which, of late years, has been forcing itself upon the attention of the United States government. They must either restrain the tide of Chinese emigration which has set in upon their shores, or amend their constitutional laws, and adopt some less liberal, though perhaps more enlightened form of special administration, enabling them to deal satisfactorily with a people who bring to their doors habits of toiling industry, the cheapest and most efficient labour, but import at the same time turbulent tempers, an objectionable religion, and some of the grossest vices that can stain the human race. In Penang, where there are few, or almost no competitors in the various occupations in which the Chinese engage, and where their vices break out in a milder form, the difficulty presses more lightly. There the Chinese, when pro-

[1] Raffles' *History of Java*, ii. 233. [2] *Ibid.* i. 253.

perly restrained, are the most useful and most indispensable members of society. True, they smoke opium, they lie without restraint, and whenever opportunity offers are dishonest, cunning, and treacherous; but for all that, those of them who have risen to positions of trust forsake their vices altogether, or—what is more probable—conceal them with Chinese artfulness.

Should you, my reader, ever settle in Penang, you will there be introduced to a Chinese contractor, who will sign a document to do anything. His costume will tell you that he is a man of inexpensive, yet cleanly habits. He will build you a house after any design you choose, and within so many days, subject to a fine should he exceed the stipulated time. He will furnish you with a minute specification, in which everything, to the last nail, will be included. He has a brother who will contract to make every article of furniture you require, either from drawings or from models. He has another brother who will fit you and your good lady with all sorts of clothing, and yet a third relative who will find servants, and contract to supply you with all the native and European delicacies in the market, upon condition that his monthly bills are regularly honoured.

It is indeed to Chinamen that the foreign resident is indebted for almost all his comforts, and for the profusion of luxuries which surround his wonderfully European-looking home on this distant island. At the fiat of his master, Ahong, the Chinese butler, daily spreads the table with substantial fare, with choice fruits and pleasant flowers—the attributes of that lavish hospitality which is the pride of our merchants in that quarter of the globe.

There is a large Malay population on the island, greater than the Chinese. It is, however, a much more difficult task to point out how they are all occupied, as they do not practise any trades or professions, and there are no merchants among them. Some are employed on plantations catching beetles, pruning the trees, and tilling the soil; but, on the whole, the Malays do as little work as possible; some own small

A CHINESE CONTRACTOR.

gardens, and rear fruit; others are sailors, and have sea-going prahus, in which Chinese trade. But I do not recollect ever seeing a single genuine Malay merchant. There are Malay campongs (villages) scattered over the island, made up of a few rude bamboo huts, and two or three clusters of fruit-trees. But many of these settlements are by the sea shore, and there they dwell, fishing a little, sleeping a great deal, but always, awake or asleep, as I believe, chewing a mixture of betel-nut, lime, and siri, which distends the mouth, reddens the lips, and encases the teeth with a crust of solid black.

There are still another class of inhabitants who are the direct or mixed descendants of Europeans. Some

A NEW TYPE OF MAN.

of these, though claiming European descent, are darker, and I should say in every way inferior to the natives themselves. Not many days after setting foot in the island I was accosted by a pigmy specimen of the human race, who declared himself to be of Portuguese extraction. His features were remarkable for the absence of any bad expression, and there were at the same time no good traits lurking anywhere in his dark physiognomy. His dress presented a strange but characteristic compromise between that of the European, the Chinese, and the Malay; his head was surmounted by a chimney-pot beaver hat, only prevented from acting as an extinguisher by a wedge formed of red cotton cloth. As I was a stranger, he politely offered to introduce me to his circle of acquaintances, who, he said, were all Europeans like himself. I felt puzzled to determine what constituted him a European, and was forced to the conclusion that it was the beaver hat.

Naturalists tell us that long residence in a certain region is apt to transform the physical appearance of an animal or insect, but when found it is at once recognised by certain attributes of its family; and so it seemed to me in this case; the transforming influence of long residence had left not a semblance of the original Portuguese parent save the uncompromisingly respectable hat. The only other relic of the civilising influence of the early Portuguese voyagers I discovered in the name 'Da Costa,' which turned out to be that borne by my little friend. Da Costa has been described as a type of men constantly to be met with in the islands, and at points on the Indo-Chinese and Chinese mainland—the result of a complicated mixture of Asiatic and European blood.

On the other hand, at all these places there exists a large and highly respectable community, the educated descendants of Europeans. Among them are government servants, merchants, and professional men, justly proud of the position they occupy; and whose wives and daughters are, many of them, ornaments to society, and boast a beauty which would be prized in any part of the world. This beauty, however, is swift to decay; like garden flowers which shoot up into early maturity, and throw all their vitality into one brilliant effort of glorious colouring, suddenly it bursts forth and suddenly it languishes and passes away.

The men are frequently of very sallow complexion. I have a lively recollection of one who made an unfair impression on me. He had been educated in Calcutta. I was green at the time. This self-introduced gentleman extended his hospitality so far as to invite me to a dinner at the baths, which lie at the foot of the Penang hills. One or two of his friends, of equally sallow and pasty skins, and appalling gastronomic powers, were included in the convivial party.

The entertainment on the whole was enjoyable, and to me new; but the reader may judge of my surprise when, two or three days subsequently, I received a bill for the entire feast.

The introduction of a snake fifteen feet long into a room full of dancers was perhaps the most extraordinary experience I ever had on any festive gathering. The event happened at a ball given by Mr. C., a gentleman who had been educated in Scotland, and fell out in this wise. My friend lived on a small plantation, and had for some time past been troubled by the nocturnal raids of this snake, which had swallowed a pig, and was gradually clearing his fowl-house. A number of natives had been on the watch, and had just captured the reptile, coiled up in a comatose state among the shrubs. The Malays, rarely excited, unless when fighting, or 'running Amok,' and knowing there was no danger, as the snake was overcome by the process of digesting a savoury meal, determined, in a fit of frantic joy, to lay the trophy at their master's feet. They had it by the tail, and dragging it to the sound of quadrille music thump, thump, up the wide staircase, rushed into the drawing-room and laid the monster down.

Motionless it gazed around upon the strange scene, and probably speculated on the prospect of still more sumptuous fare, could it only command its wonted energy and crush its entertainers in its slimy coil. Some of the gentlemen retired with strange celerity; others displayed their gallantry and daring behind a barricade of chairs; while a few stood their ground, supporting their terror-stricken partners, as the unwelcome intruder was hauled off to expiate his crime in the court below.

CHAPTER II.

A Visit to Quedah—Miden missing—The Rajah's Garden—Province Wellesley—Sugar and Tapioca Planting—Field Labour—A baffled Tiger—Wild Men—An Adventure in Province Wellesley.

An officer in Penang being about to visit the Rajah of Quedah, and to hand over to that sovereign's tender care a number of objectionable fugitives, who, quitting his dominions, had taken shelter beneath the British flag, and sought a precarious livelihood by murder and pillage, invited me to accompany his mission in a small government steamer. It was but a short run across the Straits, and about sixty miles to the north of Penang along the coast; and on the way we touched at 'Pulo Tulure,' or Egg Island, one of a group of islets, and the one which the turtles have chosen, in preference to all the others, as a repository for their eggs. On Pulo Tulure is a single hut, and close to the sea beach dwell two Malays, set there to look after the turtles and to collect in sackloads the eggs which they deposit at certain seasons of the year. A single deal table and a few sacks appeared to make up the entire furniture of the hut; and the Malays solemnly declared, as faithful children of Islam, that there was no stopping the turtles when they did commence to lay. That they first covered the beach, which shone like a pearl with their eggs, and that then the two inmates of the hut had to squat on the table, in order that the turtles might lay the residue of their offerings beneath its square wooden legs; the whole process being carried through, so they represented, in a quiet business-like manner by these strange creatures of the deep. They even went so far as to say that a sort of mutual acquaintance had sprung up, and that the turtles would strike to a turtle, and refuse to deposit a single egg, if any stranger were to settle upon the island, in hope of robbing their faithful Rajah of this deep-sea tribute. 'Banyak pandie, orang Malaiu' (cunning Malays!) said my Kling servant.

They sold us a sackload of the eggs, which are esteemed a great delicacy by the natives. They are globose in form, equal in bulk to a large duck's-egg, and are covered by a tough opalescent whitish-blue skin.

It seems strange that the turtle should always show so marked a preference for this island. Although the eggs are removed in great quantities, they never desert it for another.

The occupation of collecting turtle-eggs is one pre-eminently suited to the Malay, for in them they have genuine marketable articles deposited at their feet, without any trouble at all, free of charge. Rice requires labour for its cultivation, it is a long time in growing, and after that it still has to be reaped; even the cocoa-nut palm, which supplies food and fuel, takes years to rear its stately head and drop its treasures into its owner's lap. But the turtle (and no one need wonder) is held in veneration by the leisure-loving Asiatic, as it brings food to his table ready-made.

At the time of our visit to Pulo Tulure we saw a number of turtles swimming about. The sea was of a pure pale green hue, so clear and so placid that we could discern the marine plants and variously-tinted corals, on the rocks some fathoms below—a scene only rivalled in brilliancy by the vivid colours of a tropical flower-garden. A Malay boy caught a huge turtle for us. The capture was simply and deftly effected. He quietly slipped into the water, and swam round until fairly behind his unsuspecting prize. Then seizing it by the shell he turned it over on its back, and in this position floated it quite powerless on to the beach.

One morning at Quedah my boy Miden disappeared. He had gone ashore early, and for some hours I anxiously awaited his return, but all in vain; until at last, my patience being fairly exhausted, I landed with my friend, and after long search discovered the absentee in a village gambling-house, engaged in a violent altercation.

I dragged him at once out of the den, but not without encountering considerable opposition, for the place was filled with Malays, and they, excited by their gains or losses, clutched their krises (daggers) and made ready to resist this sudden interference. However a quiet explanation, backed by the appearance of my friend, and a party of men from the boat, restored order. I then found that Miden, with a few touches of fancy, not altogether foreign to the Indian mind, had been passing himself off as a man of considerable importance, in fact as a Hindoo of very high caste. The Malays, who are usually gentlemen in points of honour, at once conceded that, under the circumstances, I had a perfect right to intervene; and harmony being thus secured, they displayed sundry tokens of their good-will by entering freely into conversation, and exhibiting their krises for my inspection. These krises many of them have beautifully carved handles, while the blades, formed of iron and steel welded together, spring from the hafts in waved edges, and terminate in poisoned points.

My readers doubtless know that 'Amok running' is not uncommon among the Malay tribes, but I am thankful to say that I never actually witnessed this bloodthirsty revenge, which a single frantic Malay will sometimes wreak on society. I can conceive of nothing in human shape more formidable, nothing more fiend-like, than a Malay, trained to the fatal use of the kris, in his last outbreak of passion, dealing out indiscriminate slaughter. Yet the Malay, in his normal condition, is the most social, placid, and tender-hearted of Asiatics.

The Rajah of Quedah is a young man, a fine specimen of his race; his looks are full of intelligence; and indeed, since the date of my visit, he has proved himself to be a wise and careful ruler, and has earned the good opinion both of his own subjects and his foreign allies. Thus it was only the other day, when the Laroot troubles threatened to spread, that he adopted the most prompt and successful measures for the suppression of piracy, at any rate, in the dominions under his own control. The palace where he resides is a brick edifice of modest proportions; and there is an excellent road, some miles in extent, which leads from the Rajah's quarters to his pleasure-gardens. These gardens, though covering a small area, boasted a variety of products and elegance of horticultural design, unsurpassed by any which I have seen in the East.

In one orange-grove the trees were so laden with fruit that the boughs would have broken unless supported by strong bamboo stakes, and the balmy air was steeped in the aroma of the oranges and sweet perfume of the lotus in full bloom. The Rajah had tried in vain to cultivate the grape-vine. His vines grew, but the grapes never reached maturity. We were driven to this beautiful retreat in a handsome carriage of European make.

When steaming down the Quedah river we noticed a score of young alligators swimming in line upstream, and we also had the good fortune of a passing shot at as many more full-grown monsters, as they lay out in the sun on a long spit of sand. Muddy in colour, they, with their long jagged spines, were only to be distinguished from the withered leaves of the cocoa-palm, imbedded in the bank, by a very close inspection.

Province Wellesley lies opposite to Penang, on the mainland of the Malayan peninsula. It is about thirty miles long, and from five to eleven miles in breadth. This district is, at present, the most productive in the Straits, exporting annually a very large quantity of sugar, tapioca, and rice. It adjoins Quedah, and was formerly included in the Rajah's dominions, and was purchased by the British government in 1800. It contains a large Malayan population, but most of the hard work is done by Chinese labourers, or by Klings from the coast of Coromandel.

The Chinese planters were the first who reared the cane, and refined the sugar in quantities sufficient to make it a leading article of export; but European science has long superseded the rude refining processes of the less expert Chinese, and European capital has been invested to such an enormous extent in establishing plantations, as practically to shut out all but the most skilful and wealthy competitors.

The sugar plantations of the Europeans are spread over a wide area ; indeed, they cover the major portion of the cultivated lands of the province. Each plantation occupies some square miles of tilled land, and in some part of the estate there is usually a steam crushing-mill, and a refinery, where an efficient staff of European engineers are kept constantly employed.

Canes of many different varieties have been imported into the Province, but (those from the Mauritius excepted) none are found to thrive so well, or yield so high a percentage of juice, as the reputed indigenous species. Of these there are reported to be six different kinds, and one or two of them I have found growing wild in the jungle. The sugar-cane takes many months to mature after it has been planted; but the crops, whenever possible, are so timed as to come in in rotation, so that the mills may be kept constantly at work.

A quantity of cane is also raised by the Malays and Chinese, and this the growers sell at the mills for a stipulated price per acre.

When I was in Province Wellesley, many of the planters and engineers were big brawny men from the lowlands of Scotland. I spent altogether six weeks in their company, and I still look back with pleasure to a visit which introduced me to a constant variety of adventure and sport, and to so much of the warm hospitality for which my countrymen have always been famed.

In addition to sugar-growing, the planters have brought many of the less fertile tracts of land under cultivation for tapioca—a hardy plant capable of growing in almost any soil, and requiring less trenching and manuring than sugar.

In some places they alternate the crops, or rather plant tapioca after sugar, and then allow the land to lie fallow for a time.

The plant throws up a few long woody stems and large bright-green leaves, but it is from the root that the tapioca is obtained.

This root resembles most the Indian yam, or a huge potato, and in outward appearance is as unlike the snow-white delicate food it produces as coal to the flame it feeds, or tar to the brilliant dyes it yields. The roots are dug up when ripe, and conveyed to the washing-house to be brushed and rinsed in water by machinery. This process completed, they are passed by an ingenious contrivance into a grating machine, which reduces them to a brown watery pulp, and this pulp is then removed by ducts into troughs, where the fibrous matter and skin are separated from the flour, and the tapioca is next passed into tanks of water.

Workmen go bodily into these tanks, stirring up the solution with their limbs. At the end of this operation the flour is allowed to precipitate to the bottom of the tank ; the water is then drained off, and the cakes of tapioca, after sundry washings, precipitations, and cleansings, are dried in iron pans, much in the same way as tea, and finally prepared for market.

The planters in Province Wellesley lead rough and arduous lives. They have many troubles to contend against, not merely in managing their estates, but in dealing with the labour which they are forced to import.

They pass through periods of great anxiety, too, when the crops are approaching maturity, and when a sudden downfall of rain might cause the canes to burst into flower—a sight most lovely to the beholder, but deeply deplored by the proprietor of the estate, for it blights his prospect of an abundant harvest. But after all, care sits lightly on the bronzed faces and broad shoulders of these sugar planters; and they, one and all, find a real enjoyment in the vicissitudes of their adventurous lot. The most agreeable months in the year to them, and indeed to their guests as well, are probably those when the young canes are showing their vivid green blades above the high-banked furrows of the fields, when early morning reveals the heavy night-dews sparkling on every leaf, or glistening like hoar-frost on the webs of the field-spiders, over the low-lying wayside shrub. Then the dawn with rosy fingers lifts the misty veil from off the inland mountain sides, and the air comes laden with a chill and bracing breeze. Armed with a fowling-piece, the planter now sallies forth to his accustomed sport; and so plentiful are the snipe at this season that a fair marksman is certain to secure a dozen brace, at least, before he returns to his breakfast. I have been out of a morning with my friend T., a well-known shot, and I never saw him miss his bird; indeed he never fired unless he could bring down a brace, one bird to each barrel. At times, more formidable game will cross the sportsman's path. Thus, Mr. B., a big powerful fellow, had an unexpected and disagreeable encounter with a wild boar. B. was insufficiently armed. He wounded the brute and it then charged with overpowering fury, and caught its antagonist by the hand. After a terrific struggle B. at last dragged the beast to a deep pool, forced its head under water, and so compelled its drowning jaws to release his own mutilated hand, but not until the boar's tusk had made a huge hole through his palm.

Elephants in former days afforded good sport, but they were fast disappearing as their haunts in the jungle and forest made way for gardens and cultivated fields. In the wildest and more northerly portions of this section of the peninsula, elephants, tigers, rhinoceroses, deer, hogs, and other wild animals, may still be found, more especially in places where only small Chinese clearings have been effected, or where Malay hamlets are scattered at wide intervals amid virgin forests or jungle. In these sparse settlements of Malays and Chinese, Roman Catholic missionaries are at work. I once fell in with one of these priests, shod with straw sandals, and walking alone towards 'Bukit Mer-tagrim' (the pointed hill), to visit a sick convert who had a clearing upon the mountain side. His path lay through a region infested with wild animals; and when I enquired if he had no dread of tigers, he pointed to his Chinese umbrella, his only weapon, and assured me that with a similar instrument a friend of his had driven off the attack of a tiger, not very far from where we stood. But the nervous shock which followed that triumph had cost the courageous missionary his life. I gathered from my friend that he had lived for years among the natives, stooping himself, as it were, to lift them up, and he had grown old in this obscure but useful toil. I have encountered many such men in my travels, and though I do not sympathise with the religion which they preach, I have always admired their self-sacrificing devotion. Protestant missionaries one meets with nearly everywhere, many of them of equal zeal with their Roman Catholic fellow-labourers, but their chief spheres of action are situated at the ports and places of European resort, more

MALAY HUT.

frequently than in the hearts of the countries they have set themselves to convert.

As I have already stated, the supplies of labour employed in tilling the fields, and in the various processes connected with the cultivation and manufacture of sugar, are chiefly obtained from the Coromandel coast in the Madras presidency, where agreements are usually drawn up whereby the men engage to serve on the estates for a certain term, at a fixed monthly wage. On the expiration of the original term of agreement, the coolies are at liberty either to renew the contract or return to their native province. Many of them choose to remain upon the plantations—a fact which speaks well for the treatment they receive at the hands of their employers. Chinese are also used by the planters, although more sparingly, as the gangs of coolies are imported by Chinese capitalists, and only to be hired through a headman, who contracts to do a certain amount of tillage at a price fixed according to area. The Chinese are stronger, healthier, and better workmen, although they require better food, and do not perhaps stand prolonged exposure to the hot sun so well as the natives of India, and the price of their labour is consequently too high to enable them to compete successfully with the Klings; and moreover, planters are not always in a position to have their work done by the piece, nor are the guild-ridden Chinese so easily dealt with as their darker brothers in the field.

There are many Malays in Province Wellesley, but they do not work on the plantations, and indeed it is almost impossible to say how one-twentieth part of the Malay population occupies itself. As Mahometans they practise circumcision, and recite frequent prayers. The rest of their lives they seem to spend in rearing large families to follow their fathers' example, and to wait lazily for such subsistence as the bounty of nature may provide. The male Malay, in his own country, is a sort of gentleman, who keeps aloof from trade, whose pride is in his ever-ready kris, with its finely polished handle, and its pointed poisoned blade. His ancestors, some of them, knew well how to use that kris both on land and sea. There are a few timid woolly-haired races on the mountains inland, who can tell something of Malayan raids, and who still look down with longing eyes on the plains from which their own forefathers were expelled. As to these hill tribes—'Orang Bukit,' 'Orang Outan,' 'Orang Anto,' mountain men, men of the wilds, spirit men—such people, the Malays solemnly assure us, carry tails, whose tufted ends they dip in damar oil and ignite, and thereupon rushing all ablaze into the Malayan campongs, spread fire and destruction around. In this fable it is evident that the Malays have got hold of the exploits of the ape god in the Hindoo 'Ramayana.'

I may take this opportunity of assuring my readers, that the aboriginal tribes referred to, have nothing to show in the shape of a tail; not even the rudiments, so far as I know, to support the theory of progression of species, or of natural and spontaneous development of the human race. I would also ask (even supposing the progenitors of these tribes had tails) why the march of progress should deprive their descendants of such an ornament. If we are to credit the stories which some missionaries penned about two centuries ago, apes in these localities used to find the tail a highly useful appendage.[1] Thus, these ingenious apes are reported to have caught crabs by thrusting their tails into the crab-holes, and dragging out their luckless victims clinging all unwittingly to this monkey fishing-tackle.

[1] *The Oriental Islands*, by Herman Moll, i. 415.

Wild animals, as I remarked, have in a great measure been driven from the province, and were therefore by no means so abundant, as I had been led to expect. One might reside on a plantation for years, and never once be pursued by a tiger, like the fortunate Mr. MacNab. Planters of necessity live far apart, but their custom was to meet about once a week at each other's houses in rotation. This festive gathering was known as 'Mutton night,' as a sheep, when they could get one, was slaughtered for the repast. In former days planters were all bachelors, but the meetings were none the less convivial on that account. Many of them had to travel long distances for their dinner, and on one occasion, when feasting was over, when they had chatted and sung until the night was far spent, a 'dock and dorack' of Scotch whiskey was dispensed at parting to keep out the cold, and brace the nerves against the attack of a stray rhinoceros, an 'orang-outan,' or a tiger. It was rather dark, and verging on the small hours of morning, when MacNab, mounting on his trusty steed, set his face towards home. Feeling at peace with all men, and even with the beasts of prey, he cantered along a road bordered with mangroves, admiring the fitful gleams of the fireflies that were lighting their midnight lamps among the trees. But soon the road became darker, and Donald, the pony, pricked his ears uneasily as he turned into a jungle-path which led towards a stream. Donald sniffed the air, and soon redoubled his pace; with ears set close back, nostrils dilated, and bristling mane. Onward he sped, and at last the angry growl of a tiger, in full chase behind, roused MacNab to the full peril of his position, and chilled his blood with the thought that his pursuer was fast gaining ground, and that at any moment he might feel the clutch of his hungry relentless claws. Here was a dilemma ; the cold creek before him, and the hot breath of the tiger in the rear. A moment or two were gained by tossing his hat behind him, then Donald cleared the stream at a bound, the tiger lost his scent, and MacNab reached home in safety, by what he delighted to describe as a miraculous

PURSUED BY A TIGER.

escape. How frequently a man lives to discover his worst enemies in those who profess themselves his truest friends! MacNab's associates, with wicked incredulity, refused to believe in his tale of the baffled tiger; indeed, they attributed the pony's terror and the frantic headlong rush for home to the presence of a little bit of prickly bamboo which had accidentally got fixed beneath the saddle-girths.

During my visit to one of the plantations a tiger

and her cub were lurking in the jungle, not far from the house. They had been committing depredations among the cattle at a neighbouring village, and could be heard at intervals during the night.

My only unfortunate adventure in Province Wellesley occurred during a storm, when on my way to the plantation of Mr. Cain, which chanced to be the most remote in the settlement. Mr. Cain's estate lay at the foot of a range of hills, where it was said that a certain wild tribe dwelt, and my boy Talep, as he was anxious to see the 'orang-outan,' or men of the woods, was allowed to accompany me on my journey. Having selected a calm morning, we crossed from Penang in a Malay boat, and landed at a native village at the point most convenient for reaching our destination. In the village we hired two waggons, each drawn by a pair of black water-buffaloes, and set out to accomplish the twelve or fifteen miles which still separated us from my friend's plantation. Talep and the baggage were stowed in the leading waggon. I followed in the other, and occupied myself for the first mile or two in admiring the beauty of the forest and jungle along the road.

Our route at the outset took us through a mangrove swamp, which extended over an area of land that had, at no distant period, been covered by the sea. The tortuous roots of the mangrove plants rising in a complete net-work, seemed to have caught and retained the deposits of successive tides, till at last was formed the solid ground along which we were then making our way. We soon left the swamp, and took to the main road, here and there passing some Malay hamlet embowered in rich tropical foliage, and shaded with groves of banana and the broad leaves of the cocoa and areca palms.

Suddenly the sky became overcast with heavy masses of threatening cloud. The bright glare was transformed into dark twilight. The palms rocked uneasily in the breeze, the forest moaned and whispered of approaching storm, while flocks of water-fowl shot across the sky, shrieking from out of the darkness.

Hereupon Talep stopped his men and ordered them to put an extra covering of leaves over the waggons. 'Now,' he said, 'the storm will be on us in a few minutes, and we have done our best to keep the rain out.' We soon discovered, however, that the palm-thatched roofs of our conveyances were by no means watertight.

The road grew darker until night seemed to have closed in, and soon flash after flash of lightning kindled a hundred unearthly hues amid the foliage; peals of thunder shook the ground, and rolled away in echoes through the forest; a strong earthy odour announced the approach of rain, which swept with a dull sound along the road, so that for one moment we could mark its drawing near, and the next it was upon us, like a solid sheet of tepid water. The covering of my cart was useless; the water came through like a steady shower-bath. As for the large buffaloes, they plodded along heedless of the storm; but I kept shouting to the men to mind the ditches, as the road was now completely flooded over, and the carts were dragging through mud up to the axles. As long as we had a line of trees to guide us, the men kept the middle of the road; but when once we left these stately sign-posts in the rear, we were forced to flounder through the mud with ditches six feet wide and as many deep on either side. It was too dark to see far ahead, and the turbid red water was lashed into foam by the bickering rain. The interior of my cart became soaked and slippery, and I was helplessly shunted about from side to side, as the vehicle plunged into the pitfalls of the submerged road. Just as I was making a desperate effort to wedge myself into a corner, I heard a splash and a drowning cry. Talep, waggon, baggage and all, had disappeared into the ditch. I hastened through the slough of mud and water to the scene of the disaster. The driver had dived to extricate the drowning Talep, and brought him up looking little the worse.

He next proceeded to unharness his buffaloes, after which he swam them off down the ditch, and was followed by his companion and their other pair of beasts, before I had even time to remonstrate. Quite unprepared for such a piece of cool audacity, I would have fired over the heads of the vagabonds to bring them to reason, but my firearms were under water. They were off to the nearest campong, to spend the night. The Malays believe in a bountiful Providence, and wait most patiently for its gifts. They believe in fate too. It was 'Tuan Alla poonia krajah,' the work of the Almighty, the carts upsetting in the ditch; and so these men would go comfortably to sleep, believing that it was no use kicking against fate. Feeling it impossible to sustain the gravity the situation demanded, I laughed outright, much to the dismay of the unhappy Talep, who was certain that the evil influences of the 'anto (ghosts) were on him.

Something was to be done. We could not wait

until Providence should disperse the deluge, or draw the cart out of the ditch. It was equally clear we could not of ourselves accomplish either task, nor drag the remaining waggon to my friend's plantation.

To make matters worse, my note-book and directions were under water, and neither of us felt inclined for a descent into the ditch. It was growing dark, night was evidently coming on, so we made ourselves hoarse with shouting, and at length were answered by a responsive voice; and pushing on in the direction of the sound, followed by Talep, we reached a cane-field where I again paused to shout, and had not long to wait for a reply, as my friend the planter had come out to meet us, and enjoyed a hearty laugh at our disasters. As to our ruffianly drivers, they knew well enough, he said, where they were, but fearing his wrath, they decamped for the night.

Settled at last beneath his hospitable roof, I quickly forgot the day's adventure in the agreeable society of my host.

Home and the old country were what we talked of most, and midnight had already gone by, when we betook ourselves to rest. Mr. Cain lit a lamp, showed me to my apartment, and opening a chest of drawers in one corner of the chamber, produced a revolver and sword, gravely handing the weapons to me, with a request that I would stow the one beneath my pillow, and keep the other close at hand. He added confidentially, 'that he never felt quite at ease at night unless his arms were ready, for his predecessor and wife had been murdered in this very house by a neighbouring hill tribe.' Here was comforting reflection for a weary man! and with a sensation as new as it was unexpected, I lay down like a warrior to my rest 'with martial cloak around me.' Soon falling fast asleep, I dreamt of savage tribes. A prisoner in their hands I was to choose one of two alternative deaths. If I objected to being eaten while still alive, I had the liberal option of being cooked, a limb at a time. The cannibals were on the point of seizing their victim, when I suddenly awoke, and found Cain himself standing over me with a drawn sword, flashing in the feeble lamplight. The next moment he had dragged me out of bed. 'Follow me! follow me,' he cried, 'with revolver and sword, just as you are. The hill men are on us.' I slipped on my shoes, and plunged into the darkness, where I soon lost sight of my leader. I could still hear his voice calling 'Make for the fires! make for the fires! my God, they are burning the coolie houses!' I shaped my way as straight as I could towards the light of the nearest fire, plunging and floundering as I progressed now over fields, and now through swampy ground. At last I reached a house, and could distinguish the moans of some one in pain. I found that the building had fallen down, and was aflame at one end. Hailing the sufferer, he replied in Malay that he was killed. In my effort to get at him I stumbled over a huge warm body, and the next moment received a poke in the ribs, which warned me that I had narrowly escaped being impaled on the horns of a huge water buffalo stretched out in the shed. As to the man who declared himself killed, he had been slightly bruised by a falling rafter; and we found that we were the victims of a false alarm, for the storm, which burst forth with renewed violence during the night, had blown down the coolie houses and these had somehow taken fire. We were none the worse for the adventure. I certainly suffered some inconvenience from a number of leeches which I had to pick off my body, but next day I slept none the less soundly on this account.

Before leaving this strange out-of-the-way place, I was shown a huge man-eating alligator which had been trapped in an adjoining stream. It appeared that a labourer on the bank was bathing his child, when the monster caught the babe between its jaws, and disappeared. The alarm spread ; the entire gang of coolies assembled, dammed the stream at two places, and finally secured the reptile with a baited hook.

In another part of the province I fell in with a planter who proved a rather eccentric sort of character, and whom I shall call Mr. Berry. He lived quite alone, and we made up a party to pay a visit to his plantation. The roads through the fields were everywhere bad, but became more especially so as we neared the house, and we kept falling into deep holes filled up with wood and rubbish. Mr. Berry admitted on each occasion that the hole was a bad one, perhaps as bad as any to be found on his estate, 'but hearing you were coming,' said he, 'I had just put a cart-load of fire-wood into the cavity to make it good.'

Mr. Berry was a man of middle age, wearing a sa but not unpleasant expression on his face, and spoke in an accent of broad Scotch. He informed us, amongst other things, in languid tones of regret, that he had just been doctoring the fire-bars of his engine, as he had no engineer to help him. He then invited us to his house, which had an air of solitude and desolation. Berry, however, as he stepped on to his balcony said,

'Wait a bit, and I will introduce you to some of my friends.' We therefore held back, and allowed our host to walk to the front verandah alone. There we saw him stretch out his hand and, whistling gently and soothingly, a bird came fluttering from the foliage, and perched upon his finger. 'This wee birdie,' said Berry to us, 'had once a mate, and the twa used to come at my whistle and take their meals beside me; but now the hen's gone, I've not seen her for some months. She's dead, and left this lad to my care, and I feed the bonny wee thing every morning.' The scene was strange and touching; and although Berry was good-naturedly chaffed for his isolation, it was useless to endeavour to force him into freer and healthier habits. He was plainly a man of gentle and very retiring disposition, but still it was puzzling to make out by what means he had managed to tame the birds which found a home among the weeds and fruit-trees of his garden.

CHAPTER III.

Chinese Guilds; their Constitution and Influence—Emigration from China—A Plea for unrestricted Female Emigration—The Perak Disturbances—Chinese Tin-mining—Malacca—Singapore—Its Commerce and People—Stuffing an Alligator—The Horse-breaker—Chinese Burglars—Inland Scenery—A Foreign Residence—Amusements—A Night in the Jungle—Casting Brazen Vessels—Jacoons.

GUILDS and secret societies would seem almost indispensable to the individual existence and social cohesion of the Chinese who settle themselves in foreign lands. If this were not really the case, it would be hard to say why we tolerate native institutions of this sort in the Straits Settlements at all, for they have proved themselves, and still continue to be, the cause of constant trouble to the government. Avowedly established to aid the Chinese in holding their own, not in commercial circles only, but politically against the authorities, and to set our laws, if need be, at defiance, it can nevertheless hardly be doubted that some of the rules laid down for the guidance of their members are good ones, and embody precepts of the highest moral excellence; but other most objectionable instructions are to be met with, of which the following affords a good example; and from it we may perceive the reason why our officials, both in the Straits and in China, are so often baffled in detecting crime.[1] 'If a brother

[1] *Our Tropical Possessions in Malayan India.* Cameron.

commits murder or robbery, you shall not inform against him, but you shall not assist him to escape, nor prevent the officers of justice from arresting him.' In connection with the foregoing, let us take another of their regulations. 'If you do wrong, or break these laws, you shall come to the society to be punished, and not go to the authorities of the country.' From the two specimens here given, we can get some insight into the obstacles which the Chinese secret societies manage to raise up to shield offenders from justice. So far as my half-score of years' experience goes, I believe that under the rule first quoted a Chinaman is clearly enjoined to conceal the facts of a brother's crime even in a court of law; and as perjury on behalf of a friend is esteemed an undoubted sign of high moral rectitude, and as in our courts a false witness has no torture to dread, no rack nor thumbscrews, the successful disclosers of secrets in China, he lies without let or hindrance, and thus the all-powerful society so effectually conceals a member's guilt as to render Chinese testimony practically useless.

These societies are imitations of similar institutions in every province of the Chinese empire, where the gentry combine to resist the oppression of a despotic government, and the peasantry unite in clans and guilds to limit the power of local officials and of the gentry, and to promote their own commercial and social interests. The Chinaman, however poor he may be, has great faith in the infinite superiority of his own country, government and people, over all others; and when he emigrates to some foreign land he at once unites in solemn league with his clansmen to resist what he honestly deems its barbarous laws and usages. He has no belief in a liberal and pure form of administration. After years spent, it may be, in some English colony or in America, he will yet be unable to shake off the feeling, that he, in a great measure, owes his success abroad to the protecting influence of some powerful clan or guild.

Such societies were at the bottom of the disturbances that threatened Singapore in 1872, and the principal rioters concerned on that occasion were of the class described as the 'Sam-sings' or fighting men, whereof each society has always a certain number in its pay.

The immediate cause of these riots was the enforcement for the first time of a new ordinance, designed to regulate or 'suppress,' as the Chinese chose to believe, a certain class of street hawkers. These hawkers, always useful, if not always innocent members of a Chinese community in Singapore and elsewhere in the East, naturally felt aggrieved at having the prospects of their livelihood curtailed. Some of them went so far as to resist the rough interference of the police. Their case was taken up by the fighting men in various quarters of the town, the Sam-sings, whom Mr. Whampoa (an old Chinese gentleman for many years resident in Singapore) thus describes: 'They live by looting, and are on the watch for any excuse for exercising their talents. Each hoey, or society, must have so many of them, but I don't know any means of ascertaining their number. I suppose they are paid by the hoeys and brothels. They are regular fighting people, and are paid so much a month. If there is any disturbance, these people go out in looting parties; whether ordered by the head men or not,

I cannot say; perhaps they do it on their own account.' From the same report I gather that such characters are at the present time plentiful, as they have been driven out of the neighbourhood of Swatow, in the south of China. In a previous work[1] I have noticed the disturbed state of a part of the province of 'Kwang-tung,' and the strong measures taken by 'Juilin,' the present governor-general of the two Kwang, for the restoration of order. But some of the lawless vagabonds who escaped the vengeance of Juilin have settled in Singapore and other British possessions, and there under the protecting wings of their guilds they obtain frequent and lucrative employment in the shape of pillage or perhaps murder. At first sight it seems strange that the Sam-sings should find scope for their villanies in a British colony; even greater scope, one would be apt to imagine, than they find under the corrupt government of their own disorganised land.

But any disinterested observer who has travelled through China will agree with me in this, that however far behind in other respects, the Tartar rulers, when it suits their convenience, (except when the population is in actual revolt), know very well how to deal with and keep down marauders with a very strong hand; so much so is this the case, indeed, that the scum of the population is frequently driven to seek refuge in emigration to more congenial climes. One element which operates successfully in maintaining order in China, is the superstitious reverence which the Chinese have for their parents. Should a son commit a crime and abscond, his parents are liable to be punished in his stead. This law, even supposing it

[1] *Illustrations of China and its people.*

were put in force in a foreign land, would not affect the immigrants, as they seldom bring their wives or parents with them; and to this fact alone—the absence, that is, of the strong family ties held so sacred by the race—we may attribute much of the difficulty encountered by our authorities in dealing with the crime and vice of this section of the population. It must also be borne in mind that a Chinese ruffian, who would soon be brought to justice (unless he could purchase immunity) if he were practising on his countrymen in a Chinese city, enjoys, on the contrary, the countenance and support of his compatriots in a town such as Singapore. For there he commits his depredations on men of foreign extraction; and the avenger of blood from whom he is hidden away is after all only an officer of those 'white devils,' whom it is the Chinaman's delight anywhere and everywhere to oppose.

A few of the Chinese immigrants marry Malay women, and settle permanently in the Straits; but the majority remain bachelors. If any one, perchance, is unable to realise the hope of returning to his native village, if he should die on foreign soil, his friends expend the savings of the deceased in sending his body back to mingle with the dust of his forefathers in China. Thus we find a steady stream of the living and the dead passing to and fro between the Straits Settlements and the southern provinces of this 'Flowery Land.'

Surely something might be done, in framing our treaties, to alter all this, and to improve the social and moral condition of the Chinese immigrants who land in our tropical possessions. In certain districts of China the women are so greatly in excess of the men, that many girls are still sacrificed in their infancy by their parents.

A small proportion of this surplus female population is annually drawn off by native agents, who purchase them for a few dollars and ship them, often as involuntary emigrants, to foreign ports where their

CHINESE LABOURERS FROM THE KWANGTUNG PROVINCE.

countrymen abound, and where they are imprisoned in opium-dens, and brothels, until their price and passage-money have been redeemed by years of prostitution. This vile type of emigration, like everything in Chinese hands, has long been systematised, and is protected by native hoeys established at different ports. I have no doubt that the coolies, who frequently leave their wives and families behind in China, would gladly bring their partners with them if permitted by government to do so, and if they themselves felt that degree of security in their prospects abroad which the laws of a Christian country ought to inspire. The free immigration of women should also be encouraged, for Chinese girls not only make excellent domestic servants, but are useful field labourers, and they would soon find industrious partners among their countrymen. This plan would also tend to check female infanticide in those regions of China from which the tide of emigration mainly flows

I have already drawn attention to the Chinese faction fights in Perak. Perak is a Malayan state to the south of Quedah, and with a coast line which adjoins Province Wellesley.

The tin mines there have long been famous, and have attracted a large Chinese mining population. Hence it would appear that the Chinese owners of these mines found themselves strong enough to get the upper hand, and to do pretty well what they chose with the local authorities.

The original scene of the recent disturbances was a small stream at the Laroot mines. One Chinese society took upon itself to divert the stream from its old course, and thus deprive the mines, on a lower level, of its use in washing the tin. The aggrieved hoey applied to the native rulers of Perak against their rival countrymen; but the Muntrie, or inferior Rajah, proving unable to settle the dispute, either by arbitration or by force, the Chinese proceeded to drive him from the country, and settle the matter between themselves by the free use of arms.

In addition to the claims of our own commercial interests, we are bound under a treaty to protect the Sultan of Perak and the Rajah Muntrie of Laroot in the event of domestic disturbance. Accordingly Sir Andrew Clarke, the present Governor of the Straits, adopted measures to restore order in the disquieted province, where one of the contending parties had been expelled by its rivals, and had taken temporarily to piracy for a living. Peace has at length been re-established, and the country placed under the direct protection of the British flag. A provisional treaty has been drawn up, and a resident English officer is to act conjointly with the Rajah Muntrie of Laroot in the administration of the country. All this appears to be satisfactory; and I only hope that the decisive steps taken by the Governor of the Straits will meet with approval and confirmation at home, for the suppression of piracy and riot is of vital importance to trade; and the metallic wealth of the country, which passes through the hands of our merchants in Penang, is in itself something worth guarding. A small strip of the Perak coast, with a depth of five miles inland, has now been ceded to our authorities, and I hope to see the same transformation take place there which has happened in Province Wellesley, where foreign capital and machinery are busy in the production of sugar.

In Perak the tin mines are entirely in the hands of the Chinese, but there is a wide field for the introduction of modern mining appliances.

We may form some notion of the methods of Chinese mining from what a recent writer in the 'Penang Gazette' tells us on the subject. A Chinaman, when he is prospecting for the metal, fills half a cocoa-nut shell with the earth; and when he has washed this, if he finds that the residue of metal will fill a space equal in capacity to two fingers, he concludes it will pay him to work the mine.

But when he opens his mine, he will sink a shaft no more than a few feet deep, fifteen or twenty at the most; indeed, he can never be prevailed on to go down to a depth where he is no longer able to raise the water that gathers in the hole by means of his simple but ingenious chain-pump. When the shaft has become too deep for the power of this machine, he abandons it, and never dreams of tunnelling.

The wage of the common Chinese miner is about one shilling a day, and the profit per cwt. of the pure metal laid down free of all charge in Penang, is supposed to be about three pounds ten shillings.

I paid a passing visit to Malacca, but finding it neither an interesting nor a profitable field, I made but a short stay in the place. Malacca is a quaint, dreamy, Dutch-looking old town, where one may enjoy good fruit, and the fellowship and hospitality of the descendants of the early Portuguese and Dutch colonists.

Should any warm-hearted bachelor wish, he might furnish himself with a pretty and attractive-looking wife from among the daughters of that sunny clime; but let him make no long stay there if indisposed to marry, unless he can defy the witchery of soft dark eyes, of raven tresses, and of sylph-like forms. It is a spot where leisure seems to sit at every man's doorway; drowsy as the placid sea, and idle as the huge palms, whose broad leaves nod above the old weather-beaten smug-looking houses. Here nature comes laden at each recurring season with ripe and luscious fruits, dropping them from her lap into the very streets, and bestrewing the bye-ways with glorious ananas, on which even the fat listless porkers in their wayside walks will hardly deign to feed. It is withal a place where one might loiter away a life dreamily, pleasantly, and uselessly.

These are but passing impressions, and Malacca may yet, after all, develop into something in every way worthy of the Straits which bear its name. Malacca is doubtless interesting from a purely historical point of view, for it was once the seat of a Malayan monarchy, powerful probably in the thirteenth century, when the Cambodian Empire was already on the decline. At a later date, the city became one of the chief commercial centres established by the early Portuguese.

Singapore, so far as we know, has no ancient and engrossing history. I gather, from old Chinese and European maps, that the original 'Singapura' was a section of territory on the mainland of the Malayan peninsula, and not the island which now bears its name and usurps its place in ancient history. It has risen, as my readers are aware, since its annexation by Sir Stamford Raffles, to a position of great commercial and political importance.

Not many years ago it was a mere desolate jungle-clad island, like hundreds of others in the Eastern seas, with a few fisher huts dotted here and there along its coast. But there is no need for me to dwell on the recent history of the place. When I first saw the settlement in 1861 I was startled by the appearance of the European town, and since that time it has been yearly registering its substantial progress in steadily increasing rows of splendid docks, in bridges, in warehouses, and in government edifices. During these few years it has passed through strange vicissitudes of fortune. At one time the harbour and roads were crowded with square-rigged ships, Chinese junks, and Malay prahus. Now, were we to take these as the true indications of the trade of the port, we should at once conclude that its commerce had rapidly declined, for comparatively few sailing craft are to be seen there at any season of the year. But we must bear in mind that within that period the march of progress (though almost imperceptible to those who have dwelt continuously in these distant regions) has been rapid and startling in its results.

A submarine cable has brought Singapore within a few hours of London, while the opening of the Suez Canal, and the establishment of new steam navigation companies engaged in the China trade, have, to a great extent, done away with the fleets of clipper-built ships that formerly carried the produce from China and Singapore, by the long Cape route, to England. In the same way the absence of Chinese junks may be accounted for by increased facilities afforded to native, as well as foreign trade, through steam navigation in the China seas. The Chinese and the Japanese too, for that matter, are gradually learning to take the full benefit of the advantages which have thus been brought to their doors.

They travel as passengers, and ship their goods by European steamers. This is not all; they are now themselves organising steam navigation companies of their own. The trade of Singapore, save in times of unusual depression, continues steadily to advance, and since the transfer of the Straits Settlements to the Colonial Office, their commerce is reported to have increased twenty-five per cent.

In Commercial Square—the business centre of Singapore, where buyers and sellers most do congregate—the visitor will find men of widely different types, and a great variety of nationalities; among them all, perhaps, the most conspicuous is the dark statuesque-looking Kling from the Malabar coast, motionless beside his gharry, or darting out from the deep shade of the trees to present his active little pony and neat conveyance before some warehouse, which he has long been watching with a hawk's eye in the hope of a hire. Half-a-dozen at least of his fellow-countrymen crowd up as quickly to the spot as he, and vent their disappointment in noisy gabble, when one more lucky than they rattles down the road with the prize; a pleasure party, perhaps, arrayed in white, and making the most of the short time at their command in a survey of the beauties of the island, which are neither few nor far between. Let us imagine ourselves on the spot. The square rings with that babel of sounds which quarrelling Klings alone know how to raise. Baulked in their hopes, these gharry-men have it out among themselves, and deafen the passers-by with a jargon of most unmusical sounds. These Klings seldom if ever resort to blows, but their language leaves nothing for the most vindictive spirit to desire. Once, at one of the landing-places, I observed a British Tar come ashore for a holiday. He was forthwith beset by a group of Kling gharry-drivers; and finding that a volley of British oaths was as nothing when pitted against the Kling vocabulary, and that no half-dozen of them would stand up like men against his huge iron fists, he seized the nearest man, and hurled him into the sea. It was the most harmless way of disposing of his enemy, who swam to a boat, and it left Jack in undisturbed and immediate possession of the field.

Commercial Square is made up of buildings both old and new. There are the shops, the stores, the banking-houses, and the merchants' offices. There Europeans and Chinese pursue their various occupations. But the rows of new buildings, with their colossal proportions, cast a cool shade over the less assuming, antique, green-venetianed structures, erected in 'the good old days,' in times when the residents might hear once in six months from home, and when two or three successful shipments of produce from the 'spice islands' might bring a princely fortune to their proprietor. 'Those were good times indeed,' said a worthy but unfortunate old merchant to me. 'We lived then above our offices, a small but a very happy community. Now we might almost as well live in London as here ; steam and telegraph bring us daily into communication with the old world. Our Sundays are not our own. By night and by day we are at work, writing for the mail.' His words fell little short of the truth. If we follow the long, cool alleys which separate the blocks of buildings, fragrant odours of spices meet us on every side. Then suddenly we come upon an open court or warehouse, with piles of block tin glistening in the dim light, and with shiploads of pepper, tapioca, sago, gutta-percha, ratans, and other oriental products, awaiting exportation, or being carried busily by Chinese coolies to the ships. The lifting power of these Herculean coolies is startling

CHINESE MERCHANTS

even to those who have grown familiar with the scene. We next enter the office, where we may be able to exchange a few hurried words with the 'Tuan-busar,' or chief; but there is a mail signalled, expected, or going out, and dapper-looking clerks sit at their various desks engrossed with the correspondence. We retire, therefore, in haste,, not without feeling that our society, however entertaining, creates an undesirable interruption there.

Let us return for a stroll round the square, peeping as we pass through the open doors of the bank. Here our ears are almost deafened by the interminable jingle of dollars as they are rung and weighed, or counted by practised Chinese schroffs. Further on is a huge store, and the name of its proprietor, 'Boon Eng,' painted on an imposing array of signboards.

Boon Eng himself accosts you, and invites you to inspect his varied assortment of the choicest European wares. He suggests that you should be good enough to sample his sherry, or 'eau-de-vie,' as they are of number one 'brands,' while his stationery, hosiery, and saddlery, are, as he assures you, by the best English manufacturers.

A fine specimen of the Anglo-Chinese shopkeeper is Boon; tall, and portly withal; but while he courts your patronage, you find yourself instinctively turned towards the splendid carriage and pair which has just drawn up at his door; and your surprise is great when Boon Eng himself—for it is just closing time—lights a cigar, steps into the vehicle, and is driven swiftly off by his Malay coachman to some pleasant villa in the country. The coolies by this time are leaving their work, and even among them one sees many who, naked as they are, do not despair of one day wearing a silken jacket and riding in a carriage like Boon.

But now the tinkle of a bell summons us across the square, and we there find that a horse sale is about to commence. The merchants and their assistants, freed for the day, are scattered about in groups, and assume, some of them, as horsey airs as any votary of Tattersall's famous mart. An Australian ship has just brought a full consignment of horses. There they are, tethered beneath the trees, some of them likely-looking beasts, but somewhat stale after the voyage. One by one they are trotted out by Malays, or Kling grooms, and sold for, from twenty to two hundred dollars a-piece.

I remember Mr. Rarey, formerly a magistrate on one of these islands, investing, at an auction of this sort, in what was little more than the animated framework and leather of an animal. He, however, undertook, with characteristic pluck, to make a horse of his purchase in about three months, and had a small circus made near his stables, in which Rosinante was carefully exercised. He wished to prove how much good living and kindness would do to build up and beautify a jaded, worn-out animal. A few weeks afterwards my sanguine and enthusiastic friend invited me once more to examine the brute, as he thought it was now filling up. Its head and stomach seemed indeed to have become larger; its powers of eating were enormous; but I was constrained to confess that it was even less like a horse than on the day when it had changed proprietors. Ultimately, I believe, it died of a fit of indigestion.

Rarey had strange fancies about animals. I found him on one occasion stuffing an alligator over twelve feet long. I had returned from a trip to the interior, and dropped from idle curiosity into the magistrate's court. Rarey descried me from his seat on the bench, and beckoned me to a place beside him. 'Now,' he said, 'I have been here for a mortal hour, moving heaven and earth to get that prevaricating Kling rascal to tell the truth. He is a witness in rather an important case, and I really believe that for the last half hour he has been struggling against a heaven-born impulse to make a clean breast of it, and feel for once the novel sensation of honesty. But his efforts, mental and physical, have reduced him to hopeless imbecile confusion, and the wretch is perspiring so freely that he has quite vitiated the air.

'Burgoman, throw open that door!' My friend had evidently been waiting with impatience for a gleam of light from the dusky witness, and he had covered the paper on his desk with clever, but by no means flattering delineations, of his oily, shining countenance.

The case had to be adjourned, and we retired to an open space in the rear of the court. There, stretched out upon tressels, and with its capacious full-fanged jaws at their widest, lay the largest alligator I have ever seen. 'I am stuffing this monster,' said Rarey, 'and shall send it to my brother to set up in his hall; for he, like myself, is fond of curiosities which cannot be picked up every day. He has been a man-eater, this fellow; no mistake about it; but there's no stuffing the brute. I wish one or two of my peons (native police) would crawl down his throat. They would never be missed. But lend me your cane; the last lot of stuff I put in is not yet crammed down.' I lent my cane accordingly, but I never recovered it, for it stuck fast where many a daintier morsel had vanished in former days, and Rarey, in an effort to get hold of it, only pushed it further out of his reach, and in the end it was associated with the stuffing.

As I have already mentioned, some of the Australian horses are very fair specimens; but others, and those the majority, are Roman-nosed, unsightly vicious beasts; and one which I bought and tried to break for the saddle—a full-chested, fine-limbed animal—had a nasty habit of showing the white of his eyes, and used to buck until his back was like a camel's. Mr. Kugleman, a horse-breaker, undertook to cure him of this trick. Mr. Kugleman was a very powerful man; it was his boast he had never been thrown in his life. I have seen him lift a horse by the fore-legs, and back it into a carriage. Making light of the caution I was careful to administer, he proceeded without delay to mount my steed; and after about half an hour's labour, which covered the horse with a lather of foam, he got him to leave the stable and start down the road freely, at a canter, as if quite subdued. In about another half-hour they returned, the rider with his coat ripped up the back, his face cut, and bearing all the marks of a heavy fall. It turned out that the horse took fright at a stream where Bengallee washermen were beating clothes on the rocks, reared, fell backwards, rolled over, and finally got up again with his rider still on his back. So, after all, Kugleman could still continue to brag that all his life through he had never been thrown.

I must own that I was invariably unfortunate in my dealings with Australian horses. Once I had a young chestnut cob, not quite broken for the saddle, and as I rode him along the esplanade, a buggy, at a furious pace, rounded a sudden bend in the road, and one of the shafts of the buggy cut deep into his haunch. However, I had the wound sewn up, and in a few weeks' time he was well and fit for the road again. By far the prettiest specimens of horse-flesh to be seen in the Straits are the native Sumatran ponies. These are the perfection of symmetry; with small well-formed heads, full tender eyes, and necks that arch gracefully beneath a profusion of mane. Their chests are broad, their limbs fine, their hoofs round and compact; and so full of spirit are these fiery little animals that many of them, if given the rein, would keep their pace up until they dropped down.

But let me now bring my reader back to Commercial Square, and pilot him along Battery Road to the Creek, where Malay sampans and Chinese lighters abound. Crossing this creek by the newly-built iron bridge, we next reach Beach Road and the Esplanade, and may see a number of well kept European hotels peeping out amid the trees of the gardens in which they stand. The esplanade runs round a large enclosure of fine green turf—a convenient cricket-field and recreation ground—while the road itself forms a fashionable resort where in the cool of the evening, and in a double row of carriages, the wives and families of the residents move continuously in opposite directions for one or two hours at a time. In these daily circumgyrations we not only meet our acquaintances, and exchange nods of recognition, but enjoy the gentle exercise and the fresh sea breeze, which are so essential to good health in the tropics. The number of equipages is surprising, and so is the nature of their occupants. It appears to have become necessary nowadays for every resident of standing to keep his carriage, and this because the dwelling-houses are frequently a considerable distance apart. Fashion also demands that the carriage should be as costly a one, and the house as showy, as the owner's means will admit. After all, judging from the luxurious style in which the foreign residents live, we may discover, in some measure, how it comes that times are altered, and why magnificent fortunes are not piled up so easily nor so speedily as in former days.

Perhaps the change is in no way to be regretted, for I question whether it is possible, in any part of the world, to find a prettier home.

The residents, therefore, take the common sense view of the case. They are likely to remain long on the island, and determine accordingly to spend the time as pleasantly as they can. Their fine equipages must, of course, create a spirit of rivalry and a feeling of vanity, but it would be a dull and matter-of-fact world without these two instincts working everywhere around.

Starting from the square again in another direction, we enter the native quarter, or Kling bazaar, where the shopkeepers sell cotton and woollen goods, cutlery and all sorts of glass and hardware. On the opposite side of the street dwell Chinese mechanics and shopkeepers, and there you may get almost anything made which you choose.

These Chinamen are most unsightly to behold. Many of them are as nearly naked as possible, and if at all stout, they delight to expose their piggish proportions to what they believe to be an admiring public gaze. 'A large facie man' and 'large belly man' is looked upon by the Chinese as a very high type of the human race. He is sure to be good-hearted and wealthy, endowed with wisdom, and blessed with length of days. He is therefore careful to exhibit his

CHINESE TAILORS.

unrobed corporation to his admiring countrymen. Thus at mid-day his dress will consist of a pair of straw slippers, and cotton trowsers about six inches long; while if the weather is cool, his shoulders are covered with a white cotton jacket unfastened in front. But let us stop and take a look into this tailor's shop. A long table, covered with a white straw mat, runs up the centre of the apartment, and at it squat a dozen or more men, busy stitching various articles of attire. These industrious tailors are as naked as our fat friend who employs them. They make garments for others, and go themselves uncovered. Their needles are of English manufacture, although similar ones are made in China, and they stitch away from instead of to themselves, as is the practice with us.

In Singapore the Chinese far outnumber the Malays, and therefore they hold a more important position than in Penang, where the Malayan population is in excess. Were any serious outbreak to occur among the Singapore Chinese, I believe it could be suppressed most easily by arming the Malays, for they make first-class fighting men, or else by setting the members of one Chinese faction against the members of another. There are at the present time a number of Chinamen who fill responsible positions. One is an unofficial member of the Legislative Council, others are justices of the peace, and others again hold the opium and spirit farms. Many more own extensive tracts of cultivated land, or have large capital invested in commerce, and it is obviously the interest of such personages as these to promote peaceful and industrious habits among the lower orders of their countrymen.

If we knew nothing of Chinese clanship and Chinese guilds, we should think it strange that the wealthier Chinamen are rarely made the victims of the great gang robberies that, during my time, used frequently to occur. These robberies are perpetrated by bands of ruffians numbering at times as many as a hundred strong, who surround and pillage a house that is always the residence of a foreigner. Chinese thieves are thorough experts at their profession, adopting the most ingenious devices to attain their infamous ends. I recollect a burglary which once took place at a friend's house, when the thief found his way into the principal bedroom, and deliberately used up half a box of matches before he could get the candle to light. His patience being rewarded at last, he proceeded with equal coolness in the plunder of the apartment, not forgetting to search beneath the pillow, where he secured a revolver and watch. These Chinese robbers are reported to be able to stupify their victims by using some narcotic known only to themselves. I have no doubt this was done in the case just referred to, by the agency of the Chinese house-servants, who perhaps introduced the drug to my friend's bed.

Chinese, when it suits their purpose, do not stick at trifles, as may be gathered from the fact that a Chinaman, esteemed a respectable member of society, attempted, on one occasion, to poison the whole foreign community of Hongkong with the bread he supplied. The Malays have told me of cases where, as they averred, the cunning Chinese thief passes the doorway of the house to be pillaged, and tosses in a handful of rice impregnated with some aromatic drug. This drug soon sends the inmates off into a deep repose, from which they will seldom awaken till long after the robber has finished his undertaking, and that in the complete and deliberate style which suits the taste of the Chinese. For I must tell you that they at all times object to vulgar haste, whatever be the business they are pursuing; and they prefer, if possible, to avoid sudden surprises and unexpected attacks. The slightest sound will make them take to cowardly flight, dropping their booty, and their nether garments, if any, in order to facilitate escape.

But when they have a daring burglary on hand, they go quite naked, with the body oiled all over, and the queue coiled up into a knob at the back of the head, and stuck full of needles on every side. The following adventure with a Chinese burglar befel a friend of mine. About midnight, as he lay awake in his bed, with the lamp extinguished and the windows opened to admit the air, he saw a dark figure clamber over his window-sill and enter the apartment. He kept himself motionless, till the thief, believing all to be safe, had stolen into the centre of the room, and then sprang out of bed and seized the intruder. Both were powerful men, and a furious struggle consequently ensued; but the robber had the advantage, for his only covering was a coat of oil; so that at last, slipping like an eel from the grasp of his antagonist, he made a plunge at the window, and was about to drop into the garden beneath when his pursuer, with a final effort, managed to catch him by the tail. The tail, stuck full of needles, and alas! a false one too, came away by the weight of the fall, and was left a worthless trophy in the hands of the European whom its proprietor had vainly tried to rob.

The interior of the island of Singapore is less bold in outline than Penang, its highest peak, 'Buket Timor,' being only 500 feet above the level of the sea. Yet Singapore has beauties of its own such as few other lands can boast. A number of low hills lend variety to the landscape, and high-roads are carried in broad even lines along the intervening plains. Not unfrequently we may travel by these roads for miles through unbroken avenues of fruit-trees, or beneath an over-arching canopy of ever-green palms, while from the same sylvan thoroughfares we may descry the red-tiled roofs of the foreign houses, on the slopes and crowns of the hills. The long and well kept approaches to these European dwellings never fail to win the praise of strangers. In them may be discovered the same lavish profusion of overhanging foliage which we see around us on every side, besides that there are often hedges of wild heliotrope cropped as square as if built up of stone, and forming compact barriers of green leaves which yet blossom with gold and purple flowers.

Behind these fences broad bananas nod their bending leaves, and fan the hot path beneath, while cooler breezes gently ripple among the palm-trees high above our heads. A choice flower-garden, a close-shaven lawn, and a green for croquet, are not uncommonly the surroundings of the residence.

If it be early morning, there is an unspeakable charm about the spot. The air is cool, even bracing; and beneath the shade of a group of forest-trees which the axe has purposely spared, we see the rich blossoms of orchids depending from the boughs, and breathe an atmosphere saturated with the perfume which these strangely beautiful plants diffuse. Songless birds twitter or croak among the foliage above, or else beneath shrubs which the convolvulus has decked with a hundred variegated flowers. Here and there the slender stem of the aloe, rising from an armoury of spiked leaves, lifts its cone of white bells on high, or the deep orange pine-apple peeps out from a green belt of fleshy foliage, and breathes its ripe fragrance around.

Having turned the last bend of the path, we come at length upon a wide flight of steps in front of the house. The tiled roof and wide eaves cover a spacious verandah, which runs round the building on all sides. This verandah is supported by a row of plastered brick pillars of classic proportions, and is enclosed by a carved railing of hard polished wood. It has rattan blinds to shade it, and these may be let down, or rolled up beneath the eaves, as the position of the sun may require. Flowers in China vases ornament the steps, and stand at intervals on the gravel drive in front. On one side a wall of dark foliage casts its cool shade over the dwelling, and from the other we can see through some leafy spaces the rising sun, casting long shadows athwart hill and dale, or mark its faint pencillings of golden light on the distant palm-crowned islands that are gradually emerging from the morning mists in the far-off waters of the Straits.

If perfect peace can steal through the senses into the soul—if it can be distilled like some subtle ether from all that is beautiful in nature—surely, in such an island as this, we shall find that supreme happiness which we all know to be unattainable elsewhere. But here, as in other quarters of the globe—although the residents, many of them, live in princely style, although the air is balmy, and nature bountiful—cares and bitter experiences still make their presence felt. In my own time I have had friends, who, buoyant with high hopes, and in the flush of youth, have left their dear old homes to seek fortune on this distant island, and who have passed away, far from the tender hands that could smooth their pillows, gazing vacantly upon the darkening palms outside their windows, or dreaming of the sweet music of familiar voices.

But there are other special drawbacks to life in Singapore. The heat, for example, is great, and must tell on the European constitution at last. The thermometer shows an average in the shade, all the year round, of between 85° and 95° Fahrenheit, and this high temperature tends with other influences to produce a variety of the most serious disorders which flesh is heir to in the tropics, and a multitude of minor annoyances, of which prickly heat is by no means the least troublesome.

The Chinese, as they stand heat well, ought to enjoy life to the full in such a place as this. Stepping round to the servants' quarters, built on a slip of land in the rear of the house, and hidden away among the trees, we find that 'Ah-Sin,' the cook, has been gambling overnight, and is not yet astir. There he lies, stretched on the Malay mat which he has spread for himself over a bench, and his head pillowed not uncomfortably upon a billet of wood. A decided smell of opium pervades the room; but, after all, that must only be our own fancy, as no Chinese domestic ever smoked the vile drug, according to his own account. Here, too, is a long brick oven and fireplace, flanked by the usual array of pots and pans. The latter all look clean. This evidence of cleanliness in the Chinese cook is no small advantage, as I once actually found a Kling cook boiling a pudding in one end of the narrow cloth which formed his only covering, the other extremity being wound round his loins. The cook's mate, or larn 'pidgin,' as they call them in Hongkong, has already lit the fires, and is making his toilet. He must feel cool, for he wears no other apparel except his tail, and we see him busily engaged in rubbing himself down with a hot, moist cloth. At our approach he rapidly resumes his clothes, and puts on a merry look. Perhaps he has been early astir to see the sun rise. We enquire, and the answer is 'No,' he never saw the sun rise. He evidently thinks we are chaffing him, as he adds, 'he never knew any man who did.'

Perhaps he admires the scenery. No! but he would like, if we could tell him how, to make one dollar into two, and two into four, and it will probably not be long before he discovers the secret. The servants' quarters are well built, and kept clean and comfortable; for, with the exception of the groom and gardener, who are 'Bugis,' the domestics are all Chinese of the same clan from Hainan. The house-boys are now up and at work; one soothes his friends by playing a native air on a Chinese fiddle, fashioned by drawing a snake-skin tightly over about two-thirds of a cocoa-nut shell fastened on to a long handle and tail-piece, and then the strings are stretched lute-fashion outside the whole apparatus. Our friend, the owner of the bungalow, has been out for a morning ride, and has just returned to give us a hearty welcome, and to invite us to breakfast when we have completed our inspection of his abode. The house is floored throughout with polished planks of hard wood. In the centre of the building stand the drawing- and dining-rooms, which we entered from the verandah, and which are separated from each other by siken screens, reaching half way up to the ceiling. To the right and left are the bedrooms, approached through arched doorways, and shut off by similar screens, opening on hinges, and so constructed as to secure complete privacy, while they yet admit the air. In one the bed is enclosed in a huge muslin cage propped on a framework of wood, and large enough to contain also a table and reading-lamp, and an easy chair. This cage is entered by a tight-fitting doorway, and is designed as a protection against the moschettos, for even one of these troublesome insects is sufficient to banish sleep for a whole night through. There are long punkahs in the public rooms, and that luxury is not excluded even from this airy bedroom, for on hot nights a native sits up all night long fanning his lord and master to sleep. It is, doubtless, a great luxury to have a man servant in constant attendance upon one in such a place as Singapore; but at the same time I have no hesitation in saying that it, and other evils consequent upon contact with an inferior race, has a debasing effect on weak natures. Youths who have been accustomed to none of these things, having once acquired the noble science of concocting claret-cup and cocktails, their tropical education rapidly extends to requiring the most contemptible services from long-suffering domestics. When they have acquired a smattering of the Malay 'patois,' they indulge in vulgar abuse, or assume a tone of injured forbearance; and the keynote of their complaints is 'Boy! what have I done that you neglect to relieve me of my boots and coat, prepare my bath, or help me to bed, administer a sherry and bitters when I seem languid, or a cocktail (an American drink) at seasons of prostration?'

The hot climate renders some natures extremely

irritable, and I have known really good-hearted men always in a ferment with their servants; either paying them off in a moment of passion, or praying that they might return to their duties. Thus, some residents are despised by the humblest of Chinese dependents, as in their own country an ungovernable temper is accounted one of the lowest attributes of humanity.

The Singapore residents have devised many amusements for themselves. They have their clubs, their bowling-alleys and fives' courts, and their race-course. Picnics are numerous, and the frequent gatherings at private houses are pleasantly diversified by performances at the Theatre, and concerts in the Town Hall.

There used also to be a sporting club, and more than once I have been out tiger-hunting with its members, but I never encountered anything more formidable than a deer. Singapore has a great name for tigers; however, I never saw but one in its native jungle, during three years' residence on the island. I have frequently heard them roaring at night round my house at 'Bendulia,' a plantation in which I held a share. It may be safely said that tigers do not nowadays destroy a man per diem, as they are reported to have done in former times. Nor is the Singapore tiger an animal at all likely to attack a man face to face. What they usually do is to pounce upon a single unfortunate victim as he bends over his work in some lonely field. The natives say that the tiger almost always attacks from behind, and I once saw the body of a coolie who had come thus to his end. Though only slightly mutilated, it had been thoroughly drained of its blood, and showed deep ragged incisions along the back and behind the head. Herds of pigs roam wild in the jungle, the pests of the Chinese squatters, whose sweet potatoes and other produce they ravenously devour. They afford good sport to Europeans.

I once went out pig-shooting with a party, to spend the night in the jungle. We put up in a small watch-house, one of many such which are elevated in the jungle, standing on posts of bamboo about ten feet above the ground, and with a platform or flooring not more than six feet square; above is a thatched roof of palm-leaves. We were a party of four, one of us an American gentleman, the finest shot in the Straits—or supposed to be, by many. Having proceeded to a clearing close to the jungle, we entered on the business of laying in wait—a ceremony by no means the most enjoyable among those incident to the sport. These wild pigs feed in herds by night; so we spread a store of pine-apples on the ground, and then, with such patience as we could muster, we tarried to see what fortune would send us. Our clothes were of the thinnest; the stinging ants never tired of their attacks; while the bloodthirsty mosquitos buzzing about our heads, and diving into our ears, supported the invading armies of ants by light incursions, which harried our necks and heads, so that it became most difficult to maintain the silence essential to the success of our expedition. At length, after three protracted hours of weary watching and unreproachful agony, we heard the distant snorts and grunts that heralded the approach of the swine. As turtle to aldermen, so are dainty pine-apples to these denizens of the jungle. They had got scent of our bait, and were moving in our direction. They came on, but not incautiously. Now they come on in bristling phalanx, and snort for the encounter, and now they grunt a signal to halt. Swift and agile I already knew them to be ; but now, too, I discovered in them such a happy combination of boldness and prudence that I thought if undomesticated pigs could but overcome their greediness, they might rank among the noblest creatures of the forest. But, alas ! in this case as in too many unhappy instances of the past, the prospect of a rich feast was a temptation too great for their grovelling nature ! On they came crashing towards us, through the jungle in front. We grasped our rifles so as to sweep the clearing, and awaited the charge of the foe ; but unhappily preferring American to English institutions, they swept suddenly round to the field commanded by the doughty sportsman from the United States.

Then a rifle report, a yelling and a grunting, followed by the hasty pattering of the feet of our enemies, as they turned their trotters in full flight ; and lo ! when we hurried to the spot, expecting to find at least one victim to the trusty weapon of our friend, we, to our dismay, discovered him seated on the ground nursing one leg, and threatening in most unparliamentary language Baboo his native servant, who laughed, and lurked behind a tree. It appeared that the leader of the herd, a huge hog, had charged our friend before he could take aim, had ran through between his legs and toppled him over in the act of firing, and carried his followers into the jungle unscathed. Disappointed, but not discouraged, we determined to keep watch, in the hope that the pigs would return. So we fixed Baboo as a sentinel on the bamboo ladder of the hut, in such a way that he would fall off if he went to sleep, and then ourselves retired to rest. When we awoke the hot sun was shining brightly. Baboo, coiled round the ladder like a snake, was still fast asleep, and the pigs, undisturbed, had feasted upon the pine-apples beneath our feet.

There are a few Malay workmen in Singapore. One of these, a certain 'Tukang Timbago,' or worker in brass, whose shop I used to visit, was a maker of rice-bowls, teapots, and spirit-flasks. His mode of casting the brass was most ingenious, differing from any plan which I have seen employed elsewhere. His patterns were minutely made on an instrument resembling a potter's wheel; on this he placed a ball of beeswax, which, in a few minutes, he spun up with his fingers into the form of the vessel he was about to cast; by this time the material had become exceedingly thin. If the vessel was to have a narrow mouth, he made his wax model in two halves, which he afterwards joined together. This done, he next fixed on small cylinders of wax, designed to form ducts for the molten metal. After completing the wax model, he proceeded to cover it with a coating inside and outside of fine soft clay, which he followed up with a second coating when the first was dry, and by continuing this process the whole was at length enveloped in a mass of clay, which was then baked hard in an oven, and the whole of the melted wax model allowed to flow out of the ducts, leaving a most perfect mould inside the clay. A vessel cast by this method presents a wonderfully smooth surface, and is quite true, and ready for the wheel on which it is turned for use. The extreme thinness, trueness, and smoothness of the casting surpassed anything I had ever seen before.

Johore is, in many respects, the most interesting Malayan province on the mainland. It is separated from Singapore by a narrow strip of water, and it is in its wild forests and inland mountains that we meet with a type of man by far the most primitive that these

JACOONS.

regions have to show. These are the Jacoons, who, like the Orang-outan, or Mias of Borneo, are reported to dwell in trees; and yet this poor remnant of an aboriginal people has at times proved of more use to the ruler of the state than the Malays themselves.

The Tumongong, who is the Malayan chief of Johore, has steadily sought the friendly intercourse and council of his English neighbours; and in place of spending all his leisure in the time-honoured science of gambling, in cock-fighting, and in his harem, he has set himself to the task of developing the resources of his country. He has planted steam saw-mills at the point opposite Singapore, this being the place most convenient for the exportation of timber; and he has run a line of rails up to his forests, where giant specimens of the finest timber in the world are to be found. While thus making clearings on new soil, and offering facilities for the industrious Chinese pioneer to settle in his dominions, he is steadily adding to his resources by the export of wood which grows in unlimited quantities in his vast primeval jungles. But while doing all this, he is driving from their wild haunts a simple, untutored, and most interesting type of the human family, the Jacoons, to whom I have referred. This is a race living almost solely on the bounty of nature, in the food-producing trees and shrubs that grow wild in the interior. They are said to be the true aboriginal inhabitants of the land. The pure specimens among them are woolly-haired and dark-skinned; the same sort of people, indeed, whom we meet with in the Papuans of New Guinea, in the natives of many of the Pacific islands, and in the mountains of Indo-China. My only regret is that I do not know more about them. They have been used in various ways by the Tumongong, in cutting wood and clearing a route for the railway. They, however, detest the Malays, and hold no direct intercourse with them.

CHAPTER IV.

Siam—The Menam River—Bangkok—Buddhist Temples—The King, Defender of his Faith—Missions—Buddhist Priests—The Priest in his Cell—The first King's Visit to the Wats—The Court of the Dead—Chinese Speculator investing in a Corpse—The Krum-mun-along-kot—An Inventor wanted—Taking the King's Portrait—The King describes the Tonsure Ceremony—The King's Request—Mode of administering Justice—Gambling—Floating Houses—A Trip to Ayuthia—Creek Life—Visit to Petchiburee.

THE Menam, or Mother of Waters, is for some miles above its entrance a broad, sluggish, and uninteresting stream, flowing between low banks, and flat alluvial plains. When I visited Siam in the steamer 'Chow Phya,' I went ashore at Paknam, the first town on the river, and made the acquaintance of a native officer who had charge of the customs station, and who honoured me with an audience at his residence. There I found him surrounded by a group of crouching slaves, by half-a-dozen children, and by as many wives. The impression the scene made is still fresh in my recollection. The house and inmates differed from anything I had ever come across among the Malays or Chinese; nor were tokens of refinement wanting, in embroidered wedge-shaped cushions, couches covered with finely plaited mats, wrought vessels of gold or silver, and robes of silken attire. The cool and peculiar fashion of dressing the hair, adopted by both sexes, alike resembled an inverted horse-brush laid upon the crown of the head. But the sanitary arrangements were extremely defective; oppressive odours of putrid fish and garlic pervaded the establishment, while the dresses of the party, though finely wrought, were insufficient for the purposes of decency, according to our own more fastidious Western tastes. Everywhere, from Paknam to Bangkok, we fell in with numbers of the people, but with few who were not boating, or bathing themselves in the stream. Here and there a scattered hamlet stood up above the steaming, unwholesome, moschetto-haunted marshes, like some giant grasshopper sunning its back while it cooled its feet in the mud.

As we near the capital, the scenery grows more interesting and varied. Palms, fruit-trees, and groves of feathery bamboo, diversify the plains; and the latter, when covered with half-grown crops of rice, present a vast surface of vivid and beautiful green. I arrived in Bangkok on September 28, 1865, and steamed up through the floating city in the dimness of the early morning light. It is a place which other travellers have already described; yet, as I spent some time there, the reader will pardon me if I give my own impressions of what struck me as its most remarkable features. When I use the term 'floating city,' I mean to say that the dwellings of the people are for the most part afloat on rafts, and it is impossible at first sight to determine where land begins, and where it ends. Before proceeding to describe these aquatic abodes and their amphibious-looking inhabitants, I must remind the reader that my first ideas as to the splendour of this oriental city were gathered at dawn, when I was gazing upon the towers and roofs of more than half a hundred temples, standing each of them in its own consecrated ground. I enquired of what material these strange edifices were made, for their towers seemed ablaze as with jewels, and sparkled like refined gold. The thought (I confess) crossed my mind, how great a profit some powerful Christian government might secure by despoiling these heathen idols, and pulling down these 'summer-palace' looking shrines! But the reply to my enquiry somewhat modified my views, and I learnt to my disappointment that these temples are nothing more than brick and mortar embellished with gilding, foreign soup-plates, and bits of coloured glass. A trader, as I afterwards learnt, not many years back, imported a ship-load of foreign crockery, including toilet-services, dinner-services, dessert-services, and other miscellaneous china wares. But the stock was long in tempting buyers, and remained unprofitably on the owner's hands. At last, however, he persuaded a wealthy native nobleman, who was engaged in the completion of a Buddhist shrine, to invest in the lot, assuring his purchaser that in European places of worship hand-basins and other less ornamental but highly useful vessels were esteemed the most recherché adornments. The simple-minded devotee proceeded in all good faith to decorate his temple, sticking willow-pattern pudding-plates a-row in the plaster, and working hand-basins or dish-covers fantastically into the balconies and parapet ornamentation. But the deception was not long in coming out, and the trader in consequence lost his reputation, together with all future prospect of business with the Siamese. It was said, and I believe with truth, that he was even never paid for the crockery, some of which may still be seen imbedded immovably in the mortar, to point a silent moral on the consequence of commercial disingenuousness. Temple spires in Siam are decorated, most of them, with rich mosaics of glass, porcelain, and enamel, and present, as they shine in the sunlight, a dazzling coruscation which it is difficult to describe. These edifices are usually erected during the lifetime or out of the proceeds of the estate of some nobleman, as sacred and meritorious works. There were, as nearly as I could make out, sixty-five Buddhist temples in the city during the time of my visit, and the priests attached to these numbered more than nine thousand. Bangkok is one of the great Buddhist centres, and the faith there is of a purer type than in the Chinese Empire, where the teachings of Gautama are mixed up with Taouism, with Confucianism, and with the remains of a form of worship still earlier even than these. No Siamese is qualified for an official position until he has been at least three months in the cloister, wearing the yellow robes of Buddhism, and performing the services of a priest.

The King himself is High Priest, and defender of the faith. The late monarch spent about thirty years in monastic seclusion before he ascended the throne, and the distinguished reputation for his knowledge of Sanscrit and Pali scholarship, which he subsequently enjoyed, was due to his having made the Buddhist literature his study throughout this period of his career. Late in life he turned his attention to English, and attained such a proficiency in that language as enabled him to write and converse in it with comparative ease, though with an idiomatic quaintness and force of expression by which his not unfrequent communications to the 'Bangkok Recorder' were at once detected.

He disliked to have his Anglo-Siamese manuscripts mutilated or corrected; and for this reason he established a royal printing-office, where his English, probably under penalty of death, was set up just as it was written down. At one time a series of letters from his pen were published in the 'Bangkok Recorder' under the

SIAMESE BUDDHIST PRIEST.

signature of the Buddhist Champion, and in these he sought to defend and vindicate his own creed. These letters were answered by the late and much-esteemed Dr. Bradley, who spent his life as a Protestant missionary in Siam. Among other things the King maintained that Buddhist images were never set up as objects of worship. These images, always so remarkable for their expression of perfect serenity and repose, were simply designed to aid the souls of the devout in their abstracting themselves from all the cares and strife of natural existence, and in reaching that supreme inanimate repose typified by the idol, and regarded as the chief attribute of the great Gautama himself.

This is all very well for the cultured Buddhist, but then there are millions of men in Siam and China who hardly know who Buddha was, and who have an ignorant belief in the images themselves. The King admitted that the 'teveda' (or angels) of the temples were more or less mythological characters. He did not know whether they had any real existence, or what sort of duties they were designed to fulfil. 'If Christians,' he said, 'have more prosperity than any other sect, if they have more wealth, live to a greater age, have more happiness, and do not grow old, nor die, nor do not become poor, I will agree with you that the Christian religion is indeed a blessing. But this blessing I do not yet see, and how can I hold it?' Another style of argument, and one not so easy to confute, was that Christians are disagreed among themselves as to what their creed should be. There was only one Christ, and there are a great many different sects; the broadest differences existing between Roman Catholics and reformed churches, while narrower shades of faith divide the Protestant ranks. The King therefore summed up his case by the very natural enquiry as to how he was to determine which sect was in the right.

But after all there is no more uniformity of doctrine among the Buddhists than is to be found within the Christian Church; yet, I cannot forbear remarking here, that in the Buddhist countries which I have visited, the sectarianism of the Christian missions is a great bar to their success. If Missionary Societies would but unite, if they would but sink their narrow differences, and agree to abide by one scholarly translation of the Bible into the language of the land they labour in, they would by so doing command a far wider influence among the educated and influential classes than at present, unfortunately, it is in their power to do. As a rule, the missionaries who meet with the greatest respect, even among the lower orders of the natives, are the men of the highest culture and attainments; those indeed, who made the greatest sacrifices when they abandoned their home and prospects, to work on with patient long-suffering, and in obscurity, in these distant heathen lands. Each Buddhist monastery is in charge of an abbot or chief priest, who receives a small monthly stipend from the Government or noble to whom the establishment belongs. Under the abbots are the priests, the novices, and the pupils; the latter receiving their education at the hands of the monks, who are the only schoolmasters in the land. When twenty years of age, the novice, if he chooses, may be ordained a priest; and shaving his head and eyebrows anew, and donning the full canonicals of his yellow-robed order, he takes the priestly vows. Indolent persons and men of doubtful character not unfrequently take to the cloister, for reasons best known to themselves. Each Wat or temple contains as many of the sacred order as the neighbourhood can afford to feed. Every morning, at daybreak, these pauper priests may be met going their rounds by land in silent Indian file, or else sitting like Buddhas, in their small canoes, which their pupils paddle for them from house to house. Mutely they halt before each door, and await the dole of rice, fruit, and vegetables on which they depend for support, the bundles of burees (cigars) and their scraps of betel-nut and seri, with which their long hours of leisure are to be beguiled. Their chambers in the monasteries are almost like prison cells. One priest I knew well, and was in the habit of visiting, divided his attention between the pursuits of literature, perfect self-absorption, and the taming of a colony of white rats and mice. This devotee's cell was lit by a small window, and screened by a faded filthy Buddhist robe, which allowed a feeble streak of sunshine to struggle into the cold interior. At one end of the apartment there was a simple platform of wood, covered by a straw mat. On this he slept at night; on this he sat, wrapped in silent meditation, brooding over his sins by day.

Above, in a dark corner, was a cage where his little favourites were busily at work upon a tread-mill. These rats and mice he tended with the most peculiar care, because their white skins have a sacred significance for the Buddhists, and each tiny body may contain, as is supposed, the spirit of some Buddha of the future.

A number of sacred books on a shelf, one or two bowls of brass or coarse eathenware, and a mat on the clay floor, completed the furniture of the dwelling. This recluse had a taste for drawing, and was occupied in decorating the inner wall of a royal Wat with objects of Buddhist mythology. The cartoons produced were remarkable for gracefulness of outline, richness of colouring, and strange imagery; the faces of several he copied from photographs, and other pictures which I supplied to him; and he would experiment sometimes with my water-colours, though, on the whole he preferred his own, or those of Chinese make. The majority of the Buddhist priests in Siam are, I suspect, but moderate scholars. They can read Siamese of course, and possess, some few of them, a smattering of Pali; but, though they profess greatly to venerate Sanscrit, theirs is the reverence of the ignorant, rather than an admiration for that which they really comprehend. I make this remark from the fact that, after my visit to Cambodia, a number of the most noted priests translated one or two of the inscriptions found on the ancient temples in that country. But although the original texts were in every case the same, the renderings were never alike. My fellow-traveller, Mr. Kennedy, who is now at work translating these inscriptions, has found them to be in an ancient Pali character, much allied to the Kawi of the Javanese; and had the priests been able to travel at all beyond the strict language of their own sacred books, they would assuredly have made these inscriptions out. The late King of Siam was a man of a different stamp; had he given his attention to this subject, I feel no doubt that he could have translated the inscriptions into Siamese, at any rate, if not into the English tongue.

It is the annual custom for the King, in the month of November, to visit certain royal temples, and to make offerings to their priests. On these occasions the monarch may be seen arrayed in all the splendour of his jewelled robes, enthroned in his state barge, and paddled by about a hundred men. Behind him follow the nobles of his court, almost as grand, and thus the

THE KING OF SIAM'S STATE BARGE

pageant moves in long procession down the river or along its network of canals. This 'progress' in boats was one of the most imposing spectacles I ever beheld in the East. I do not, however, suppose that either the first or second Kings ever visited Wat Seket, or even the outer precints of that temple. The principal building at Wat Seket is a huge unfinished pile of bricks and mortar—intended, as I suppose, to symbolize Mount Meru, the centre of the Buddhist universe—the summit of which commands an extensive view of the palm groves, and house roofs of Bangkok; but the special and most melancholy feature of this sacred edifice is a court in the rear, where the bodies of the dead, who have no friends to bury them, are cast out to the dogs and vultures to be devoured. I paid one visit to that place. Few would willingly turn their steps thither a second time! Following a narrow path through an avenue of trees, we came at length upon a walled-in enclosure intended for the reception of the dead. In the centre stood a small charnel house, while the pavement round about was covered with black stains and littered with human bones, bleached white by the sun. An overpowering stench of carrion pervaded the atmosphere of the place. On a sudden the light was obscured, and down dropped a troop of vultures from the trees above, lazily flapping their dry parchment-looking wings, and sweeping a pestilential blast into our faces as they rustled slowly through the air. Next a hungry pack of mangy dogs rushed howling into the enclosure. And then, tardily wending its way up the avenue, followed a procession of slaves and mourners, bearing a naked corpse upon a bier. We made way for this funeral train, and saw them deposit the dead body upon the ground; the vultures meanwhile limping forward with a whistling, jerking noise, thrusting out their bare scaly necks to within a few feet of the corpse, and only kept off by an attendant with the aid of a bamboo rod. At length, when the funeral train had withdrawn, the leader of the vultures ran forward, tapped the corpse on the forehead to make sure that life was extinct, and then, in an instant, had scooped out its eyes. Horror-stricken, we rushed away from the spot, and left these ill-omened birds to feast and squabble over their prey. This was by no means the only sickening sight I encountered in Bangkok. One day, when passing along the main thoroughfare in the city, I found a Chinaman seated by a temple gate, with a naked corpse at his feet. His object was to collect contributions from the devout to defray the costs of cremation. The Siamese responded well to his appeal, as they believe that by practising acts of charity they will win favour in a future state. But as for the Chinaman, he had purchased the body as a pure speculation. He was, indeed, bound to burn it, and he had paid the bereaved family about half-a-crown, promising to remove their deceased relative and burn him at a Wat. Out of the money collected by an exhibition so sensational, this curious undertaker supplied funds for firewood, and pocketed a handsome balance.

I applied, through the British Consul, for permission to photograph the first King's palace. This was at once conceded, and his majesty was pleased to appoint a day on which I should take his own portrait as well. The King requested me to visit his abode on Monday, October 6, in the company of the Krum-mun-alongkot, a nobleman holding the position of chief astronomer, that is, the head of the astrologers attached to the palace. His majesty's letter informed me, among other things, that his royal brother 'was well understanding of the work of taking photographs, and being with Mr. Thomson will have good opportunity to do according to his pleasure in and about this palace.' Here was indeed a fine sample of 'Siamese king's English.' I found the Krum-mun an agreeable old mandarin, but, if anything, a little inclined to boast of his own scientific attainments. He stood about five feet four inches, and was 53 years of age; but he wore a very haggard expression, and indeed looked much older than he really was. He was dressed, when at home, in a light jacket, much too small to cover him, and wore a band of silk around his loins. His shrunken limbs were bare, and his feet encased in richly-embroidered slippers; but on other occasions, when he paid me a visit, for example, he assumed much more ample and costly attire, putting the last finish to the whole toilet by covering his head with a European cap, braided all over with gold lace. Mahomet Ali, a Malay in the service of Mr. Ames, the commissioner of police, acted as my interpreter, translating the Siamese into Malay. Ali was, however, sometimes at a loss to make out the prince's words, as his mouth was frequently stuffed with a ball of seri-leaf and betel. Although kind and hospitable, the prince was not a man calculated to inspire awe into his beholders. Around his singular figure were grouped a number of his attendants and slaves, who crowded reverently on their hands and knees. The room in which we were received was filled with foreign ma chinery, scientific instruments, and articles of domestic use. In one corner there was a telegraphic machine, backed by a statue of Buddha. In the lap of the image there was a Siamese flute (the idol was off duty and under repair), and an electro-plated coffee-pot, which had evidently been forced into some unnatural use. There were also watch-tools, turning-lathes, and telescopes, guitars, tom-toms, fiddles, and hand-saws; while betel-nut boxes, swords, spears, and shoe-brushes, rifles, revolvers, windsor-soap, rat-paste, brass wire, and beer bottles, were mingled in heterogeneous confusion.

Having been dismissed to a sumptuous native repast, served up for me in one of the smaller apartments, I rejoined my conductor at the King's palace gate.

Before leaving this subject, I must confess that I was surprised at the ingenuity which this royal astronomer displayed, and at his honest desire to understand the foreign instruments which he set up in his apartment for contemplation. One day he took a very fine sextant to pieces in order to discover how it had been constructed, and having fathomed the mystery, he felt very grateful to me for helping him to set it again together. Another time he called upon me with a royal letter in a splendid gold case, which set forth that his brother the King (who was a decided wag) had commanded him to find a foreign inventor, a man who could invent anything, and he wished to know how much monthly salary such a genius would require. The King, he said, desired when taking an airing of an evening to indulge freely in shooting his subjects; but the gun must be planned so that the progress of the ball would be arrested when it had just penetrated half an inch beneath the skin. He only wanted, in this way, to strike terror into the hearts of his people by firing at them and then miraculously saving their lives. My noble friend Krum-mun-alongkot may have been a very accomplished Siamese astronomer, able to determine, from the march of the heavenly bodies through stellar space, whether the year, as it passed, was that of the rat, the hog, or the goat; but although he had a number of our finest instruments, he had made but little progress in the science as we understand it. His sextants and quadrants were out of adjustment, his chronometers refused to keep time, and the lenses of his telescopes were dimmed with oxidation. I found him one day busily studying 'Thomson's Tables;' but the book was upside down, and he gave it up in despair as he was called off to put a fresh spoke in a wheel of a royal carriage.

After we had become better acquainted, he introduced me to his family circle. He had, I believe, sixteen wives, although I never saw more than twelve at a time; some of these were young and pretty, but no less timid in their behaviour, than unhappy in their looks. He told me it was a difficult task to keep his wives cheerful; they were modest and graceful ladies, and they expressed their surprise that a foreigner was after all a very harmless sort of animal. They were usually engaged in embroidery, and their needlework displayed both beauty of design and skill. I thought it a pity to see them smoking cigarettes, or chewing betel-nuts, the teeth blackened with the incrustation, and their mouths disfigured with blood-red juice; they had also perforce a nasty habit of spitting into golden vases which their slaves held up dutifully for the purpose. As for the children, they seemed to be born with a cigarette in their mouths. I have actually seen a child leave its mother's breast to have a smoke. This buree or cigarette is made of native tobacco, rolled up in a strip of dried plantain leaf, and cut even at the two ends. These cigarettes may be bought in

SIAMESE LADY.

bundles of one hundred for a few cents, and are really very good smoking.

But to the palace. In front of the entrance gates we found a guard of soldiers drawn up, who presented arms to the Prince as he passed through. Soon we reached an inner court, and there fell in with a group of nobles, who crouched upon the pavement before our royal guide, and seemed, many of them, as if vainly anxious to render their portly figures invisible to a personage of such exalted rank. After a pleasant refreshment of fruit, cake, and wine, we were informed that his majesty was engaged in his morning devotions, and that during his absence we could amuse ourselves by examining the objects of interest in the audience hall. This palace has been constructed partially in a foreign style. A flight of broad marble steps conducts us within the audience hall, and facing us, as we enter, is the throne of state, ablaze with gold and jewels, and erected in the centre of the back wall of the apartment. The furniture in the room made up a miscellaneous collection of Chinese, Siamese, and European wares; the pillars were covered with polished brass to the height of four feet above their bases. At one end of the hall were life-sized portraits of Napoleon III. and the Empress of the French, while a well-executed picture of the late Siamese King adorned the opposite side of the apartment. A shrill blast of horns heralded the approach of the King, and caused us hastily to descend into the court. His majesty entered through a massive gateway, and I must confess that I felt much impressed by his appearance, as I had never been in the presence of an anointed sovereign before. He stood about five feet eight inches, and his figure was erect and commanding; but an expression of severe gravity was settled on his somewhat haggard face. His dress was a robe of spotless white, which reached right down to his feet; his head was bare. I was admiring the simplicity and purity of this attire, when his majesty beckoned to me to approach him, and informed me that he wished to have his portrait taken as he knelt in an attitude of prayer. I accordingly adjusted my instrument, but not without a feeling of some surprise, for I had thought, incorrectly, as I afterwards discovered, that a Buddhist had no need of prayer. All was prepared beneath a space in the court, which had been canopied and carpeted for this special purpose; when, just as I was about to take the photograph, his majesty changed his mind, and without a word to any-one passed suddenly out of sight. I thought this a strange proceeding, and fancied I must have given him some offence; but it was possibly only one of his practical jokes. I appealed to the Prince; but his reply was simply that 'the King does everything which is right, and if I were to accost him now he might conclude his morning's work by cutting off my head.'

As that would have been a result distasteful to his royal highness, we patiently waited, and at length the King reappeared, dressed this time in a sort of French Field Marshal's uniform. There was no cotton stuff visible about his person now, not even stockings. The portrait was a great success, and his majesty afterwards sat in his court robes, requesting me to place him where and how I pleased. I consulted the Prince, who said—'Yes, place him, but do not for the life of you lay hands on him, more especially on his thrice sacred head.'

Here was a difficultty. How to pose an Oriental potentate who has ideas of his own as to propriety in attitude, and that, too, without touching a fold of his garments? I told the King, in plain English, what I wanted to do, and he said, 'Mr. Town-shun, do what you require for the excellency of your photograph.' He enquired my nationality. I told him I was born in Edinburgh. 'Ah! you are Scotchman, and speak

English I can understand; there are Englishmen here who have not understanding of their own language when I speak.'

When all had been finished, his majesty thanked me and retired, and then the Krum-mun-alongkot invited me to join him at a table spread with Siamese and foreign delicacies. The nobles also, at his highness's invitation, added their presence to the repast.

By request of the King I afterwards attended the great Tonsure Festival, or So-Kan, as the Siamese call it, when the heir-apparent, Prince Chowfa Chul-along-korn, who has since come to the throne, was deprived of the top-knot of his boyhood for the first time—a solemn hair-cutting ceremony conducted with all the pride, pomp, and circumstance of a sacred Brahminical rite. The festival lasted six days, and was concluded on January 6, 1866.

Within the grounds of the first King's palace, there is a large paved quadrangle surrounded by picturesque buildings of an architecture purely Siamese, and shaded, here and there, by the wide-spreading banyan and other umbrageous trees; flowering shrubs adorn this enclosure, and in the centre there had been erected, by the King's command, an artificial hill known as Mount Khrai-lat, and bearing a tiny shrine upon its summit. In this shrine were deposited the sacred vessels, a throne for the reigning sovereign, and a font of holy water which the priests of Brahma had blessed. As to the hill itself, it rested on a strong substructure of teak-wood, and was entirely made up, externally, of thin sheets of lead; so fashioned as to represent a variety of rocks and fantastic caverns with tanks for water hollowed here and there. The whole had been artfully painted and patched with moss, while living trees and flowers were stuck about it in a profusion that far outstripped nature in her most gorgeous tropical luxuriance.

Perhaps the most important, certainly the most conspicuous feature, in the pageant was the procession which each afternoon escorted the young Prince thrice round the sacred Mount Khrai-lat. This procession was got up on a scale of great splendour. The chief members of the nobility marched in its ranks, arranged in costumes of an ancient type ; hundreds of the King's wives followed, glistening in silks of varied hues ; while female slaves dressed up to represent the women of various foreign nations brought up the rear of the phalanx. The imitations of English ladies were particularly ludicrous, for while the contrast between the graceful, modest native costumes and the huge crinoline and chignon of the West, could not fail to strike every beholder, the awkward carriage and the faces stained a golden colour till they looked like harvest moons, gave a rendering of the pretty English originals, of which their country is so justly proud, rather less faithful than a stiff painted Dutch doll. The most attractive element in the whole procession was a white-robed band of children, the daughters of the nobility, who bore peacocks' feathers, or other emblems, in front of the young Prince's palanquin. Three of the ladies were dressed in cloth of gold jewelled with a dazzling array of precious stones, and dancing in front of the throne. Among other photographs which I took on the spot, one represents his majesty as he receives his son and places him on his right hand, amid the simultaneous adoration of the prostrate host. Mrs.

Leonowens, who ought to have known better, has made use of this photograph in a work on Siam which recently appeared under her name, and described it wrongly as 'Receiving a Princess.'

After this ceremony two ladies, here in waiting, conduct the Prince down the marble steps of the Pavilion, and two pretty young damsels are in readiness below to 'bathe his feet in a silver urn.' Thence he betakes himself to a temple hard by, where the top-knot is solemnly removed. The next business is to dedicate the sacred hill, by a sort of baptism of fire, the priests carrying lighted tapers thrice round its base on three successive nights. The entire ceremony is long and tedious; but I think the most interesting feature was the purificatory ablution, which the Prince performed in a tank at the foot of Mount Khrai-lat. I believe, however, that I was the only European who witnessed this important part of the Brahminical ceremony. It is curious to remark, throughout these ancient Oriental rites, the importance attached to the sacred numbers three and nine. Thus we find that the circle of fire which is carried round the Mount is completed three times each day for three days in succession, in all making up nine circles of fire. The same mystic reverence for certain numbers may be observed in parts of the Chinese Alar as well as in the ceremonial at the Temple of Heaven, in Peking. There we have a triple terrace and triple roofs, while nines, or multiples of nine, may be counted in the steps and balustrades, and even in every circle of stones with which the terraces and top are paved. In Cambodia, also, we find a kindred symbolism in the three chief approaches on the outer cruciform pavement of Nakon-Wat, in the three gateways on each side, in the three terraces leading to the central tower, and in the three ornaments which crown the brows of the Teveda (angels) sculptured on its walls. Many of the great stone images of Cambodia are still called 'Phrom' or Brahma by the natives, and there can be little doubt that the three galleries of this temple were designed for the use of the priests in carrying out Brahminical ceremonials, after the pattern of the Sokan and other Siamese festivals. I shall perhaps have more to say on this point when we reach the succeeding chapter.

After I returned from Cambodia I witnessed the actual ceremony of cutting the top-knots of five of the second King's sons. The first King having sent for me, I had accompanied the Prince Krum-mun-alongkot, to await his majesty in an outer court in the palace of the second King. There, at length, I fell into the procession of soldiers, priests, and Tevedas or angels, marching to the temple in which the ceremony was to be performed. In the front court of this temple we were detained for about half an hour, and then his majesty came out, walked up to me, and gave me his hand. He enquired kindly about our journey, said he was glad to know that we had got safely back, but could not forbear wondering why two rational Englishmen should undergo so long a journey, at the risk of being either devoured by wild animals, or carried off by jungle fever, only to see some stone buildings very much out of repair, and this more especially as he placed no restriction upon our looking at his own magnificent Wats in Bangkok. I presented his majesty with a set of my photographs of the Cambodian antiquities, with which he seemed very much astonished. 'What can I do for you, Mr. Tomo-shun?' said he. 'I will give you, if you wish, a free passage to Singapore.' Perhaps he took me for a 'yak' or evil spirit, and wanted me well out of his dominions. At any rate he may have honestly thought that anyone who would take the trouble to go so far to examine dilapidated specimens of ancient masonry had better be looked upon as insane, and treated as a dangerous character. This conversation ended, the King led me by the hand to the door of the Wat, and there described to me the hair-cutting ceremony. I was startled by the unexpected beauty of the scene within. The walls were frescoed with cartoons, their bright colours softened by the dim religious light; while at the inner extremity was a pyramid decked with flowers, and surmounted by a gilt image of Samana Khodôm. The floor was of marble, and there was a low altar in the centre, on which a number of slender tapers burnt. The five royal children sat to the left of this altar, robed in white, and having nobles of high rank on their right hand. Arranged in circles around the central group were others of the King's children, many of them of rare beauty, and all perfectly motionless and silent. At length, and as if prompted by the monotonous strains of music that broke on the ear, the most venerable noble took a lighted taper from the altar, and delivered it to the outer circle of priests, who, in their turn, passed it on from hand to hand, until the fire had completed the circuit. This was repeated three times, and thus the objects of the ceremonial were consecrated by what the King told me was an ancient Brahminical ceremony, and which we have seen above as the rite most prominent in the dedication of Mount Khrai-lat. His majesty then asked me if I thought that the ancient temples of Cambodia belonged to Siam. I said I supposed they did, and he promised to give me some information on that subject before I quitted his dominions. Faithful to his word, the King afterwards paid my passage to Singapore, and presented me, in addition, with two golden mangoosteens and a cigar-case elaborately inlaid with gold. He also sent me a letter in English, from which I take the following extract:

'I beg to take from you a promise that you should state everywhere verbally, or in books, and newspapers, public papers, that those provinces Battabong and Onger, or Nogor Siam, belonged to Siam continually for eighty-four years ago, not interrupted by Cambodian princes or Cochin China. The fortifications of those places were constructed by Siamese Government thirty-three years ago. The Cambodian rulers cannot claim in these provinces, as they have ceded to Siamese authority eighty-four years ago.'

Space will not admit an exhaustive account of my travels and experiences in Siam. I must leave out much that might interest the reader, and as briefly as possible conclude this part of my subject, before I proceed to Cambodia. The physical characteristics of the Siamese have been frequently described; I need only say, therefore, that they resemble the Chinese more closely than is the case with the Malays, and on the other hand there is something so purely Indian in their appearance as to forbid our classing them with the Mongolian or Tartar races. They are indeed Indo-Chinese, and their institutions, political or religious, their manners and their customs, partake of the same mixed character. The state ceremonials are of ancient Brahminical origin, while in their mode of governing, and in their code of laws, they have borrowed much from China in former days. As in the Celestial Empire, many of the magistrates of Siam receive but a nominal salary (or practically, no salary at all), and they undisguisedly make up for the lack of revenues by a not unrecognised system of corruption, a handsome bribe being found to be a powerful witness in favour of a client in the court where his case is tried.

Polygamy, too, flourishes among the Siamese with greater vigour even than in the Flowery Land. Opium is a luxury in both countries, and gambling among each nation is a ruling vice. I remember visiting a magistrate's court in Bangkok, where a case of some importance was under investigation, and I noticed the same agencies at work there as in China, only that in the latter country the system of corruption is managed, by subordinates appointed for the purpose, with a degree of subtle polish and refinement, which almost persuades the grave and sober judge himself to believe in his own absolute integrity, though he knows full well that a little gold dropped mysteriously into the scales will make the balance of justice kick the beam on one side or the other. But it was not so in Siam. There, in an open court, we found the fat judge, a single silken cloth around his loins—his only judicial robe—seated at a small window, with one flabby leg hanging over in the sunshine; a slave girl fanning him, his mouth filled with betel-nut, and thus snorting out his enquiries from time to time. The prisoners were shut up in a sort of cattle-pen in front, while their friends and supporters, laden with gifts of fruits, cakes, or other produce, crawled through the court in a continuous procession, and presented their offerings for inspection as they passed the judge's chair. The latter—when some fat side of pork, or other similar delicacy, won his special approval—would squirt out a mouthful of saliva, grunting and pointing with his nose or chin to some ever-watchful slave, who thus understood that the tit-bit referred to was to be retained for his master's table. The train of tribute-bearers thus passed on through a gateway into the magistrate's house, and thence to deposit their burdens upon the stalls of a small market kept by the family of this impartial ornament of the judicial bench. With these influences at work, we may be sure that a prisoner, if his friends were numerous and liberal, had little or nothing to fear. But, in justice to the government and the late King, I must add, grave offenders were not allowed to escape unpunished. I shall never forget the scene I witnessed inside a Bankok prison. The public executioner lived close by, so we paid him a visit before we entered the jail. He was a hideous-looking fellow, but proudly conscious of his brawny chest and sinewy arm, that with one fell swoop of the sword had closed many a luckless criminal's career. He readily produced his fatal weapon, bright with recent polishing, passed his fingers lightly, nay, almost lovingly along its sharp-edged blade, grinned, and disappeared. I meanwhile watched his retreating figure, and then took a long breath. I thought the fellow eyed me professionally; he certainly looked at my neck, which was thicker than the average of those with which he had commonly to deal. In one part of the prison grounds men heavily ironed, and covered, one or two of them, with old sores, were making bricks in a mud pool. Some had been in chains for years, and their condition reminded me of pictures of the Buddhist hells which I had seen on the walls of their temples. The air was filled with the wails of distress and the clank of fetters. Seated on a bench there was a condemned woman, who had been implicated in a murder. She seemed to be treated with mercy, and even indulgence, as she wore no chains but those which bound her to a pretty little child that lay smiling and crowing in her lap, and struggling to bring back the sunshine to its mother's worn and haggard brow. It was afterwards reported that she had been reprieved, partly for the sake of the child; and I can readily believe the rumour, as the King had a passionate affection for his own children, and devout Buddhist potentates deem it a merit rather to save life than to take it away.

The Siamese are great gamblers; they amuse themselves also with cock-fighting and betting, not perhaps so unrestrainedly as the Malays, for the Buddhist laws forbid the wanton destruction of life; but they sink at times to depths much lower than this, and I have been present in a gambling-house in Bangkok and seen an unfortunate player gamble his family one by one into slavery. A great variety of games of chance are known in Siam, for the most part imported from China. Among them are dice, cards, and dominoes. Sometimes we meet men playing the simple game of odd or even; at other seasons they will bet upon the number of pips in an unopened durian or other kind of fruit; and there is, besides these amusements, the ever-recurring lottery, an institution purely Chinese. In Bangkok at least two-thirds of the native population pass their lives in their boats, or else in houses which float on the surface of the river. These floating houses are built upon platforms of bamboo, for the hard durable stems of this useful plant grow to great dimensions in that country, and offer special advantages in the construction of a raft. Thus the long hollow stem is divided naturally into a certain number of water-tight compartments, separated from each other by solid diaphragms of wood. The bamboo, too, will remain for a great length of time under water without deteriorating; and even should the stem by chance spring a leak in any one of its compartments, this still will not affect the buoyancy of the rest. It may have been from that fact alone that the Chinese derived the idea of building their boats in water-tight compartments. The bamboos of the foundation or raft are piled up one above the other, in longitudinal and transverse layers; these are then lashed together with ratan, and when sufficient buoyancy has been obtained to float the dwelling above, the platform is launched and moored in the stream. The raft, when moored, is fastened at each of the four corners to a strong pile which has been driven into the river bed for that purpose. The fastening consists of a loop of stout ratan rope, which will move or 'travel' freely up and down the pile, and thus the abode will rise or sink with the ebb and flow of the tide. When the raft has been got into position, the house is then erected above its surface, and may be constructed of teak-wood or bamboo, according to the taste or means of its proprietor. Not uncommonly the eaves, the windows, the panels, and the balustrading, are carved and varnished; often they are painted and gilt, so that they form highly picturesque objects on the water. As to the interior apartments, these are so comfortable and well arranged as to furnish a cool and suitable dwelling even to the most fastidious tastes. From a sanitary point of view these 'river dwellings' offer many advantages. Thus they do away with the need of a borough engineer, and the complicated systems of subterranean drainage which burden the rate-payers in Europe. The Siamese, too, are much addicted to bathing, and like to have their water close at hand. These floating houses are generally moored close together in compact lines, and are difficult to deal with in case of fire—a calamity happily of rare occurrence. Not many years ago one of the houses in a long row having caught fire, the neighbours immediately cut it adrift, and let it go blazing down the stream. It was not long before it fouled a barque at her anchorage, and the latter was soon in flames and burnt to the water's edge. Floating houses are rather in the way of unskilful pilots, especially at points where the river narrows, and if the current is strong. I remember once lifting a part of the roof off one of these abodes with the bowsprit of a steamer. Two merchants, an engineer, and myself, having had a steam-launch placed at our disposal, determined to visit the ancient capital of Ayuthia. We armed ourselves with a chart of the river, and took turn about at the helm, leaving the engines to the charge of our professional friend.

Things went on pretty smoothly during the first day, until at night we reached a district where the country was flooded, and it was difficult to keep to the main channel of the stream. About eight o'clock, when, of course, it was already dark, I found we were steering bow on for a green mount, which loomed up in the distance. By reversing the engines and altering the course we just cleared the obstacle, but having rounded and taken bearings, we discovered to our dismay that we were in the centre of a paddy (rice) field. Here we halted till daylight, and, enabled to regain the bed of the channel, soon after arrived in safety at our destination. Having examined the Kraal and the Sala or 'Grand Stand,' whither the King repairs periodically to see the wild elephants driven in, and the most promising specimens secured, we took our way to the Royal Elephant Stables, where about a dozen of these huge animals are usually to be seen. Near to the river a splendid buffalo cow was feeding tethered to a stake, and with a calf at her heels; she looked up fixedly and steadily at the white faces of our party; so steadily, that I determined to photograph her. But the sight of the camera, and the mysterious dark tent, disgusted the brute more than ever, and she began to assume a disagreeably threatening look. 'Now,' I said, 'let one of you open out your umbrella suddenly, just as I am about to photograph, and we shall have an attitude of surpassing grandeur.' One of my friends, therefore, cautiously approached her and fired off his umbrella. This was too much for the buffalo, and, with a wild toss of her head, she broke the rope, and I just got a glimpse of her in full career, as she charged in the direction of her aggressors. The next moment I found that the owner of the umbrella had tumbled into an elephant midden, and though in a disagreeable position, was safe from harm. As for my China boy, he had consigned himself to the river, and only consented to crawl out of his place of refuge on being informed that a huge alligator was at his heels. We started for home shortly after, and came down beautifully with the flood, but the steering required constant attention; and, finally, at a most unfortunate conjuncture, when we were just entering the city of Bangkok, we lost all command of the helm; the steamer would not steer; first she stuck her nose into the reeds on the bank, then she turned round with the flood, came out again into mid-channel, and at last crossed to the opposite shore, and carried the roof away from the floating house aforesaid. When we had leisure to look for the cause of this strange behaviour, we found that the steering-chain had got displaced. Things were put to rights at last, and we reached the jetty without further disaster.

Siam has greatly changed since the time of my visit to that country. The first and second Kings have both been gathered to their fathers, and their sons now reign in their stead. Antiquated laws and objectionable customs have passed out of date, and a liberal policy is being steadily pursued. Slavery has been abolished, and the custom of crouching in the presence of a superior has been discontinued by the express order of the Sovereign. His majesty lately visited Singapore and Calcutta, and the experiences which he gained there seem to have been taken to heart. The education which this young King received from the English Governess, Mrs. Leonowens, at his father's court, must have had its effect in forming his character, while constant intercourse with foreigners, together with his own manly ambition to make the most of his inheritance, have all contributed to render his career an exceptional one in the history of his country. One might almost suppose that he has in his veins some of the blood of those ancient Cambodian rulers who built their marvellous cities and temples, who conquered and subdued the surrounding countries, and founded for themselves a mighty empire, of which no traces save their stone monuments remain. The influence of a newspaper, published partly in English and partly in the vernacular, must not be overlooked when we take account of the progress of Siam.

The late Dr. Bradley kept this newspaper, the 'Bangkok Recorder,' afloat for many years, sometimes under difficulties which would have effectually swamped the undertaking in the hands of anyone less devoted and zealous than he. I had the pleasure of joining the venerable doctor in a trip to Petchiburee, a southern province of Siam. At the start we passed first through the Bangkok-yai canal of 'Great Bangkok,' and then turning to the left we travelled along the Klong-Bang-luang, or 'Creek of the King's Hamlet.' The people on the banks of these creeks dwelt either in floating houses or in cottages built on piles, so that they overhung the stream. And thus, from the window of our boat, we enjoyed a series of views of humble city life. Yonder we could see a Siamese shopkeeper lazily smoking his cigarette, while his wives assorted and sold his wares, or else tended a troop of naked children that never seem to tumble into the water, although they are reared and dwell within a foot of it all their days. Women were to be observed on the verandahs of nearly every house, lolling about, nursing children, smoking, or asleep. Few of them could pretend to any beauty, but all for the most part were as lightly clad as Siamese decency would permit; for, with the exception of a silken langouti wrapped round the loins, tucked up between the legs, and fastened in the waist behind, they sought for no other adornment than their own bright olive skins; and yet these women are both modest and chaste. In other verandahs were groups displaying their fair proportions, and indulging their passion for gambling. At length we came upon the pretty floating harem of a noble. The cut represents two of his Lakon, or dancing-girls, wearing the masks and costumes in which they appear on festive occasions. The façade of this house was elaborately carved, painted, and varnished; an ornamental wood rail swept round the broad platform in front, and we could there see a number of female slaves and concubines crouching before their master, who had but just arrived, and was listening to the musicians on his barge. The leader of these native musicians was performing a jubilant Siamese air on the 'whong kong,' a circle of musical bells, supported by the 'cluae' (flageolet), and the Laos reed organ, on which the performers kept up a running accompaniment, intermingled with the woody tones of the bamboo harmonican or 'Ranat.' The combined effects of these instruments, when softened by distance, was very pleasing at times. But there appears to be nothing of a soul-stirring nature in the Siamese music; it is too vague. One hears a few notes, and fancies them the prelude to some sweet soothing measure. The illusion lasts but for a moment; the effect is cut short by a tumult of sounds, and the sweet fragment of melody flies off the instruments like a nightingale startled by the howling of a menagerie let loose. We passed a number of rice-mills on the banks of the creeks, where enslaved debtors were working out their redemption. A number of these unfortunates had dragged their chains

DANCING GIRLS.

down to the water's edge, and laughed and joked as they bathed, as if they were the happiest of mortals.

It requires a careful study of the tidal influences upon the network of creeks of this region to make a quick trip to Petchiburee. Thus we quitted Bangkok about an hour before the tide had ceased to flow, and carried it with us as far as Banban, from which place the ebb of the current swept us twenty-five miles onward down the Tacheen river and to the mouth of the Ma Klong. At Ma Klong village we had to wait twelve hours. This was the birthplace of the Siamese twins, but the people there seemed to have forgotten their existence. At the local temples we found a "lusus naturæ" in the shape of a biped pig, which was fed and tended by the priests. Besides the pig, there were two pitiable idiots at large in the temple grounds, and a herd of starving pariah dogs. It is contrary to the Buddhist creed to take away life; hence many of their temples become places of refuge for troops of famished dogs, who remain there till they die. For though the priests give them what food they can spare, there is never enough for them all. These dogs, then, are usually animated skeletons, their skins destitute of hair, and covered with many sores. I tossed them a little food; it gave rise to the most savage fight I ever witnessed. One or two wretched curs limped away from the strife torn and lacerated, probably to lay down and die. This canine community—fierce, hungry, and diseased—must surely be one of those many Buddhist hells where sinners expiate their crimes. The animals are deemed to be animated by the spirits of the departed, and are undergoing a lifetime of torture. The priests, if they are *good men*, look on at their misery with pious complacency, and probably take the lesson to heart, lest they too in the next stage of their existence should be condemned to howl for offal or garbage to satisfy the hungry fangs and sore-eaten frame of starving pariah dogs. The male idiot whom we encountered here was constantly beating his head and muttering, 'The trouble is here—is here; beat a little more and it will be out.' He had been beating thus for years, until the palm of his hand and a patch on his forehead had become as hard as horn. The female manifested what to the Siamese mind seemed a very aggravated sort of madness; she was simply striving, with the few rags which did not cover her, to hide her nakedness from the public gaze. Not long after we left Ma Klong we noticed a certain conical hill, which appeared to be taking a morning walk round and round our position—an extraordinary fact in geology, only to be accounted for by the windings of the stream.

Petchiburee is one of the finest and most productive provinces in Siam. The chief town, unlike Bangkok, was mainly built on land, and in some parts bore quite an English look. Thus, there were rows of well-built brick cottages, and a stone bridge across the river, broad enough and strong enough to sustain the traffic even of a metropolitan thoroughfare. The builder of this new town was a very clever young noble, who had visited England with the Siamese embassy, and who, at the time of my visit, was the deputy-governor of Petchiburee. It was he, too, who designed and erected the king's new summer palace, after the model of Windsor, on the top of an igneous mountain which rises boldly above the plains about two miles beyond the town. To build this palace was no easy task, for the road to the summit of the hill, and the foundations for the edifice itself, had all to be cut out of porous volcanic rock, nearly as hard as flint. A line of rail was laid along the plain for the transport of stone and timber to the mount, and an iron aqueduct had also been constructed to supply the palace from the river. At the palace end of the aqueduct a bath has been constructed for the special use of the King, the water flowing into it from the mouth of a serpent. There is also a sala or grand stand, whence his majesty may witness wrestling-matches, foot- and cattle-races, or the other out-door amusements of the country. From the palace on 'Khow Phra Nakon Kiree' we obtained an unbroken view for at least twenty miles across a plain as level as a billiard-board, and presenting an almost continuous expanse of pale green fields of rice. These fields are banked off into squares for the purpose of irrigation, and fringed in many places by tall Palmyra palms. As for the rice-plants, they were partially covered with the still pools of water that lay between the rectangular ridges which divided field from field. Far away on the verge of the horizon we could descry a dense forest of dark sugar-palms, and about two miles to the north of us stood Khow Sang, a volcanic hill, hollowed with magnificent grottoes, which the natives at great cost had converted into Buddhist shrines. The avenue leading to the principal grotto is shaded by kamboga-trees, whose many flowers shed a delightful fragrance, and are employed by the devout as offerings, which they reverently deposit on the palms of Buddha's hands. At the mouth of this grotto stand natural pillars 30 feet in height, and we found the dimensions of the great cave to be 180 feet east and west, and 140 feet north and south.

The floor has been paved, and the whole interior adapted to the purposes of a magnificent temple, the light being admitted through an old volcanic vent in the apex of the roof above. From the ceiling depended a number of huge pure white stalactites, while the crevices and cells in the rock were filled with images and votive offerings. Part of the area is occupied by large golden statues of Buddha. I descended, against the advice of the local priests, into a rent which dipped down through the rock, but I had to return quickly, half suffocated by strong sulphurous fumes.

In the vicinity of Petchiburee are a number of pretty Laos villages, the abiding places of four or five thousand captives who have been planted there in former times. The Laos bondsmen are permitted to grow their rice on crown lands free of impost, but are taxed immoderately in other ways. Thus, at times they are compelled to give six months unpaid labour to the government. It was the Laos slaves of Petchiburee who built the palace for the King, and they had to find their own maintenance during the whole of that employment. But they are a frugal and industrious folk, simple and honest in their ways; and although this burden must have pressed heavily upon them at the time, they soon recovered from its effects. The building is so well put together as almost to make one imagine that these Laos slaves have inherited something of the skill of the ancient Cambodian craftsmen. There can be, I think, little doubt that they are in many respects a superior race to the Siamese; they are taller and handsomer. They weave fine cloth, and wear more of it to cover them, as only the feet are left bare. They are more painstaking and successful cultivators of the soil; their musical instruments are ingeniously constructed, and their native airs are full of tenderness and pathos. I never spent a more pleasant day than when paying a visit to one of the Laos villages. One always feels a certain degree of sympathy with captives in a strange land.

Mr. McFarlane and myself set out on horseback. The Prapalat had kindly furnished us with royal steeds. I had also six men bearing my photographic instruments.

The road was in parts flooded, but every available foot of ground around was taken up with rice. On either side were thick hedges of the sweet-smelling gum-arabic tree, or of the 'Mai Phi' or wood-bamboo, a plant studded with formidable prickles, and which forms, owing to its great strength, an impenetrable barrier.

The bridges over the creeks were formed by single bamboo stems, so rather than risk our limbs upon them we made the best of our way through the water, and at length reached the Laos village, where I was favourably impressed with the fine appearance of the people. The men were larger and more muscular than the Siamese, while the poorest among them were completely clothed in dark blue cotton, closely resembling the dress worn by the labourers in some parts of China, and made up of a loose jacket, and trousers falling to two or three inches below the knees. The women, some of them, were of fair complexion and exceedingly pretty, having their long dark tresses coiled up so as to form an ample and picturesque covering for the head. Their costume consisted either of an embroidered jacket or long strips of cloth covering the bust, and a petticoat of striped red, yellow, and blue (primary colours), manufactured by themselves, and peculiar to the Laotian tribes.

The houses of the village were raised five or six feet above the ground on strong posts, and built of wood and bamboo; the roofs were tent-shaped, and thatched with long dried grass. With the exception of a few articles of Chinese manufacture, everything about the village, and for domestic use, was of native make. Viewed from a distance, the settlement, hidden among palms and fruit-trees, rose from the wide expanse of level plain like a green island in the sea. Everywhere around, the fields were cultivated with rice; and the same evidence of ceaseless industry was carried to the very threshold of the dwellings, where each household had its well-tilled kitchen garden, and plot of tobacco, and cotton. The latter they dye with native vegetable and mineral substances, and weave on their own looms into fabrics for family use.

There were huge bamboo baskets for holding produce, and small baskets of straw, utensils made of varnished wood, harrows, ploughs, and various other implements used in husbandry. The Laos of Petchiburee and their surroundings bore a stronger resemblance to the Pepohoan of Formosa than to any other race I have encountered during my travels. The Laotian is the higher type of the two, as the Pepohoan is solely occupied in cultivating the soil. The villages of both races are characterised by the same peaceful surroundings, while the inhabitants of these primitive settlements are remarkable for their simple honesty, and for the absence of crime among them. In the Formosa Pepohoan villages I do not remember ever having seen either a prison or a pauper. The rapid inroads which the Chinese are making on that beautiful island will soon furnish both, as their trade and ancient civilisation will disturb the social equality which only recognises the rank conferred by grey hairs and wisdom. Craft and duplicity will ere long invade their humble abodes that nestle in fertile valleys, watered by clear mountain springs, and shaded by primeval forests.

CHAPTER V.

An Expedition to Cambodia—Bang Phra-kong Creek—Prairie on fire—A Foreign Sailor—Wild River Scenery—Aquatic Birds—Kabin—Kut's Story to the Chief—A Storm in the Forest—The Cambodian Ruins—Their Magnitude—Siamrap—Nakhon Wat—Its Symbolism—The Bas-reliefs and Inscriptions—The Hydra-headed Snake—The Ancient Capital, Penompinh—The King of Cambodia—Dinner at the Palace—The whole Hog—Overland to Kamput—Pirates—Mahomet's Story—The Fossil Ship—The Voyage up the Gulf of Siam.

I HAD already been in Siam several months before I could carry out the project which had originally taken me to that country. My plan was to cross overland into Cambodia, and there photograph the ruined temples and examine the antiquities which have been left behind by the monarchs of a once powerful empire. Mr. H. G. Kennedy, of H.B.M.'s consular service, consented to accompany me on this expedition, and we got away together on January 27, 1866. We had first intended to sail down the Gulf of Siam to Chantaboon, and thence to cross over the forest-clad mountains of that province to Battabong. But the Siamese Government declined to grant a passport for that route, which they reported as dangerous and impracticable. We were therefore reduced to the necessity of making a tedious, and, so far as health was concerned, more dangerous journey by the creeks and rivers, and across the hot plains and marshes of the south-eastern provinces of the interior.

We started in a long boat manned by eight stalwart Siamese, with Mohammed Ali, a Malay, a Siamese named Kut, and two Chinese men-servants, Ahong and Akum. Our way lay along the Klong Sansep, a creek cut some fifty years ago, and which penetrates from the left bank of the river Menam nearly due east, till it emerges, after a course of fifty miles, in the river Bang Phra-kong. This creek, at Wat 'Tam Phra,' about ten miles from Bangkok, was only three or four feet in depth, and its banks were choked in many places with high prairie grass, through which we had to force a passage. It was harvest time, and the vast plains of Sansep district were covered with a golden crop of rice. Here and there we could descry groups of reapers among the grain, or isolated slaves stationed as scarecrows about the fields.

At Wat Sansep, a small temple where we halted for dinner, the festivities of our evening meal were enhanced by the howling accompaniment of some dozen famished pariahs. The kindly curs barked for our entertainment with a skill and assiduity that did them infinite credit, willingly repeating the choice passages at the barest hint for an encore. Jolly dogs these; and yet, as I have already stated, the canine tribes who flee from worldly sorrows to consecrate their voices to the exclusive service of the Buddhist faith, are generally miserable skeletons, veritable ascetics indeed; and it is difficult to make out why so many dogs, endowed as they are with singular sagacity, should drift into these temples, unless indeed they love the seclusion and liberty of these monastic retreats, where they may die of starvation, or, maddened by hunger, devour each other. Here we fell in with an American sailor. Ali was the first to see him. He said 'Ah! Orang puti de blakang poko, ada' ('There is a white man behind the trees').

He had deserted from his ship for the purpose, he said, of going to Saigon hospital overland, to have a broken arm reset. For several days he had been wandering about the country, meeting with some kindness from the natives, but suffering fearfully from the bites of moschettos and other insects. When we met him he was literally one mass of sores, and his broken arm was much swollen and inflamed. After doing what we could to relieve his immediate wants, Mr. Kennedy called upon the nearest native official, who promised that the fugitive should be sent back to Bangkok. It appeared that some judicious friend had advised him to walk over to Saigon, some four hundred miles away, without food, without a passport, and without a cent in his purse.

We spent our first night in the creek, to the joy of the moschettos, which attacked us in myriads, and effectually banished repose. We tried to sleep at a Wat (temple), but it was no good; and then the boatmen, who were nearly as badly off themselves, volunteered to pull all night, in order to get clear of the marshy haunts where these vile insects abound, and to reap the benefit of a little breeze by keeping the boat constantly in motion. All night long the buzzing of our invisible foes sounded like the discordant notes of an orchestra as it sets its stringed instruments in tune. Moschetto-nets were useless, and wrapping one's head in a blanket only drove them to sing on, and sting on, until they dropped off bloated and intoxicated with blood. Next morning our hands and faces were swollen, painful, and distorted ; but we had now reached a wider part of the creek, and were free from further persecution. The plain hereabouts was covered with grass which stood ten feet high. Some of this had caught fire, and was blazing with great fury when we passed. The flames were swept before the wind, roaring, crackling, and sending up a dense column of smoke in their wake, followed by vultures ready to pounce down upon the hapless victims of the devouring fire. We landed, and had some sport; but it was arduous, unprofitable work. Ali fell into a mud pool up to the neck, while my friend and I had to wade through marshes covered with water, and were obliged to undress and pick the leeches off our bodies when we returned to our boat. But it was quite by accident, and after some short interval of time, that we discovered the presence of the leeches. They fasten silently and without pain upon the flesh, where they at length produce a disagreeable itching sensation, which leads to their detection.

The Kabin branch of the Bang Phra-kong river formed one of the most attractive parts of our route. No more romantically beautiful little stream is anywhere to be found in the world. When we passed into its placid waters, we seemed to have entered a region unknown to man, and inhabited only by the lower orders of creation. Monkeys walked leisurely beside the banks, or followed us with merry chattering along the overhanging boughs, while tall wading birds with tufted heads, snow-white plumage, and rose-tipped wings, paused, in the business of peering for fish, to gaze with grave dignity upon the unfamiliar intruders. Some were so near that we could have struck them down with our oars, but to avoid this outrage they marched with a calm stately stride into the thickets of the adjoining jungle.

The first report of our rifles wrought a change in the scene. The forest rang with voices of alarm; the monkeys gibbered and scrambled out of sight, the tall storks rose slowly upon their giant wings and soared away in their flight till they looked like a curved line of light against the blue face of the sky. We made an attempt to preserve the skins of a number of rare aquatic birds, including one or two varieties of the kingfisher, which are to be found in great abundance in this part of Siam. Unfortunately our arsenical soap, and the facilities for drying, were insufficient for the purpose. Coming suddenly upon a wide reach in the river, we found its surface whitened with a fishing party of pelicans. Some, with pouches well stocked, lolled lazily along; others skimmed the surface, elevating their bills from time to time, and indicating by the glittering of their finny prey that the flock had chosen happy hunting-grounds, and were busily engrossed with their enterprise. Two fell victims to our rifles; one of them escaped; the other was of such colossal proportions that it took two men to haul him into the boat. Our Chinaman, with the masterly assistance of Kut, who had a keen appreciation of the delicacies of the table, produced a savoury breakfast of soup and pelican-steak. Ahong was heard to remark just before falling asleep for a forenoon nap, 'Ah yah!' The fat of this king of birds is delicious. It recalls to my mind the pleasures of a pork dinner. Anyone unacquainted with the lower orders of the Chinese can form but little notion of the bliss implied in the above brief sentence. To be overcome by a full meal of pork, and to sleep off the effects of the repast, comes very near filling the cup of Chinese happiness to the brim.

On the morning of the 30th the maximum temperature in the shade was 91° Fahrenheit, but at 6 P.M. it had fallen to 68°, while strangely enough the water of the river showed a temperature of 85°. We passed a place called Bang-Sang, where a royal palace had been erected for the reception of a sacred white elephant, which died, it was reported, of a champagne dinner, on its progress to the capital. The untimely end of this brute was esteemed a national calamity, and was a cause of deep mourning to all devout Siamese Buddhists.

On the same evening we passed a Chinese trading-boat, bound with a cargo of rosewood to Paknam. At Prachim we presented ourselves before the Prapalat or deputy-governor, and handed in our credentials. The old gentleman examined the King's letter with great reverence; his chief clerk, meanwhile—a powerful-looking functionary, well up in years—devoting his whole attention to a bottle of 'eau-de-vie,' which he would have finished on the spot, had it not been for the timely precautions of Ali.

The river had cut a deep channel through this part of the country, and the exposed strata on the banks showed that the plain was made up of a series of thin argillaceous and sandy deposits, resting upon a substratum in which I noticed marine shells. During our journey across the country, I found constantly recurring evidence that the plains of Siam had gradually emerged from the bed of ocean. The thin alternating upper strata were accounted for by the annual floods which still inundate the land, depositing the alluvium upon which the rice crops depend.

At a small Wat at Lan-yang-we, we noticed a venerable priest engaged in shaving his head and face without either mirror or soap, and wonderfully he managed it too. About a mile from Ban-hat-yai-kow we came upon a Laos settlement, where the women were weaving silk and cotton fabrics; the latter of fine quality and long staple, and the former of the coarse yellow sort peculiar to Cambodia and the Laos States.

They evidently took us for Yaks (wood spirits) or Teveda (angels), as they had never seen white men before. Angels of the Siamese mythology are quite different from anything we picture them. They are more like satyrs; some have the tails of apes and claws of birds.

On the 31st of the month we reached Paknam Kabin, or the port of Kabin, the only place which we had as yet encountered of any commercial pretensions. Here, as might be expected, we found the pioneers of trade in the shape of Chinamen from Bangkok. There is great competition among these sons of Han, who carry on their transactions by barter, waylaying the elephant trains from Battabong and the far interior, and exchanging salt and Chinese and European wares for horns, hides, silk, dammar, oil, cardamums, and other products.

At the town of Kabin there were no elephants to be had, so we were forced to content ourselves with ponies and buffalo-carts for the overland journey before us. Here it was that we gained our first experience of vexatious delay. We ourselves reached our halting-place by 9 A.M., but we had then to await the arrival of our men and baggage, who turned up at last in the afternoon at about 4 o'clock, and discovered, when they arrived, that they had left the cooking-utensils in the boat, and we had not yet had breakfast!

Hiring a pony, I started at once for Paknam, which lay about six miles off. But the journey was an arduous one, as my steed had no saddle, and only a bit of cord by way of bridle. The animal took its own way, and that, unfortunately for my clothes and skin, lay through the thickest of the prickly jungle. At last, just after dark, I met another of our carts, and returned with it to Kabin; but there were still neither cooking-pots nor lamps. We, however, found a teapot and tin of salmon, and these supplies furnished us with breakfast, dinner, and supper, all in one. We called on the governor of Kabin, and presented him with a cadeau of European wares; among other things, we gave him a micro-photograph in a small ivory telescope, and a bottle of perfume. Kut, whenever he made official visits, put on an old suit of his wife's uniform (she was an officer of the King's amazon guard). We afterwards discovered also that he dealt largely in fiction, and had informed the Prapalat that the photograph (one of Her Majesty the Queen) had been sent specially as a mark of royal favour to this renowned chief; and as to the perfume, it was the breath of a thousand beautiful English women put up in a bottle, and reserved exclusively to reward all governors who rule well and wisely. The Prapalat only remarked, 'he could never have supposed it, as the breath of his own women was so very different.' He smelt, and wondered as he smelt, what manner of women those could be who breathed such sweet fragrance forth. He thought it strange, too, that our country should be ruled over by a woman; and I have no doubt, from the questions he asked, the notion crossed his mind that we had come to Siam to pay tribute, and that we probably wanted the King to take our State under his protection. The people of his town, city, or village, were not remarkable for honesty. We slept in a sala, or open bamboo shed, erected on a clearing in the forest. This sala was raised about six feet above ground, and there were cracks between the boards which formed the flooring, large enough for us to insert our feet through if necessary, which was a very convenient arrangement. One morning early I was about to put on my nether garments, when I saw them depart mysteriously through one of these openings in the floor. This was ungenerous in the trousers, for I had been on friendly terms with them for some time previously. I have reason to suspect that some villain persuaded them to desert me—at least, a dark shadow flitted soon after across the clearing into the forest. Anyhow, my garment left me, and I never saw it more. As for the natives, they put an absurd story afloat that the trousers had been stolen, but they did not go the length of suggesting a human thief. They concurred in saying that it must have been a spirit or a tiger, and no doubt great weight ought to be attached to their opinion.

I set out again in a bullock-cart for Paknam, where I discharged the boatmen, while Kennedy made arrangements for our overland journey. The boat's crew behaved well the whole way, and two or three of them, as we parted, carried me on their shoulders back to the cart.

In the evening we enjoyed an entertainment at the governor's house, where a band of Laos musicians exhibited their skill, and a Laos girl sung a plaintive pleasing air to the accompaniment of a reed organ, and a soft-toned flute.

About this time our two Chinamen, finding that pork was a rare luxury, their meals rather irregular, and their work rough, while the danger of being devoured by tigers was daily increasing as we penetrated further into the interior, thought that a little insubordination might not be wholly thrown away. By threats and coaxing, however, we calmed them for a time, and prevailed on them to proceed with us on our journey.

At last, one evening, towards 5 o'clock, with two wretched buffalo-carts and a pair of ponies, we set out for Cambodia. I had also engaged two extra carriers specially for taking charge of my chronometer, sextant, and other instruments. Our way, at first, lay through a stunted forest; but it was not long before we reached a shrine on a small clearing, and halted for the night. At 3 on the following morning we again set out, ourselves in advance, and our baggage-waggons following slowly in the rear. We had not proceeded far before the forest was wrapped in deep gloom, and a thunder-storm burst upon our party. The rain was still falling in a deluge, when one of the buffaloes took sudden fright and upset our cart, our Chinamen, and our stores. Alarmed at the crash and uproar, we rode quickly back, gathered our men and provisions out of the mud and water as well as the darkness would permit, and then pushed on again till 8 o'clock. By this time the rain had abated; but Ahong discovered, when we halted, that he had lost his box and all his cherished possessions. The box was recovered, but its contents had gone. Ahong and Akum next tried to make their escape, and at all hazards return to Bangkok; but we intercepted them, and again persuaded them to carry out their agreement. We had little reason to complain of them afterwards, as to our surprise they faced the remaining difficulties of the journey with a pluck and manliness of which we had thought them destitute.

Camping at night beneath forest-trees, or on the open arid plains; halting at short intervals to repair our carts with the materials which the jungle afforded (for there was not a single nail in these vehicles), or to exchange them for others at the various settlements on the route; we thus spent over a month in lumbering across the country, and, as may be imagined, had to endure some hardships from want of proper food, the bulk of our supplies having been lost or damaged in the storm when we quitted Kabin. At 'Ban-Ong-ta Krong' I had a sharp attack of jungle fever, which left me so utterly prostrate that I had to hire a small bullock-cart to take me on. Kennedy, with regular doses of quinine and kind nursing, effected a rapid cure, but I could not take to my feet for some days. Had we succeeded in procuring elephants at Kabin, as we were led to expect, the whole journey might have been accomplished in half the time.

It was our custom, when camping for the night, to make an enclosure with the carts, and branches of trees, placing the cattle inside, and keeping up a fire in the centre. Wild animals were sometimes seen near our halting-places, and I brought away the skin of a huge leopard, shot close to a sala where we slept.

On one occasion I remember being roused, and Ali, who slept beneath my cart, cried out that there was a tiger prowling round. The night was dark, but I could make out a black object not many paces from where we lay. The cattle were active too, and snorted uneasily. I raised my revolver, and would have fired, had Ali not arrested my arm, and advised me not to risk a shot in the dark, as had I only wounded the brute we should have been certain of a furious attack. At the sound of human voices it speedily disappeared into the forest.

From Mrs. Leonowen's account of her expedition into Cambodia, I gather that she must have travelled along the same route as ourselves; but I cannot make out, if that was the case, how her elephants could have 'pressed on heavily, but almost noiselessly, over a parti-coloured carpet of flowers.' As to parti-coloured carpets, the convolvulus and other flowers, found in these regions, are of remarkably beautiful kinds, but it is on account of their extreme rarity that they are most highly prized. For my own part, I should have expected a longer and more detailed account of her journey from a lady who observes so accurately and describes so well. Can it be possible that it was she, after all, who aided in compiling M. Mouhot's posthumous narrative, where some of the passages which treat of the Cambodian ruins read like extracts from Mrs. Leonowen's own valuable work. For example, we find, on p. 305 of 'The English Governess at the Court of Siam':—

'The Wat stands like a petrified dream of some Michael Angelo [what is a petrified dream?], more impressive in its loneliness, more elegant and animated in its grace, than aught Greece and Rome have left us.'

In M. Mouhot's work, vol. i., p. 279, the same Wat is thus described :—

'One of these temples—a rival to that of Solomon, and erected by some ancient Michael Angelo—might take an honourable place beside our most beautiful buildings. It is grander than anything left to us by Greece or Rome,' &c.

There is a slight difference between the two passages. In the one the Wat is simply pronounced the work of some great master; while in the other it resembles an animated, petrified dream, whatever that may be. But other ideas, on the pages quoted, will be found expressed in nearly identical words, furnishing an example of one of those strange coincidences which so startle us occasionally in our experience of life. We regret, however, to discover this authoress, when she describes the Cambodian ruins, falling into a number of grave errors which might, some of them, have been avoided had she studied my photographs more carefully when she did me the honour of selecting them to illustrate her work.

On the higher waters of the Sisuphon river we fell in with the first trace of ancient Cambodian civilisation in the shape of a ruined shrine, which had been built of exquisitely finished grey bricks, like blocks of freestone both in texture and appearance. The stream, at this point, was still faced with a strong stone retaining wall, and a broad flight of steps gave us access to a narrow path terminating in an elevated mound of earth, where

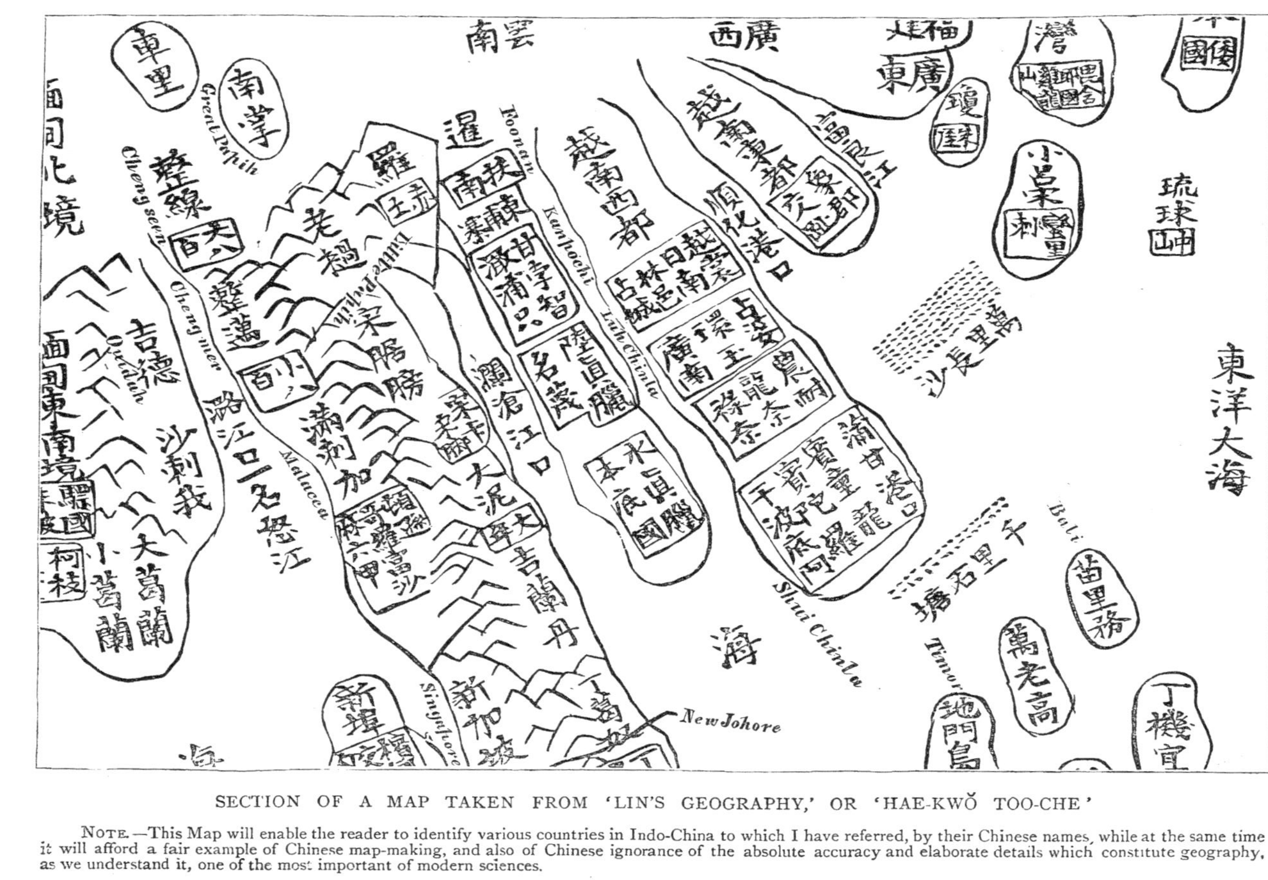

SECTION OF A MAP TAKEN FROM 'LIN'S GEOGRAPHY,' OR 'HAE-KWŎ TOO-CHE'

NOTE.—This Map will enable the reader to identify various countries in Indo-China to which I have referred, by their Chinese names, while at the same time it will afford a fair example of Chinese map-making, and also of Chinese ignorance of the absolute accuracy and elaborate details which constitute geography, as we understand it, one of the most important of modern sciences.

giant trees now grew. Buried beneath this overgrowth of jungle lay the foundations of an ancient edifice. I took the bearings of the mound with my azimuth; and the men, when they saw me adjusting my instrument, concluded that I was after hidden treasure, and set to digging until they reached the wall, and unearthed some bricks. In the centre of the mound there was a thick brick wall built above arched vaults, while, beneath a rude shed hard by, we found the remains of two idols finely sculptured in stone. These idols were life size, and modelled in very accurate proportions. One, a male figure, had been decapitated; and we found the head with its stony diadem still lying among the rubbish close at hand. The features wore a calm benignant look, reminding one of the Hindoo type. The second figure, a female, was in much better preservation; both the contour of its bust, and the expression of its face, showed traces of an accomplished sculptor's hand. The Chinese annals of the Sui dynasty tell us that the then Queen of Chinla [1] was married to a Hindoo, and that it was he who taught the people Deva worship. There were no inscriptions to be found among the ruins here; but it is just possible that these images may have been the statues of that Queen and King who reigned about the beginning of the seventh century, and to whom the historians of China allude.

Fragments of sculptured stone everywhere met the eye, and impressed us with the conviction that the ancient temple-building race of Cambodia had reached a high pitch of civilisation. There was nothing rude, unfinished, or elementary about the work. The simple

[1] See Chinese Map.

bricks of the wall had been carefully and honestly finished, and their plain even surfaces were so true that when placed in position and fixed together without mortar, they left only a delicate line to mark where the joins occurred.

But one ought to be careful in asserting that square honest work, and good material betoken a high pitch of civilisation, lest in some future age it may be said of ourselves that our much-vaunted progress and nineteenth century civilisation were but empty shadows; that our domestic architecture, at least, was designedly deceptive and dishonest; that our greatest ambition was to please the eye with spurious imitations of sculptured marble and stone, to supply tinsel in place of gold, paint and veneer for the tough fibre of the solid oak. But what shall we say of the stone cities and sculptured palaces which we were now approaching—monuments of human labour with which even our greatest modern edifices can hardly be worthily compared; of those cities where, as ancient travellers tell us,[1] there were images of pure gold within the palaces, and looking down from above the city gates.[2] Another Chinese historian relates that the people of Bonam, or Siam, as early as the third or fourth century, were noted for their commerce, their honesty, and their thrift. All that we can say in regard to their buildings, in the absence of any historical records of their own, is that these old Cambodians must have built their towns and temples by the taskwork of slaves, or by cheap labour of some sort. And yet, as I have said, there is a

[1] *History of the Tsin Dynasty*, A.D. 265–419.

[2] It is stated, in the History of the Chinese Sui Dynasty, that a Chinese general carried off from the capital of Limyip (probably Siamrap) eighteen golden images.

thoroughness about their edifices, and a genuine love of art evinced in all their sculptures—in the tender tracery lavished without stint upon the stones, in the uniform grace of every curving stem, in each delicately chiselled lotus, or lily—such as never could have come out of the lash of the slave, out of ill-requited, unwilling hands, or out of the crushed spirit of a bondsman. We see a love of art in every line of ornament, which speaks of the enthusiasm of a master sculptor glorying in his work, and straining every effort of his hand and head that nothing might be lacking which could confer excellence on his toil.

But I am anticipating. At 'Dan Simah,' on the Tasawi river, the chief of the district would have had us wait until he could find a suitable craft to convey us across the lake. But as we observed a boat which would suit our turn at his very door, we took possession of it at once, agreeing as usual, to pay for its use.

This arrangement was concluded much too suddenly to enable the chief to take it in. He would have required at least a week to think over it. As we left in the vessel, he looked good-naturedly bewildered. The notion had not yet dawned upon him that it was all right, as our men pulled away out of sight, and had soon crossed the head of the Great Lake 'Tale Sap,' and entered the Siamrap stream, whence we sent on our letters under Ali's charge to the Chow-Muang, or governor of the province where the chief antiquities are to be found. The great freshwater lake of Cambodia I shall leave for the present undescribed; but I may here mention that Battabong and Siamrap are two provinces which were wrested by the Siamese from the Cambodians eighty-seven years ago. Ali returned in the afternoon, bringing a favourable account of his reception. The Governor had indeed done us the honour to despatch two elephants for our own riding, and five buffalo waggons for our baggage. The elephant howdahs were dome-shaped, of a kind used only by persons of a superior rank. My friend had had experience of elephant travelling in Korat, but the sensation was new to me. The colossal, soft-eyed brute was requested, in Siamese, to give me a lift. Whereupon he bent his huge right fore-leg, and then looked me over slowly from head to foot, before venturing to hoist me on to his back. I placed one foot firmly on his knee, and he then gently raised me until I could reach his neck, keeping me steady with his trunk until I had fairly scrambled into the howdah. This business finished, he then marches with a steady step onwards to his destination, knowing, apparently, all about the country. On he goes through pools and marshes, but keeping an eye the while on the spreading branches of the trees above ; for somehow, with a marvellous exactness, he knows the howdah's height, and if a branch would barely clear it, he halts, raises his trunk, and wrenches it off before he ventures to proceed.

When he comes to the steep bank of a stream, he sits and slides down into the water, and if hot and teased by the flies, he will duck howdah and all beneath the cold surface as he swims across. He charges his trunk with water whenever an opportunity occurs, and this he carries along with him to quench his thirst or to squirt over his body and drown the unsuspecting flies. Thus he plods on in perfect safety over obstacles which no other quadruped could surmount.

If he sees afar off some tempting tree, he shapes his course for it, in order to have a passing mouthful of its leaves. For all that, he is perfectly docile, and seems by his implicit obedience to understand every word his keeper utters. His attendant sits astride his neck, and guides him gently, when needed, with an iron-spiked staff. The elevated position, the straight course one shapes through forest and jungle, and the commanding view one obtains of the surrounding scenery, have at first a rare charm; but after a time we feel that it would be a decided relief could we stay the regular gyration of the head, and seek another axis of motion than the small of the back. So we form some excuse, and descend to 'terra firma;' but even then the motion still goes on, or appears to go on at any rate, for some time.

The Chow Muang of Nakhon Siamrap received us with great courtesy, placing a house at our disposal for two or three days, until a Laos chief, who had come with a considerable escort on a pilgrimage to Nakhon Wat, should have started on his homeward journey, and left room for our accommodation. The old town of Siamrap is in a very ruinous state — the result, as was explained to us, of the last invasion of Cambodia—but the high stone walls which encircle it are still in excellent condition. Outside these fortifications a clear stream flows downwards into the great lake some fifteen miles away, and this stream, during the rainy season, contains a navigable channel. On the third morning of our stay we mounted our ponies, and passed out of the city gates on the road for Nakhon Wat, and the ancient capital of the Cambodian empire. One hour's gentle canter through a grand old forest brought us to the vicinity of the temple, and here we found our progress materially arrested by huge blocks of freestone, which were now half buried in the soil. A few minutes more, and we came upon a broad flight of stone steps, guarded by colossal stone lions, one of which had been overthrown, and lay among the *débris.* My pony cleared this obstacle, and then with a series of scrambling leaps brought me to the long cruciform terrace which is carried on arches across the moat. This moat is a wide one, and has been banked with strong retaining walls of iron-conglomerate. The view from the stone platform far surpassed my expectations. The vast proportions of the temple filled me with a feeling of profound awe, such as I experienced some years afterwards when sailing beneath the shade of the gigantic precipices of the Upper Yang-tsze.

The secret of my emotion lay in the extreme contrast between Nakhon Wat—rising with all the power which magnitude of proportions can give, a sculptured giant pyramid amid forests and jungle-clad plains—and the grass-thatched huts, the rude primitive structures which are all that the present inhabitants have either wish or ability to set up. Nakhon Wat, like the majority of the buildings of 'Inthapatapuri' and the other cities of Cambodia, is raised upon a stone platform. It is carried upward from its base in three quadrangular tiers, with a great central tower above all, having an elevation of 180 feet. The outer boundary wall encloses a square space measuring nearly three-fourths of a mile each way, and is surrounded by a ditch 230 feet across. This ditch is spanned on the west by the causeway (already described), having sculptured flights of stone steps leading to the water. These were pro-

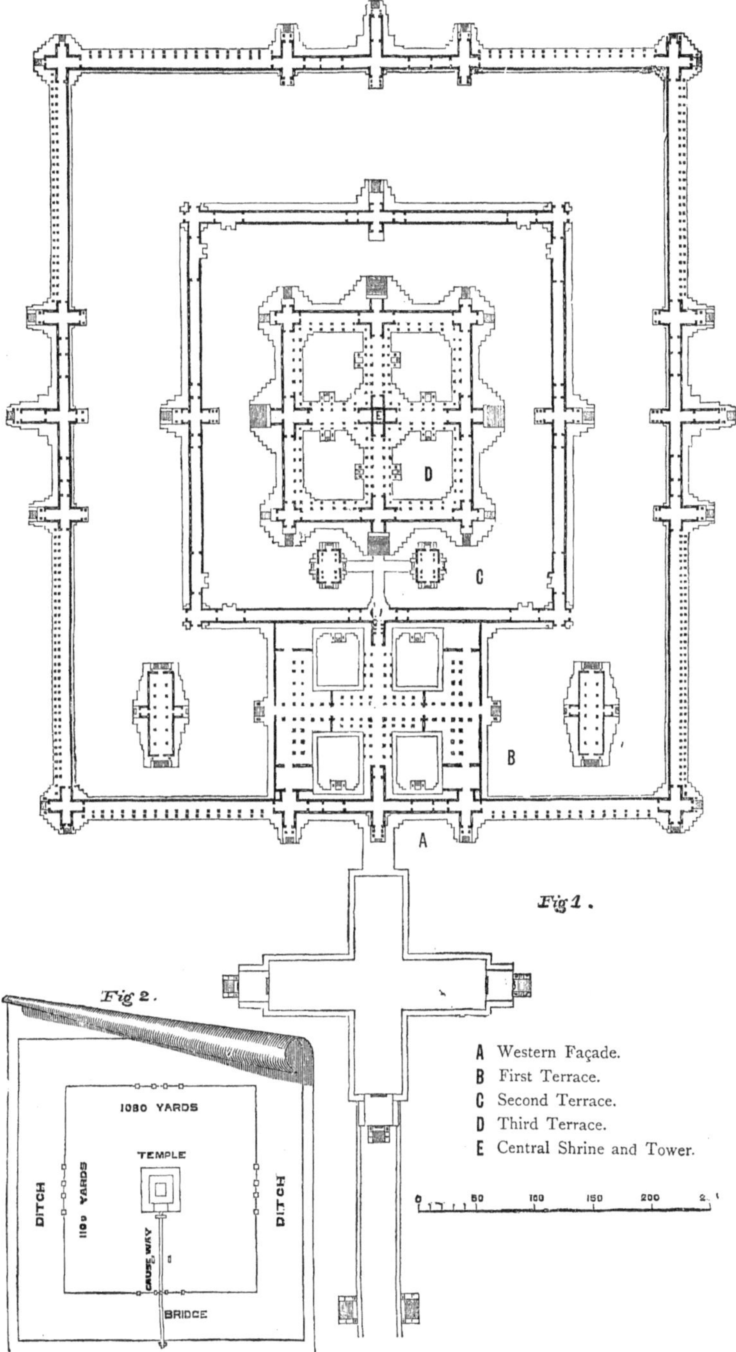

Fig. 1. Plan of Inner Temple of Nakhon, from a survey by the author.
Fig. 2. Plan of area enclosed by outer wall, Nakhon Wat.

bably intended for the first ablutions of the worshippers at this Brahminical or Buddhist shrine. Facing the cardinal points of the compass, and in the centre of each side of the boundary wall, there are long galleries with arched roofs and monolithic pillars, which present a striking and classical appearance. Entering the main gateway through the western boundary, and passing up a broad inner causeway, paved like the outer one with blocks of polished freestone, we approach the western front of the temple proper. Ascending to a cruciform terrace by a flight of steps sculptured with the most beautiful ornaments, and guarded on either side by colossal stone lions, we stand before the principal entrance of the shrine. The façade on this side is more than six hundred feet in length, and is walled in, in the centre, for a distance of some two hundred feet. This walled space is divided into compartments, and each compartment is lighted with windows. In every window there are seven ornamental stone bars, uniform in pattern and in size throughout. The floral ornamentation on these bars appear to represent the sacred lotus, and the flowers are as carefully repeated as if they had been cast from a single mould. These compartments recur in the centre of all the galleries; the remaining two-thirds of the space always consisting of open colonnades, the back walls of which are adorned with the bas-reliefs which form one of the chief attractions of Nakhon Wat.

The building, as I have already observed, rises in three terraces, one above the other, and it is out of the highest of the three that the great central tower springs up; four lower or inferior towers rise around it, and the whole structure is probably meant to symbolise

Mount Meru, or the centre of the Buddhist universe. This is all the more apparent when we consider that Meru is surrounded by seven circles of rocks;[1] that there are seven circles on the central tower; that the sacred mount is supported on three platforms (corresponding to the three terraces) one platform or layer of earth, one of water, and one of wind; and that it rises out of the ocean. This part of the symbolism is indicated by the temple being surrounded with a moat, and indeed during the rains, when the plain is flooded, the whole stupenduous structure would rise (like Meru from the ocean) out of an unbroken sheet of water.[2]

[1] See Dr. Eitel's *Sanscrit Chinese Dictionary*, Art. Sumeru, p. 136.

[2] The accompanying note by the Rev. Joseph Edkins will show that in some of the Buddhist monasteries of Peking the ordination of the priesthood takes place on a triple terrace, similar to the triple terrace of Nakhon Wat.

Admission to the Buddhist Vows on the Triple Terrace.

Buddhist priests are received into the monastic community of that religion in great numbers at the monastery called Chiay tăe sze, near Peking. This beautifully situated monastery commands a fine view of the Hwun ho and the Peking plain.

The name Chiay tăe means Vow terrace. The Vow terrace is in a square building on the east of the hall, in which are placed the principal images. It is built of carved stone, and is triple. The disciple ascends the lower terrace at the back. Going round it, he ascends the middle terrace, and after going round it in the same way he ascends the upper. On reaching the top, after three times making the circuit, he finds himself in front of the abbot and his assessors. The abbot sits on a throne which faces the south, and the assessors, two on each side, face the east and west. The ceremonies for the reception of neophytes are here carried through to their completion.

I expect that there is a Chiay tăe in every large monastery, or in most of them, but this is the best-known in the neighbourhood of the capital.

At small monasteries priests are admitted with less formalities than in large ones.

The first terrace is for Buddha, the second for the written law, and the third for the monastic community.

The neophyte enters into a responsible relation to all three. He leaves the sea of misery where he was without a helper and attaches him-

In many of the ancient temples of Java we find the same symbolic architecture. The shrine of Kalisari,[1] for example, we are told, is an oblong square divided into three floors, and there are many others of exactly the same design. On the ancient Buddhist temple or monument at Bóra Bódo, there are, I believe, seven terraces (and no central tower) which would correspond with the seven circles of Meru. But the three terraces of Nakhon Wat may have another significance; they may have been designed originally for the sacred rites and processions still practised in the ceremonials at the royal tonsure festivals of Siam; for example, at the coronation of a king the priests march thrice, on three separate days, round the sacred 'Khao Khrai-lat,' the Siamese Buddhist Mount Meru. It is difficult to say what may have been the origin of the sacredness attached in many heathen religions to the number three. We have them in the Holy Trinity of our own Christian faith—a doctrine which does not claim a high antiquity; in the supreme principle of creation; in the Orphic Mythology,[2] Council, Light, Life; in On, Isis, and Neith of the Egyptians; in the Magian trinity Mithras, Oromazdes, and Ahriman; the Indian triad Brahma, Vishnu, and Seeva; while in China we have the classic doctrine of the powers of nature—Heaven, Earth, and Man; and the Buddhist Past, Present, and Future. We also find

self to Buddha, who occupies the position of a Redeemer. He escapes from ignorance into the knowledge of Buddhist doctrine. He gives up worldly enjoyments and sins in order to enter on what he expects to find—the pure life of the monks, far from the turmoil of city crowds.

It is to symbolise this threefold refuge that he is made to pass along the railed pathway round three terraces rising successively in height before he arrives in the presence of the venerable robed abbot who admits him to the Buddhist spiritual life.

[1] Sir S. Raffles' *Java*, ii. 25.

[2] See Hale's *Chronology*, iv. 472.

in the Temple of Heaven at Peking, where state wor ship is performed, an altar of three terraces, on which at certain times of the year three sacrifices are offered. These are the Ta-sze,[1] or great sacrifice; the Choong-sze, or medium sacrifice; and the Seaon-sze, or lesser sacrifice. The symbolism of this Chinese temple is a subject full of interest, and has been very carefully examined by the Rev. Joseph Edkins.[2]

To return to Nakhon Wat. The ancient Chinese traveller says something in his narrative of a tradition relating to the worship of the snake in early times;[3] but he, at the same time, tells us that Buddhism was the religion which then prevailed in Cambodia. It is possible that this great building has been erected to the snake god (and this was the view taken by Prof. Ferguson after I had placed my plan, my photographs and the information I had gathered, at the disposal of that most distinguished authority on architecture); but after visiting China, and viewing the Hindoo deities which guard the gates of Buddhist temples there, and the mythological objects which adorn these shrines, I have been led to believe that Nakhon Wat is a Buddhist edifice, decorated about the roofs and balconies with effigies of the seven-headed snake, who is honoured for ever, because he guarded Gautama when he slept. 'Nagas (snakes) appeared at his birth to wash him; numbers of nagas conversed with him here and there, protected him, and were converted by him, and after the cremation of his body an eighth portion of the relics was allotted to the custody of nagas.'[4]

[1] Sir J. Davis, *The Chinese*, p. 210

[2] *Journeys in North China*, Rev. A. Williamson, ii. 353.

[3] 'Chinla Tung-too-ke,' by Chow Ta Kwan.

[4] *Sanscrit-Chinese Dictionary*, Art. Naga, 78, Dr. Eitel.

The snake plays an important part in the Buddhism of China, and is represented, when on the earth, as man's great enemy; and again, when a river god, as his great protector. It would appear, then, that the snake which guards the temple of Nakhon was nothing more than the natural protector of Gautama spoken of in the ancient Sutras.

I cannot, however, do justice to this question here; I must leave it in the hands of those who are better able to sift the evidence brought forward in elucidation of a deeply-interesting subject.

I believe that a richer field for research has never been laid open to those who take an interest in the great building races of the East than that revealed by the discovery of the magnificent remains which the ancient Cambodians have left behind them. Their stone cities lie buried in malarious forests and jungles, and though many of them have been examined, not a few are still wholly unexplored; and indeed it is impossible for anyone who has not visited the spot to form a true estimate of the wealth and resources of the ancient Cambodians, or of the howling wilderness to which their country has been reduced by the ravages of war, the destructive encroachments of tropical jungle, and the ignorance and sloth of its present semi-savage inhabitants. The disappearance of this once splendid civilisation, and the relapse of the people into a primitiveness bordering, in some quarters, on the condition of the lower animals, seems to prove that man is a retrogressive as well as a progressive being, and that he may probably relapse into the simple forms of organic life from which he is supposed by some to have originally sprung.

The bas-reliefs of Nakhon Wat which are sculptured on the walls of the galleries are extremely interesting. They are contained in eight compartments, measuring each from 250 feet to 300 feet in length, with a height

INTERIOR OF WESTERN GALLERY, NAKHON WAT.

of 6½ feet, and in a square space of 6½ feet the average number of men and animals depicted is sixty. The majority of these representations are executed with such care and skill, and are so well drawn, as to indicate that art was fostered and reached a high state of perfection among the 'Khamen-te-buran,' or ancient Cambodians.

The chief subjects represented are battle-scenes, taken from the epic poems Ramayana and Mahabarata (which the Siamese are said to have received from India about the fourth or fifth century). Disciplined forces are depicted marching to the field, possessing distinct characteristics soon lost in the confusion of battle. In the eager faces and attitudes of the warriors,

CAMBODIAN FEMALE HEAD-DRESS. ANCIENT SCULPTURE.

as they press forward past bands of musicians, we see that music then, as now, had its spirit-stirring influence. We also find humane actions represented—a group bending over a wounded comrade to extract an arrow, or remove him from the field. There are also the most animated scenes of deeds of bravery—soldiers saving the lives of their chiefs; chiefs bending over their plunging steeds, and measuring their prowess in single combat; and finally, the victorious army quitting the field laden with spoil, and guarding the numerous captives with cavalry in front and rear.

Perhaps the most wonderful subject of all the bas-reliefs is what the Siamese call the battle of 'Rama-kean.' This is one of the leading incidents of the Ramayana, of which Coleman says, 'The Grecians had their Homer to render imperishable the fame acquired by their glorious combats in the Trojan war; the Latins had Virgil to sing the prowess of Æneas; and the Hindoos have their Valmac to immortalise the deeds of Rama and his army of monkeys.' The Ramayana (one of the finest poems extant) describes the incidents of Rama's life, and the exploits of the contending foes.

In the sculptures of Nakhon Wat many of the incidents of the life of Rama are depicted; such as his ultimate triumph over the god Ravana, and the recovery of his wife Sita. The chief illustration of the poem, however, is the battle-scene which ensues after the ape-god Hanuman had performed several of the feats which formed the everyday incidents of his life, such as the construction of what is now known as Adam's Bridge at Ceylon. This he accomplished by a judicious selection of ten mountains, each measuring 64 miles in circumference; and being short of arms, but never of expedients, when conveying them to Ceylon, he poised one on the tip of his tail, another on his head, and with these formed his celebrated bridge over which his army of apes passed to Lanka.

In another compartment the subject appears to be the second avatar of Vishnu, where that god is represented as a tortoise supporting the Earth, which is submerged in the waters. The four-armed Brahma is seated above. A seven-headed snake is shown above the water, coiled around the Earth, and extending over

ANCIENT CAMBODIAN BAS-RELIEF, NAKHON WAT

the entire length of the bas-relief. The gods on the right, and the dinytas on the left are seen contending for the serpent. Hanuman is pulling at the tail, while above a flight of angels are bearing a cable to bind the reptile after the conflict is over.

The example given in the woodcut will convey an idea of the accurate nature of the battle-scenes, and will also enable the reader to judge for himself not only regarding the art which they display, but also of the constructive mechanical skill which the Cambodians possessed, and which enabled them to build their war chariots at once strong enough for the rough usage of war, and light enough to secure that degree of speed upon which the issue of a conflict might depend.

Take, for example, the wheel of the chariot. It must have been strong, and nothing lighter or more elegant could be constructed at the present day among ourselves. Part of it at least must have been made of metal, and had we no further proof, the inference may hence be fairly drawn that the builders were skilled in the use of metals. In another compartment of the bas-reliefs however, we find mechanical appliances for the torture of human beings, such as a double-handed saw, or knife, a lever, the wedge, pestle and mortar ; and a number of other contrivances, which must have been in common use then, and are still, in our own land.

It is impossible here, in the space of a single chapter, to give anything like a complete account of the information we gathered during our expedition to Cambodia. I may say, however, before I leave this region, that the ruins are found to spread over an area very much larger than was at first supposed, which has since been broken up into, and occupied by different independent States ; and which, judging from the similarity of the ruined buildings found in Siam, Laos, and Annam, and the identity of the characters with which they are inscribed, leaves little doubt as to the magnitude of the empire over which the ancient Cambodian dynasty must in former centuries have reigned. Much may yet be learned as to the true history of the race, when the inscriptions found carved upon the ancient temples shall have been made out. I took rubbings of some of these, but my efforts to obtain translations of them have hitherto been unsuccessful. Mr. Kennedy has, however, already been able to interpret some portions, and perhaps I cannot do better than quote what he says concerning them. 'There are, at any rate, three styles of writing adopted; I do not say that the languages differ, I suspect that they will be found to be in all cases identical; but the characters are fundamentally the same, and as more competent men than I have assured me, are modifications of the Devanagari alphabet. In reference to the difficulties to be encountered in translating, he says: 'There is this peculiarity to be noticed, which is probably one of the secrets of the failure hitherto of all attempts at interpretation. These men of monosyllabic speech cut down their long Pali or Sanscrit terms to the shortest possible dimensions. Thus Indra becomes In, a disciple of a priest (Samanera) becomes Nen, and the name for a camel is not ushtra, but ut; akshara (letters) becomes akson. But when these words are written down, in many cases their derivation is shown by a number of mute terminals, with an accent superscribed, denoting that that portion of the word is left without articulation. Now when we examine these inscriptions, it becomes necessary to inquire whether the engraver expended the time and labour requisite to write down the unpronounced part of the word which he had to engrave, or would he simply cut the letters of the shortened form, the word as pronounced, and not the word as written?'[1] If this be indeed the case,

ANCIENT ARCH AT KEU-YUNG-KIVAN, NANKOW PASS.

it is strange and interesting to find inscribed on an old arch in the defile of the Nankow Pass, on the road to the Great Wall of China, a Buddhist prayer, which Mr. Wylie tells us is also in one section, at least, written in

[1] See paper read by H. G. Kennedy, *Indian Section of Society of Arts*, May 1, 1874.

the ancient Devanagari characters, and bearing the date 1345. It was probably somewhere about this date that the temple of Nakhon Wat was erected; and when we further find it recorded that the ancient Cambodians were in the habit of sending ambassadors to China to obtain imperial titles for their religious edifices, it is possible that Cambodian sculptors may have been employed to construct this memorial, and more especially as we find on its keystone the same seven-headed snake which forms a leading ornament of the great Cambodian temple.

At any rate we have here the seven-headed snake adorning a purely Buddhist structure, inscribed with a Buddhist prayer, engraved in a number of different languages. The bas-relief representations of the Hindoo gods found beneath the arch are the finest examples of the sculptor's art I found in China, and resembled more closely the work of an ancient Cambodian sculptor than of a Chinese artist.

It would appear from the Chinese annals that the Cambodians, at an early period, were an exceedingly warlike race, and that they annexed many surrounding kingdoms.

Thus, in the history of the Sung dynasty, there is a reference to the kingdom of Sanbotsi. That country is there described as conterminous with Cochin China (Cheng Cheng), and lying between Cambodia (Chinla) and Java! It is further represented as highly civilised, owning both Hindoo and Chinese institutions, and making use of Chinese state documents. Lastly, we are told that the education of the country was conducted by means of Pali writing.

In the year A.D. 1003, it is stated that the reigning

monarch sent an embassy to inform the Emperor of China that he was building a Buddhist temple, in the hope that so meritorious a work might add something to the length of his years. The edifice referred to might have been Nakhon Wat, but evidence from

UNFINISHED PILLARS, NAKHON WAT.

other quarters points to a later date for its construction. It would appear to have been built after the visit of the Chinese traveller of the thirteenth century (whose narrative M. Remusat has translated), as he makes no mention of it. He visited Cambodia in 1295, but the final overthrow of the empire by the Siamese did not take place (according to M. Garnier's account, p. 139) until 1373, when the still unfinished temple was abandoned, and the King fled to Annam.

Nakhon Wat itself bears evidence that during the progress of its construction the Cambodian empire must have been overthrown by some crushing disaster. At any rate the building was never finished, and in the interior of an outer pavilion I found some pillars which were still rough hewn. They had been placed in position, it is true, but we could almost point out the spot at which the sculptor's hand had been arrested, leaving his task for ever incomplete. The plan followed had been to fit the rough monolithic stones into their places, and then to cover them with sculpture—a system adopted now-a-days by our own builders when elaborate ornaments have to be carved.

But I must quit a subject over which I fain would linger, and hurry forward on my journey. We spent several days at the ruined city of Nakhon, on the verge of the native jungle, and amidst a forest of magnificent trees. Here we were surrounded on every side by ruins as multitudinous as they were gigantic; one building alone covered an area of vast extent, and was crowned with fifty-one stone towers. Each tower was sculptured to represent a four-faced Buddha, or Brahma, and thus 204 colossal sphinx-like countenances gazed benignly towards the cardinal points—all full of that expression of purity and repose which Buddhists so love to pourtray, and all wearing diadems of the most chaste design above their unruffled stony brows. At the outer gate of this city, I experienced a sort of modern 'battle of the apes.' Reared high above the gateway stood a series of subordinate towers, having a single larger one in their centre, whose apex again displayed to us the four benign faces of the ancient god. The image was partly concealed beneath para-

SCULPTURED TOWER IN NAKHON THOM, THE ANCIENT CAPITAL OF CAMBODIA.

The cut represents a single example out of fifty-one stone towers which adorn the ancient temple 'Pres-sat-ling-pown,' in the heart of Nakhon Thom or 'Inthapatapuri.'

sitic plants, which twined their clustering fibres in a rude garland around the now neglected head. When I attempted to photograph this object, a tribe of black apes, wearing white beards, came hooting along the branches of the overhanging trees, swinging and shaking the boughs, so as to render my success impossible. A party of French sailors, who were assisting the late Captain de Lagrée in his researches into the Cambodian ruins, came up opportunely, and sent a volley among my mischievous opponents; whereupon they disappeared with what haste they might, and fled away till their monkey jargon was lost in the recesses of the forest.

On our return to Siamrap we found our old friend the Chow Muang busily engaged in the cremation services of the deputy governor, who had deceased not long before. The funeral pyre was set beneath an imposing catafalque, with a spire that reminded us of some Gothic church. A pavilion had also been erected to accommodate the spectators, of whom there were two hundred or thereabouts. The ceremony began with a procession of Buddhist priests, behind whom followed a band of musicians, a troop of hired mourners bringing up the rear. These mourners kept to their work bravely, the chief leading off with a shrill wail, and his associates supporting him with a chorus of sobs. While the body was still burning, the townsfolk gave themselves up to the delights of a banquet, or occupied their time with the theatricals and a variety of other amusements which had been provided for their entertainment, but gambling was the pastime most in vogue. The comic evolutions of a dwarf and a giant were received with general approbation, while a troop of pretty Lakon girls, who danced to native music, came in also to show that the burning of the body of a chief was by no means a subject to call forth intense mourning, any more than the burning of a house would with us, when one felt certain that the owners were safe and their effects insured. The deceased chief they supposed had gone, leaving behind nothing more than his old tenement of clay, that in his future state he might take possession of one better fitted for a being one degree nearer Nirvana. The only objection to the practice of cremation in our own Christian country that can be reasonably urged, is the feeling that the relatives of deceased persons would be sanctioning, or taking part in, what to them might seem to be a barbarous destruction of familiar and much-loved forms, in place of consigning them to the silent, slow, but equally certain and more loathsome process of decomposition in the grave. Some, again, would ask, what if our real bodies are, one day, to be raised up from the dead?—putting no faith in the theory that the dust of the dead mixes with its parent soil, and is constantly being redistributed among living plants and animals; and that the gases of the body pass into the air, and are carried with the wind over the wide world. Such persons would thus seek to limit the power of the Almighty by supposing that the process of cremation would in some way affect the ultimate designs of God. But this is a subject on which I cannot enter here. It seems to me, however, that no valid objections can be raised to cremation as a rapid means of disposing of the bodies of the dead in overcrowded cities, in the neighbourhood of which extensive and overstocked burial-grounds have proved detrimental to the health of the community.

Next day we mounted our elephants and started for the 'Richi Mountains,' about thirty miles distant from Siamrap. It is said that these mountains contain the quarries from which ancient Cambodians obtained their supplies of stone. On our route we passed more ruins, the most remarkable being a broad causeway which led right up to the foot of the hills, and which was still in very serviceable repair. The officer who accompanied us made a series of devout offerings at the shrines in the forest, in order to gain the favour of the malignant spirits that infest these wilds. We then set out bare-backed upon the elephants, to attempt to penetrate the thick jungle of the mountains.

But riding bare-backed upon an elephant was by no means as agreeable as it was new to us.

The loose skin on the back had a nasty way of carrying one over the hard spine of the animal. However, there was nothing for it but to submit and push on, as howdahs could not be used; and we soon discovered that even the elephants themselves could not make way through the gigantic wall of jungle and forest that closed us round on all sides. We had therefore to return, but not before seeing what we imagined to be traces of ancient stone quarries. The expedition occupied nearly three days, after which we pushed on for the head of 'Thale Sap' lake.

This lake rises during the rains to a very considerable depth, and forms a sort of back-water to the river Mekong; but when we crossed it, which it took us about five days to do, we found that the water was seldom more than three or four feet deep, whereas, at the end of the wet season, it becomes so full that even the forests on its banks are submerged. A number of fishermen's villages studded the lake, some of them far from the shores, and supported on piles which had been driven into the soft bottom of the lake. These villages, from their situation and general appearance, reminded me of the accounts given of the pre-historic Lake-dwellings of Switzerland. The houses are erected above a platform of bamboo, common to the entire settlement, and used also for drying and curing fish. After descending Thale Sap, and entering the stream that connects it with the Mekong, we discovered that a great trade in fish-oil was carried on in the Annamese settlements along the banks. It surprised us to see the enormous quantities of fish that were caught in this lake, and then sent to the Annamese villages to be boiled down into oil.

The trade is a lucrative one, and gives employment to thousands of families—the only really industious ones in this quarter. We came into contact with European civilization once more when a sudden bend of the stream brought us in sight of a small gunboat, which was there awaiting the return of M. de Lagrée from Siamrap. The meeting was as welcome as it was unexpected, and I shall be ever grateful to those kindly French officers for cordially receiving us on board. On March 26th we landed at Campong Luang, the first trading-place of any pretensions which we had yet reached on our downward voyage. There are many Malays settled in this town, as might be expected from the name it bears. Malay settlements, indeed, are common on both banks of the stream; but regarding the date at which they came into the country, the village chiefs whom I interrogated could give no certain information. They adhere to their own customs, are governed by their own chiefs, and are followers of the Mohammedan religion.

The bazaar at Campong Luang presented a most animated scene, and we saw few there who were not well-dressed and busy, and to all appearance prosperous.

We reached Penompinh on the night of the 27th, and anchored off the palace, in the centre of the town. Just below this place there is a point at which several streams converge. Of these confluents the most important is the great river Mekong, and after that the artery which drains the lake at one season and fills it at another, and down which we had been shaping our course. The King treated us with great courtesy, assigning us a house within the palace grounds, and entertaining us repeatedly at his table, where excellent dinners were specially prepared for us in completely European style. The fact is, his majesty had a French cook in his pay ; and this was the secret of a culinary skill which at first took us somewhat by surprise. These dinners were a real enjoyment, for we had not had a good meal for some time; as my readers will understand when I tell them that at Nakhon Wat—thinking we should be all the better for some strengthening food, and not being familiar with the American plan of cutting a steak as we required it, and keeping the animal going alive—we had to purchase a whole bullock to secure a joint of beef. The animal afforded us about three good meals, and caused us to be looked upon as demons by the devout Buddhists for slaying an ox. We then tried to preserve portions of the carcase, but it was a failure.

His majesty honoured us with a long performance of his dancing women. However, it was truly a tedious affair when the first novelty of the exhibition had worn off. As for the King, he lay stretched out in a nearly nude condition, betel-chewing and smoking, till the whole entertainment came to an end. Truly, the cares of state must sit easily on his royal breast.

In return for a number of presents we laid at the feet of this easy-going potentate, he one morning sent us a whole pig. He must have done this without consulting the members of his Cabinet, for otherwise a monarch so enlightened would hardly have been guilty of so inconsiderate an act.

The sight was too much for our way-worn Chinamen. Here was an entire fat porker, all our own, handed over to us as a free gift. Their masters would not eat of it, and that they well knew. Almost mechanically they stripped their jackets off, and whetted their knives, stopping every now and then to gaze and grin, and smack their lips in a sort of delirium of joy. After three days of uninterrupted feasting there was very little left of the pig; but our celestial serving-men made a touching appeal to us to pay them their dues, and suffer them to remain behind in a country where pigs are given away.

I photographed the King in his native robes of state, and a second time in the uniform of a French field-marshal. In the latter instance, I remember, there was some difficulty about the boots, which I think ended in his majesty borrowing a pair from his cook.

One night during our stay a fire broke out in a large Malay settlement on the other side of the stream. The spectacle was a grand one, and we hurried across the river, to see whether we could be of any use. Judge our surprise to find the Malays—men, women, and children—coolly sitting at the water's edge watching the devouring flames. At length we made up to the 'Orang-datu,' or chief, and prayed him to rouse the people to do something to save their effects; but he laconically replied, 'Teda tuan!' (No, sir). 'Why not? Have they then, themselves, set fire to the village?' 'Teda tuan' (No, sir), again. 'Tuan Alla poonia krajah! Kinappa bullie baut?' (It is God's work! What can we do?) The old man afterwards informed me, when the fire had done its worst, that it was customary for good sons of Islam to allow a conflagration to take its natural course, as it was simply one of God's most direct ways of punishing a much-loved community for their sins. 'Praised be God,' he said, as the last house fell among the ashes, and the inhabitants prepared to spend the night beneath the cloudless sky. Had he said that the fire was the work of the devil, he would have been much nearer the truth. For there were others in the town who assured us that conflagrations of this sort are brought about by incendaries—men who have just brought a large stock of bamboos to the place, and who will get a better sale for their wares if a fire brings building-material into brisk demand. Such conflagrations, therefore, are by no means uncommon, the simple inhabitants invariably setting it down to their own sins, while crafty Chinese speculators grow fat on the misery which their own mischief entails. The authorities are aware of this; probably some of them get hush-money out of the nefarious traffic.

Provided with elephants by the King, from whom, as well as from the French officers at Campong Luang, we received every kindness and attention, we set out for Kamput. The district crossed on our five days' journey overland abounded in forest-clad mountains and richly cultivated alluvial plains; but, as it was now the very height of the dry season, we suffered extremely from scarcity of water. The districts which lie between Pe-nompinh and Kamput are perhaps the most productive of any in the present kingdom of Cambodia. Rice is grown there in such abundance as to admit of a considerable export trade, although that grain is the staple food on which the people depend for their sustenance. Palm-sugar is another important article of commerce raised in this quarter. Silk also is produced and manufactured into the rich langoutis, prized no less for the brilliancy of their dyes than for the durability of their texture. At one spot in a plain which we crossed, a band of rebels had formerly been overthrown, and the skull of a ring-leader who had been captured and put to death was still to be seen impaled upon a post, as a warning to evil-doers. The intense heats of the day were followed by a clammy night air, and by heavy falls of dew. Once, after a heavy day's march, we stretched ourselves out, as usual, to pass the night on the open plain; and at daybreak, when I awoke and turned round to where my companion lay, I felt my limbs stiff and racked with pain, and I saw how my friend, where he still slept, had his head and hair glistening with a thousand drops of dew. After a while the rheumatic pains wore off, but we took care henceforward to observe greater caution in the selection of a resting-place. Passing through a rocky defile between mountains clad in evergreen forests, and rising five or six thousand feet above the plain, we emerged on April 9 on the cultivated lands around Kamput, having spent about five days in the accomplishment of our journey.

Kamput stands on the coast near the southern extremity of the Gulf of Siam, and is approached by a small shallow river not easily navigable, and having a bar at its mouth which obliges the ships that trade at the port to anchor in the road outside. The chief merchants at Kamput are, as a matter of course, Chinamen. It is the Chinese, too, who cultivate the rice, sugar, and pepper which form the chief articles of the local export trade. But the business of the place had fallen off, and the port, at the time of our visit, was said to be blockaded by a piratical fleet of junks, owned and manned by men of the same race as the merchants whom they sought to plunder, but hailing from different provinces; the merchants belonging mostly to Fukien, and the pirates to the island of Hainan. It was reported to us that some of these junks were bound for Bangkok; and one of our own servants, a Hainan man, who brought us the information, suggested to us to embark among his piratical kinsmen; but an old Malay chief, whom we fell in with at Kamput, gave us a hint of the danger, and we therefore declined the proposal.

This Malay chief was an officer in the service of the King of Cambodia; one who, with his trusty sword, had aided more than once in suppressing rebellion in the land. I enquired of him if, for any consideration, he would part with that sword. Bending the blade nearly double, and allowing it to spring out to within an inch of my throat, he replied 'No, sir! when I part with my sword I part with my life.' There is at Kamput a Malay settlement, of fighting men as far as I could make out. But our friend Mohamet, as I shall call him, though I did not learn his true name, told me a long story about a peaceful mission with which he had been entrusted, and one affecting the prosperity of the kingdom. He said, 'I was despatched to the distant mountains to search for a white elephant reported to have been seen by some "Orang Outan" or "Orang Bukit," wild men of the mountains, who dwell there.' 'But who are these wild men?' I said. Mohamet, assuming an expression of compassion at my ignorance, replied, 'Ah, you seem to know a good many things, and yet you don't know that.' 'Did you ever see one yourself, Mohamet?' 'No, sir, not exactly, not altogether, but I have seen them flying off through the forest. They are very black and hairy, have a language of their own, eat nuts and fruit, just like monkeys, and shoot game with the bow and arrow.

'Come with me and I will show you them. Moreover, if you are fond of sport, there are the elephant, rhinoceros, tiger, deer, besides a multitude of other animals which inhabit these wilds, and on which the "Orang Bukit" feed. More than that, if you give me ten days, as you hold the King's letter, I will take you over yonder mountains to a place near the summit of them, where sacred lotus pools are to be seen, and lilies big enough to sit in. There, at night, you hear the whisperings of strange beings around the pools, and see the weird lights of the "Orang Anto" (spirits), as they feed the reptiles that dwell in the waters. On the summit of the mountain there are foot-prints of animals of all sizes in the solid rock, some three feet in diameter, some smaller; some cloven, and some with toes and nails; all of them perfect, as if they had been moulded in clay. But I am coming to what I desired to tell you about, and by the holy prophet of Mecca it is true!' Here he made a gesture, as if to cut his throat, as a token of his veracity. 'On the mountain top there stands a ship made of stone. It wants the masts, it is true; but there, on the deck, is a coil of rope, also of stone. It is an immense ship, worn in places; but it is still complete, and who can say for how many tens of thousands of years it has stood where we may see it now.' As to the white elephant, he was not to be found, nor could he open communication with the 'Orang Bukit.'

It was difficult to know what to make of such a story as this. Mohamet spoke as one who was recording only what he had actually seen, and sketched me an outline of the stone ship with the point of his sword on the sand.

Perhaps he may have seen what he related in some dream, and told the story repeatedly, till belief in its reality had ultimately taken possession of his mind. Perhaps he had discovered Noah's Ark, and the true Mount Ararat. Perhaps it was a pure fabrication, founded on the account of the deluge contained in the Koran.

At any rate he volunteered to take us to the spot, and the offer was a tempting one; but we decided that we were both of us much in want of change, for our health had been somewhat impaired by the heat of the climate, by the scarcity of pure water, and by the absence of nutritious food. So we hired a boat with six men on board her, and set sail up the Gulf for Bangkok, a distance of about 500 miles. Trusting to a small map of this region, and to our compass, we kept watch and watch, Kennedy and myself, and made the run to the mouth of the Menam in rather less than five days.

Some of the islands where we landed on our route were uninhabited, save only by birds, insects, and wild animals. On one we found the spoor of the elephant, where that animal had been recently feeding; and this fact is valuable, in so far as it tends to corroborate the theory that these islands were originally attached to the mainland, and were separated probably by the subsidence consequent on volcanic action, as Mr. Wallace suggests when endeavouring to account for the natural history of the regions through which he travelled. There is hardly a bare spot on these islands. They are clothed with an evergreen foliage to their summits, and rise from the sea a glorious confusion of gigantic trees, tangled shrubs, and parasitic plants; save when bold red cliffs peep out, here and there, amid a drapery of pendant creepers. Among the boulders and bright sand on the beach are found clear pools, filled with beautiful marine plants and sparkling shells. The surrounding bed of the ocean, seen many fathoms down through the glassy water, rivals the island in the rich colours of its corals, shells, and plants.

On the night of the 18th we steered, as we thought, to fetch the mouth of the Menam; but it was unfortunately dark, and the land lay so low that we ran inshore about five miles to the eastward, and had to come to anchor with a heavy sea running, which favoured us with cold baths at short intervals throughout the night.

We made sail again next day at daybreak, and reached Bangkok in safety, much to the surprise of some of our friends, who had recommended, when we left, that we should take with us our coffins, and have the Burial Service read before starting.

CHAPTER VI.

Saigon; its Harbour—The Town—The Resident Foreign Community—Cholon, the Chinese Town—River Dwellings—Customs of the Cochin Chinese—Chinese Traders—The Cochin Chinese Village of Choquan—The Sorcerer—Plaine des Tombeaux—Petruski.

SAIGON, in French Cochin China, is approached by an offshoot of the great Mekong river, narrow and tortuous indeed, but nevertheless navigable for vessels of the heaviest tonnage. The town itself has a gay look about it, or had, at least, during the time of my visit; but it has a somewhat straggling appearance. Facing the settlement there is a spacious haven, containing a floating-dock, and a fleet made up of ironclads, steamers of the 'Messageries Maritime' line, and other private trading companies, besides many square-rigged ships awaiting cargoes of rice, the chief product of the vast alluvial plains of southern Cochin China. Along the banks run a long low line of cafés and mercantile or government offices, surmounted by the flags of the different consulates, while by far the most conspicuous building was an hotel in progress of erection, which promised to become a very imposing edifice.

The wide level roads, edged with rows of trees, and penetrating for miles in perfectly straight lines through the country, were an attractive feature in the settlement; showing also that the Government had lost no time and spared no expense in adopting measures which materially contributed to the health and enjoyment of the community. As for the residents themselves, they have provided their dwellings with many of the comforts and luxuries of home. As far, however, as I could judge, the bulk of the Saigon commerce is in the hands of the English and Germans. At the same time, there were a large number of French houses; yet the French merchant, somehow, seems to carry on his trade with a degree of polite ease and light but elegant deliberation, which constitute his business a means of supplying a comfortable pleasant livelihood, rather than an instrument which, after days of weary toil, sleepless nights, and continuous struggle, will enable him to wrest a competency from the hands of fortune. It is interesting to note how the day was usually portioned out. About half-past five or six o'clock in the morning the man-servant (Chinese) would tap at the door. 'Tuan bangon adda copee!' 'Awake, sir, coffee is ready,' is the announcement he brings, in Malay, a language spoken by the Singapore Chinese. Refreshed with a cup of coffee—of the true Parisian flavour, by the way—and with a plate of freshly-gathered fruit, the merchant would descend in bajo and pajamas (sleeping costume) to the office on the ground-floor; and there, having lit his cheroot, he would sit down to business till about half-past nine o'clock. To bathe and complete the toilet is the next duty to be fulfilled, and after this follows breakfast, with its rice, curry, and so forth; such a repast, indeed, with slight variations, as are the breakfasts which we know everywhere in the East. The meal concluded, time is whiled away with reading, sleeping, smoking, and lounging, until the cool of the afternoon has arrived. Then tiffin (luncheon) is served up, and after tiffin work is renewed for two or three hours. Some time is then spent in a promenade, to listen to the band; in a game of billiards, or 'écarté' at the club; or in sipping a glass of absinthe at the favourite café. After dinner the evening would be spent at home, or it might be at the club or café, where card-parties were made up and play carried on to a late hour.

This sort of existence is, of course, varied by private balls, dinner-parties, and state receptions at Government-house. I remember meeting one or two of the representative Chinamen at a Government ball, and among them one who had never before been present at such a gathering. Some one had informed this gentleman that the dancing carried on with great seriousness and ceremonial was part of our European burial service, and he was gravely enquiring whether he should not have appeared in white (deep mourning) as a token of sympathy for the bereaved, till he discovered that he had been the victim of a hoax. But the imaginative Frenchmen sometimes will themselves fall a prey to delusion. On one occasion, at a quiet dinner given by a French merchant, I found the guests could talk of nothing else but the untimely end of a devoted naturalist and distinguished traveller who had filled the position of director of the 'Jardin Botanique' in Saigon. It was reported that this unfortunate gentleman had been robbed and murdered by a band of natives in a hill district, where he had for some months been prosecuting his botanical researches. Our party was truly a sad meeting; the young martyr to science was loved and esteemed by all who knew him, and those present, one and all, vowed to wreak a speedy vengeance on the heads of the assassins, a number of whom—so the rumour ran—had already been secured. The tide of sympathy was now at its height, when a light foot was heard on the stairs—in a moment the door flew open, and the murdered savant rushed into the arms of his sorrowing fellow-countrymen. He had, as it turned out, lost all his property, but a well-disposed native had saved his life.

Cholon, the native quarter of Saigon, is separated from the European settlement by a distance of three miles. Let the reader join me in a morning walk to this half Chinese, half Annamese town. Our course is along the footway of the 'Grand Canal'—grand in nothing but its name, for the banks are overgrown with rank weeds, and the waters at high tide are muddy, and at low tide mud. A pack of pariah dogs rush madly across the road, and through the cloud of dust which they raise we can discern the outlines of a train of Cambodian carts, each cart having a pair of bullocks tethered by a rope through their nostrils to the conveyance immediately in front. The whole train is managed by a little boy, for the traders are still asleep among the tusks, hides, horns, gum-dammar and gamboge, which they are bringing to market for sale. The cart-wheels creak hideously around their dry wooden axles, and indeed would make the fortune of any speculator who should be enterprising enough to drive them up and down some quiet London neighbourhood. We had now entered the main Cholon road. Yonder is the Gendarmerie on the left, and here come a long row of barefooted women, bringing fresh vegetables to the town. Their dress is similar to that of the Chinese peasant girls, excepting their hats, and these resemble huge baskets poised above their heads. Hats of this sort are made of dried leaves, and measure two feet in diameter, by six inches in depth. The men wear head-pieces even larger still, conical in shape, and descending over the shoulders; these huge extinguishers are tilted up in order to enable their wearers to see their way, and are of a sort well suited to the Annamese character, for they afford shelter from rain, and this is everything among a people who deem pure water to be their deadliest foe. During a residence of three months in Cochin China, I do not recollect ever having seen a native wash himself, unless when requested to do so, that a fair photographic representation of his face might be obtained; and even then the operation had to be carefully watched, for the washing was managed in such a way that it left a rim round the physiognomy, like an earthwork, thrown up to protect the features from further violence.

Let us, however, proceed in our excursion. There has been no rain for months, the hedges and shrubs are bronzed with dust, but enlivened also by the varied colours of the convolvulus. There is nothing of peculiar interest to be seen on the road at this early hour, until we get within a mile from the town; and then we come upon the 'Plaine des Tombeaux,' a burial-ground covering an area of about twenty miles. This ground was chosen by the native rulers hundreds of years ago, as a resting-place for the dead, in obedience to the advice of the court astrologers. The telegraph which skirts the road now tells of new life, and a new era in the history of the country. Cholon is now before us; the principal inhabitants are Chinese, and Chinese characteristics are to be discovered everywhere around, no less in the temples and the houses than in the industrious activity of the population. The town was astir hours ago, and in the faces we encounter so full of business we recognize only Chinamen.

In order to see something of the Cochin Chinese we must go to the river-side, where there are hundreds of boats grouped together, forming a native floating village. Many of the Chinese merchants are already down to the boats, treating for the rice which they contain, while others have closed their bargains, and are paying the natives in basket-loads of copper cash. A few steps beyond we come upon the river dwellings. Can any style of life be more primitive than this? The caves which our British forefathers inhabited were castles when compared to these abodes, and the Swiss Lake-dwellings were palaces. Here a family of seven may be found domiciled in a hut which measures five feet by seven. The sanitary arrangements are simple. The structure is elevated on a platform a few feet above the stream, into which all the refuse and garbage is allowed to fall. The capitalist, if he proposes to build a river residence of this sort—one offering every advantage to a large family in search of cheerful society, a commanding view of the stream, good fishing close at hand, unencumbered by tolls and ground rent, and boasting a drainage system so unelaborated and cheap—has to launch out the sum of two-and-a-half dollars, or twelve shillings, in the construction and decoration of the edifice. When built, the proprietor will let it on a repairing lease. By referring to the picture it will be noticed that the 'Paterfamilias' has modestly retired behind his children. As the morning is hot, his only article of clothing is a conical hat, the badge of parental dignity. He would, as he is partially civilized, have removed this ornament when we approached, but as it might have led to a severe cold and an untimely end, I requested him to keep it on. Clothing in this neighbourhood is one of the most expensive items in the maintenance of a family, although articles of dress are usually unknown to the children until they become five years old. In front of these huts we may see the canoes, scooped out of solid logs, and used for friendly visits, marketing, or fishing. These natives, as I have already said, are not cleanly in their habits. They are near water, but I fear soap would find a poor market among them, unless they took a fancy to eat it, which sometimes occurs. They labour as little as they possibly can, and spend their leisure in smoking, in chewing as much betel-nut as they can afford to buy, and in the chase; but their hunting-ground is a 'caput humanum,' and the tiny game is esteemed a great delicacy. Here, in Cholon, the Chinese is the dominant trading Asiatic race, and this is indeed the case in all the Malayan and Indo-Chinese nations to which they have emigrated. They are almost invariably found not only carrying on a direct import and export trade on their own account, but also acting as middle-men between the foreign merchants and the natives. I made the acquaintance of one or two China merchants in Cholon, who not many years ago arrived in the country as ordinary day labourers, and who by their reputation for energy and honest dealing won for themselves the support and confidence of the European traders in Saigon.

During the Chinese new-year holidays, I had an invitation to the house of one of these traders. The place was built in semi-Chinese, semi-European style. The front warehouse had changed its usual aspect.

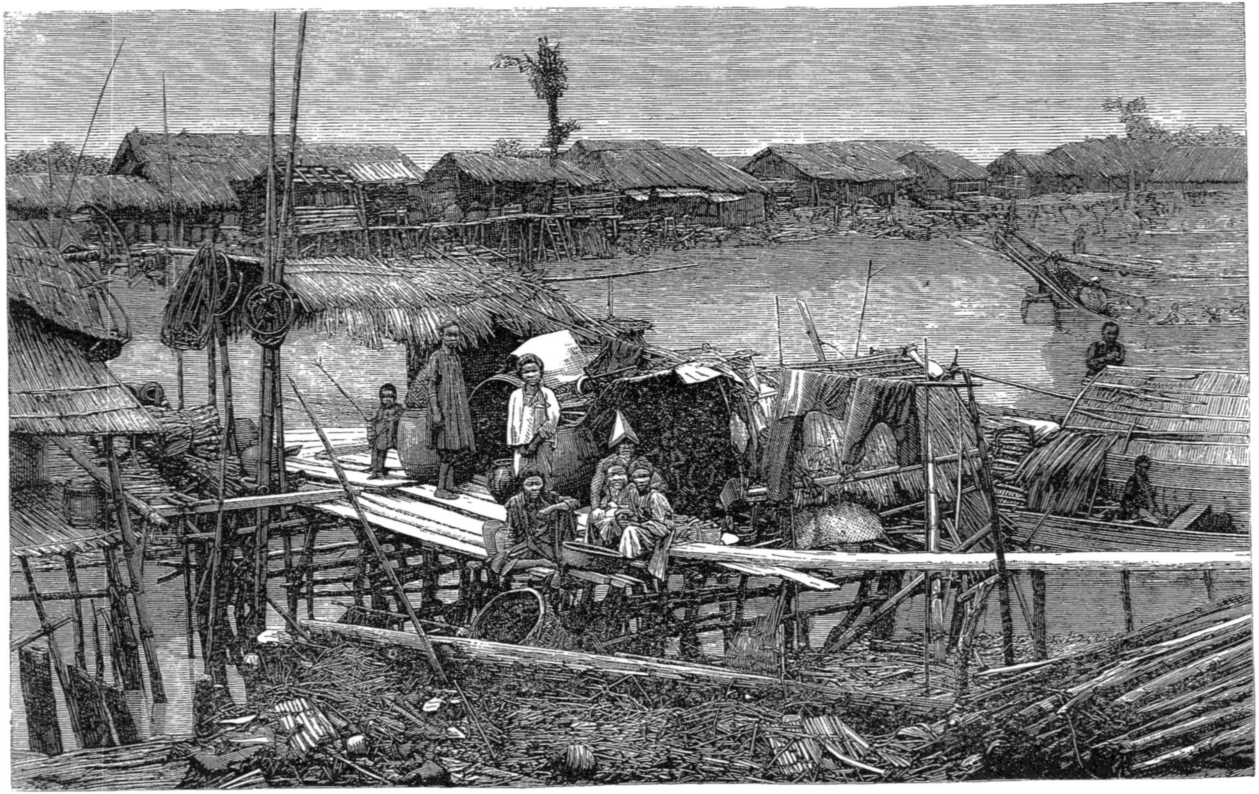

VIEW OF SHOLON, COCHIN CHINA

Tables with embroidered covers had taken the place of bales of piece goods and bags of produce, and were laden with substantial fare. Some hundreds of vermilion visiting-cards, each about the size of a sheet of note paper, and inscribed with Chinese names, adorned the walls. In a spacious apartment on the upper story a table was spread with European ware, wines, and delicacies. Our host apologised for the absence of certain plates and knives by saying that his Cochin Chinese friends had begged to be allowed to carry them off as curiosities. Some of these sons of Han settle permanently in the country, but the majority return to China, where, having purchased a petty title and personal security with a portion of their savings, they will retire, or resume business with what is left.

The village of Choquan stands about half way between Saigon and Cholon. On the right of the pathway by which it is reached there is a well-grown bamboo hedge, and on the left, in the centre of a rice-field, a deep pool in which buffaloes delight to wallow, plastering their hides with mud to prevent the attacks of the moschettos. Upon approaching Choquan there is nothing to be seen of the village, save the fruit-trees that cluster round the houses; and at the time of my visit, orange and pumeloe-trees (*Citrus decumana*) were in full fruit, bending down over the enclosures with the burden of their crops. The village, in so far as I could make out, is entered through a narrow lane between two walls of prickly cactus; this lane led to a labyrinth of other lanes, so I was puzzled to know which to take to find Choquan. But I had passed through the heart of the hamlet several times without being aware of it, as the scattered houses were each shut in by high hedges of cactus or bamboo. The natives love privacy; every prickle in the hedges that encompass their dwelling is, as it were, a token that the family within would rather be alone. If one be not satisfied with this, the outer doorway has only to be opened, when one or two ill-conditioned pariah dogs will show their fangs, and use them too. Groups of naked children roll about in the dust in the lanes, or loll in the shade smoking, inflating their chubby cheeks with the fumes of the cigarette and blowing them out again through mouth and nostrils with that air of intense satisfaction which belongs usually to maturer years. Men, too, block up the way squatting or (as the hedge is not an inviting object to lean against) lying down in the dust to have a talk, or else—as there are no 'Swans,' 'Wheat Sheaves,' or 'Royal Oaks,' one of which always seems to be the next house we come to in our village streets at home—they betake themselves to their own abodes, bar the outer gate, get into the verandah, into seats, or upon matted benches furnished with wooden pillows, and then, in a recumbent position, with tea, cigarette, sam-shu and betel-nut within reach, resume the topic of discussion, the interest in which has carried them so far through the listless day.

Now let us enter one of these dwellings. The two men (for what I relate I have actually witnessed), now prostrated with their conversational efforts, are landowners in the village, and their estates measure about an acre apiece. The pair of pleasant-faced unwashed little girls who fan their masters are domestic slaves. The lady of the house sits smoking and dandling her child in a dark corner of the interior. The edifice itself is well built, and the floor stands upon brick pillars

A VILLAGE ROAD, COCHIN CHINA

about three feet above ground. An ornamental framework of carved wood supports the tiled roof, and the interior is partitioned off into apartments for the decent accommodation of the family. In front there are verandahs on each side of the doorway, and above the lattice is a board inscribed with the owner's name or title, while suspended from the doorposts are additional boards bearing texts from the Chinese classics. If the owner be a man of wealth, the entire front of his house is carved into open work, which with the addition of paint and gilding presents an imposing aspect, and serves to screen the defects within, where the family are kept lively by the vermin that revel in the darkness and dirt. The fetid air of the interior deters one from a prolonged inspection. Let us notice, however, the unique arrangement of a boudoir where an old woman is seated on a table sewing, and an elderly gentleman reclines on a neatly-covered couch. A few chairs of Chinese make are ranged round the apartment. On one of them stands a rice-pot filled with oranges, a bowl of rice, a cup of sam-shu, and one or two disused idols. On another we may see sundry articles of horse harness, and above it a Roman Catholic picture in red and yellow. Beneath the chair are a bag of fruits and a lot of agricultural implements. Chinese and European pictures are hung about the walls; and one or two mirrors, which give most hideous contortions of the human face, make up the adornments of the dwelling.

Now for a breath of pure air, and I will take you to another quarter of Choquan, where a sorcerer resides. His house is situated in a retired part of the village, and is surrounded by a thick cactus hedge.

There is only one way by which this curious retreat can be entered, and that is by ascending a tree which bends over the hedge, then walking along a branch, and dropping from it to the doorway of the hut. When we have got inside we find the doctor, soothsayer, and magician, bent over a volume. Strewn on a rough deal table before him are the herbs by means of which he works some of his potent spells. One herb there is in frequent demand, and is a love-philter; and this, when used by some ardent but disappointed swain, must be reduced to a powder, and applied to the end of a cigarette which he presents to the unsuspecting but fickle fair one. When the first few whiffs of the enchanted vapour have been puffed through her nostrils, she loses her heart to its assailant, and is conquered. The posture of profound study assumed by the magician is altered at intervals, and the mysterious medicine-man at last reminds us that he is mortal by reaching forth his hand to refresh himself from a bowl of sam-shu (native whiskey). Now he pauses to take a whiff of his pipe, or to rivet his gaze upon nothing material, while he ponders over the most dangerous symptoms of his last patient, considering whether in the event of his succumbing to his disease, or his physician's treatment, the friends of the deceased will be able to pay the full fee. It may be he is then interrupted by a fresh patient dropping down upon him with a broken head, or heart, the victim of a quarrel or the sufferer from disappointed love. But the branch of his profession on which he mainly depends to fill his cash-box is the exorcism of the devils, which find a home in the hearts of his countrymen, When a poor man is troubled with a malignant spirit, it can be got rid of for about a dollar; while, on the other hand, if the patient be a man of property, the demon is certain to prove refractory, and to require at least sixteen or twenty dollars' worth of spells to bring about his ultimate expulsion. When called to a patient's bed-side, the doctor begins his operations by bleeding—not the sick man, however, but himself. Into his own cheeks he first fixes two small skewers having lighted candles attached to their ends; then bending over the bed, he recites the praises of the good spirit, Châu-xuong, and solicits its aid. Should this exorcism fail, he calls in his attendant who does the drudgery, stretches out the lad's right arm, and in his hand next places an idol, which is supposed to create involuntary motion in the extended arm. After the first hour or so, the involuntary motion resolves itself into one that takes the nearest bowl of sam-shu provided for the idol deity, who, on such occasions, has an intense thirst, producing strangely enough, a variety of complex and involuntary motions in the limbs of the assistant who supports him. The natives attribute all this to a kind of animal magnetism, not unknown in other parts of the world. Should the treatment described be unsuccessful, the physician, priest, and sorcerer is supposed to sleep on thorns, walk through fire, drink boiling resin, and accomplish a variety of feats, wherein the only visible spiritual agent is sam-shu. Another source of income to this mysterious quack is derived from the 'Plaine des Tombeaux,' or 'Dông-tâp-trâu,' where tens of thousands of the Cochin Chinese lie buried. He has simply to declare to some afflicted family that the cause of their affliction is the unfortunate position of the body of a deceased kinsman in relation to the terrestrial dragon; he will then be engaged by the suffering survivors to remove the body to a more lucky site.

The Cochin Chinese, like the Chinese, have many superstitions connected with the burial of the dead; one of these accounts for the uniform direction of the graves in Dông-tâp-trâu, and another for their general structure. As in China, the dragon is frequently seen sculptured on their tombs. When death takes place in a family, this sorcerer or master of the mysteries of 'Feng-shui' is called in to superintend the burial of one who, it may be, has been a victim of his quackery; and, as a matter of business, he is expected to dispose of the corpse in such a way that the spirit in its new state will aid the fortunes of the house. He therefore proceeds to Dông-tâp-trâu, with a Chinese compass in the one hand, and an idol in the other. His first care is to find the position of the head of the terrestrial dragon, in order that he may rest the head of the body upon it. He then carefully takes the bearings of the stream that flows through the plain, so that the body may be placed with its feet towards the source. Were it placed with its head towards the source, it is believed that the spirit would be eternally engaged in striving to make way against the current, and thus suffer, through the neglect of surviving relations, the torments of a perpetual watery hell.

The Cochin Chinese gentleman, like his prototype among other and more enlightened nations, generally exhibits in his physique and manners the evidences of superior breeding. When nature has had fair play, he is taller and more erect than the average specimens of his countrymen of the humbler orders, while they are infinitely his superior in muscular development. He has never done a day's work in his life. His hands are small, well formed, and soft like a woman's, while, as an indication of their utter uselessness, the nails of his third and little fingers are permitted to grow, or are cultivated, until they rival vulture's claws. Some of his actions, too, might be aptly compared to those of the king of birds. If he be a government official, he is frequently severe in the treatment of subordinates; for it is he, together with his chief, who are responsible for their behaviour. In consequence of this system, clannish outbreaks are less frequent in French Cochin China than among the Chinese of Singapore and Penang. The life he leads is an indolent one; when at home, he lolls on a couch or chair, surrounded by half-a-dozen attendants, one probably hunting for insects in the hair of his head, another fanning him; while a third, who watches the inanimate face of his lord, anticipates a wish, lights a pipe or cheroot, and quietly places it between his master's lips. Should a friend drop in for a chat, he fills his mouth with betel-nut and seri, as a polite intimation that anything like an animated conversation is not to be thought of, and only suited for the vulgar. The friend is then invited to do likewise; and when both have the nut sufficiently chewed, gurgling growls, emitted through the plash of mastication, are interchanged, intelligible only to their own highly-tuned ears. A notable exception to the above type of native gentleman was Monsieur Petruski, a Cochin Chinese Christian, occupying the post of professor of his own language in the College des Interprètes of Saigon. He had been educated in a

Roman Catholic college at Penang, and I shall never forget my surprise when first introduced to him. He addressed me in perfect English, with just a slight French accent, while in French he could converse with the same purity and ease. He was equally at home, I believe, when he spoke, or wrote in Spanish, Portuguese, or Italian; and it was to his scholarly knowledge of Oriental tongues that he owed the distinguished position which he filled. On one occasion I visited his study, and I found him engaged on a work which had cost him years of labour—'A Comparative Analysis of the Languages of the World.' He was surrounded by a collection of rare and valuable books, some of which he had gathered when travelling in Europe; others—Sanscrit, Pali, Siamese, and Chinese—he had obtained in various parts of the East. During the evening one of the Cholon missionaries joined us, and when I left he had engaged Petruski in a theological discussion in Latin. He is the author of a number of works; among others, an Annamite Grammar, which opens by tracing the affinity between the most ancient symbolical characters and those of the modern written language of Annam.

CHAPTER VII.

Hongkong—Description of the Island—The City of Victoria—Its present Condition—Its Foreign and Native Population—The Market-place—Hongkong Artists—Grog-shops—Tai-ping-shan—Expense of Living—A Strange Adventurer—A Mormon Missionary.

AFTER leaving Cochin China I spent a short time in Singapore, and thence took voyage to the British colony of Hongkong. Hongkong was the first island I visited in Chinese waters, and it was there that I obtained my earliest impressions of the Chinese on their native soil, and formed the determination, which I afterwards carried out, of making myself acquainted with the manners and customs, and the wide-spread industries, of this ancient people in various provinces of their land.

Hongkong, with its mixed population, its British rule and institutions, its noble European edifices, and Chinese streets, its Christian churches, and Buddhist temples, stands alone, on the verge of the great continent of Eastern Asia. This spot, moored to our little island by an electric cable that sweeps half round the globe, rises like a political beacon out of the China seas, and has by no means been without its influence in preventing the Tartar dynasty from foundering, in maintaining peace, and in casting the light of a higher civilization over some dark corners of the Flowery Land.

We may justly be proud of the policy which planted the British flag on this desolate island, and constituted it a Crown colony in 1843. A like praiseworthy enterprise since those days has built a splendid city out of its granite rocks, cleared the surrounding seas of piratical hordes, and crowded the spacious harbour with a merchant fleet of all nationalities; and yet, in some respects, the change is a disappointing one. Our liberal administration, and the freedom, and protection afforded by our laws, have rendered the place an asylum for the scum of Chinese cities and for ruffians too poor, or actually too depraved, to be able to purchase immunity from the penalties of crime by entering the Buddhist cloisters of their own land. Happily some of these *mauvais sujets*, finding a wider scope for honest energy, become respectable citizens, but the bulk of them are either supported in our prisons, or else prey upon the European and native community.

Although the geographical position of the island is well known, it may not be out of place here to give some account of its general appearance before we disembark. On the average it is about ten miles in length and four miles broad. A central rocky spine runs from east to west, rising in a series of jagged peaks, whose greatest elevation is 1,900 feet, and falling away towards the shore in a multitude of low hills, or bold crags. It is no longer the barren place of thirty years ago. There are wood-covered heights and grassy slopes, gardens in the valleys, and picturesque fisher villages nestling beneath the shade of umbrageous trees; while on the north, the city of Victoria rears its granite buildings, like the side of a richly-sculptured pyramid, on the terraced cliffs beyond Victoria Peak. Below the town the shore curves round towards the mainland of British Kowloon, where a high ridge of hills encloses one of the finest harbours in the world, approached from the east by the Ly-ee-moon Pass, and entered through the Lama passage on the west, The view of Victoria from Kellet's Island, a small fortified rock in the east of the harbour, presents a striking scene, more especially during the rainy season, when the setting sun casts a deep purple veil over the town and over the peak,

HONGKONG, FROM KELLET'S ISLAND.

which lie partly in shadow. At such a time I have seen the hill capped with a wreath of pearly cloud with a fringe of rose-pink or gold, and the edges of the stone buildings beneath gilded with sunshine looming out through the deepening gloom. The islands in the distance seemed like ruby clouds resting on the horizon, while near at hand a tangled forest of masts and spars rose up darkly against the face of the sky. The harbour was ablaze with light, broken by the sombre hulls of the ships, or the picturesque forms of native craft, with their huge sails spread out like wings to catch the evening breeze.

Let us suppose that we land from a steamer that has just come to her anchorage. It is early morning, and there is a great tumult on deck. Passengers hurry, to and fro, in quest of baggage that had been consigned to the hold, and about which the officers seem to know nothing and care less.

Trunks and boxes are all the while being speedily got up and arranged on deck, and the yells and imprecations of a hundred boatmen announce, not that they have come from the lower regions, but that celestial labourers are discharging cargo in their own way. Soon the ladder is let down, and up it scramble a number of petty traders arrayed in straw hats, long white cotton, or silk jackets which reach to the knees, dark blue breeches, white cotton leggings, and embroidered shoes with thick flat soles. To your surprise, one accosts you familiarly as captain, and says, with a look of recognition, 'Tsing! Tsing! too muchee long tim my no hab see you!' This is the pidjin English for 'I greet you! it is a long time since I have seen you!' It is no use telling the fellow he is mistaken, as you have only arrived for the first time in China. He will reply, 'Ah, my sabby your broder, you alla same large facie mun; he blong my good flin;' or, 'Ah, I understand, I know your brother, you have the same broad benevolent face as he who was my friend.'

They have a notion, some of them, that England is a very small outside settlement on the borders of the Chinese Empire, and that we Englishmen all know each other, or are in some way akin. Hence they think they cannot go far wrong in asserting that you are some member of the family. These men are floating tailors, shoemakers, jewellers, washermen, artists, and curio-dealers; but we will have a better look at them ashore. They are certainly very enterprising, and there is no end of competition among them. Others, a trifle more enlightened, imagine that Hong-kong represents our greatest possession, and that the bulk of our people are merchants, who pass, to and fro, in ships engaged in the Chinese trade. We go ashore in a native boat, which is the floating dwelling of an entire family. There are, in Hongkong alone, more than 30,000 such people as these, who make their homes in their boats, and earn their subsistence by fishing or attending upon the ships in harbour. These folks carefully study the indications of the weather, and can calculate with great shrewdness the near approach of a storm. They usually verify their own observations by ascertaining the barometrical changes from foreign ship-captains in port; and when they have settled in their own mind that a typhoon is at hand, they cross the harbour *en masse*, and shelter in the bays of Kowloon until the fury of the hurricane is past. The men in the boats are naked to the waist, and bronzed with constant exposure; but the women are decently clothed, pretty, and attractive-looking. Some of them, if we may judge by their pale skins, their finely-formed features, and their large lustrous eyes, are not of purely Chinese blood. We have just time to observe that the Praya, or Bund, is faced with a retaining wall composed of huge blocks of granite—which, as we shall see by-and-by, are not of sufficient dimensions or weight to resist the violence of a typhoon—when we are landed opposite the Clock Tower at Peddar's Wharf, and find ourselves mobbed and jostled by a crowd of Chinese coolies, who, if you don't look about, will tilt you into a chair and bear you off, *nolens volens*, to the nearest hotel.

A FAMILY PARTY, KOWLOON.

These sedans take the place of our flys, and are the only public conveyances in the town. They are licensed, and bear, each one, a printed tariff of charges, fixed at about half the cost of London cabs. Each chair will hold one passenger. It is made of bamboo, roofed over with oilcloth, and is carried on two long poles that rest on the shoulders of the bearers. It is by no means a disagreeable mode of travelling, and affords, at the same time, a good opportunity for seeing the streets. If of a sensitive temperament, you are apt to feel compassion for the men who bear you through the hot thoroughfares, or toil up the hill paths in order that, without an effort of your own, you may breathe the fragrance or enjoy the wonders of the Flowery Land. These sedans are to be found at every street corner, also in front of the hotels and public-houses. The bearers make it their constant study to find out the habits of the European residents, so that a new-comer only requires to be about a week in the place, and it is ten chances to one, should he be dining out, and hail the first chair to take him home, the chair-coolies, without a word spoken on either side, will land him in front of his domicile. Nay, they have learned more; they already know something of his personal character, and whether they ought to trust him and accept the paper which he offers. It is customary, in most transactions with the Chinese, to pay them with an order on the schroff, or Chinese cash-keeper of the house to which one belongs, while the schroff, in honouring these chèques, whenever he has the opportunity, will discharge the debt in light dollars, and charge full weight to his employer's account.

This is the first sample of the systematic squeezing and overreaching process which is the keynote of Chinese society over the whole land. The system is so minute in its ramifications, that it is quite impossible for the European merchant who employs Chinese compradors and schroffs to place a check upon it.

Besides this, the value of the dollar in copper cash is subject to constant fluctuations. To-day it may be 110 copper cash; but should the cook, house-boy, or coolie be sent to market, he only accounts to his master for 100 cash each; the difference in exchange he pockets as his own legitimate squeeze. We are now in Queen's Road, which runs east and west through the town, and to the right, and left, a labyrinth of streets conduct us to the Praya, or to the upper terraces and roads cut along the face of the hill. Every available spot of ground in this quarter of Hongkong is taken up with shops, stores, offices, and banks. The Hongkong Club and Hotel are stone-built edifices, whose imposing proportions would not disgrace the best part of London; and as for the shops and their array of valuable contents, Falconer the jeweller's, which is but a trifle more showy than the rest, looks like an establishment in the heart of Bond Street. The Chinese, on their part, vie with each other in the display of costly wares, Canton silks, carved ivory, jewellery, porcelain and paintings. Entering 'Sun-Sing's,' a Cantonese shop, we are welcomed by the proprietor himself, a Kwangtung gentleman speaking English. His attire is a jacket of Shantung silk, dark crape breeches, white leggings and embroidered shoes, and he displays all the pondorosity and ease of a prosperous Chinaman. His assistants are dressed with equal care, and stand behind ebony counters and glass cases—the latter of spotless polish, and filled with curiosities, ancient and modern, from Canton. One side of the shop is occupied with rolls of choice silks, and samples of grass matting, all labelled and priced. The floor above is taken up with a cleverly arranged assortment of ancient bronzes, porcelain and ebony furniture and lackered ware. We invest in an ivory fan, and Sun-Sing designs and engraves on it a pretty English monogram. This shopkeeper, really a fine specimen of his race, much respected by the European community, and scrupulously fair in his dealings, will furnish one with the cheapest toy in his stock with as great politeness, and apparent satisfaction, as if receiving an order for a shipload of embroidered silks.

Crossing the street we enter the market-place, but there the chief business of the day was concluded by about seven in the morning. Here the avenues are rendered picturesque by painted and gilded signboards inscribed with characters, Chinese or English, though the dealers are all of them Chinamen. Thus 'Ah-Yet' 'Sam-Ching,' 'Canton Tom,' and 'Cheap Jack,' announce that they are prepared, as ships' compradors, to supply poultry, beef, vegetables, and groceries of the best quality, at the lowest rates, and solicit a trial, or at least an inspection of their stalls. Such men keep monthly market-books for their customers, and these, with each item supplied and its price jotted down, are settled at the end of each month. Apart from the well-filled shops of these useful members of society, there are a great variety of stalls which supply special commodities ; preserved European provisions, for example—fruit, fish, and so forth. Perhaps the most interesting of them is the fishmonger's. This establishment consists of an arrangement of tanks, or aquariums, filled with clear running water, and teeming with living sea or river fish, for the most part reared in the Canton fish-breeding ponds, and brought to market in water-boats. The purchaser stands over the tank, selects some finny occupant which takes his fancy, and this is immediately caught and supplied to him. I have never seen any of these fresh-water fish in Europe ; they revel in the most beautiful and varied colours, blue, green, brown, red, yellow, mottled, striped or spotted ; and there are others plain and uniform in tint, though no less curious in form. Then, at the butcher's, there are sundry delicacies to be met with unknown to European palates, but which the natives delight in ; rats strung up by the tails, temptingly plump, and festoons of living frogs fattened for the epicure. Some say that here and there we may see small legs, and ribs, undoubtedly canine, but of this I am by no means certain. I have, indeed, in cities purely Chinese, seen dog's flesh sold for food ; the practice, however, is not a common one. As a rule, the Chinese are not very particular as to the kind of food they eat ; but they are cleanly in their modes of preparing it, and we might well learn some valuable lessons from them in this branch of domestic economy. Thus they are skilled in making very palatable and nutritious dishes out of odds and ends, and are far less wasteful and extravagant in the use of their food than we are.

A number of our best European vegetables are sold in the Hongkong market ; beef and mutton, fowls, eggs, fish and game, are also to be procured at prices which seldom exceed what we pay for the same commodities at home. Besides all this, there are about fifty different kinds of fruit, nearly the half of them indigenous, and peculiar to China. Retracing our steps to Queen's Road, we pause before a display of huge signboards, each one glowing in bold Roman letters with the style and title of some Chinese artist. The first we come to is that of Afong, photographer ;

to this succeeds Chin-Sing, portrait painter. Then follows Ating; and many others make up the list of the painters and photographers of Hongkong. Afong keeps a Portuguese assistant to wait upon Europeans. He himself is a little, plump, good-natured son of Han, a man of cultivated taste, and imbued with a wonderful appreciation of art. Judging from his portfolios of photographs, he must be an ardent admirer of the beautiful in nature; for some of his pictures, besides being extremely well executed, are remarkable for their artistic choice of position. In this respect he offers the only exception to all the native photographers I have come across during my travels in China. He shows not a single specimen of his work at his doorway, whereas his neighbour Ating displays a glass case containing a score of the most hideous caricatures of the human face that it is possible for the camera obscura to produce. Ascending a narrow staircase we reach the showroom of this celestial artist; and there, in another case of samples, we find representations of men and women, some looking as if they had been tossed against a wall and caught in a moment of intense excitement and alarm; others with their heads to all appearance spiked on the iron rest; while, as far as the natives were concerned, the majority wore the Buddhistic expression of stolid indifference, and were seated all of them full front, with limbs forming a series of equal angles to the right and left. A Chinaman will not suffer himself—if he can avoid it—to be posed so as to produce a profile or three-quarter face, his reason being that the portrait must show him to be possessed of two eyes and two ears, and that his round face is perfect as the full moon.

The same careful observance of symmetry is carried out in the entire pose of the figure. The face, too, must be as nearly as possible devoid of shadow, or if there be any shadow at all, it must be equal on both sides. Shadow, they say, should not exist; it is an accident of nature; it does not represent any feature of the face, and therefore should not be pourtrayed; and yet they all of them carry fans in order to secure that very shade, so essential to existence in the South of China, and the element—though they fail to recognise it as such—to which, in conjunction with light, they are indebted for the visible appearance of all things animate and inanimate which make up the Chinese Empire.

The walls of Ating's studio are adorned with paintings in oil, and at one extremity of the apartment a number of artists are at work producing large coloured pictures from small imperfect photographs. The proprietor has an assistant, whose business it is to scour the ships in port in search of patrons among the foreign crews. Jack, desirous of carrying home a souvenir of his visit to the wonderful land of pigtails and tea, supplies a small photograph of Poll, Dolly, or Susan, and orders a large copy to be executed in oils. The whole is to be finished, framed and delivered within two days, and is not to exceed the contract price of four dollars, or about one pound sterling in our own money. The work in this painting-shop, like many things Chinese, is so divided as to afford the maximum of profit for the minimum of labour. Thus there is one artist who sketches, another who paints the human face, a third who does the hands, and a fourth who fills in the costume and accessories. Polly is placed upon the celestial limner's easel—an honour, poor girl, she little dreamt of—and is then covered with a glass bearing the lines and squares which solve the problem of proportion in the enlarged work. A strange being the artist looks; he has just roused himself from a long sleep, and his clothes are redolent of the fumes of opium. He peers through his huge spectacles into poor Polly's eyes, and measures out her fair proportions as he transfers them to his canvas. Then she is passed from hand to hand until, at last, every detail of her features, and dress, has been reproduced on the canvas with a pre-Raphaelite exactitude, and a glow of colour added to the whole which far surpasses nature. But let us examine the finished work. The dress is sky-blue! flounced with green. Chains of the brightest gold adorn the neck. There are bracelets on the arms, and rings on the fingers gleaming with gems. The hair is pitchy black, the skin pearly white, the cheeks of vermilion, and the lips of carmine. As for the dress, it shows neither spot nor wrinkle, and is as taut, Jack will say, as the carved robes of a figure-head. On a very square table by the side of this brilliant beauty stands a vase, filled with flowers that glow with all the brilliant hues of native art.

Surely all this will please the lover, and indeed it does. John Chinaman, he declares, màde more of the lass than even he thought possible, and there is a greater show of colour within the frame than he ever beheld before. He proudly hangs the picture above his bunk; but still, at times, he has his grave misgivings about the small hands and feet, and about the rainbow-hued sailor's goddess into which Poll has been transformed.

We will now descend to the open street from

Ating's gallery of horrors. On the other side of the way there are numerous ivory-miniature-painters. These men also devote themselves to copying photographs, and their work is decidedly better than when the copies are enlarged, as in the latter the defects of the original are frequently exaggerated. It is, however, only on rare occasions that the miniature-painters produce fairly good work. Their paintings are always highly finished ; but during my residence in the colony I fell in with one man only who, from his knowledge of art, could venture with any success beyond a mere servile imitation of a photograph. He was a sort of genius in his way, and, at the same time, a most inveterate opium-smoker. When I first knew him he was a good-looking dandy, in full work as a miniature-painter, fond of good company and high living, a frequenter of the music-halls and gambling clubs of Victoria. He used to smoke opium in moderation at first, but it gained upon him to such an extent, that when the hour for the pipe came on, no matter where he was, or how occupied, he had to rush off and abandon himself to the use of the drug which was bringing him fast to his grave. He used to work at my rooms, and when the moment arrived (never having a cent of his own), and he could hold out no longer, he would demand an advance of money with the fierceness of a man suffering the death-pangs of starvation.

Passing westward along Queen's Road, we come upon a quarter of the town much frequented by seamen of all nations. Here spirits are sold in nearly every second shop, and bands of common sailors may be seen spending their time and money on questionable drink in more questionable company, roaring out some rough sea-song in drunken chorus, or dancing to the time of a drum and flute, accordion or cornopean.

The keepers of these grog-shops might be mistaken for respectable members of society were it not for their bull-dog, battered, and damaged countenances, which betray sundry evidences of recent bruises and black eyes, received in taking the change out of their customers. The piles of Chinese houses which rise above this locality embrace Tai-Ping-Shan, or the hill of great peace. The name is a fine one, but a fine name will not hide the sins of the place. Tai-Ping-Shan is inhabited, for the most part, by Chinamen; but men are found there belonging to all the nations of the East. As for women, these are principally Chinese; they are numerous enough, but of the lowest type. There are strange hotels in this quarter, besides music-halls and lodging-houses, the haunts of vagabonds well known to the police. I once accompanied an inspector of police on one of his periodical rounds through this region of darkness, and I should not like to describe everything I saw there; but it proved that all which has been alleged of the immorality of the lower orders of the Chinese is perfectly true; while, on the other hand, that the more respectable part of the community, had there many places of rational amusement, with which, in so far as I could judge, one could find no fault whatever. One great difficulty of our government in this new colony has been how most effectually to curb the crime and vice common to all great seaport towns, and avert its consequences. The policy adopted has been to licence, and bring within direct government supervision, whatever they have found themselves powerless to suppress;

and the result, so far as statistics show, has proved the wisdom of the system. From a few particulars which I have gathered on the spot, but which it would serve no good end to publish here, I found no difficulty in estimating the magnitude and gravity of the question, how best to bring under control an evil which has always hitherto appeared inevitable.

Among the largest music-halls there was one which had been but recently erected, and it may serve as a type of the more attractive sorts in a list of about one hundred and eighty similar establishments. The hall I speak of stands at the end of Holywood Road, and is extensively decorated externally with porcelain floral ornaments. At the entrance we find an altar crowned with votive offerings, and dedicated to the god of pleasure, whose image surmounts the shrine. To the right and left of this hang scrolls, on which high moral precepts are inscribed, sadly at variance with the real character of the place. Half-a-dozen of the most fascinating of the female singers are seated outside the gate. Their robes are of richly-embroidered silk, their faces are enamelled, and their hair bedecked with perfumed flowers, and dressed in some cases to resemble a teapot, in others a bird with spread wings, poised upon the top of the head. On the ground-floor all the available space is taken up with rows of narrow compartments, each one furnished apparently with an opium-couch, and all the paraphernalia for the use of the drug. Here there are girls, in constant attendance, some ready to prepare and charge the bowl of the pipe with the opium, and others to strum upon the lute or sing sweet melodies to waft the sleeper off into dreamland under the strangely fascinating influences which, ere long, will make him wholly their slave. On the first-floor, which is reached by a narrow flight of steps, there is a deserted music-hall, showing traces of the revel of the preceding night in the faded garlands which still festoon its carved and gilded roof. There were two more stories to the edifice, partitioned off both of them in the same way as the ground-floor.

At another house we visited we found a goodly company in the music-saloon. The whole interior had been freshly decked with flowers, festooned from the ceiling, or suspended in baskets made of wattled twigs; while mirrors, paint, gilding, and all the skill of Kwangtung art, had been lavishly bestowed in the more permanent wall-decorations. At a table spread with the choicest delicacies, and the finest fruits, sat a merry throng of Chinamen—young, middle-aged, and old. Hot wine in burnished pewter pots was passing freely round the board, and the revellers were pledging each other in small cups of the fuming draught. We had, in fact, dropped in upon a dinner-party, where, under the influence of native wine, melon-seeds, and pretty women, the guests were engaged in a noisy, but at the same time, friendly contest, in the art of versification. Behind each guest, as is customary at such gatherings, a young girl sat; and many of these girls might fairly claim to be called handsome, while all were prettily dressed in the most fashionable silks of Canton. Their hair was wreathed with flowers, and their faces painted until they resembled their native porcelain ware. An old Chinese merchant present, whom I knew, informed me that these women were all highly respectable. That might be the case; at any rate, he assured me that they were not unfrequently carried off by the visitors, and raised to the rank of second wives or concubines.

Music, of a high Chinese order, was being performed in the four corners of the room by four independent female bands, each accompanying the shrill piping voice of an old woman, who sang the adventures of an ancient hero of romance, a personage famous alike for his unscrupulous dealings, and for his ardent and amorous heart.

During my residence in Hongkong that passion for gambling which characterises all Chinese communities got the credit, probably with justice, of being at the root of much of the crime and petty larceny among servants and subordinate office employés. The police were found incompetent to keep the popular vice in check, and as a consequence it became more and more in fashion throughout the island.

At last the authorities determined to try the experiment of licensing gambling-houses, and instituted a gambling-farm, in order to bring the evil under the tri ctest surveillance and control. The experiment was a bold one, and as a matter of course was received in many quarters with violent opposition. So strongly did the current of public opinion pronounce against the policy, that no very long time elapsed before the new ordinance was suppressed.

The licensing system, during its short career, contributed about 14,000 dollars a month to the treasury; and judging from local government statistics, materially aided in the suppression of crime. It was besides supposed to maintain a higher moral tone among the native police, who, when secret gambling-houses flourish, are seduced continually by bribes into dereliction of duty and corruption. One of the first practical difficulties in carrying out the newly inaugurated plan was the conscientious scruples—which, apparently, even affected the promoters of the measure—as to the application of a constantly accumulating fund derived from so polluted a source. It was even suggested to drop it silently into the sea, and be done with it. All I would say is, if the policy of sheltering this particular vice, in order to effect diminution of crime in the colony, was sound, the proceeds of the gambling-farm might have been worthily employed in rendering the police force still more efficient, and in lightening the general burden of taxation borne by the colonists. But the ordinance, as I have already stated, was suppresed probably before the efficiency of such a hazardous and unpopular experiment could be thoroughly put to the test, as a means of suppressing crime. The Hongkong police force is numerous and expensive, and its reputed inefficiency has been a subject of frequent comment in the press of Victoria; but the last of these characteristics may not impossibly be, in a very considerable degree, due to other and simpler causes than the wiles of Chinese gambling parties. The constables were, many of them, Chinese under the command of European inspectors, who, for the most part, knew nothing of the language and habits of the men under their charge. One section of the force was made up of Indians, who, with rare exceptions, were alike ignorant of Chinese, and therefore of very little service in detecting crime; while some of them were sufficiently well up in Chinese manners to know something of the security and dignified silence procurable by a judicious use of the coin of the realm.

Gambling is a luxury in which all Chinese more or less indulge. During the time when gambling-houses were under Government supervision, they became the open resort of most respectable-looking Chinamen—men whom one might take for patterns of native virtue, and yet who must needs have acquired their secret passion for this vice when it was still under the ban of the law. It took me by surprise, when visiting a gaming-house, to find one or two Chinese shopkeepers, otherwise noted for eminent respectability, busily engrossed at the table; indeed I should hardly have been more amazed had I beheld an elder of the Scotch Kirk cautiously staking his savings after church hours on Sunday.

These establishments were well worth inspection. As you approached one from the street, you would notice an European seated at the outer doorway. This individual was supposed to select and admit the men who ought to gamble, and to exclude those whose morals were of greater importance to the community; among the latter were included domestic, and office servants. He must have been endowed with rare powers of perception to be able to determine the occupation of each visitor to the house (it would have been called a hell before the new ordinance came into force, but now it was a sort of heaven with a gate-keeper who separated the wheat from the chaff) for tickets could afford no protection, as they might be passed from hand to hand. This watchman could also test for himself the power of the new law to suppress bribery and corruption. At the top of a narrow wooden staircase we found an apartment lit by a smoking oil lamp. This room was nearly square, and the ceiling above it had been pierced in the centre with a large square opening leading to the next floor, or gallery. Above the gallery is a contrivance to accommodate the upper ten, some of whom are bending over the railing and looking eagerly down upon a long gambling table spread before us.

One would scarcely, at first, suppose it, but we were pressing forward for a good place amongst some of the most desperate ruffians of Hongkong. But let me now bring you to the spot to watch the game; the stakes are being made. That close-shaven, smooth-visaged, fat, placid Chinaman on the right, is the banker; see how orderly is his array of coins and bank notes, and how deftly he reckons the winnings and interest on the smallest sums, deducting a seven per cent. commission from the gains of every transaction. Behind him is his assistant, weighing the dollars, broken silver, or jewellery of the players. Then at his side is the book-keeper, and on the left the teller. On the centre of the table is a square pewter slab crossed with diagonal lines, and the sections thus formed bear the numbers one, two, three, and four respectively. The player is at liberty to stake on any of these numbers, when, unless he stakes on two numbers separately, and at once, he will have three to one against him, plus seven per cent. on his winnings, if he succeeds. Some of the players spend the entire day in the house, and on starting open an account with the bank, which is kept carefully posted on a pewter slab before them, and balanced at the end of the day. All the stakes have now been made, including those dropped from above, in a small basket attached to a cord. The teller—sleek, fat, and close-shaven, like his confrères—

sits there conducting the vital part of the game with an air of stolid indifference; a man to all seeming, of the strictest probity and honour, and yet, if report be true, he knows tricks in his trade which defy the detection of the hundred hawk-like eyes that watch his every movement. His sleeves are short, nearly up to his armpits, and in his right hand he wields a single thin ivory rod. Before him on the table there is a pile of polished cash. From this he takes up a huge handful of coin, places it on a clear space, and covers it with a brass cup. When all the stakes are made, the cup is removed, and the teller proceeds, with the extreme end of his ivory wand, to pick out the cash in fours, the remaining number being that which wins. Before the pile is half counted, provided there are no split coins or trickery in the game, a habitual player can always tell with puzzling certainty what the remainder will be, whether one, two, three, or four, and it is at this stage of the game that we observe a striking peculiarity in Chinese character. There are no passionate exclamations, no noisy excitement, no outbursts of delight, no deep cursing of adverse fate. It is only in the faces of the players that we can perceive signs of emotion, or of the sullen desperate determination to carry on, at all hazards, until fortune smiles once more, or leaves them beggared at the board.

Gambling, in those days, was not entirely confined to the licensed houses. It was still carried on secretly in clubs and private abodes; even by the coolies, in their leisure moments, at the corners of the streets. Dice, too, were in constant demand among petty traders and hawkers; and I have seen children form a gambling-ring round some byeway vendor of sweets, and eagerly stake their cash in the attempt to win a double share of his condiments. I have found coolies, too, in my own employment, sit down deliberately and gamble away their next month's wages, till their very clothes were held in pawn by the lucky winner.

Lotteries are also in great vogue in China at all times. For these there are tickets sold, upon which a series of numbers have been engrossed. The purchaser pays his cent and marks ten of the numbers—those which, by some secret process of his own, he may have fixed on as the lucky set. The marked ticket is then paid in, and the holder receives in exchange a duplicate ticket marked in the same way. On the day of drawing the numbers are supposed to be dealt with by a mystic being, who dwells perpetually in darkness. He who holds three of the winning numbers receives back his even money, and he who holds the ten numbers receives six thousand times his stake. Assuming that the whole transaction is honestly carried through, the banker not unfrequently pockets as much as fifty per cent. as his profit for managing the lottery.

Although gambling is a common Chinese vice, it does not, so far as I am aware, meet with direct recognition from the Chinese Government, although it might be made to contribute largely to the imperial revenue.

Following Queen's Road through 'Wong-nei-chong,' or passing along the Praya to the east of Victoria, we reach the shady approach which leads to the Happy Valley, where the race-course and the cemetery are to be found. This European burial-ground lies behind the grand stand, where all the gaiety and fashion of the island assemble annually to view the races, which have long been one of the institutions of the place. The turf-loving residents look forward to the race-meeting from year to year as the crowning pleasure of the whole twelvemonth, making up to them for all the heat and hardships of a place which has been termed the grave of Europeans. Although, strangely enough, but a step divides the living from the dead in this truly picturesque valley, the island itself is accounted one of the healthiest stations on the coast of China. The present style of living has probably something to do with the improved health of the community. The houses are better adapted to the climate than they were some twenty years back. The sanitary arrangements are also more complete; whereas, when first the city was being built, vast surfaces of decomposed granite were laid bare as the workmen cut into the face of the hill; from the exposed spots noxious miasmas were exhaled, and to them are attributed those maladies which prevailed so fatally at that time, and which proved themselves the worst enemies our troops had to contend against in China. Even now, whenever the soil has to be opened anew, we still hear cases of this Hongkong fever occurring near the spot. The Chinese geomancers attributed the prevalence of this disease to our ignorance of the laws of 'Feng Shui'—literally 'wind and water,' but denoting something like good luck brought about by a knowledge of astrology and geomancy—and it must be acknowledged that they correctly foretold the results which befel the colony as soon as the hill-sides were opened.

Tree-planting was carried on vigorously under Sir Richard MacDonnell's administration; and this, while it adds greatly to the picturesqueness of the island, has done not a little to promote the good health of its inhabitants.

Europeans in Hongkong live in a very expensive style; much more expensively, one would think, than they need do, when we consider that many of the necessaries of life are to be had at prices very little in advance of our market rates at home.

Beer and wine, however, and the countless other little luxuries which one has to purchase at the European stores, make up a startling monthly bill; and, after all, the dollar which would be four shillings and sixpence in London is equal to little more than a shilling in Hongkong, in exchanging it for such commodities as are brought from home. The newly-arrived resident may furnish his dwelling cheaply enough by buying at the constantly recurring auction sales of the householders who are leaving the colony; or else of a Chinese tradesman, who will fit up his house for him throughout at a comparatively moderate charge. But then servants are indispensable, and add greatly to the expense of living. The following is a list of those required for an ordinary family, where there are one or two children to be maintained:—

	Monthly Wages.
Cook	10 dollars
Two chair-coolies	14 "
One nurse or amah	10 "
One house-boy	8 "
One house-coolie	7 "
	$49

This, at a low rate of exchange, is equal to one hundred and twenty pounds a year for domestic servants alone. Then all the washing is done by a Chinese laundryman, whose charge is the same as we pay in London. As for the doctor, he will make a contract to attend the family for an annual retaining fee, say forty pounds, or thereabouts, and no end of medicine has to be bought at prices which, if need be, will afford your medical adviser a consideration of twenty-five per cent. The doctor is not supposed to have anything to do with the dispensing chemist; but, nevertheless, the enormous quantity of drugs ordered, and at times tossed out at the window by the patient, leads people to draw conclusions which are not always just. Rent would be about one hundred and forty pounds a year for such a house as may be obtained in London for sixty; and altogether, the expense of living in Hongkong may be fairly set down at something more than double what it is at home.

Strange characters are not rarely to be met with here; men who, from time to time, turn up with wonderful schemes for the benefit of the human race, but quite unable to tell you how their projects are to be carried into effect, or by what means the money is to be provided. Mr. Gabriel was an adventurer of this sort. I knew nothing of him, and had never seen him before the night on which he came to my house as a stranger, and requested permission to bring his baggage into my rooms until he could find some suitable lodgings elsewhere. This I granted, and about an hour afterwards he returned, saying he had not succeeded, and that he would feel grateful if I would allow him to sleep in any corner. A couch was prepared for him, and he settled himself for the night, but not before he had detailed to me his plans for rendering the island of Borneo one vast coffee-plantation, and bringing its coffee-coloured people out of the darkness of savagedom into the light of civilisation.

Appearing to find pleasure in my society, Gabriel had remained under my roof for ten days, when I suggested to him that Borneo was all this while a howling wilderness, and its inhabitants still preying on each other for the want of schools and coffee. He had come from the Sandwich Islands, where he had been a schoolmaster, but his occupation there was unremunerative, as he had brought no money with him. At length he persuaded a ship captain that it was his duty to afford him a free and comfortable passage to Singapore, and he accordingly left for that port, where he found out some of my friends, and got them to help him on his way to Borneo. In about two months Mr. Gabriel again appeared at my door with his cotton umbrella in one hand, a hymn-book in the other, and a decidedly crest-fallen expression in his face. He had landed on Borneo, but strange to relate, everybody there, even to the Bishop and the European community, so he said, were of opinion that he had made a mistake; and the very natives themselves seemed disinclined for coffee, commerce, and schools. How he managed to get back I never clearly made out. Gabriel's countenance was a good one, and he always appeared in all he did to be actuated by the purest motives, and the deepest sincerity. He had a mild, dreamy eye, and he would sit for hours alone, picturing to himself the results of the great reformation which he was destined never to accomplish. Again taking up his abode with me, he professed his willingness to do anything, or to go anywhere to do good; his life in one hand, his umbrella in the other, to gain a living. At last I got him into the police force; he wore their uniform for about two days, and then he returned to me again, and in a state of the deepest depression. He had resigned; he could not stand the rough work, and rougher talk, to which he had been exposed. He was next employed at the sugar factory, and when he paid me his last visit it was to plead for the loan of eighteen dollars to settle his rent, for the ruthless landlord of the small house he occupied was about to seize his all for debt, as he could not appreciate his philanthropic object in desiring to live rent free. I lent him the money, but never saw any more either of him or it. I feel sure he would have paid me if he could, and I should really like to have heard what was his ultimate fate.

A well-known clergyman told me of another character, who accosted him one day as he was leaving his church, and announcing himself, in a tone of mysterious confidence, as the bearer of a divine message, summoned to Hongkong to publish what had been thus revealed, requested permission to occupy the pulpit during the afternoon. My friend, noted no less for his caution than distinguished for his learning, said, 'Where are your credentials? If you have a mission direct from heaven, you are no ordinary person; and seeing you have been sent to Hongkong, you have doubtless been gifted with the Chinese tongue; so if you will just repeat what you have stated in Chinese, I will let you have the chapel.' This he could not accomplish; but he did what surprised my worthy friend nearly as much—he confessed to being a faithful follower of the Mormons, and asked the clergyman if he had an old pair of trousers to bestow, as those he wore were not his own.

Like other small communities at home and abroad,

Hongkong has a little artificial society of its own divided into sets or cliques; but on the whole the inhabitants pull well together in all matters where they have common interests at stake. The trade of the port is divided among men of different nationalities; American, French, German, Dutch, Chinese, Parsees, Hindoos, all enjoy a share of the commercial prosperity of our little colony. Next to the English and Americans, German merchants hold the foremost place. They have just built a splendid new club, and they are our close and successful competitors in almost every avenue of trade. Some of these German houses have a very high standing indeed, and their undoubted successes are spoken of at times with feelings not unmingled with bitterness. Nevertheless, we cannot but award them just praise for conducting their business with thoroughness, economy, and energy—qualities which have secured them a not unimportant position in commercial circles in the East, and have also brought them to the front rank among Continental nations at home. There are, doubtless, times when the British merchant imagines he has just cause to complain of the manner in which the petty German trader secures his ends, and probably he is right. But if he is, it is ten chances to one that the trader who, like a mole burrowing in the soil, seeks the shady and doubtful paths of commerce, will be found out in the long run by the Chinese with whom he has to deal, and turn out a loser in the end. Be this as it may, it seems to me that the Germans are masters of some elements of success with which even a Scotchman, with all his thrift, can boast but a rudimentary acquaintance; in a word, they manage their business more cheaply than we do. They are, many of them, less expensive in their mode of living. Their assistants are not so numerous; they board together in their houses comfortably, if not quite as luxuriously, as in the English establishments; and often they are masters of more than one European language; at any rate most of them not only know their own tongue thoroughly, but can speak our language well enough, if need be, to occupy posts even in an English house. This in itself enables them to join a British firm, for the express purpose of adding to their already extensive experience a knowledge of the English trade. Many of them have been in houses in London, Manchester, or Liverpool, and while there have made the most of their opportunities. Few of our countrymen, on the other hand, have had similar facilities for acquiring German, or have even thought it worth their while to fit themselves to translate a simple German document.

Nothing surprised me more in Hongkong than the expensive way in which English assistants were housed, and the luxuries with which they were indulged. Indeed few more luxurious quarters were anywhere to be found than the 'junior messes' of the wealthy British firms. There the unfledged youth, coming out from the simplicity of some rural home, was apt to develop into a man of epicurean tastes, a connoisseur in wines, and to become lavish in his expenditure; proud of his birthright, as a Briton; honest, hospitable, extravagant; despising meanness, and, alas! even thrift. This sort of education was not calculated to prepare the merchant of the future for the cheese-paring shifts of modern times, when markets are overstocked, when competition runs strong, when Chinese companies and

German economy are set in array against us, and when to trade and win a share of the wealth, that seemed almost forced upon us in the olden times, requires now patience, self-denial and determination. But Hongkong is rapidly shaping itself to the nervous energy of the times, and her English merchants still hold their own in the great trade of China. Their assistants still live well, although not so lavishly as in former days; they are still hospitable, still liberal, and no unfortunate fellow-countryman is ever left destitute in their streets. Often in my time old residents have died and left penniless families behind them; then subscription lists were opened, and responded to with such liberality that the widow and children went home with a very comfortable pension. But as I said, the times have changed; now there are constant telegrams and steamers, and no less constant anxiety and care. The luxury and the extravagance have abated, but yet the style of life is higher and the amusements of the residents are more varied; and altogether society in Hongkong resembles more closely what one is accustomed to see at home.

The climate of this quarter of the globe is for about six months of the year dry, with cool nights, and an almost cloudless sky; but when the hot weather and the rain come round, the sky seems to descend and rest like a sponge on the top of the hill; and this sponge, always full of moisture, is frequently squeezed over the town, and the rain falls in a sheet, and floods the streets and rises in hot vapour with the sun; books and papers become limp and mouldy, and the residents feel as in a vapour-bath, while reclining in their chairs and languidly watching the flying ants that settle in thousands in the lamps, or alight on the table, when, casting their wings, and, crawling like worms, they seek an asylum in one's soup-plate, or in the various dishes of the dinner-table. But after all one gets used to these things and the place is by no means an unhealthy, or a disagreeable one, to reside in.

I happened to be in Hongkong in 1869, when His Royal Highness the Duke of Edinburgh visited the colony. He was the first English Prince who had roamed so far and wide over the world, and who, according to the Chinese notion, had braved the dangers of the deep in order that he might, for once, feast his vision on the glories of the 'Great Middle Kingdom.'

Whatever may have been his impressions of the Celestial Empire and her rulers, any feeling of disappointment on that score must have been dispelled by the hearty British welcome he received when the 'Galatea' steamed through the throng of native and foreign craft, and moored in the smooth waters of Hongkong harbour.

I well remember his landing. Ships of all nations vied in the splendour of their decorations; long lines of merchant boats guarded the approach to the wharf; and on a thousand native craft, adorned with flags and shreds of Turkey red cloth, appeared dusky multitudes of the floating population, swarming over the decks or clinging to the rigging of their vessels. The wharfs, too, and landing-stages, were covered with a sea of yellow faces, all eager to catch a glimpse of the great English Prince. Nor can I forget the regret expressed by some at finding he was only a man and a sailor after all. Some even ventured to suggest that 'sailor-man no saby proper Prince pidjin,' and indeed he was only attired in a captain's uniform, with no display of purple and fine linen, and with none of the mystic emblems of royalty to hedge his dignity around. A different being, this, surely, from the offspring of their own great Emperor, who is brother of the Sun, and full cousin to the Moon, and on whose radiant countenance no common mortal may look and live.

The Prince's sojourn on the little island furnished a gay and festive episode in its history. The Prince and his gallant officers were never behindhand in contributing to the enjoyment of the residents. Their crowning effort was a theatrical performance given by them in the pretty City Hall Theatre, where they not only displayed histrionic skill, but where the orchestra, under the able leadership of the Prince himself, proved a great attraction.

CHAPTER VIII.

Snakes in Hongkong—A Typhoon—An Excursion up the North Branch of the Pearl River—Fatshan—The Fi-lai-sz Monastery—The Mang tsz-hap, or Blind Man's Pass—Rapids—Akum's Ambition—The Kwan-yin Cave—Harvest—From San-shui to Fatshan in a Canoe—Canton—Governor Yeh's Temple—A Tea Factory—Spurious Tea—Making Tea—Shameen—Tea-tasting.

'Beware of snakes' is a caution very necessary to the new comer who may delight in morning rambles over the hills or through the grassy valleys of the island. Indeed the snakes we find at Hongkong belong some of them to the most venomous sorts. Thus I once myself encountered a hooded 'cobra' among the rocks at Wong-nei-Chong. When taking a photograph I suddenly noticed a dark object moving close to my feet. I raised my camera in order to use the tripod as a weapon of defence, whereupon the reptile reared its head, erected its hood, and with a hiss slid down off the rock into the underwood. A well-known doctor in the colony captured three live cobras one after the other in the hospital grounds; these he kept for some time in a cage, and instituted a series of interesting experiments to test the best mode of treating the wounds which they inflicted. At one time he had a fine specimen in his possession. It had been but recently secured, and was an object of great interest to his acquaintances. But I confess my own curiosity was somewhat marred when one afternoon, before dinner, my medical friend informed me with much gravity that he hourly expected a visit of the cobra's mate, as they were frequently found in pairs. 'If you should see it about the room,' said he, 'just sit quiet and don't bother yourself. It might be beneath the table, you know, but it would'nt attempt to bite unless you happened to tread on it, and even then you might hear it hiss, and have time to get out of its reach. At any rate if the wound was treated at once you probably would not be a whit the worse for it.' Suddenly the dispenser appeared, to announce that the snake had arrived, and was in the adjoining room. 'Now,' he said, 'coolness and a quick eye are all that we require for his capture. Come along, and mind your legs, for the cobra is very quick in his movements.' We accordingly proceeded to the scene of action, and found the enemy beneath a chest of drawers, from which he was successfully dislodged and secured in spite of his forked tongue, his ferocity, and his poisonous fangs. These snakes never survived long, so that the experiments which promised to yield important results could not be carried to a satisfactory issue. The doctor was a man of wonderful resource. During the intense heat of summer he was troubled with sleepless nights, so in his bath-room, near the chamber where he slept, he fitted up two bathing-jars, one above the other, and fixed a water-wheel between them. This wheel had originally belonged to a bicycle, but was soon metamorphosed and became the driving-wheel which kept a punkah continually at work, fanning him on his bed all night. The water falling on the wheel descended to the lower jar, and was ready for his morning ablutions.

I had for long been anxious to see a typhoon, and I had my wish gratified in Hongkong on more occasions than one. The strength of the wind at such times, is greater than I could ever have thought possible. It whirls ships helplessly adrift from the firmest moorings; and I have seen them emerge from the storm with canvas torn to shreds, spars carried away, and masts broken off nearly flush with the decks. In Hongkong the wind with a sudden blast has riven away the corners of houses, and sent projecting verandahs flying across the streets. During the height of the gale the residents for the most part shut themselves closely in their houses, carefully securing their windows and doors, and so remain with constant apprehension and dread, lest the dwelling should in a moment be swept away, and themselves entombed beneath the ruins. Once, while the storm was at its worst, I ventured down to the Praya in time to see the crowd of Chinese boats and trading craft that had been blown inshore, and piled up in a mass of wreck just below the city, at the western extremity of the beach. One or two intrepid foreigners had been there, and had rescued a large number of the natives, but many more had gone down with their boats. The sky was of dark leaden colour, and there were moments when the fierce strength of the wind abated, but only to gather fresh violence, catching up the crested waves and sending them in long white streaks of vapour across the scene, through which the dismantled ships were dimly descried drifting from their moorings, and the steamers with steam up ready for an emergency. Besides, the heavy stone-faced wall of the Praya had given way, and the great granite blocks of which it was composed had been washed in upon

A TYPHOON IN HONGKONG HARBOUR

the road. Half blinded by the waves as they leapt over the road and dashed in angry foam against the houses, and leaning forward in the efforts, often fruitless, to make headway against the tempest, I at length reached the east end of the settlement, where a number of foreigners were attempting to rescue two women from a small Chinese boat. These boatwomen were using the most desperate exertions to keep their tiny vessel in position, and to prevent it from being dashed to pieces against the breach in the Praya wall, where jagged blocks of stone were interspersed with the fragments of boats that had already been destroyed. So strong was the wind that the wild raging ocean seemed reduced nearly to a level, for the tops of the waves were caught up by the tempest in its fury and hurled in blinding spray into, and even over the houses. We had to cling to the lamposts and stanchions, and to seek shelter against the doorways and walls. Advantage was taken of a slight lull in the storm to fire off rockets, but these were driven back like feathers against the houses. Then long-boats were dragged to the pier, but the first was broken and disabled the moment it touched the water, while the second met a like fate, and its gallant crew were pitched out into the sea. In short, every effort proved abortive, and as darkness set in the boat and the unhappy women were reluctantly abandoned to their fate. Next morning the whole length of the Praya presented a scene of wreckage and desolation. Many of the Chinese, notwithstanding their shrewdness in predicting storms, had been taken quite unawares, and hence the fearful sacrifice of life and the loss of property which had ensued.

In 1870, accompanied by three Hongkong residents, I made an excursion up the north branch of the Pearl River of Canton. This northern affluent joins the main stream at a spot called 'San-shui' or 'three waters,' lying above the city about forty miles inland. To reach it, we must pass through the Fatshan Creek, where Commodore Keppel fought his famous action in the year 1857. The town of Fatshan exceeds a mile in length; the creek passes right through its centre. It is said to be the nucleus of the greatest manufacturing districts of Southern China. Cutlery and hardware are the two chief industries, hence Fatshan is sometimes designated the Birmingham or Sheffield of the Flowery Land. It seemed a strange thing to me when I examined the knives, the scissors, and the pans of brass and copper which find a ready market all over the country, that similar articles of a superior English make have done so little to paralyse the industry of these Fatshan factories. This is partly caused by the cheapness of Chinese labour, and partly by the suitableness of the articles manufactured to the local popular requirements. Chinese scissors, for example, are quite different in form from those in use with us, and, if we were to attempt to cut with them, we should be apt to tear the cloth. In the hands of a native tailor they are made to work wonders, and indeed use had taught the latter to prefer them to our own. I have no doubt it would be well worth the while of an English manufacturer to visit Fatshan and make himself acquainted with the exact form of all the different kinds of tools in use among the Chinese, so that afterwards he might imitate and export them himself. The iron used in this district is imported from foreign countries, although it has been said that ore abounds in the Yan-ping division of the province,[1] of a quality so good, as to yield 70 per cent of the pure metal, and contiguous also to deposits of valuable coal. So long, however, as 'Feng-shui' and shortsighted Government interest hold their sway, mines are certain never to be opened up. As we pass through the city we notice numerous imposing edifices substantially built of brick, the residence of native merchants, temples with a grotesquely sculptured granite façade, and a large customs station; but the houses in the suburbs which border the creek are raised above water on piles, and their temporary miserable appearance is in striking contrast to the princely abodes and evidences of wealth which we encounter in the heart of the town. These poor propped-up tenements suggest the idea of a procession of invalids, staggering forth on their way into the country, much the worse for the dissipation of city life. The creek is the principal thoroughfare, and is crowded with thousands of junks and boats, all busily engaged in loading or discharging cargo, or else in bearing passengers to and fro along the extremely narrow channel which winds its way through this floating Babel, where endless discord reigns. This creek is evidently much too contracted for the traffic of the place; and I can readily imagine how, seventeen years ago, the Chinese squadron, fleeing before a handful of British tars in their small boats, drew up like a wall across this narrow passage, and poured a hailstorm of shot upon their gallant assailants, spreading death and destruction among the little band. As for the Com-

[1] *China Review*, 1873, p. 337.

modore, with his boat shot away from under him, 'with his coxswain killed, and every man of his crew wounded,'[1] he calmly retired to await reinforcements and returned at last from a severe attack, with five of the largest junks in tow. The Chinese themselves, who are by no means destitute of courage, are said honestly to have acknowledged their admiration for the pluck, and daring of the man who started with seven small boats to capture Fatshan and its 200,000 inhabitants, and who destroyed their entire fleet—the terror, as was supposed of the 'foreign fire-eating devils,' who were held never before this to have fought a fair fight; but to be always taking their foes in the rear of their forts, instead of bravely coming to the front and facing the guns which had been set up with so much pains for the very purpose of receiving their assaults.

Whenever a block-up among the boats in the creek takes place—which happens frequently, and is protracted indefinitely for a long period of time—one has leisure to notice the numerous floating tea and music-saloons, and many flower-barges moored close against the banks. These boats carry elevated cabins on their decks, and are very prettily painted, gilded, and decorated throughout. The windows and doors are curtained with silk; and through one of these, which stood conveniently open, we could discern gaily-dressed young dandies, and even elder sybarites, flirting with gaudily-painted girls, who waited upon them with silver pipes or Chinese hookahs, or served up cups of tea. There were pleasure-boats, too, fitted up with private cabins, in which families were being conveyed into the

[1] *China*, G. Wingrove Cooke, p. 35.

country to enjoy a glimpse of the green rice-fields and orchards.

At San-shui we entered the north river, passing into a picturesque district, in some places not unlike the Scottish lowlands, covered with ripening fields of barley. Halting not far from the town of Lo'pau, at Wong-Tong village, on the right bank of the stream, I prepared to take a photograph, and my intention was to include a group of old women who were gossiping and drawing water; but when they saw my instrument pointed towards their hamlet, they fled in alarm, and spread abroad the report that the foreigners had returned and were preparing to bombard the settlement. A deputation soon set out from the village, led by a venerable Chinaman, the head man of the clan, and to him we explained that we had come on no hostile errand, but only to take a picture of the place. He gave us a hearty welcome to his house, spreading tea and cake before us. This was one of those many instances of a simple genuine hospitality which I experienced all over the land; and I feel assured that any foreigner knowing enough of the language to make his immediate wants understood, and endowed with a reasonable even temper, would encounter little opposition in travelling over the greater part of China. But there is always a certain amount of danger in the larger and more populous cities. We offered one or two small silver coins to the children of the house, but the old gentleman would not permit them to be accepted, until it had been carefully explained to him that they were simply gifts to be worn as charms, and not intended as a recompense for his hospitality.

On the bank of the river in the Tsing-yune district

I narrowly escaped sinking into a quicksand. We spent a night before Tsing-yune city, but were kept awake by the noise of gongs and crackers, by the odour of joss-sticks, and by the smoke of cooking from the adjoining boats. At length we reached the monastery of Fi-lai-sz, perhaps the most picturesque and one of the most famous of its kind to be seen in the south of China. The building is approached from the brink of the river by a flight of broad granite steps; this conducts us to an outer gate, whereon is inscribed in characters of gold, 'Hioh Shan Miau.' The monastery has been built on a richly wooded hill-side, and half way up to it, on the verge of a mossy dell, we reach the Fi-lai-sz shrine. Three idols stand within this shrine, one of them representing, or supposed to represent, the pious founder, who is said to have been transported hither, shrine and all, on the wings of a fiery dragon, more than two thousand years ago. A favourite resting-place this for travellers, one where they are hospitably entertained, and where the monks, with impious sympathy for human weakness, supply their guests with opium, and sell carved sticks, cut from the sacred temple groves, as parting relics of their visit.

The Tsing-yune pass, in which the monastery lies, is in great repute as a burial-ground. There, thousands of graves front the river and stud the hill slopes to a height of about 800 feet. To every grave there is a neat facing of stone, something in the form of a horseshoe, or like an easy-chair with a rounded back. The interior of the temple cloister is paved with granite and decorated with flowers set out in vases and ornamental pots; thus art lent its aid to a scene of natural loveliness the most romantic and beautiful. On the opposite bank of the stream a narrow path leads to a wooded ravine, whither the monks retire when they seek to abstract themselves from the world, forgetting existence, with its pleasures and sorrows, and cultivating that supreme repose which will bring them nearer Nirvana. It seemed to me, when I inspected the cell-like chambers of these devotees, that some among them were not unfamiliar with the fumes of the opium-pipe, and that they must, poor frail mortals ! at times endeavour to float away to the western heavens steeped in the incense of that enslaving drug. I cannot picture anything more dreary and depressing, than the unnatural existence which these recluses are supposed to lead, droning their dull lives away in chanting a tedious, and to some of them, meaningless ritual ; seeking to attain the perfect holiness of doing nothing, learning nothing, and feeling nothing ; struggling, indeed, to crush out all consciousness of life, and to resolve themselves into the inanimate material out of which all things have been created.

We next halted at a village called Lien-Chow-Kwong. It was a miserable specimen of its kind, planted in a desolate neighbourhood, and with an air of poverty and destitution pervading both it and its inhabitants. The wretched unwashed peasant, in his tattered coat, leant from sheer weakness against a wall, in order to get a steady look at us, while the lean and ill-conditioned fowls were plucking their own feathers out to appease the pangs of hunger ! The passes in this river present some bold rock and hill scenery, while the short reaches and sudden bends of the stream remind one of Highland lochs. In other places the hills slope gently downwards towards the water, and terminate in a bank of glittering sand, not unfrequently a mile broad. These sand-banks glare like miniature deserts beneath the blazing mid-day sun, but are happy in the association of a refreshing stream which flows clear and cool along the margin. The Mang-Tsz-Hap, or Blind Man's Pass, is one of the finest on the river. Here the bold crags shoot up in precipices that are lost in shreds of drifting mist, as if the heavy clouds, sweeping across jagged pinnacles of rock, were riven into a hundred vapoury fragments. The weather was now cold and stormy, but fitful gleams of sunshine broke in upon the darkness, now lending its brightness to a patch of vivid green among the rocks, now shooting a solitary beam through clouds and haze, to light up some distant spot upon the waters. Once, caught in a rapid by a sudden gust of wind, our boat seemed like to have been shattered in the breakers ; but her crew in a twinkling slipped the tracking-line, and she drifted safely down mid-stream. At another time we ran aground, and the sudden shock sent one of the boatmen headlong overboard. He was thoroughly exhausted when we picked him up again ; but after a glass of brandy he speedily recovered, and expressed his willingness to be rescued from drowning, and revived in the same way, as frequently as we chose to repeat the dose.

The Chinese get the credit of being exceedingly-temperate, and in the majority of cases this is true ; but at the same time, among the lower orders, especially the boating population, temperance is only observed because sheer necessity compels restraint ; and many of the boatmen on the rivers along which I have travelled will drink sam-shu to excess during the cold weather, whenever they can win a few extra cash. These men are about as poor and miserable a class as one can meet in the most poverty-stricken districts of the land. In the southern provinces their sole food is steamed rice flavoured with salt, or rendered more savoury with a fragment of salt fish ; and when times are good, they even indulge in the luxury of a little bit of pork fat. It is surprising how they stand the cold, more especially in the northern regions, and how a drop of spirits will send the warm blood tingling through their veins and cause them to display a muscular power and a strength of endurance not easily accounted for, when one considers the simple nature of their food. Millions of these hardy sons of toil live from hand to mouth, and are only kept from starving, from piracy, and from rebellion, by the cheapness of their staple food, and by the constant demand for their labour. But there are pirates to be found in this very river; our crew themselves told us of it, and added, that for anything they knew to the contrary there might be a swarm of them in the boats among which we moored at night.

At Ying-Tek city I fell in with a spectacle which fully confirmed this assertion, and at the same time produced in me a sensation of horror that it will be impossible ever to forget. Ying-Tek stands on the right bank of the stream. Beneath its outer wall there stretches a bank of reeking filth and garbage, which at mid-day must pollute the air for miles around. We picked our way over slimy treacherous paths and across putrid-looking pools, till we passed through the gateway into the main street of the town.

It was an exceedingly narrow thoroughfare, and had at one time been paved, but the pavement was now broken and disordered ; while, as to the people, they looked sickly, sullen, dirty and dispirited. But it was in the market-place we beheld the most shocking sight of all. There the bodies of two men were exposed to the public gaze, their position indicated by swarms of flies, and the air telling that decomposition had already set in. One of these malefactors had been starved to death in the cage in which he stood, and the other had been crucified.

Beyond the rapids of this part of the river we reach vast cultivated plains, out of which isolated limestone rocks and parallel ranges of mountains rise up in shapes most fantastic, and disorder most picturesque. It was from a hill above the Polo-hang temple that we obtained the finest view of the country. The cultivation hereabouts was of a kind I had never seen before. In the foreground were a multitude of fields, banked off for the purposes of irrigation, but already shorn of their crops. Here and there was a mound covered with temples and trees ; and beyond, reaching to the base of the distant mountains, were groves of the pale green bamboo rocking their plumage to and fro in the wind, like the waves of an emerald sea. The bamboo is reared in this and other districts, and forms a valuable article of commerce, the wealth of a landowner being frequently estimated by the number of clumps which he has on his estate. Its growth is rapid and independent. It requires neither care nor tillage, and is a source of abundant riches in this part of the country.

When looking on this scene my old Chinaman, Akum, came up. I do not think he has yet been introduced to my readers. He was a faithful servant, or boy, as they are here called, about forty years of age, who had been in my employment in Singapore, and afterwards turning trader, had lost his small capital. 'Well,' he said, 'what are you looking at, Sir?' 'At the beautiful view,' I replied. 'Yes,' he said; 'I wish I had the smallest of these hills; I would settle

LOOKING NORTH FROM THE PO-LO-HANG TEMPLE, KWANG-TUNG.

there, on the top, watching my gardeners at work below, and when I saw one labourer more industrious than the rest I would reward him with a wife.'

He spoke to me often afterwards about this ideal hill on which he hoped one day to sit, and reward the virtue of his servants.

Hereafter I may say something as to the multitudinous uses to which the bamboo can be applied.

There is good snipe and pheasant-shooting in this quarter.

We noticed quantities of the reeds employed for making Canton mats. Mats of this sort are manufactured extensively in three places,[1] viz. Tun-kun, Lin-tan, and Canton. They afford occupation to many thousand operatives, and are indeed an important industry of the province of Kwang-tung. About 112,000 rolls, measuring 40 yards apiece, are said to be annually exported from Canton.

About two hundred miles above Canton we visited the most remarkable object which we had encountered in the course of our journey. This is the celebrated grotto of Kwan-yin, the goddess of mercy, formed out of a natural cave in the foot of a limestone precipice which rears its head high above the stream. The mouth of the cavern opens on the water's edge, and the interior has been enlarged in some places by excavation, and built up in others so as to render it suitable for a Buddhist shrine. A broad granite platform surmounted by a flight of steps leads us into the upper chamber, and there the goddess may be seen seated on a huge lotus-flower; sculptured, so they tell us, by no human hands, and discovered *in situ* within the cave. The priests placed implicit faith in the story, but they could not be persuaded to believe that the flower might be the fossil of a pre-historic lotus of monstrous dimensions. Barbarians might credit such childish fables as that flowers or fishes can be turned into stone, but not the enlightened followers of Buddha: No; they say the lotus was created in the

[1] *China Review*, 1873, p. 255.

cave for Kwan-yin to sit upon; there was no getting over that.

According to their account, this goddess of mercy has a marvellous history. She first appeared on earth in the centre of the world, that is China, as the daughter of a Chinaman named 'Shi-kin,' and she was made visible to mortal eyes as a child of the Emperor Miao-Chwang. The sovereign ordered her to marry, and this she steadfastly refused to do, thus violating the native usages, whereupon the dutiful parent put her remorselessly to death. But this measure, contrary to Miao-Chwang's expectation, only caused his daughter to be promoted into the proud position she now fills. Afterwards Kwan-yin is said to have visited the infernal regions, where the presence of such transcendant goodness and beauty produced an instantaneous effect. The instruments of torture dropped from the hands of the executioners, the guilty were liberated, and hell was transformed into paradise itself.

The goddess now looks down with a benign expression from her seat upon the lotus throne, but she seems to be urgently in need of repairs.

The priests who dwell within the cave sit overlooking the river from an opening in the upper face of the rock, which serves the purpose of a window. As we see them with the sun at their backs they appear to be like a row of badly-preserved idols, so motionless do they sit, and so unconscious, to all seeming, of the presence of foreigners. But when we confront them and display a bright coin, they wake up, and manifest an unholy zeal to appropriate it.

The money is offered and accepted, and then a venerable member of the order shows us through the interior of the cave. A number of smaller idols, the attendants of Kwan-yin, are ranged along niches in the rock; a little lighted taper burns in front of each, while cups of sam-shu and votive offerings of food are spread out before them. A group of stalactites hangs in front of the window; above and around them hover a number of pure white doves, that descend at the call of the aged priest, and feed out of his hand. It was interesting to notice the outstretched hand of the old man; it was withered, shrunken, and encumbered by a set of long yellow nails that looked dead, and were already partly buried beneath the unwashed encrustation of a lifetime. This recluse said that the spotlessness of the doves is emblematic of the purity of the goddess, and admitted that for anything he knew to the contrary these doves might contain the departed spirits of former monks. Judging from the appearance of our venerable unwashed friend, the spirits of departed monks would feel extremely uncomfortable in their new quarters, having exchanged their filthy robes and filthier bodies for the spotless plumage of the dove.

It is harvest-time, and the grain in many places is already cut, and has been piled up in farm-yards in stacks, to be thrashed with flails, or trodden beneath the heavy-footed ox. The season has been a plenteous one, and the farmers are full of joy, praising the god of agriculture for the abundance of this their second crop, from a soil which has yielded produce during centuries of constantly recurring harvests. The Chinese are careful farmers, and were probably the first to understand that their land requires as much consideration as their oxen or their asses; that the substnce which it gives up to a crop has to be replaced by manure, and that it requires a time of rest after a season of labour, before it will yield its greatest increase. How the Chinese acquired this knowledge, and at what epoch, are questions which Confucius himself would probably have been puzzled to answer. There is no doubt that they succeed in raising green crops and grain alternately from their fields at least twice in the year. But this extraordinary fertility is due in part to the small size of their farms, which are, most of them, of so limited an area that the proprietors can cultivate them personally with unceasing care, and partly also to the abundant use of manure in fashion among the peasants of China. We see evidences of the social economy of the people in a multitude of instances and a variety of ways. Thus, when the farmer is near a town, he pays a small sum to certain houses for the privilege of daily removing their sewage to his own manure-pit. This sewage he uses, for the most part in a fluid state, often to fertilise poor waste lands which have been leased to him at a low rental. If his farm is some distance from villages or towns, he is careful to use every opportunity for securing cheap supplies of the manure which he so much needs, and accordingly he erects small houses for the use of way farers along the edge of his fields. His neighbour is equally careful to have houses of the same description; and they vie with each other in keeping them as clean and attractive-looking as possible.

I returned to Canton alone from San Shui, in a small boat, leaving my friends to find their own way leisurely back. At one place there were only a few inches of water above the bed of the stream, so I had to hire an open canoe, while my baggage was carried overland to the next bend of the river. In this canoe I descended, or rather raced, down to Fatshan amid a number of similar craft whereon Chinese traders were embarked. The distance was about twenty-five miles. We contrived to reach the town about half an hour ahead of the rest, and passed at once down the narrow channel between the crowded boats. This was by far the most disagreeable experience of the journey. Attempting to land quietly and have a look at the town, I was assailed on the bank by a mob of roughs, who drove me into the river, where I was taken into a boat by a couple of good-natured women, and by them rowed down stream till I could succeed in engaging a fast-boat to convey me as far as Canton.

Canton and the Kwang-tung province, as my reader is doubtless aware, continued for many years to be almost the only places in the vast Chinese Empire with which Europeans were acquainted. I need hardly do more here than refer those of my readers who take an interest in the obscure and checquered history of Canton to an elaborate and interesting account, translated and published in China by Mr. Bowra, of the Imperial Customs. In this narrative it is stated that the first authentic notice of Kwang-tung province is found in the native writings of the Chow dynasty B.C. 1122. The fifth century of our era is set down as the date at which Buddhist missionaries introduced their religious classics, and not only founded the sect which now predominates in the country, but led to the establishment of commercial relations between the Empires of India and China. The intercourse which the Chinese have ever since that time carried on with other nations has been subject to periodical interruptions, and its history has been one of endless strife; China, on the one hand, adhering steadfastly to her policy of exclusiveness, and throwing all kinds of barriers in the way of foreign trade; while outside communities, with equal persistence, applied a pressure to which the Chinese have been gradually giving way, and thus the mutually advantageous treaty relations have by tardy steps been established.

The city of Canton stands on the north bank of the Chu-kiang or Pearl River, about ninety miles inland, and is accessible at all seasons to vessels of the largest tonnage. Communication between the capital and the other parts of the province is afforded by the three branches which feed the Pearl River, and by a network of canals, and creeks. A line of fine steamers plies daily between the city and Hongkong, and the submarine telegraph, at the latter place, has thus brought the once distant Cathay into daily correspondence with the western world. It is a pleasant trip from Hongkong up the broad Pearl River. From the deck of the steamers one may view with comfort the ruins of the Bogue forts, and think of the time and feelings of Captain Weddell, who, in 1637, anchored the first fleet of English merchant vessels before them. From this point the gallant captain, through the misrepresentation and slander of the Portuguese, had to fight his way up to Canton, where he at last obtained cargoes at rates so unprofitable that the trade was abandoned for a quarter of a century afterwards. The Chinese cabin in the Canton steamer is an interesting sight, too. It is crowded with passengers every trip; and there they lie on the deck in all imaginable attitudes, some on mats smoking opium, others on benches fast asleep. There are little gambling parties in one corner, and city merchants talking trade in another; and viewed from the cabin-door the whole presents a wonderfully confused perspective of naked limbs, arms and heads, queues, fans, pipes, and silk or cotton jackets. The owners of these miscellaneous effects never dream of walking about, or enjoying the scenery or sea-breeze. I only once noticed a party of Chinese passengers aroused to something bordering on excitement, and it was in this Canton steamer. They had caught a countryman in an attempt at robbery, and determined to punish him in their own way. When the steamer reached the wharf, they relieved the delinquent of his clothing, bound it around his head, and tied his hands behind his back with cords ; and in this condition sent him ashore to meet his friends, but not before they had covered his nakedness with a coat of oil-paint of various tints.

My readers will remember the celebrated Governor Yeh of Canton, who was carried prisoner to Calcutta. He would almost be forgotten in this quarter were it not for a temple erected to his departed spirit. It may be seen on the bank of a suburban creek. A very pretty monument it is to remind one of our lively intercourse with the notorious Imperial commissioner in 1857, an intercourse marked by trouble and bloodshed throughout, and which ended in the capture of that unfortunate official in an obscure yamen. Yeh's temple is a handsomely finished, pretty edifice, among the best of its kind in Canton, and it conveys to a visitor an excellent notion of the temple architecture now in vogue at that city.

The Fatee gardens, so often described, are still to

YEH'S TEMPLE, CANTON

be found, almost unchanged, at the side of a narrow creek on the right bank of the river. These gardens are native nurseries for flowers, dwarf shrubs, and trees. Like most Chinese gardens they cover only a small area, and have been contrived to represent landscape gardening in miniature. Thus the walks are intentionally narrow. Here and there are dwarf trees and stunted shrubs, little rockeries crowned with temples and pagodas equally diminutive in their proportions, while small pools set out like lakes are spanned with dainty little marble bridges in their narrower parts. In the Fatee nurseries, besides rare and beautiful flowers, a great attraction is found in the shrubs trained to form small barges, dwellings, and dragons; some have even been turned into bird-cages, where living birds might find a more congenial home than in the bamboo cages in common use. It is interesting to notice the dwarfing of trees. An ordinary tree is selected, and around a suitable branch the gardener binds a bag of mould, which he is careful to keep moist until, at length, the branch strikes roots into the mould. It is then cut from the parent stem and planted to form the trunk of the dwarf, that soon bears leaves, and flowers, and fruit.

Some distance below the Fatee creek, on the same side of the river, a number of Tea Hongs and tea-firing establishments are to be found. To these I now venture to introduce the reader, as he must needs feel more or less interest in the tea-men, and their mode of preparing this highly-prized luxury. Passing up the creek along the usual narrow channel, between densely-packed rows of floating craft, we land on a broad stone platform, cross a court where men are to be seen weighing the tea, and enter a large three-storied brick building, where we meet 'Tan Kin Ching,' the proprietor, to whom we bear an introduction from one of his foreign customers. One of the clerks is directed to show us over the place. He first ushers us into a large warehouse, where thousands of chests of the new crop are piled up, ready for inspection by the buyer. The inspection of this cargo is an exceedingly simple process. The foreign tea-taster enters and places his mark on certain boxes in different parts of the pile. These are forthwith removed, weighed, and scrutinised as fair samples of the bulk. The whole cargo is shipped without further ceremony should the parcels examined prove satisfactory ones; and, indeed, nowadays it seldom happens that shortcomings in weight and quality are at the last moment detected, for the better class of Chinese merchants are remarkable for their honesty and fair dealing. I am the more anxious thus to do justice to the Chinese dealers, because the notion has recently got abroad that, as a rule, they are most notorious cheats; men who never fail to overreach the unsuspecting trader when an opportunity occurs, and upon whose shoulders must fall the full weight of the charge of preparing and selling those spurious or adulterated teas which have recently reached this country in a condition not fit for human food. It seems clear to me that the Chinese manufacturer of this sort of rubbish is by no means the most reprehensible party in the trade. He it is, indeed, who sets himself to collect from the servants of foreigners or natives, and from the restaurants and tea-saloons, the leaves that have been already used, and to dry them, cook them, and mix them with imitations of the genuine leaf. This process completed, he next adds pickings, dust, and sweepings from the tea-factory, and mixes the whole with foreign materials, so as to lend it a healthy surface hue. Lastly, he perfumes the lot with some sweet-smelling flower—the chloranthus, olea, aglaia, and others; and thus provides a cheap, fragrant, and polluted cup for the humble consumers abroad. They, poor souls, are tempted by the lowness of the cost; while, as for the grocer from whom they buy their pennies'-worths of the dear herb, or whatever we ought to call it, he probably knows about as much of the chemistry of tea and of the science of tea-tasting as he does of the spectroscope and the composition of a comet. He might just as reasonably, in some instances, be fined for ignorance of the chemistry of the stars as for unacquaintance with the properties and composition of the tea he sells. I must not, however, be understood to say that the retail dealer is ignorant of the market value of the tea he buys. I only affirm that he is fairly entitled to take it for granted that tea on which duty has been paid, and which is offered to him for sale, is fit for human food. The evil will only be cured when the market for such stuff is closed in China, and when those who traffic in it shall be content to follow the legitimate course of trade, and to compete with the foreign tea-merchants who are armed with a staff of highly-trained, honest assistants, and who buy only what they themselves know to be sound and good. The tea-trade is more or less a speculative one, always full of risks (as some of our merchants have found out to their cost); and though a vast amount of foreign capital is annually invested in the enterprise, it is probably only every second or third venture that will return, I do not say a handsome profit, but any profit at all.

Tea-mixing is also carried on, to a certain extent, at home, in order to meet the taste and means of European consumers; but the materials which form the spurious class of teas to which I have already referred are brought from the Central Flowery Land; and it may be set down as a guide to the public that tea pure and simple cannot be sold in England at much under two shillings, or two shillings and sixpence a pound, although cheaper teas or mixtures may at the same time be obtained of a perfectly harmless quality.

We will now proceed to another apartment and see the method adopted in the manufacture of gunpowder teas. First the fresh leaves of black tea are partially dried in the sun. These are next rolled either in the palm of the hand, or on a flat tray, or by the feet in a hempen bag; then they are scorched in hollow iron pans over a charcoal fire, and after this are spread out on bamboo trays, that the broken stems and refuse may be picked out. In this large stone-paved room we notice the leaves in different stages of preparation. The labour required to produce the gunpowder leaf is the most curious and interesting of the many processes to which the plant is subjected. We are surprised to notice a troop of able-bodied coolies, each dressed only in a short pair of cotton trousers tucked up so as to give free action to his naked limbs. One feels puzzled at first to conjecture what they are about. Can they be at work, or is it only play? They each rest their arms on a cross beam, or against the wall, and with their feet busily roll and toss balls of about a foot in diameter (or the size of an ordinary football) up and down the floor of the room. Our guide assures us it is work they are after, and very hard work too. The balls beneath their feet are the bags packed full of tea leaves, which by the constant rolling motion assume the pellet shape. As the leaves become more compact, the bag loosens and requires to be twisted up at the neck, and again rolled; the twisting and rolling being repeated until the leaf has become perfectly globose. It is then divided through sieves into different sizes, or qualities, and the scent and bouquet is imparted after the final drying or scorching.

Most of the tea shipped from Canton is now grown in the province of Kwang-tung; formerly part of it used to be brought from the 'Tung-ting' district, but that now finds its way to Hankow. Leaves from the Tai-shan district are mostly used in making 'Canton District Pekoe' and 'Long Leaf Scented Orange Pekoe,' while Lo-ting leaf makes 'Scented Caper and Gunpowder' teas.

In order to see the foreign tea-tasters prosecuting a branch of science which they have made peculiarly their own, we must cross the river to Shameen, a pretty little green island, on which the foreign houses stand; looking with its villas, gardens, and croquet-lawns, like the suburb of some English town. There is a neat home-like church there, too, and near it resides the Archdeacon, who is constantly being found engaged in some tender-hearted self-sacrificing mission to the poor foreign sailors that frequent the port. We ascend a flight of steps in a massive stone retaining wall with which Shameen is surrounded; and this done, we might wander for a whole day, and examine all the houses on the island, without discovering a trace of a merchant's office, or any outward sign of commerce at all. Those who are familiar with the factory site, and who can figure what that must have been in olden times, when the foreign merchants were caged up like wild beasts, and subjected to the company and taunts of the vilest part of the river population, and to the pestilential fumes of an open drain that carried the sewage of the city to the stream, will be surprised at the transformation that has, since those days, been wrought.

The present residences of foreigners on this grassy site (reclaimed mud flat raised above the river) are substantial elegant buildings of stone or brick, surrounded each by a wall, an ornamental railing, or bamboo hedge, enclosing the gardens and outhouses in its circuit. Except the firm's name on each small brass door-plate, there is nothing anywhere that tells us of trade. But when we have entered, we find the dwelling-house on the upper story, and the comprador's room and offices on the ground-floor; next to the offices, the tea-taster's apartment. Ranged against the walls of this chamber are rows of polished shelves, covered with small round tin boxes of a uniform size, and bearing each a label and date in Chinese and English writing. These boxes contain samples of all the various sorts of old and new teas used for reference and comparison in tasting, smelling, and scrutinising parcels, or chops, which may be offered for sale. In the centre of the floor stands a long table bestrewed with a multitude of white porcelain covered cups, manufactured specially for the purpose of tasting tea. The samples are placed in these cups, and hot water of a given temperature is then poured upon them. The time the tea rests in the hot water is measured by a sand-glass; and when this is accomplished, all is ready for the tasting, which is a much more useful than elegant operation.

The windows of the room have a northern aspect, and are screened off so as to admit only a steady sky-light, which falls directly on to a tea-board beneath. Upon this board the samples are spread on square wooden trays, and it is under the uniform light above described that the minute inspection of colour, make, general appearance, and smell, takes place. All these tests are made by assistants who have gone through a special course of training which fits them for the mysteries of their art. The knowledge which these experts possess is of the greatest importance to the merchant, as the profitable outcome of the crops selected for the home market depends, to a great extent, on their judgment and ability. It will thus be seen that the merchant, not only when he chooses his teas for exportation, but at the last moment before they are shipped, takes the minutest precautions against fraudulent shortcomings either in quality or weight. It is possible, however, for a sound tea, if undercooked, or imperfectly dried, to become putrid during the homeward voyage, and to reach this country in a condition quite unfit for use. This I know from my own experience. I at one time was presented with a box of tea by the Taotai of Taiwanfu in Formosa, and when I first got it I found that some of the leaves had a slightly green tint, and were damp. I had intended to bring this tea home to England; it was of good quality, but it spoiled before I left China. Judging from the quantites of tea that have been recently condemned, the importation of spurious cargoes can hardly be a lucrative trade, and it might probably be done away with altogether were competent public inspectors appointed to examine every cargo as it arrives.

Although Chinese commercial morality has not run to such a very low ebb as some might imagine, yet the clever traders of the lower orders of Cathay are by no means above resorting to highly questionable and ingenious practices of adulteration, when such practices can be managed with safety and profit. Thus the foreign merchant finds it always necessary to be vigilant in his scrutiny of tea, silk, and other produce, before effecting a purchase. But equal care requires to be observed in all money transactions, as counterfeit coining is a profession carried on in Canton with marvellous success; so successful, indeed, are the coiners of false dollars that the native experts, or schroffs, who are employed by foreign merchants (Mr. W. F. Mayers assures me), are taught the art of schroffing, or detecting counterfeit coin, by men who are in direct communication with the coiners of the spurious dollars in circulation.

In many of the Canton shops one notices the intimation 'Schroffing taught here.' This is a curious system of corruption, which one would think would be worth the serious attention of the Government. Were counterfeit coining put down, there would be no need for the crafty instructors of schroffs; and at the same time the expensive staff of experts employed in banks and merchants' offices could be dispensed with.

But the dollar in the hands of a needy and ingenious Chinaman is not only delightful to behold, but it admits of a manipulation at once most skilful and profitable. He will set to work and saw it in two, rewarding himself for his patience and labour by appropriating everything but the silver shell and superscription. He will then fill up the two halves with baser metal, and solder them together in such a way that, both in sound and appearance, the coin will seem good to all but the trained expert. Devices more daring still he frequently resorts to, when only the outer mould and colour of the dollar are furnished to resemble the true coin.

CHAPTER IX.

Canton—Its general Appearance—Its Population—Streets—Shops—Mode of transacting Business—Signboards—Work and Wages—The Willow-pattern Bridge—Juilin, Governor-General of the two Kwang—Clan Fights—Hak-kas—The Mystic Pills—Dwellings of the Poor—The Lohang-tang—Buddhist Monastic Life—On board a Junk.

CANTON is by no means the densely packed London in China which some have made it out to be. The circuit of the city wall very little exceeds six miles, and if we stand upon the heights to the north of the city, and turn our faces southward, we can trace the outline of these fortifications along a considerable portion of their course. This, then, is the entire area strictly included in the limits of the town; but there are large straggling suburbs outside the walls which spread for no little distance over the plain. In these suburbs there are many open spaces. Some, shaded by trees and orchards, form the parks and gardens of the gentry; others, again, display the carefully tended produce of the market-gardener; while military parade grounds, rice-fields, and ponds where fish are bred, are scattered at intervals between more thickly populated ground. There is, indeed, nothing in the whole picture of this southern metropolis suggestive of a teeming land population, save the centre of the city itself. But to the south of the wall there is the broad Pearl River, and communicating with this stream a network of canals and creeks, the whole more densely populated perhaps than the city. In the boats which crowd these water-ways a vast number of families pass their lives, and subsist by carrying merchandise or conveying passengers to different parts of the province. The population of Canton is computed at about a million souls, although the official census returns it at a figure considerably higher.

As in Peking, so at Canton, the space within the walls is divided into two unequal parts, the one occupied nominally by the Tartar garrison and official residences only, and the other containing the abodes of the trading Chinese population. But the descendants of the old Tartar soldiers, too proud to labour, and too haughty to stoop themselves to the mean artifices of trade, have become impoverished in process of time, and have disposed of their lands and dwellings to their more industrious Chinese neighbours. As to the houses themselves, they everywhere preserve one uniform low level, but the monotonous appearance thus produced is at rare intervals broken by some tall temple which rears its carved and gilded roof from amid a grove of venerable trees, or by the nine-storied pagoda, or lofty quadrangular towers that mark the pawnshop sites. The pawnshops in this strange city rear their heads heavenward as proudly as church steeples, and indeed at first we mistook them to be temples. What was our surprise, then, to discover in them the Chinese reproduction of that money-lending establishment which is found in the shady corners of our own bye streets, beneath a modest trinity of gilded balls, and whose private side entrance stands invitingly open—the refuge of the widow or the fatherless, when they creep thither at the last moment, in the twilight, to part with jewels whose paltry lustre perhaps gleams with many a bright memory to them. But there is no romance about these Canton pawnshops. They are square bold-looking edifices, lifting their benevolent grey brick heads to a height which positively, in Chinese eyes, invests them with sanctity.

Ah-sin, and Ah-lok, indeed look up with something akin to veneration at their plastered walls, narrow stanchioned windows, and at the huge rock boulders poised on the edge of the roof above, ready to drop down upon any robber who might dare to scale the treasure-sheltering sides. I recollect visiting one of these places for the purpose of seeing within, and to obtain a view of the city. Armed with an introduction from a leading Chinese merchant, I presented myself one morning before an outer gate in the high prison-looking wall which encircled the tower. My summons was answered by a portly gate-keeper. who at once admitted me inside. Here I found a number of military candidates going through a course of drill; the porter was himself an old soldier, a sort of drill-sergeant, and was now instructing pupils in the use of the bow, and how to lift up heavy weights. After exhibiting one or two specimens of their powers, we were taken to a narrow barred gate at the base of the tower. The office for transacting business was on the ground-floor, and above this a square wooden scaffolding, standing free of the walls, ran right up to the roof. This scaffolding was divided into a series of flats, having ladders which lead from one to the other; the bottom flat was used for stowing pledges of the greatest bulk, such as furniture or produce; smaller and lighter articles occupied the upper flats, while the one nearest the roof was devoted to bullion and jewellery. Every pledge from floor to ceiling was catalogued, and bore a ticket denoting the number of the article, and the date on which it was deposited. Thus anything could be found and redeemed at a moment's notice. Such towers are places for the safe custody of the costly gems and robes of the wealthy classes of the community, and are really indispensable institutions in a country where brigandage and misgovernment expose property to constant risks. Besides this, a licensed pawnbroking establishment makes temporary advances to needy persons who may have security to lodge; the charge being three per cent. per month on sums under ten taels, save in the last month of the year, when the interest is reduced to two per cent. If the amount of the loan exceeds ten taels, the rate is uniformly two per cent. per month. The pledges are kept for three years in the better class of pawnshops. It is the custom of the poor to pawn their winter and summer clothing alternately, redeeming each suit as it may be required.

Not far below the Heights in the Tartar quarter of the city, is the British Consulate or Yamen. This edifice stands in the grounds of what was once a palace, and is made up of diverse picturesque Chinese buildings, environed by a tastefully laid out garden and deer park. Hard by is the ancient nine-storied pagoda ascribed to the reign of the Emperor Wu-Ti, in the middle of the sixth century of our era. It is octagonal in shape, and 170 feet high. In 1859 some British sailors, weary of shore life, and longing to go aloft, managed, at the risk of their necks, to scale this crazy-looking monument—an event which greatly disgusted the Chinese, for they hate to have their dwellings overlooked from a height, more especially by a pack of foreign fire-eating sailors. Descending from the height, and passing southwards down to the main street of the town, we are struck by the appearance of the closely-packed shops, which differ from anything we have ever seen before. We observe that the folks who lounge about, even in the meanest looking dwellings, are, most of them, good-looking—the men tall and shapely, and the women in no instance disfigured by small bandaged feet. There are also a number of soldiers, not far from the parade ground—fellows who, erect and muscular, carry themselves with a dauntless military air. These are the remnants of the once powerful Tartar camp. They have been instructed in foreign drill, and are said to make good soldiers. They certainly contrast favourably with many of the troops I saw in other quarters of the Empire. As to the shopkeepers, they are all Chinese, but their small-footed consorts are nowhere to be seen; the fact is, they keep them strictly secluded. Some of these handsome Tartar matrons have their children seated in bamboo cages at their doors, and pretty little birds they make, too.

One is almost bewildered by the diversity of shops, and the attractive wares which they display. There are so many things that one would like to carry home. Everything is so beautiful, everything so costly, and not unfrequently cumbrous too. Then the shop-keepers are so very fascinating in their manners. Have a good look at them; they are about the best class of men in China—honest, industrious, contented, and refined too, some of them. A short time back a curious though not uncommon sort of lottery was got up among the shop keepers of Canton.[1] Wang-leang-

[1] See *China Review*, 1873, p. 249.

chai, of the Juy-Chang boot shop in Ma-an street, seized with a passion for poetry, organised a sort of literary lottery, and offered the stakes as prizes to the successful composer of the best lines on five selected subjects.

Frequently, on entering a Canton shop, you will find its owner with a book in one hand and a pipe or a fan in the other, and wholly absorbed in his studies. You will be doomed to disappointment if you expect the smoker to start up at once, all smiles and blandness, rubbing his hands together as he makes a shrewd guess of what he is likely to take out of you, and receiving you obsequiously or with rudeness accordingly. Quite the reverse! Your presence is apparently unnoticed, unless you happen to lift anything; then you hear that the fan has been arrested, and feel that a keen eye is bent on your movements all the while. But it is not till you enquire for some article that the gentleman, now certain you mean to trade, will rise without bustle from his seat—show you his goods, or state the price he means to sell at—with a polite yet careless air which plainly says 'If it suits you, we make an exchange, I take the money, you the goods, conferring a mutual benefit on each other: but if not agreeable, depart and leave me to my pipe and book.' After all, by adhering to this independent style, I believe they sell more, and make better profits, than if they were perpetually soliciting patronage by word and gesture. On our way homewards we pass through Physic Street, or Tsiang-Lan-Kiai. Here the shops are nearly all uniform in size, a brick party-wall dividing each building from its neighbour. All have one front apartment open to the street, with a granite or brick counter for the display of their wares. A granite base also supports the tall upright signboard, the indispensable characteristic of every shop in China. Opposite the signboard stands a small altar or shrine, dedicated to the god who presides over the tradesman and his craft. This deity is honoured regularly when the shop is opened, and a small incense-stick is lighted, and kept burning in a bronze cup of ashes placed in front of the shrine.

The shops within are frequently fitted with a counter of finely-polished wood and finely-carved shelves, while at the back is an accountant's room, screened off with an open-work wooden partition, so carved as to resemble a climbing plant. In some conspicuous place stand the brazen scales and weights, ever brightly polished, and adorned with red cloth. These scales are used for weighing the silver-coin bars, and fragments of the precious metal, which form part of the currency of the place. When goods are sold by weight, the customer invariably brings his own balance, so as to secure his fair and just portion of the article he has come to buy. This balance is not unlike an ordinary yard-measuring rod, furnished with a sliding weight. It is a simple application of the lever. But the tendency of this simple mechanical contrivance is not calculated to elevate the Chinese in our estimation. It proves a universal lack of confidence, which finds its way down to the lowest details of petty trade, for which the governing classes may take to themselves credit. The people are in this, as in many other matters, a law unto themselves. A ceaseless struggle against unfair dealing has, therefore, like other native institutions, become a stereotyped necessity.

A STREET IN CANTON

It is by no means pleasant to be caught in one of these narrow streets during a shower, as the water pours down in torrents from the roofs and floods the pavement, until it subsides through the soil beneath. The broadest streets are narrow, and shaded above, in some places, with screens of matting, to keep out the sun. So close, indeed, are the roofs to each other in the Chinese city, that, viewed from a distance, they look like one uninterrupted covering—a space entirely tiled over, beneath which the citizens sedulously conceal themselves until the cool of the evening, when weary of the darkness and of the trade and strife of the day, they swarm on the housetops to gamble, or smoke, or sip their tea until the shades of night fall, and they retire again to the lower regions, to sleep on the cool benches of their shops.

The signboards of Cantonese shops are not only the pride of their owners, but they are a delight to students of Chinese. The signboards in the engraving may be taken as fair examples of Chinese street literature. In the high-flown classical, or poetical phrases by which public attention is drawn to the various shops, one fails to see, in most instances, the faintest reference to the contents of the establishment. Thus, a tradesman who sells swallows' nests for making soup, has on his board simply characters signifying Yun-Ki, sign of the Eternal. But here is a list, translated by Mr. W. F. Mayers from the signboards in the picture.

Kien Ki Hao—the sign of the symbol Kien (Heaven) Hwei-chow, ink, pencils, and writing materials. This is, indeed, a very high compliment to literature.

Chang Tsi Tang (Chang of the family branch designated Tsi). Wax, cased pills of select manufacture. Chang is evidently proud of his family connection, and probably offers it as a sufficient guarantee for the quality of his pills.

Tien Yih (Celestial advantage). Table-covers, cushions for chairs, and divans for sale. Now what 'Celestial advantage' can a customer be supposed to derive from table-covers or cushions, unless, indeed, one supposes that the downy ease conferred by the use of these cushions is almost beyond the sphere of terrestrial enjoyment. There must be some notion of this sort associated with upholsterers' shops, as we have here another sign embodying a high-flown phrase, flavoured with a little common sense.

Tien Yih Shên (Celestial advantage combined with attention). Shop for the sale of cushions and ratan mats.

Yung Ki (sign of the Eternal). Swallows' nests. Money-schroffing taught here.

K'ing Wēn T'a'ng (the hall of delight in scholarship). Seals artistically engraved.

Notwithstanding the narrowness of the streets of Canton, they are extremely picturesque; more especially those in which we find the old curiosity-shops, the silversmiths, and the silk-mercers; where the signboards present a most attractive display of brilliant and varied colours, as, indeed, in the one through which we have just been passing.

Striking thence by a narrow alley into a back lane, we find ourselves in a very poor neighbourhood, with dingy, dirty hovels filled with operatives, who are busily at work; some weaving silk; others embroidering satin robes; others, again, carving and turning the ivory balls and curios which are the admiration of foreigners. Entering one shop, we are shown an elaborately carved series of nine ivory balls, one within the other. It is commonly believed that these balls are first carved in halves, and then joined together so perfectly as to look solid. But as we watch a man working on one of them the mystery is gradually solved. The rough piece of solid ivory is first cut into a ball; it is then fixed into a primitive-looking lathe, and turned with a sharp tool in various positions, until it becomes perfectly round. It is then set again in the lathe and drilled with the requisite number of holes all round. After this one hole is centred, a tool bent at the end is passed in, and with this a groove is produced near the heart of the sphere; another hole is then centred, and after that another; the same operation being carried out with all the holes until all the grooves meet, and a small ball drops into the centre. In this way all the balls one within the other are ultimately released. The next operation is carving the innermost ball; this is accomplished by means of long drills and other delicate tools and in the same way all the rest of the balls are carved in succession, the carving gradually becoming more easy and elaborate until the outside ball is reached, and this is then finished with a delicate beauty that resembles the finer sorts of lace. Close by these ivory-turners are men designing patterns for embroidery, and shops full of children, sewing the most beautiful patterns of birds, butterflies, and flowers on satin robes. The wages of the people who do this lovely work are very small indeed. The artist who furnishes the designs receives about 1*l.* 5*s.* a month, and the following table gives the average at which skilled labourers are paid.

	£	*s*	*d*	
Shoemaker		15	0	a month, with food.
Blacksmith	1	0	0	"
First-class ivory carver . .	2	8	0	"
Skilled embroiderer . .		15	0	"
Silversmith	1	12	0	"
Painter		18	0	"

It takes about ten days to complete the embroidery of a pair of shoes; and these, when soled and finished, fetch fifteen shillings a pair. The wages of the embroiderer, according to this calculation, would amount to six shillings or thereabout, and the balance, to cover cost of material and making, would leave but a modest profit to the master; but then embroidered shoes are in constant demand, and a lady of rank will require some thirty pair for her marriage trousseau alone. Some ladies embroider their own shoes, but the practice is by no means a common one. The dress shoes of the men are embroidered too, and are used by all except the poorest class. It will be seen from the foregoing notes that skilled labour is so cheap in China as to give artisans a great advantage in all those various branches of native industry which find a market abroad; and this will one day render the clever, careful, and patient Chinaman a formidable rival to European manufacturers, when he has learned to use machinery in weaving fabrics of cotton or silk.

Many of the beautifully embroidered stuffs we see in our shops at home are made by hand in China, and yet they can be sold in London at prices that defy competition. The opposition to the introduction of the machines used in Bradford and Manchester comes mostly from the operatives themselves. The masters, who understand the foreign markets, would many of them be glad to set up European looms, and even to use steam to drive them. But the poor operatives, who earn their miserable pittance by their handwork, would strike and starve rather than tolerate two or three new wheels and spindles, which, as they believe, would throw them out of employment. I was assured by one Chinese silk merchant who accompanied me to his factory in the country, that he once tried to introduce a foreign contrivance to his reeling machines; but his people left him in a body, and perseverance in the innovation would simply have involved him in ruin—so at least he said. This gentleman employed the greater portion of the men, women, and children, of a whole village—a rare thing in China, where labour is so minutely divided, and where nearly every householder is his own master. But these villagers were only hired to reel and dress the silk during certain months of the year; and they, most of them, had small farms where they cultivated the raw silk on their own account. It is perfectly astonishing to see what these Cantonese can accomplish on their own inferior looms. Give them almost any pattern or design, and they will contrive to weave it, imitating its imperfections with as much exactness as its beauties. I like to linger over these shops, and to meditate on these scenes of ceaseless industry, where all goes on with a quiet harmony that has a strange fascination for the observer. Amid all the evidences of toil, the poorest has some leisure at his command. Then, seated on a bench or squatting tranquilly on the ground, he will smoke or chat with his neighbour, untroubled by the presence of his good-natured employer, who seems to grow fatter and wealthier on the smiles and happy temperament of his workmen. Here, too, one can see how the nucleus of this great city is more closely populated than at first sight one would suppose. Most of the workshops are kitchen, dining-room, and bed-room too; here, the workpeople breakfast on their benches; here, at nightfall, they stretch themselves out to sleep. Their whole worldly wealth is stored here too. An extra jacket, a pipe, a few ornaments which are used in common, and a pair of chopsticks—these make up each man's total worldly pelf; and, indeed, his greatest treasures he carries with him—a stock of health and a happy contented mind. Surely, one would think, such men as these, accustomed to nothing but endless toil and simple fare, would be tolerably wretched at times; that there would be moments when they would call to mind their barren prospects, and resolve to make a struggle to raise themselves above their fellows. But then we must recollect that Chinamen, for the most part, only become wretched and ambitious when they leave home and go to a foreign country. Here, in their own land, they seem to think little about the future, save when some one among them, more provident than the rest, hoards up cash, and invests in a coffin for use after his own decease. The Chinese operative is completely content if he escape the pangs of hunger, endowed with health sufficient to enable him simply to enjoy the sense of living, and of living, too, in a land so perfect that a human being ought to be happy in the privilege of residing there at all. It is a land, so they seem to suppose, wherein everything is settled and ordered by men who know exactly what they ought to

A PAVILION IN PUN-TING-QUA'S GARDEN

know, and who are paid to keep people from rising, or ambitiously seeking to quit the groove in which Providence placed them at their birth. Many will say that the Chinaman is not without ambition, and in a sense they will be right. Parents are ambitious to educate their children, and to qualify them for candidature at the Government examinations; and there are probably no men who lust more after power, wealth, and place than the successful Chinese graduates, simply because they know that there is no limit to their prospects. If they have interest and genius, the poorest of them may fairly aspire to become a member of the Imperial Cabinet; but then these are the men of letters, and not the poor labouring masses, the populace whom I have just described.

Before I quit Canton I must give some account of a spot there which I visited more than once, and which is commonly known as the garden of Pun-ting-qua. Pun-ting-qua or Pun-shi-cheng, the original owner, had been a wealthy merchant at Canton, but his Government ultimately drained him of his wealth, by compelling him to pay a certain fixed sum for the monopoly of the trade in salt. Falling into heavy arrears, and being unable to raise the amount, his property was sequestrated, and his splendid garden raffled in a public lottery. A notable instance, this, of the danger of becoming too rich in China. His house, a singularly beautiful place, was sold to the anti-foreign anti-missionary society of Canton; and at the time of my visit to this quaint pleasure-ground traces of decay had already set their stamp upon the curious structures that adorned it. I first made my way up Sulphur Creek, which sweeps round to the west of the city, and passed many a strange crazy-looking edifice rising above the dull water, and bending over a frail wooden jetty which divided it from the stream. Most of these jetties were themselves decayed, and had been propped up only at the last moment, as their green mouldy timbers were about to settle down and bury themselves in the muddy bed of the creek. Small barred windows pierce the gaunt walls of the moss-covered brick buildings, and sundry garments dangle from bamboos and ropes, which are stretched from wall to wall. Women are washing, and children sit upon the steps and jetties in a way that makes one tremble for their safety. Dogs bark and snarl at the doorways, domesticated pigs or fowls look out upon the throng of boats, while the men are busy dipping dark blue cotton fabrics into the stream. A three-storied pagoda marks the site of Pun-ting-qua's garden, which we enter through a gateway in the outer wall. Once arrived inside, we seem for the first time to realise the China pictured to us in our schoolboy days. Here we see model Chinese gardening; drooping willows, shady walks, and sunny lotus-pools, on which gilded barges float. Here, too, spanning a lake, stands the well known willow-pattern bridge, with a pavilion hard by. But we miss the two love-birds; there is no dutiful parent, with the fishtail feet, leisurely, and with lamp in hand, pursuing his unfilial daughter as she, with equal leisure, makes her way after the shepherd with the crook. I photographed this willow-pattern bridge, but when I look at my picture, I find it falls far short of the scene on our soup-plates. Where, for example, is the pavilion which is all ornaments, the tree above it which grows nothing but foot-balls, and that other tree, too, on which only feathers bloom. Where

THE WILLOW-PATTERN BRIDGE

is the fence that meanders across the platform in the foreground? And yet these gardens have a quaintness all their own. Their winding paths conduct to cleverly contrived retreats; and tunnels cut through mossy fern-covered rocks land us in some pavilion or theatre, on the edge of a glassy pool, where gold-fish sport in the sunshine, and glistening frogs sit gravely on broad dew-spangled lotus-leaves; or else we discover some spacious open saloon, where a party of native gentlemen, seated on square, cool, marble-bottomed, ebony chairs, enjoy a repast of tea or cake, or listen to the strumming of a lute, and to the shrill song of some lady in attendance.

Juilin, the governor of the province of which Canton is the capital, and of the adjoining province of Kwang-si as well, is an officer who has seen distinguished service, and one as widely known to Europeans as any dignitary in China. A man of singular administrative ability, he has done much to promote the prosperity of the provinces which he controls, and it is probably owing, in a great measure, to his influence that peaceful relations with foreign nations have been so well maintained. Besides this, he had organised a steam gunboat service, which had already made its presence felt among the pirate vessels on the coasts. Juilin is a Manchu by birth, and at an early age was employed in public functions at the capital. Here he won the goodwill of the Emperor Tao Kwang, and rose to be cabinet minister. He was afterwards degraded, owing to the defeat of the Chinese troops at Pa-li Chiao, when the allied forces made their advance upon Pekin, but was subsequently restored to favour and appointed general of the Tartar garrison of Canton. From this post he was transferred shortly afterwards to the office which he at present holds. His career as governor-general has been marked by signs of progress and by an enlightened or even liberal policy. He has restored order in the distracted district near Chao-chow-fu, and rendered life and property secure there, successfully suppressing the village clans which for many years previously had set all authority at defiance. These villages were each like a garrisoned fortress, inhabited by one large family or clan, and at feud with all the other surrounding villages and clans. Thus wars on a tiny scale were for ever being carried on, the youths of the villages being the fighting men, and their pay being provided by the elders.

When in Chao-chow-fu I visited several of these villages, and got some notion of their style of fighting. Those unfortunates who were carried off as prisoners of war were frequently detained in slavery, or met a fate even worse than this, for their captors would dispose of them to be sent, as involuntary emigrants, to foreign shores. At harvest-time one village would make a midnight raid upon its neighbour, and carry off all the crops; and at Sinchew I found an old feud existing between that village and a number of smaller hamlets. One Aching and his brother, tired at last of fighting, and of being constantly interrupted in more peaceful and profitable pursuits, resolved to go into the Fukien Province, and there to seek for work. With their bundles on their backs they started from their native place, but halted when not far on their journey to fish in a neighbouring stream. While thus engaged, a boat full of their enemies carefully disguised made its approach, and one of the crew offered to buy their stock of fish. The two brothers falling into the snare, were thus carried off to the hostile village, and there killed and mutilated in an open space in front of the settlement. Aching's heart was cut out, boiled, and eaten by his savage captors, under the notion that they would become more daring and bloodthirsty in consequence of this revolting deed. This occurred in 1869. Another example of native treachery and cunning will suffice. Two men of opposite clans had made up their minds to quit the province with the loot they had gained in war; they, both of them, went to Cheng-lin at the same time, in search of the same object, viz. a boat. The one, hearing of the other's presence, hired a number of ruffians to slay him, promising them six pounds for his enemy's head and heart. The gang, tempted to the crime by the prospect of this liberal reward, soon caught their man; but he, enquiring how much they were to receive for his head, at once offered them, on better security, double terms for the capture of his crafty foe. They had no hesitation in accepting the proposal, and it was their first employer, therefore, who fell a victim to their guile. In the end a small army was sent into the provinces, and all who refused to come to terms, and obey the law, were mercilessly put to the sword. So it came about that at the time I visited the place a well-dressed man might walk abroad, and no longer fear lest he be stripped and sent adrift without a rag to cover him, or else sold into slavery or even killed.

There is a hardy race of people found in this and several other districts. These are known as Hak-kas, and some are of opinion that they are a people distinct from the Chinese, as they speak a language of their own, and resemble Indians in physical appearance, rather than the Chinese type. Others, again, hold that the Hak-kas emigrated some eight hundred years ago from the Ning-hwa district in the Fukien province, and a recent writer in the 'China Review' undertakes to prove from the Hak-kas family records that Ning-hwa was really their original home. Be their origin what it may, they have carved out an important place for themselves in the rich province of Kwangtung. I also met them increasing, multiplying and spreading their industry in the island of Formosa. It was they who, having no sympathies in common with the Puntis of Canton, formed the Coolie corps to the allied troops, and won a high reputation for perseverance and bravery. They have even been known to rescue British soldiers, when wounded and drowning, amid a perfect storm of bullets. Dr. Eitel, who laboured among them for many years, and who kindly furnished me with some of his experiences, described them as the hardest workers and the most industrious men in Kwangtung; and when the interests of Hak-kas and Puntis, or natives of the province, clashed, the former have always distinguished themselves by their readiness to fight For more than two centuries a stream of Hak-ka emigration has been flowing into the Ka-ying-chow department, taking its course more especially through the mountainous and thinly populated parts. This movement is still going on.

The process, in individual cases, is more or less as follows. A couple of Hak-kas come to a Punti village, and there they hire themselves out to labour on the farm. In process of time, when they have laid up a little money, they rent a few acres of mountain land, or unredeemed bog. The insecurity caused by robbers and banditti makes it difficult in sparsely populated districts to cultivate land far from a village. The Hak-kas, therefore, easily find landowners willing to rent their outlying acres at a merely nominal rate. All further difficulties are gradually overcome, and at last the persevering Hak-kas send for their families and friends, and settle down in mud huts, which they build like forts, surrounding them with ditches, with thorny thickets, and impenetrable bamboo. Success in most cases follows, the hamlet grows rapidly, and a flock of immigrants from their native province crowd in to plant a settlement in the neighbourhood. These scattered settlements form a confederation among themselves, and forthwith demand a reduction of the ground rent. If this be not acceeded to, things will progress pleasantly for a short time longer, until the confederation feels itself strong enough to wage war with the original owners, and refuse to pay any rent. But, lest the Government should interfere, they are careful to inform the mandarins beforehand that they will pay lawful ground-rent to them. Besides, in many public offices in the Kwangtung province, the subordinate employés are Hak-kas. This always enables them to judge of their own strength, to meet intrigue with intrigue, and to keep their quarrels outside the limits of Government intervention. As this class of village wars is looked upon as harmless by the authorities, they only interfere to squeeze both parties. The Punti employ braves to fight for them, while the Hak-kas fight their battles for themselves, and that is why the latter always win.

It is impossible to say whether this distinguished soldier and diplomatist Juilin entertains any kindly feeling towards foreigners, or any desire to encourage friendly intercourse with outer nations. If he has one or the other, he is an exception to the general race of Chinese statesmen; and I expect that he adopts a careful conciliatory policy, partly because his duty to the Imperial Government constrains him to that course, and partly because he well knows the power and resources of European nations. Recent occurrences in the Kwangtung province prove that there still exists, among the governing classes, a deep-rooted hostility to foreigners. The latest development of this feeling was in the Shan-shin-fan outrage in 1871, when the movement, had it not been checked in time, might have led to a wholesale massacre of the native and foreign Christians of the province, as well as to bloodshed in our own colony at Hongkong. Certain individuals belonging to the so-called literati class are said to have been at the root of the whole affair; through their instrumentality inflammatory placards were printed and put extensively into circulation; pills also were manufactured, and freely distributed to the populace; pills, it was said, concocted by the missionaries, and possessing the power to bewitch innocent women, and to proselytise foolish men; they were besides this accounted capable of working miracles of a character too disgusting to be described. The results of all this trickery were riots in different quarters. A chapel was burnt at Fatshan, and a feeling of intense repugnance and bitter hatred to foreigners was stirred among the simple, superstitious, and peacably inclined peasantry. Public feeling, indeed, was just as excited as before the Tientsin massacre; but the prompt action of the lieutenant-governor of Hongkong, who despatched a gunboat to Canton, backed by the strong representations of the acting British Consul on the spot, roused the native authorities to a recognition of the danger, and led them to take such vigorous steps that order was speedily restored.

Before I quit Canton, it may be worth while to glance at a quarter of the town which has undergone improvements within the past ten years. Not far from the old factory site, and close to the river, there stands a row of well-built brick houses. In 1869 these houses had not yet been built, and the ground was occupied by a strange mixed population of the poorest classes. Too poor to live in boats, or in the houses of the city, they squatted on this waste land between the river and the wall, existing, most of them, nobody knew how. Some of the hovels in which they dwelt would not have made decent dog-kennels; and yet, amid all their poverty, they seemed a tolerably contented lot. I remember one hut which had been pieced together out of the fragments of an old boat, bits of foreign packing-cases, inscribed with trade marks that betrayed their chequered history, patches of decayed matting, clay, mud, and straw; a covering of odd tiles and broken pottery made all snug within. In the small space thus enclosed accommodation was found for a lean pig that lived on garbage, two old women, one old man, the old man's daughter, and the daughter's child. A small space in front was arranged as the kitchen, while part of the roof, and one or two pots, were taken up with vegetables or flowers. I have seen the inmates, in the morning sunshine, breakfasting off a savoury meal of mixed scraps that they had picked up in their perambulations about the city. There were many such dwellings in this neighbourhood, and the district physician lived not far off. The doctor had a very aged look, as if, at some distant period, he had been embalmed and preserved in a dried-up state, though still alive. He might be consulted at all hours, and would be found at his doorway among his herbs and simples, dressed in a pair of slippers and cotton breeches, and with ponderous spectacles across his shrivelled nose. But the door and wall of this public benefactor's abode were covered with an array of black plasters, to which the old man pointed with great pride as incontestable evidences of his professional skill. These plasters had a wide celebrity among his poor patients, and many a man, as a token of deep gratitude for some signal cure, had brought his plaster back as a certificate to adorn the residence where his deliverer dwelt.

Leaving this quarter, and striking for the suburbs north of the foreign settlements, we come upon a temple perhaps the most interesting in Canton. This is the temple of 500 gods; said, in Mr. Bowra's translation of the native history of the province, to have been founded by Bôdhidharama, a Buddhist monk from India, about the year 520 A.D. It is Bôdhidharama whom we frequently see pictured on Chinese teacups, as he ascends the Yangtsze river on his bamboo raft. The temple was rebuilt in 1755, under the auspices of the Emperor Kien-lung. It contains the Lo-hang-tang, or hall of saints, and with its temple buildings, its houses for priests, its lakes and its gardens, covers altogether a very large space. Colonel Yule, in his last edition of Marco Polo, says that one of the statues in this temple is an image of the Venetian

TEMPLE OF THE FIVE HUNDRED GODS

traveller; but careful inquiry proves this statement incorrect, for none of the images present the European type of face, and all the records connected with them are of an antiquity which runs back beyond Marco Polo's age. I made my first visit to this temple about five years ago, in the company of a Chinese gentleman attached to the customs department. The aged abbot, who is the centre figure in the group of chess-players on page 266, received us with great cordiality, and showed us into his private apartments, where we enjoyed a repast of tea and cake, and spent some time in examining a collection of dwarf trees and flowering shrubs, which he had arranged in a court in front of his sitting-room. In the centre of this court stood a tank containing fish, and a group of sacred lotus-flowers in full bloom. The golden fish darted in and out among a multitude of brilliantly-green aquatic plants that floated on the surface of the water. The old gentleman had spent many years of his life in seclusion, and seemed to be devoted to his garden, expressing his delight to find a foreigner who could share in his love for flowers. The apartments of this prelate impressed me with a sense of cold squareness and rigid uniformity. The flooring was marble, and the tables and chairs were either wholly of marble, or ebony and marble combined. If the chairs sent too rheumatic a chill through your blood, you could test the comfort of a block of polished rock in the corner, or try one or two cold glazed porcelain stools. Sundry texts from the sacred classics were hung about the dim walls, the strange characters looking like huge spiders marching in Indian file to the ceiling. Everything was in order, and everything scrupulously clean. But at length we discovered, when a number of the monks had joined our party, that the shaven, silent, thoughtful-looking inmates of the cloister, could unbend if they chose, and take a natural and ardent interest in the current gossip or scandal of Canton. Nay, they conducted us to a snuggery in an inner court, where a table was sumptuously spread, embowered beneath plantain-trees, and shaded by their huge waving leaves.

CHESS-PLAYING IN A BUDDHIST MONASTERY.

Round a lotus-pool, in the centre of this court, ran a paved pathway, and an ornamental railing, draped with the green leaves of a creeping plant. Here we left the monks engaging their venerable abbot in a game at chess, while I took my way to the interior of the shrine to obtain a photograph of the central altar. I found a number of people at worship within, making votive offerings to the idols whose aid they sought.

Some ladies were there, decked in their finest silks; and my entrance so startled these fair devotees that they would have fled but for the intervention of the priests, who gave me a high character as one in search of knowledge, who had wisely come from an obscure island to view the greatest temple in all the 'Central Flowery Land,' and to carry pictures of its wonders home. The images in this temple, though most of them are remarkably grotesque, yet, in the diversity of their attitudes, in their modelling, and in the varied expressions which their faces wear, reveal to us a knowledge of this particular branch of art, to be found perhaps nowhere else in China, and rather Indian in its character than Chinese.

Wending our way back to the river through narrow tortuous streets, and passing third-rate tea establishments, where men mix the fragrant leaves and toss them about with their naked feet on mats spread out in the sun, we at length embark in one of the many small boats which ply for hire at the jetties.

The crew of the little craft consists of three young girls, and these boatwomen are the prettiest and most attractive-looking of their sex to be met with out of doors in this part of China. They never paint, and are therefore set down by their countrywomen as of doubtful respectability. This is really true of some of them, although in the presence of Europeans who may hire their boats they behave with uniform modesty and decorum. Their boats are the perfection of neatness, and their dress as simple as it is picturesque. There is a hue of health, too, about their olive cheeks, and sparkling in their lustrous eyes, while the darkness of their raven tresses is charmingly heightened by a crimson flower in the hair. They scull or row with great dexterity, skimming in and out among the crowd of shipping, or along the narrow ways that form the thoroughfares in the floating town of boats, where natives in their tens of thousands pursue their various avocations quite apart from the dwellers on shore. A brisk trade is carried on in many of these narrow avenues, and the small merchants who engage in it have their shops in the bows of their boat, and their residences at the stern. If business happens to be dull at one end of the town they move to the other, or else take a tour in the provinces, carrying their whole establishment to a region where the family can enjoy balmy air, and where they will delight the hearts of the rustics with their display of city wares.

Steering clear of a floating market in one of the main alleys of this aquatic Babel, we come in front of a row of flower-boats, the floating music-saloons of this quarter of the stream. It is growing dark, and the numerous lamps which hang round these boats produce a very striking effect. Each saloon rears its head high above the water, and is carved into the most elaborate representations of the animal and vegetable world, of the beauties on earth, or the wonders in the heavens above. Through the interstices of the carving we can make out some exceedingly pretty female faces, and suddenly a crowd of fine young damsels rise above the woodwork, looking like a pretty continuation of the ornaments beneath. Suddenly again they disappear, as a gay group of youths in silken robes step out of a boat, and pass into the nearest saloon. Then we hear the warble of the lute, and the damsels piping in shrill treble tones; for these maidens have descended from their perch above, and are entertaining the city youths, who are come to dine in the saloon, to enjoy a whiff of opium, and to bask in smiles so sweet that they seem like to crack the enamel off the faces of the fair musicians.

Pulling back is hard work for the crew ; but they redouble their efforts, for as they say, 'Plenty piecee bad man hab got this side, too muchee likee cut throat pidjin,' and soon we are once more in mid-stream. Here we pass close under the dark frowning hulks of a fleet of old weather-beaten junks that lie moored in a long double line. As everyone already knows all about these junks—what they look like, with their big eyes set in front to scare off the demons of the deep—I need not attempt to describe them here ; but I may inform the reader that the accompanying picture of the deck of a junk was one which it cost me some trouble to obtain. I got it under the following circumstances. Two artistic friends and myself were one day pulling about Hongkong harbour in quest of a good subject for a picture, and after having scrambled by the aid of a convenient rope on to the deck of a junk at anchor there, we found the crew busy with a complex machinery of ropes, poles and windlasses, and indeed on the point of making sail. Suddenly they forsook their work, confronted us with angry gestures, and threatened to bar our advance. We enquired for the captains, of whom not uncommonly there are half-a-dozen on board, for these junks are built in water-tight compartments, and each owner of cargo is a captain so far as concerns that compartment, where his own goods have been separately stored. Thus, if the compartments be six, the captains are six, and each captain has a sixth part of the vessel under his own command. The result of this equitable arrangement is that the craft is sometimes required to travel in six different directions simultaneously, and to stand for six different points at a time; and in the end the crew take the steering into their own hands, or else consult Joss, who stands in his shrine in the cabin unmoved though tempests rage. As it happened in our case, there were but two captains on board, the one anxious to be civil and the other ready to pitch us into the sea. At length they requested us to remain, while they referred the case to Joss. The idol, it appeared, gave us a hearty welcome, for captains and crew returned from the interior to unite in helping me to get up a successful picture.

DECK OF A CHINESE JUNK

CHAPTER X.

The Charitable Institutions of China—Macao—Description of the Town—Its Inhabitants—Swatow—Foreign Settlement—Chao-chow-fu—Swatow Fan-painters—Modellers—Chinese Art—Village Warfare—Amoy—The Native Quarter—Abodes of the Poor—Infanticide—Manure-pits—Human Remains in Jars—Lekin—Romantic Scenery—Ku-lang-su—The Foreign Settlement.

THE charitable institutions of China are far from numerous, and but ill organised as a rule. In 1871 an establishment under Chinese supervision, and supported entirely out of Chinese funds, was about to be opened in Canton for relieving the sick and destitute, and supplying coffins to the poor. The intention of its founders, so it is supposed, was to counteract the influence of the hospitals and charities supported by the foreign Christian Missions in their city. But when I left Canton the place was still unopened, although a house had been already bought, which had been occupied as a private residence by Pun-ting-qua, the last of the Hong merchants whose property, as I have said already, had been confiscated by Government. This house was one of the finest I have seen in China, and its magnificent costly decorations conveyed some notion of Pun-ting-qua's great wealth, which had been quietly absorbed by the authorities. Strange to relate, a similar charity exists in Hongkong; similar in so far as it is a hospital supported by the Chinese community. It is stated in the Report of the Medical Missionary

Society of China for 1867 that the Chinese themselves contributed 47,000 dollars, and the Colonial Government 15,000, towards the expenses of founding this establishment, and providing it with a site. Native physicians are to be employed at this hospital—men who have never taken a degree of any sort, and whose chief qualification for the post will probably rest on their skill in mixing quack nostrums, and in their knowledge of the days most lucky for administering doses to patients; and there they will be able to enjoy the luxury of either curing, or killing their sick fellow-countrymen, and yet escape the danger, imposed upon them in Chinese cities, of losing their fee if they should not achieve a success. It is not too much to say that the Chinese know comparatively nothing of medical science. Good luck and favourable omens are all-important in their eyes; but a sound constitution, that will pull a patient through the effects of their worst medicines, has a great deal to do with the recovery of the unfortunate sufferer who in Hongkong may fall, or rather be deliberately delivered, into the hands of a celestial quack. Perhaps after all they follow a sound principle when they administer to a patient, who obstinately refuses to get well, a little of everything, in order that his disease, whatever it be, may select its own remedy from the heterogeneous compound. This Hongkong hospital is, or ought to be, under European supervision, and it is probably intended that native practitioners may gradually be led to adopt our medicines, and to study our system of therapeutics. But with the Chinese blind belief in their own superiority as men and as physicians, they cannot fail to account our meeting them thus half way as a tacit acknowledgment of the excellence of a system made up in reality of ignorance and superstition. On the other hand the Chinese Government appear to have returned the compliment by appointing Dr. Dudgeon to a lectureship in the college at Peking, where, from what I know of that gentleman's abilities as an English physician, and from his intimate acquaintance with the language, I feel sure that the students will be so systematically trained that they may one day prove themselves the founders of a new school of medicine in China.

Among the charities in Canton there is a Leper Village. These sort of asylums for plague-stricken men and women are found in various quarters of the Empire, but as I only visited one place of the kind I shall reserve what I have to say about them for a future page. There are also institutions for the aged and infirm, and a foundling hospital, in which the poor children, who may be left at its door, are nursed on the slenderest fare. Dr. Kerr gives some interesting details as to the management of this hospital in the 'China Review' for September 1873. One wet nurse, so he tells us, has at times as many as three infants to feed, and she must herself be reduced to starvation allowance, as her pay is only about eight shillings a month. Many of the nurslings die, as might be expected, while those who survive are sold for about three shillings a-piece. It is mostly female children that are brought to this benevolent institution, for girls are esteemed nothing but encumbrances to poor parents in China, the reproach of their mothers, who ought to give birth to boys alone. These foundlings are bought by the wealthy, and brought up as servants or concubines; or else they are disposed of to designing hags, who purchase them on speculation and reserve them for a more miserable fate. This custom of investing in girls as speculative property, and of rearing them carefully till their personal attractions will command a high market value, is one of the worst aspects of that traffic in slaves which is carried on without shame or concealment all over Chinese soil, and more secretly by the natives residing at Hongkong, as the police reports will show. The evil might be mitigated if we could but persuade the Chinese Government to encourage female emigration by any means in their power, more particularly to those lands where as yet only males have found their way from China; lands where there is valuable work for female hands to do, but where, as for instance in California, their vices could well be dispensed with. Besides this there are countries in which the Chinese are as yet almost unknown—Africa, for example—where, with wives and children around them, a congenial climate, and a rich soil to cultivate with produce which they have been accustomed to grow, vast tracts of the waste lands of the earth might be colonised and redeemed. Thus would the parent country be relieved from the pressure of over-population, which hitherto has been mainly kept in check by famine, infanticide, and civil war. Colonel Gordon—better known as Chinese Gordon—of the ever-victorious army—is now on a mission to the heart of Africa; and he, perhaps, should he ever think of such a scheme, might be able to open up new sources for the enterprise of the toiling husbandmen of Cathay, to whom once already he has appeared as a deliverer in years now gone by.

Macao is interesting as the only Portuguese settlement to be found on the coast of China. It may be reached by steam, either from Hongkong or Canton, and it is a favourite summer resort for the residents of our own little colony. In that pretty watering-place we may enjoy the cool sea-breezes, and almost fancy, when promenading the broad Praya Grande, as it sweeps round a bay truly picturesque, that we have been suddenly transported to some ancient continental town. Macao is a magnificent curiosity in its way. The Chinese say it has no right to be there at all; that it is built on Chinese soil; whereas the Portuguese, on their part, allege that the site was ceded to the King of Portugal in return for services rendered to the Government of China. These services, however, cannot have been properly appreciated, for the Chinese in 1573 built a barrier-wall across the isthmus on which this town stands, to shut out the foreigners from Cathay. The place has had a chequered history since the time of its original foundation, sometimes being under its own legitimate Government, and at others being claimed and ruled by the Chinese. But its history, however important to the parent country, had better be left alone, more especially as there are passages in it which reflect no great lustre on the nation whom Camoens adorned. We will, therefore, content ourselves by a look at the chief objects of interest in the settlement. From the Praya Grande, with its fine pier, Government-house, and painted buildings, we pass up one of the numerous small streets, shut in by high walls on either side. It is mid-day, and there is nobody to be seen abroad. You remark many iron bars about the windows; yes, those prison-like dwellings are 'barracoons;' the offices, that is, of various emigration agents. These agents have a strange way of watching over the innocent emigrants. There are savage-looking men on guard at the doors, set there to prevent any of the coolies from getting out and running the risk, poor things! of losing themselves in the town. Alas! for these unfortunate 'emigrants;' they have been kidnapped most of them; and I have seen them at early morning taken down in gangs, forced into the boats, and pulled off to the ship lying out yonder in the glassy bay. They have all to be conveyed to make their fortunes by digging guano on the islands of Peru. One ship left Macao in 1865 with 500 emigrants on board. On touching at Tahiti the number had dwindled to 162. That cargo of slaves, for slaves they practically were, turned out a bad speculation; but the traffic has been recently put a stop to under the enlightened administration of a very unpopular governor—unpopular because he has thus seen fit to abolish an exceedingly lucrative sort of trade.

The Chinese Government, too, are looking after the interest of native emigrants, and have recently sent a deputation to Peru to enquire into the condition of Chinese labourers in that quarter. We pass the gaol, and through the stanchioned windows see a number of wretched native prisoners, who beg of us to befriend them. An American captain with whom I afterwards ascended the Yangtsze-kiang, told me the following story connected with this prison, which seemed to him to corroborate his belief in spiritual agency. His father, who had been a skipper too, was one morning about to make sail from Macao, and passed the prison on his way to join his ship. Arrested by the desparing cries of the men within, he turned aside to make enquiries, and learned that three of the captives were condemned to be executed next day. Tossing a quantity of cents inside, he took his departure, and thought nothing more of the incident. But when he reached San Francisco he hastened to his owner's office, and was surprised to find no letters awaiting him from home. He concluded something must be wrong, and the merchant advised him to visit a certain spiritual medium who resided in the town. This he did, and when the séance commenced the medium informed him of the presence of certain spirits around him, reverently bowing before him, and thanking him for some great boon he had conferred on them. They carried their heads beneath their arms, and were declared by the medium to be the spirits of Macao Chinamen beheaded the day after the captain left that port, now come across the ocean to thank him.

The main streets in Macao are deserted. The houses there are painted in a variety of strange colours, some of the windows being fringed with a rim of red, which gives them the look of inflamed eyes in the painted cheeks of the dwellings. But there are magnificent staircases, wide doorways, and vast halls, though the inmates for the most part are a very diminutive race; they are called Portuguese, but they suffer by comparison with the more recent arrivals from the parent land, being darker than the Portuguese of Europe, and darker even than the native Chinese. There is trade going on in the streets, but it is of a very languid kind, and the gambling-houses or the cathedral are the chief places of resort.

The forts are of course garrisoned with troops from

Europe, and the sounds of trumpet, kettledrum, or bugle, which issue uninterruptedly from these strongholds would make a stranger fancy that the soldiers were being constantly mustered to repel some invading Chinese host. Macao must be a very devout place indeed; the church bells there seem never to be tired of ringing; and at morning, noon, and eventide, the townsfolk may be met flocking to the cathedral or the chapels, to renew their religious worship. At 4 P.M. or thereabouts the settlement wakes up; carriages whirl, along the road; sedan-chairs struggle shorewards, that their occupants may taste the sea-breeze; and the midday solitudes of the Praya Grande have been converted into a fashionable promenade. Ladies are there, too, attired in the lightest costumes and the gayest colours; some of them pretty, but the majority sallow-faced and uninteresting, and decked out with ribbons and dresses whose gaudy tints are so inharmoniously contrasted that one wonders how Chinnery the painter could have spent so many of his days among a community so wanting in artistic tastes. The young men—for there seem to be no old men here, at least all dress alike, quite irrespective of years—are a slender race, but not more slender than diminutive. On the adornment of their persons these pigmy dandies bestow no inconsiderable study and care, striving to conform to fashion to the utmost their moderate incomes will admit, and some of them—so I know for a fact—living sparingly, and having their salaries mortgaged, to provide the gay neckties, the kid gloves, and patent leather boots, in which they worship at the cathedral, or on the Praya at the shrine of the fair. Meanwhile from the windows or balconies glancing eyes look down behind their fans, and send a thrill through the blood of each admiring devotee below. But if Macao is interesting as a Portuguese settlement, and the only one which now remains to Portugal of those which her early traders founded in China, it can also boast of historic associations giving it a special, and independent attraction. Here the poet Camoens found a retreat, and here, too, Chinnery produced a multitude of sketches and paintings which have really had some influence on art in the south of China.

Swatow is the next place on our route northward, and to reach it we take steamer from Hongkong. There is, I must tell you, almost daily a service of magnificent steamers up and down the Chinese coast. The splendid passenger accommodation, and the facilities for conveying merchandise supplied by these vessels, are of a kind not easily surpassed; and considering the nature of the coasts they navigate, and the dangerous typhoons to which they are exposed, very few accidents occur.

Swatow is the port of the city Chao-chow-fu, and lies, as I have said already, in the province of Kwan-tung. Chao-chow-fu ought really to have been an entrepôt for foreign trade, but this idea was given up in consequence of the turbulence of the surrounding clans. The town is built upon the banks of the Han, and the district through which that river flows is one of the most fertile in the province. Swatow has a harbour available even for vessels of the largest tonnage; and so far as that point goes, therefore, the place is better suited to foreign trade than Chao-chow-fu would have been; for the latter place stands some thirty miles up the river, and can only be reached by lighters of a shallow draught. The foreign settlement, or rather the residences of foreigners, are perched upon a low range of hills which reminds one of the barren cinder-looking hills of Aden. Huge boulders of granite are planted up and down these hilly slopes in the most extraordinary positions; some are like Druidical circles, others resemble great obelisks. Not unfrequently, too, they bear inscriptions in Chinese characters; and thus, supposing that the Chinese were ever to be driven from the region, a rich field would present itself for antiquarian research. Many theories would be forthcoming to account for these sacred circles and carved obelisks, which have simply been left in their positions as the soil around disintegrated, and was washed away from the slopes of the hills. As for the inscriptions, they are nothing more than the productions of Chinese who have sought to gain an unprofitable immortality by graving their names, or their poetical effusions, or else a record of some local incident, upon the imperishable surface of these stones. Here the foreign houses, and many of the native ones too, are built out of a local concrete made of the felspar clay which abounds in the neighbourhood, combined with shell-lime. In process of time this compound hardens into a stony substance producing solid and durable walls. The interiors of these dwellings are no less remarkable, for the ceilings are adorned with the most beautiful stucco cornices, representing birds and flowers, in endless variety and profusion. The men who execute this sort of artistic work are to all appearance coolies, receiving for their labour but little more than they could earn by tilling the soil or drawing water; and yet, to fit themselves for their tasks, they must undergo what is a high art training at least to a Chinaman. When at work they squat on the floor with a hod full of stucco before them, and a sort of small baking-board at their feet. On this board, with their fingers and a trowel, they model flower after flower—stems, foliage, fruit and all—besides birds of one or two kinds; passing the portions, as they complete them, up to a workman whose business it is to group the bits together and fix them in position. No moulds are used, no wooden pattern of any sort; all is done with the unaided hand and eye, and exquisitely done to.

Of the native settlement of Swatow I need only say that it is more or less like the river quarters of Canton, or Fatshan, or any other town in the south of China; but I cannot refrain from introducing the reader to the Swatow fan-painters, as they, too, are most remarkable men. There are a number of fan shops in the main street, and one which is perhaps more celebrated for the beauty of its work than any of the others can pretend to be. To this shop, then, I repaired, in the company of an English merchant, whose warm hospitality proved him to be no exception to the majority of his associates in China. We were here shown some of the most beautiful and delicate fan-painting that I have ever come across, representing, for the most part, garden scenes. Asking to be introduced to the artists, I was shown into an apartment at the back of the premises, where I found three occupants. Two were seated before a table, engaged in designing on the yet unpainted fans, while the third lay stretched on a couch, indulging in an opium-pipe. They were all of them opium-smokers; and it struck me that their most finely imaginative paintings were executed under the influence of the drug. As I have said, the pictures produced by these men were remarkable for their beauty, and that because the drawing and perspective were excellent, and the designs full of delicacy and tender feeling. Here, then, we find Chinese art pure and simple, without the admixture of any foreign element, as in Hongkong; and my opinion is that it is a higher class of art than we are apt to suppose the Chinese to possess. But then we must bear in mind that after all we do not know much about China and her art. It was only the other day, when in Peking, that I picked up one or two old pictures which had formed part of the collection of a private Chinese gentleman, and that alone gave me a much higher opinion than before of, at any rate, the ancient school of Chinese artists. One specimen, a series of original sketches, representing children at play, was as remarkable for its quaint humour as for its clever execution; yet the pictures are nothing more pretentious than unelaborated pen-and-ink sketches. In a postscript attached to his book, the artist modestly tells his readers, 'I have made up a portfolio of twelve sketches, consecutively illustrative of the four seasons of the year, beginning with a representation of new year festivities, and ending with the drawing of the snow lion; and, though I cannot pretend to the perfection of the artists of bygone days, perhaps I may aspire to six or seven-tenths of their talent. Written on the 4th day of the 4th month of the year Woo-shin, by Se Hea of Hang-chow.' There can be no doubt that art has declined in China, and this the Chinese themselves confess, as the above note will serve to

CHILDREN AT PLAY. *(From a Chinese Drawing)*

show. Moreover, as with ourselves, the wealthy and cultivated classes in China will expend large sums of money in collecting the works of the ancient masters, which they carefully preserve. Many of these old paintings have been executed on silk scrolls, and thus a Chinese picture gallery is quite unlike what we should expect to see, for the pictures are not framed and exposed on the walls, but are kept carefully rolled up and protected against the light or air. It is only by some rare chance that Europeans are permitted to view any of the art treasures which are thus kept sacred by a host of private collectors. My friend Mr. Wylie, who is well known to Eastern scholars, when examining several old pictures which I had brought from Peking, made some interesting remarks on this point. He said, 'Many anecdotes are on hand regarding the achievements of the old masters. Thus, in the third century we are told of a painter, Tsaou Puh-ying, who, when he had finished a screen for the Emperor, added some flies to the picture by a few touches of the pencil here and there; great was his gratification at seeing his majesty take up a handkerchief to drive these flies away. Not less celebrated was Hwan Tseuen, who flourished about A.D. 1000, and who introduced several pheasants into a mural decoration in one of the halls of the palace. Some foreign envoys, who had brought a tribute of falcons, were ushered into this hall; and no sooner did the birds of prey get sight of the pheasants on the wall than they made a precipitate dart at their victims, more of course to the detriment of their heads than to the satisfaction of their appetites.' The fan-painters of Swatow are about the most worthy representatives of the ancient masters to be found in the south of China; and were the old practice still in vogue of recruiting the royal harem from a portrait gallery of the belles of the Empire, the talents of these Swatow artists might find lucrative employment in picturing the future favourites of the palace. Fans of the very best workmanship are in great demand, and consequently difficult to procure; and yet it seems strange that this should be the case, in a district where we may frequently see most respectable-looking natives cooling themselves by an expedient much more simple than the use of a fan. Between Swatow and Chao-chow-fu I have met wayfarers on a hot day stripped to the skin, every article of their clothing bound around the head, and thus marching along, to all appearance, without the slightest sense of impropriety. The higher one ascends the Han the more savage-looking are the people we encounter there; but, as I said before, the clan-fights had been suppressed, and peace re-established in the province, at a very recent date. At one village, called Oting-poe, the natives some short time previously, attacked a boats' crew from the English gun-boat 'Cockchafer,' and had their village blown about their ears in retaliation. The whole affair, indeed, was settled with a promptness and despatch that took the semi-savage clansmen by surprise, and rendered them civil even to us within a five-mile radius from the ruined walls. At Chao-chow-fu my experience was somewhat different. I got up one morning before daybreak to photograph an old bridge across the river there, and I fondly thought that, being so early astir, I should get clear of the city mob; but, as it happened, there was a market held on the top of the bridge, and even before it was quite light long trains of produce-laden coolies were pouring in from every side. I had just time to show myself and take a photograph, when a howling multitude came rushing down to where I stood near my boat on the shore. Amid a shower of missiles I unscrewed my camera, with the still undeveloped photograph inside, took the apparatus under my arm, and presenting my iron-pointed tripod to the rapidly approaching foe, backed into the river and scrambled on board the boat. I lost the cap of my camera, and the bright lens received a black eye of mud in exchange. However, the picture turned out a good one, and I may make it my boast that I took the bridge at the point of the tripod. Chao-chow-fu bridge is not unlike that at Foochow which spans the river Min. It is built of stone, and contains a great many arches, or rather square spaces, for the passage of boats beneath. On each side of the causeway above a row of houses has been erected, and these project beyond the parapets, and overhang the stream for as much as three-fourths of their entire depth. There seems, indeed, to be no part of each house, except the brick wall in front, which rests upon the bridge; while as to the fabric itself, it is held up by a series of long stout poles, which abut upon the projections of the buttresses below, and thus serve to support the dwelling like the under-props of a bracket. This was what one would call a break-neck sort of architecture, and yet the great market of the town is held on this bridge, and there we find the dwelling-houses and shops of the merchants. There they trade and there they sleep, calmly awaiting the hour which shall drop them and their frail tenements into a muddy grave. But they had other means still to ensure safety both for property and life. Suspended between each archway hang two slender wooden frames, and these barriers the householders piously let down at night to deter malignant spirits from passing beneath their dwellings —a device, I need hardly say, universally successful.

Chao-chow-fu is open to foreign trade, and on one or two occasions the attempt has been made to establish a British Consulate in the town; but it has always hitherto been a failure. Turbulent mobs continually stone foreigners, and during the time of my visit the Vice-consul was the only European in the place. He, when I told him how I had been attacked by the rabble, said quietly, 'You are no worse off than your neighbours; it is just what every white man must expect at the hands of the lawless ruffians of the town.' So I was not sorry when I turned my back upon this part of Kwang-tung, and descended once more to Swatow. Every year sees an increase in the number of emigrants who leave this part of China to work on the plantations in Siam, Cochin China, or the Straits. More than 20,000 such persons are computed to have sailed from the port in 1870, and we may be sure that the price of labour in China is at a very low ebb when we find that wages running from two to four dollars a month are all the inducement held out to allure the coolies from their homes; and that such a sum as this even is, by the toiling poor, esteemed sufficient to enable them to save money to invest in a farm on their return to their native land. It was up into this region that Juilin sent a military mandarin with a force of 2,000 men. This officer, at the time of my visit, was in the district known as Chao-Yang. His task was approaching completion, and there was consequently more of peace and prosperity in the country than had been its lot for many previous years. Fang-Yao, for that was the mandarin's inharmonious designation, pursued a rough and ready sort of system in the conduct of his operations for putting matters to rights. Thus, at the village of Gò-swa, near Double Island, he seized a man named Kwin-Kong, well known to foreigners, and required him to surrender 200 of the chief rebels of his village. Kwin-Kong produced 100, many of them, poor wretches, innocent substitutes for the true offenders. Under pressure and threats a few more victims were ultimately given up, and the whole were then beheaded, Kwin-Kong's own skull being tossed into the pile to swell the number of the sufferers. It must have been bloody work; more than 1,000 are said to have been decapitated during Fang-Yao's memorable march.

Swaboi, one of the most powerful villages in the province, stands about two miles distant from Swatow, and for many years has monopolised the right to supply coolies to that town. About ten years ago, seventeen other villages combined against Swaboi, and resolved by force, if necessary, to put a stop to its monopoly of labour. The war lasted four years, and terminated in favour of Swaboi. At such times the villagers practise the most heartless cruelties on each other, burying their enemies, for example, while still alive, and head downwards, in graves prepared with quicklime and earth. It was, indeed, in this district that I gathered a notion of the inhuman treatment of idiots practised in some parts of China. The late Dr. Thomson, of Swatow, in one of his excursions, observed a small-footed woman limping along without her staff. She showed that she was a lunatic by making for his sedan, for there is no sane Chinawoman in this quarter who would not flee from a foreigner. Arrived in his presence, she prostrated herself at his feet, as if he were some official high in rank. Her hair was hanging in wild disorder, and her head was fearfully bruised and wounded; her arms, too, were cut and bleeding, and her dress hung in rags about her shrunken limbs. Dr. Thomson wished to convey her to the nearest village to have her wounds dressed, but the Chinese chair-bearers would have nothing to do with her; they said 'She is mad! she is mad! let her herd with the crows.' I myself have seen an idiot exposed outside a village in a wooden cage, and there left for the passers-by to feed him, or better still, to starve and die. I afterwards went a second time to see this being, that looked more brute than man, but he had died in his cage.

Amoy is the next open port in our northern route; and though situated in the province of Fukien, its geological features resemble those of Swatow. Thus the same decomposing hills, crowned with huge granite bare boulders, are to be seen at the entrance of the harbour; and one of these boulders, which faces the port, has some passages connected with the local history of the place engraven in huge characters upon its stony sides. Several of them rear their grey heads to a great height out of the water, or above the shore close by, and these the natives look up to with reverence and awe, as objects intimately connected with the Feng-shui, or good luck of the port. But in such a place as this it is but seldom that good luck waits upon the lower and most superstitious classes. The

Amoy men make good soldiers, so at least it is said; they certainly fought well for their independence, and were the last to yield to the Tartar invaders, and those upon whom the conquerors seemed to have pressed most heavily. To this day they wear the turban which they assumed to hide the tonsure and queue imposed on them by the conquerors. The dialect here is so different from that spoken in Canton as to lead my boys to imagine that they were once more out of China, and in some foreign realm. But a glimpse of the town quickly reassured them. There they fall in with men from their own province, and with odours and appearances so unmistakably Chinese that there is no getting over the fact; and they soon acknowledge that this indeed could still be no other than their own Chinese land. At Amoy, as in Swatow and most other Chinese seaport towns, the houses in the native quarter are huddled together like a crowd of sightseers, all eager to stand in the front row along the water's edge. Many of these dwellings are in a sad state of decay and dilapidation; and the long, dark, narrow street which runs the length of the settlement is paved with cross flags of stone so worn and loose, that they rest for the most part in treacherous pits of mud; and thus, if a foot be placed hastily on the rocking flag, a shower of most offensive dirt is splashed up over one's clothes. Every second shop reeks with a smell of roasting fat and onions. Mangy dogs and lean pigs yelp and grunt as we disturb their occupations. These are the sanitary authorities of the locality, and to them the duty falls to clear up the refuse and garbage. Nor were these the only inconveniences; on nearly every occasion when I waded my way along the uninviting thoroughfare, I found it blocked at some point by a strolling band of players, hired to perform in public by one of the more liberal-spirited tradesmen. The approach to the foreign merchants' establishments can hardly be accounted better than the miserable Chinese alley which I have just described; but the offices themselves, when the difficulty of reaching them is overcome, are found to be venerable structures, filled with all sorts of produce beneath, and showing all the evidences of business above.

The trade of this port has grown, and is likely to continue growing, just in proportion as the rich island of Formosa opposite is developed, and its tea, sugar, and other products increase. The import trade, and the distribution of foreign goods inland, is pretty effectually choked off by the illegal system of transit duties levied at the various stations, and regulated chiefly by the need or avarice of the local officials at the various points along the route. There is also a grievous charge called Lekin, originally imposed as a war tax on foreign goods, and never since withdrawn. The only other ports similarly heavily burdened are those of Formosa.

The American Consul, in writing on the subject, said:[1] 'At Swatow the local taxes levied on imports remain unchanged; that is to say, about one-fortieth of what they are in Amoy;' and he goes on to observe 'that natives can still bring foreign goods overland from Swatow to the Amoy districts, and sell them at a cheaper rate than if they were imported and sold direct in Amoy.' This Lekin tax was instituted to defray the expenses either of the Taiping rebellion or of the 'small knife' rebellion, or both. The

[1] *Report on Amoy and the Island of Formosa*, by A. W. Le Gendre.

'small knife' rebellion of 1853 was a serious affair for Amoy. The rebel chief, or ringleader, of this dagger society was said to be a Singapore Chinaman of the name of Tan-keng-chin. The outbreak was, in fact, a development of one of the secret societies that have been a source of continual trouble to all the countries into which Chinese labour has flowed.

In 1864, a few months after Nankin fell into the hands of the Imperialists, and when the cause of the Tien-Wang or Heavenly King was all but crushed, the last remnant of his followers made a final effort and captured Chang-chow-fu, a city which stands in the same relationship to Amoy as Chao-chow-fu to Swatow. The place was eventually retaken by the Imperialists after a protracted struggle; and this barbarous war then closed, amid scenes of cold-blooded massacre as inhuman as any that have stained the annals of the Taiping revolt, whose overthrow was brought about by foreign intervention, and by one or two powerful decisive blows dealt at the strongholds of the rebel towns. Alas! these successes were but too frequently followed up by indiscriminate slaughter, for those are the means by which a weak government seeks to strike terror into the hearts of the people.

Occurrences such as that which I am now about to describe were accordingly by no means rare. The fight was ended, and the fruits of the victory were being reckoned up. It was reported to the conqueror that there were 254 heads, and 231 queues and ears of people supposed to be rebels. At any rate they were heads and ears and queues, and these the Imperialist troops had to lay at the feet of the authorities. It is astonishing how some of these mutilated wretches survived. Thus I myself saw a man who reported that his head had been nearly severed from his body, and he had actually to hold it on until he reached Amoy. There were certainly marks of a severe wound on the neck, similar to those described by Mr. Hughes in the 'China Review' for June 1873. I have also seen a man enjoying good health who had both ears chopped off and part of the scalp carried away. Mr. Hughes again tells us, in another paper, that female infanticide is perhaps worse in this part of the Fukien province than in any other quarter of the Empire, and this corroborates the conclusion I myself had come to from enquiries I made on the spot.

Mr. Hughes one day met a stout well-to-do looking man of the coolie class, carrying two neat and clean round baskets slung on a pole, which he bore across his shoulder. 'Hearing the cry of a child, I stopped him, when I found he had two infants in each basket;' and it is recorded that this crafty old speculator in innocents was on his way to sell his living burden at the Foundling Hospital, where he would receive 100 cash, or about fivepence for a female child, and as much as three pounds for a boy.

This Foundling Hospital was organised by a native merchant whom I had the pleasure of meeting, and it is a lamentable fact that the prospect of receiving fivepence will tempt a mother to part with her babe.

The Amoy Hospital is, however, conducted on rather more liberal principles than that in Canton; for if any one wishes to obtain a child, he may get one here free of charge, provided that he can deposit suitable credentials as to his own respectability. One of the resident Christian missionaries informed me that he felt convinced that 25 per cent of the female children of Amoy were destroyed at birth. The natives themselves make no secret of this crime, and I saw one old woman who confessed to having made away with three of her daughters in succession. They excuse their misdeeds on the ground of extreme poverty, and they certainly are poor and wretched to a degree I had no conception of before I visited their abodes. The district around is naturally barren and unproductive, and plundering raids of rebel and Imperial troops have most effectually crippled the energies of the needy inhabitants. War, it is true, has thinned the population, but not to such an extent as materially to affect its density.

An able-bodied man can here earn only fivepence a day, and skilled workmen, of whom there are many, are paid about eightpence per diem. There is a great trade carried on in one quarter of the town, or rather in a suburb, in the collection and preparation of manure, which is afterwards sold to the farmers to fertilise their poor lands. The people who deal in this commodity dwell on the edge of the foul pits into which filth of all sorts is thrown, and for the use of the hovels in which they reside many of them pay about fivepence a month in rent.

Close to this spot is a hill on which the poor are buried. There is no lack of recent graves, but all such are covered with lime, mixed with fragments of glass and pottery, in order to keep pigs and dogs from digging up the bodies. How the people subsist here it is hard to say! Judging from the multitude of graves they must die in great numbers, and who can wonder at it, in an atmosphere that smells so putrid? I looked into one or two of the dwellings; they were single-roomed huts, reared above the naked sod. Often they contained no furniture at all, and their ragged lean occupants were filthy in the extreme; and yet numerous children were to be seen running about, pitching pebbles into the pools, or chasing the pigs and pariah dogs, to prevent them from eating up the only article of trade in the locality. Most of the children were boys, and boys after all cost as much to nurse and rear as females would; so that the pressure of immediate want will not suffice alone to account for infanticide. Want is doubtless one of the causes, an indirect as well as a direct one, and this because it induces a supreme callousness, and a savage stony selfishness of heart, which petrifies the instincts of maternity, and renders a mother capable of selling or even destroying her child.

There was another hill not far off, and commanding a view of the harbour. On this I found a row of glazed earthern pots, each containing a skeleton; one had been broken, and the bones lay scattered over the face of the rock, while a number of children were playing catch-ball with the skull. What mean these dishonoured relics, over which some Ezekiel might prophecy, lamenting the degradation of his people? These are the remains deposited here to await interment—a ceremony which can only be properly accomplished by attending to the times and places which the Feng-shui may prescribe. But alas! too many of these unsepulchered skeletons will never know any resting-place more hallowed than the pots in which they were originally stored. There they crumble unfriended and forgotten, for their surviving kinsmen are perhaps themselves cut off from the land, or else too poor to pay the expenses of the for ever deferred burial rites. Now, then, my readers can appreciate the true motives of a Chinaman who, as I have said already, will devote his earnings to the purchase of a coffin, funeral raiment, and a burial site in anticipation, many years before his death.

My sketch of Amoy thus far has been a dark one, and yet the true picture is not without some glances of light, striking down even into the lowest quarters of the town. Thus, in one of my many perambulations, I came to a very narrow and very dark lane, where I found the humble tenants of the houses engaged in what, to me, was quite a new industry. Men, women, and children were all busily occupied in the manufacture of most beautiful artificial flowers, from a pith obtained in Formosa, from the same plant (*Aralia papyrifera*) as that out of which the so-called rice-paper is made. I entered shop after shop, and everywhere found thousands of flowers spread out on trays, and each one so life-like that it might almost be mistaken for nature herself. But tiny hands were at work here too, and roses, lilies, azalias or camelias, grew up with wonderful celerity beneath them. The workshops are the dwellings, the offices, and the warehouses of each firm, or family; and the workers within are so closely packed that strangers not unfrequently must watch the process, or make a purchase, by taking up a position outside. I bought a great many of these flowers from a man in a very mean shop indeed. He was extremely poor, and he asked me for an advance of money, offering to furnish security if I wished. I lent him a few dollars without troubling him for securities; and though I knew nothing about him, he carried out the transaction with the most scrupulous honesty.

There are many wealthy Chinese merchants in Amoy, who live in good style and in superior houses on the hills above and beyond the town. On those hills, too, we may find temples and monastic establishments, built in the most romantic situations among great granite boulders which tower in some places many hundred feet above the plain. Thus from the rock on which the 'White Stag' monastery stands one obtains a commanding view of the town, harbour, and island of Ku-lang-su. It is on Ku-lang-su that European settlers chiefly reside; and there the houses, environed with parks and gardens, are second to none in China. Some Christian missions also are established in the same quarter, and not unfittingly, for there is a wide opening for mission labour in a field so benighted and so woe-stricken as Amoy. I may add, however, that in spite of all I have related of the townsfolk and their peculiar institutions, one may pass a month very agreeably in Amoy, and the warm hospitality of the merchants there will add, not a little, to the pleasure of the trip. I had every facility afforded me for visiting places of interest. Thus one gentleman would place his boat at my disposal, and another would lend me his pony for a little exercise on the race-course. This race-course is situated on a narrow plain, close under some of those forts which fell one after the other into our hands in 1841. A few huge rusty guns still remain on the spot to mark the scene of a struggle which ended in the capture of the island of Amoy. This island has been a favourite foreign trading resort for two or three centuries past, but it is only of late years that its commerce has become important. I saw a number of old European grave-stones on the hills, some dating back to the fifteenth century.

From Amoy I crossed over by steamer to Formosa on April 1, 1871; but before I left the harbour I had time to pull off to the steamship 'Yesso,' and take a hurried leave of an esteemed friend, broken down in health, and then homeward bound. I never saw him again, for he died before reaching home. His is, alas! a too frequent case; the invalid lingers on in a climate that is undermining his health, in the hope that the cold season may set him up again for work. Too late he discovers that he can bear no further delay; the cold season is long in coming, and at last he hastens to seek the sea-breezes in the homeward-bound steamer, which only carries him to his grave. I had a pleasant companion in Dr. Maxwell, the medical missionary of Tai-wan-fu, in Formosa, and from him I heard some interesting accounts of the savages on this strange island. Leaving the harbour at 5 P.M., we passed the Pescadore group of islands at daybreak next morning. The wind all the while blew strongly from the north, forcing me to forego my dinner, and to confine myself a prisoner in my berth, until I was summoned on deck to see land. It was a grateful sight, very, but how the ship was rolling! and the land, alas! the only thing that struck me about it was that it must be a very long way off. Having once gained my sea legs, I had one or two hours leisure to scrutinise the coast and the inland mountain ranges, which lost themselves in the clouds above. A narrow rocky inlet was pointed out to me as the only harbour accessible in this quarter; and it was abreast of this spot, some two miles from shore, that the steamer came to her moorings. Here on a sudden I found myself keenly interested in the experiences of a Malay on board, who informed me that vessels were constantly being wrecked along this shore, and that their crews were invariably eaten to a man by the bloodthirsty savages, who perpetually scoured the beach in search of prey. He had probably heard of the wreck of the schooner 'Macto' in 1859, and how the crew were massacred on this very beach by the natives; or else he may have been referring to the murder, at a later date, of a number of American castaways by the Aboriginies further south. That certain native tribes here are cannibals there can be little doubt; and they have assuredly robbed and murdered unfortunate men and women who have from time to time been wrecked upon their shores. It is to punish outrages of this sort that a Japanese army has lately been despatched to Formosa, in retaliation for some particular barbarities which chance to have been practised upon a Japancse crew; so say the Japanese. As Formosa is a Chinese possession, it is hard to tell how, or where this armed interference on the part of the Japanese may end. I predicted, in my previous work, the probability of coming difficulties between Japan and China, as the former is now beginning to look upon her Chinese neighbours in the light of inferiors.

We are told by the 'Pall Mall Gazette' that when the Japanese fleet anchored off Formosa, and before a single soldier landed, a Chinese corvette and a gun-boat steamed into sight with guns run out, men at quarters, and everything prepared for action. Between them, these two vessels, as they assure us, might have sunk the whole Japanese squadron; but after some palaver, the Chinese men-of-war quietly steamed off again, and the Japanese troops were landed.

Before we disembark and proceed on our journey inland, it may be as well to give the reader some general notion of the island and its position. Isla Formosa, or the Beautiful Island, as the Portuguese named it, lies at the distance of about one hundred miles off the mainland, and was discovered by an enterprising Celestial, who, getting up one morning before his neighbours, a few hundred years ago, to see the sun rise over the ocean, discovered the mountain peaks of Formosa.

In time the Chinese crossed over and planted a settlement on the island, driving the savages high up into the almost inaccessible mountains.

Formosa runs nearly north and south, its length is about 250 miles, and it is about 84 miles broad across its widest part. Down its centre a rocky spine of lofty mountains stretches longitudinally nearly from sea to sea, with peaks, in some places, about twelve thousand feet high. The Chinese occupy only the western half of the island and a small portion at its northern extremity, while the whole of the mountainous region to the east is held by independent tribes of Aborigines. The island is ruled over by a Taotai resident at Taiwanfu, and appointed by the Central Government. The Taotai of Formosa is the only officer of the same rank in the Empire who enjoys the privilege of direct appeal to the throne. The population is about three millions, viz., two and a-half million Chinese, and half a million Aborigines.

Naturalists suppose that Formosa has originally been joined to the mainland; and what confirms them in this view is the great similarity of its flora and fauna to that of the nearest provinces of China. But let us land and see for ourselves.

CHAPTER XI.

Takow Harbour, Formosa—La-mah-kai—Difficulties of Navigation—Tai-wan-fu—The Taotai—His Yamen—How to cancel a State Debt—The Dutch in 1661—Sylvan Lanes—Medical Missions—A Journey to the Interior—Old Watercourses—Broken Land—Hak-ka Settlers—Poah-be—Pepohoan Village—Baksa Valley—The name 'Isla Formosa'—A Long March—The Central Mountains—Bamboo Bridges—'Pau-ah-liau' Village—The Physician at Work—Ka-san-po Village—A Wine-feast—Interior of a Hut—Pepohoan Dwellings—A Savage Dance—Savage Hunting-grounds—La-lung Village—Lakoli Village—Return Journey.

A Chinese pilot, named Opium, came off to the steamer, and brought her to a secure anchorage about a mile from shore. There was a pretty heavy sea on at this time, rendering it dangerous, even in a surf-boat, to make for the mouth of the harbour; so Dr. Maxwell and I determined to go ashore with Opium, trusting to his local knowledge to land us safely somewhere along the coast. This pilot was a cool, imperturbable seaman, a daring specimen, who had been out in all weathers, and who was said to have earned his singular cognomen of Opium from his notoriety as a smuggler of that valuable drug. It is truly wonderful how in California the genius of the Chinese race has been times without number equal to the task of carrying on an untaxed opium traffic, and that too under a system of police surveillance that only falls short of submitting the Chinaman and his effects to a process of sublimation, which would leave the hidden juices of the narcotic behind. Nevertheless, their dodges have been detected one by one; a layer of opium glued in between the polished sides of a trunk will never reach shore, nor pass unnoticed though wrought into the well-made soles of a silken boot, or stitched into the skirts of a padded robe. But we are now on the top of the breakers, plunging as if the boat were going bow-foremost to the bottom. Opium is looking calmly on the while, with a countenance at once soothing and reassuring. We soon roll over the last billow, and are swept into a small haven amid the rocks. These rocks are of igneous formation, and look like molten metal suddenly chilled while in a state of violent ebullition. We land, and scramble over a multitude of cell-like cavities, with edges hard as flint and sharp as splintered glass. Many of these cavities have the hollows filled up with a little sandy soil, in which luxuriant shrubs and a sort of dwarf date-palm grow. The wet sand along the beach was of a deep black hue.

As we made our way through the native town of Takow I was much struck with the tropical appearance of the place, and with the shady palms, which reminded us of the villages in the Malayan Archipelago. But evidently neither Mohammedans nor Malays dwelt here, for huge porkers roamed free about the settlement, or kept watch around the cabin doors. At length we reached the Mission Station, and met with a cordial welcome. Here the Rev. Mr. Ritchie gave me some notion of the lawless state which prevailed in this portion of the island. One day, when on a mission-trip inland, he fell in with the deputy magistrate (Chinese) of the Tung-shan district, returning to his 'Yamen' from a place called La-ma-kai, with a troop of armed retainers at his heels. Passing this official, and proceeding on to

La-mah-kai, my friend there met a band of ruffians carrying spears, daggers, and firearms ; and behind them followed an old woman, who besought the marauders to return her son's matchlock, which one of them had just stolen from her house. The first question asked of Mr. Ritchie, when he reached the Chinaman's hut where he proposed to sleep, was whether these armed men had been seen, as they were a band of highway-robbers that had been plundering the neighbouring settlements. The magistrate, it appeared, had been despatched by his superior officer to seize on a rich relative of one of the bandits, and to hold him as a hostage ; but the crafty knaves had been forewarned of the threatened surprise, most probably by one of the servants in the mandarin's train, and had forthwith met their enemy with so overwhelming a force as to compel him to an undignified and speedy retreat.

A wholesome dread of Europeans, inspired by the vigorous action of Lieutenant Gordon at Tai-wan-fu, saved my friend from falling an easy prey into the hands of the gang.

Two or three of the European firms at Amoy have branch establishments in Takow, or had at the time I speak of (April 1871) ; and behind these foreign houses there rises a hill more than 1,000 feet high, and commonly known as Apes' Hill, from the large apes, its only inhabitants, which may be seen in great numbers about the crags. From this hill I obtained a commanding view of Takow harbour, and the observations which I made here, as well as closer inspections carried out from other points, led me to the conclusion that, in the hands of a civilised foreign power, a portion of the soft sandy lagoon, which is gradually invading and narrowing the available anchorage of the harbour, might soon be added to the now limited accommodation for shipping; while the bar at the mouth of the port might no less easily be removed. As the case now stands, with wind and tide favourable, a barque drawing twelve feet of water can find her way through the rocky entrance. Rapid physical changes have taken place within a recent period on this the western side of Formosa, as I shall be able to demonstrate conclusively when we get to a point further north. It struck me, however, that the natural formation of the harbour of Takow belongs to a modern date. Thus when the Dutch occupied the island a considerable river existed at the southern extremity, and the channel, now nearly dry, is still known as 'Ang-mang-kang,' or estuary of the red-haired race. The combined action of the sea silting up *débris* on the one side, and of the river on the other, has formed a natural barrier several miles in extent, now covered with a belt of most luxuriant tropical trees. This bar is joined at its northern extremity by a ridge of igneous rocks; and it is in this ridge that the break or flaw occurs which forms the mouth of the harbour. Much of the six or seven miles enclosed by this natural wall consists of a shallow lagoon, with a bottom of extremely soft mud. It is only towards the northern end that a depth of water is obtained sufficient for ships trading to the island.

Owing to the disturbed state of the country I deferred my visit to the aboriginal tribes of the south, and went with Dr. Maxwell to see Tai-wan-fu, the capital, twenty-five miles further north on the coast. Starting at daylight in the steamer 'Formosa,' we reached the outer roads at 8 o'clock. It is singular to observe that there is now no harbour at Tai-wan-fu. We could descry the old fort Zelandia, erected there by the Dutch in 1633, about two and a half mlles from where we lay, and surrounded by water so shallow as to render any nearer approach impossible; and yet in the Dutch accounts of Formosa it is stated that Zelandia was an island where a spacious haven was formed; and further, that on April 31st, 1661, Koksinga's fleet appeared before Tai-wan-fu, ran into the spacious haven between Zelandia and Provincia, and came to anchor between the two forts. The two forts referred to are Zelandia and Provincia, separated by a distance of more than three miles; and the haven in which the Chinese invader anchored his fleet is now a dry arid plain crossed by a high road, and having a canal cut through it, communicating with the old port of Tai-wan-fu. A small portion of the plain is flooded at high tide, while off the fort the water is now so shallow that vessels have to anchor, as we did, two miles out to sea. Neither is it an easy or a safe business to cross these vast shallows, at least when the sea is rough; and if there is a strong south-west monsoon blowing, it cannot be done at all. As for ourselves, we went ashore in a catamaran, a sort of raft made of poles of the largest species of bamboo. These poles are bent by fire so as to impart a hollow shape to the raft, and are lashed together with ratan. A strong wooden block, made fast to the centre of this surf-boat, supports the mast, which carries a large mat sail. There is not a nail used in the whole contrivance, and the most curious feature about the strange vessel is the accommodation provided for passengers. This is nothing more than a capacious tub. I thought it possible at first that these were the boats of the local washerwomen ; but, so far as washing is concerned, the natives of Formosa confine themselves to washing their customers occasionally ashore in the tub and mangling them on the beach—a very simple process, for the tub is in no way fixed to the raft, so that a heavy sea would, and does frequently, send it adrift. The tub into which we descended would hold four persons, and when we squatted down inside it we could just see over the top. Not feeling very comfortable, we came out and sat on the bare raft, to which we had at times to cling *manibus pedibusque* as the waves broke over us.

Tai-wan-fu, the capital of Formosa, is a fortified city of 70,000 inhabitants. The walls enclose a space of about five miles round, planted to a great extent with fields and gardens, and still showing traces of the ancient Dutch occupation, in the ruins of Fort Provincia and in the extensive parks shaded with fine old trees or groves of tall bamboo. The suburbs are intersected by a multitude of green lanes, which run between walls of cactus, interspersed with the brilliant flowers of the wild fuschia, and clusters of major convolvulus, or else shaded by bamboo hedges, which form a pointed archway above the path. The inhabitants of this part of the island are chiefly natives of the Fukien province, and the Hak-kas already described. These between them are daily carrying arts and agriculture further into the territory claimed by the aboriginal tribes.

Armed with an official introduction I paid a visit to the 'Taotai' (or governor) of Tai-wan (Formosa). Waiting in my chair outside his yamen while my card—a red one, the size of a large sheet of note paper—was sent in,

I found myself surrounded by the idle crowd that is always certain to collect about a stranger in China—whence the gazers came, and whither they go would be difficult to tell—and all sorts of conjectures being thrown out as to the nature of my business. A little naked boy, with a face full of perfectly untutored innocent curiosity, ventured a trifle too near, so I leaned slightly forward and frowned at him. Bursting into a fit of screaming terror, he fled from the yamen, while the mob looked grave, and wondered what devilry I could have practised on the child. Soon an officer appeared, and behind him followed a train of yamen attendants, who wore the usual conical hats with red feathers that suggested the idea of flames burning through the top of an extinguisher. Thus escorted, I was ushered into the yamen. Passing through the hall of justice, I noticed various instruments of torture, the substitutes for our sacred oath, to extract truth from a witness, or confession from the lips of a prisoner. Here I met a more venerable official, dressed in a long silk robe, a stiff girdle, and heavily-soled satin boots. By him I was conducted through a court, and along a series of corridors, and finally presented to the Taotai, with infinitely greater official ceremony and pomposity than when I was introduced to Prince Kung, or Li-hung Chang. Indeed it seems to me that the Chinese are not exempt from the peculiarity which makes small officials everywhere self-important, and fearfully exacting in all matters touching their personal dignity. The private quarters of the Taotai and his retainers were prettily laid out, the open courts being shaded with palms, and decked with flowers in vases, besides shrubs, ferns, and creepers;

and the whole interior was surrounded with saloons or pavilions.

Into one of these last I was led, and there presented to a full-faced pleasant-looking Chinaman who, to my surprise, held out his hand, and addressing me in perfect English, said, 'Good morning, Mr. Thomson, I am glad to see you here; when did you come over?' I recognised the speaker, after a time, as a man whom I had met in Hongkong as a compradore, or a schroff in a bank. He told me he was the nephew of the Taotai, and I have a strong suspicion that that functionary himself had at one time been engaged in trade, and that he had somehow obtained this post, out of which, if report spoke true, he was making a very good thing indeed. After partaking of tea and fruit, my friend, whose mind was evidently imbued with the notion that I had come to the place on some secret mission, tried all he could to gain exact information as to my intentions. I told him plainly that my purpose was to go into the heart of the island to see the aborigines. He wanted to know why I should take the trouble to trudge so far on foot, through a region where no proper roads existed, merely to see the place, with the chance perhaps of being killed. 'Depend upon it,' he assured me, 'you will never get near them; you will be shot with poisoned arrows, or lose yourself in the forest paths. But come and see the Taotai.' This gentleman was rather a good-looking man, of middle age, and said to be remarkable for his administrative ability. At any rate, although apparently affected with suspicions as to my design in visiting the aborigines, he showed me some kindness, and, in return for a portrait which I took for him, he sent me a small box of tea and some dried lichees. The tea unfortunately spoiled before I reached Hongkong, but the lichees were very good.

A curious incident occurred in this town during the rule of the preceding Taotai. When the fort of Anping had been stormed by Lieut. Gordon and his party, the military mandarin in command of the troops at Anping was supposed in some measure to have failed in his duty. To this charge was added an accusation of treason; for it was known that he had saluted Mr. Gibson, the late British Consul, with three guns, when that functionary left for Amoy. This unworthy commander, then, was dining one night with the Prefect, when a message was sent from the Taotai, directing the Prefect to detain his military guest until morning. At daybreak a second messenger arrived, who brought instructions for the Prefect to repair with his prisoner to the Taotai's yamen, and forthwith, as the business was urgent. When they reached the yamen, a servant came out to say that the Taotai would not receive the military mandarin, and ordered him to prepare for instant death. The unhappy officer insisted on an interview, and with his men forced his way into the yamen, where he demanded an appeal to the Emperor. The Taotai informed him that the edict had been received from Peking, had him stripped of his official clothes, hurried off, and put to death on the spot. In another such instance of summary vengeance a wealthy mandarin, who had aided the government with loans of money, determined, as he saw no probability of repayment, to withhold a certain proportion of the local taxes. Shortly after he had taken this step an official was dispatched by the Governor-general to inquire into the matter. The district governor hereupon invited the defaulter to a quiet dinner to meet the governor-general's emissary, and during the course of a convivial evening the host and his friend between them so managed to outrage the feelings of the guest that a quarrel finally ensued. Then the 'yamen runners' were called in, the expostulating guest was cut down, and this was the new way in which an old state debt was paid.

A large tract of land outside Tai-wan-fu is known as the execution-ground, and this spot I visited in company with Dr. Maxwell. I tried to make a picture out of it, but there was nothing to lend pictorial grace to the scene; for the plain here is a perfectly flat one, whence the grand old trees of Tai-wan may be seen crowding away into the background, as if they shrunk from rooting themselves in unhallowed earth. Hardly a shrub relieves the monotony of this gloomy place of death; and yet with what a fearful interest it must have been gazed on by that band of Europeans, 160 in number, who were led out there to execution one morning in August 1842! The mob of the city followed behind them with yells of exultation; but before the terrible massacre had closed, their savage laughter was changed into panic terror, for the sky became overcast, and a dire storm burst upon the scene. The watercourses were filled with impetuous torrents that flooded the land, sweeping trees, houses and produce before its swollen streams, while the cries of perishing people were drowned in the fierce tumult of the tempest. Thus, say the thoughtful and superstitious natives, God wiped out the bloody stain from the ground. It is alleged that about 2,000 persons perished on that eventful day. A tragic history attaches to Tai-wan-fu, apart both from the incident which I have just related, and the storming of Anping fort, more recently still—an event too full of details to permit description here.

In olden times the city was the scene of the fierce struggle which ended in the expulsion of the Dutch from Formosa in 1661, after a nearly twelve months' siege. Koksinga, who drove the doughty Hollanders from this beautiful island, must have been a bold adventurer. He was indeed a sort of Chinese sea-king, levying black mail from all the surrounding islands. China now-a-days needs just such an admiral to command her new steam fleet. With resources so great at his command, he would teach the ambitious inhabitants of the small kingdom of Japan that their safest policy is to keep their troops at home. As the case now stands we see 2,000 Japanese soldiers actually landed at Lang-kiau in southern Formosa, while the authorities of China are looking on from the mainland, in a sort of dreamy amazement at the audacity of the enterprise. But when I took my rambles through the sylvan lanes of Tai-wan-fu, no feature so much struck me as their perfect repose; not a sign or a sound recalled the fearful conflicts which they too often witnessed. The languid air was filled with no noise more warlike than the hum of insects, the creak of produce-laden carts on their way to market, or the merry prattle of children at play. Alas! the quiet glades of Formosa may soon be stirred once more with the din of a vital struggle for supremacy, between two races who for the first time will confront each other with modern weapons in their hands. The conflict, if it ever takes place, will without doubt be protracted and severe; and its issue may lead to important results in opening up the vast continent of China; or perhaps the Chinese, in the flush of victory, may be hurried into a final attempt to close their country for ever against the hated intrusion of foreigners. The latter, however, is not a probable contingency, for China will find that her only safety lies in keeping herself always fit to cope on terms of advantage with her restless Japanese rivals.

I cannot leave Tai-wan-fu without noticing the medical mission over which my friend Dr. Maxwell presides, and expressing my regret that hospitals of the same kind are not more numerous in other quarters of China. One who lives at home in an English city —where the poor are always with us, but where they are tended and cared for in an infinite variety of ways, quite unknown to the ancient civilisation of the 'Flowery Land'—cannot picture the train of miserable diseased wretches who daily drag their way to the Mission hospital. Many who have heard of the fame of the good foreign medicine-man, accomplish long weary pilgrimages; almost believing, poor souls, like the woman of old, that they have but to touch the hem of the physician's garment, to be cured of diseases that have made their lives, for years, one prolonged cry of pain. Sometimes the maladies are simple in themselves, though beyond the power of native skill, and a single probe of the lancet will send such a heaven of relief, as almost to tempt the poor sufferer to fall down and worship his deliverer. The scenes I myself witnessed in a single day at that hospital made me feel perfectly appalled when I reflected on the groans of unalleviated pain which must constantly rise from the poverty-stricken millions who swarm over the plains of China. Here, in this small sanctuary, it is but the faint echo of the great unheeded wail which we hear rising from the breasts of sufferers that find relief at last. Much of the sickness common in this quarter is due, directly or indirectly, to poverty, insufficient or unwholesome food, and to neglect. The medical missionary thus enjoys many opportunities for spreading a knowledge of Christianity, for gaining converts, and for doing good in a variety of ways—which, let me assure my reader, are seldom left untried. In a place like this the life of such a man is no enviable one, and the only pleasure he can enjoy must come of the consciousness of doing good work. His is a lifetime devoted to self-sacrifice and systematic toil. Day after day crowds of fresh patients flock to the hospital, and their cases are treated in rotation, leaving little leisure to the missionary save what is stolen from meal-times, or from the hours of rest by night.

Dr. Maxwell and I determined to make an excursion into the interior, and to visit the outlying mission-stations, where my friend hoped, if possible, to open new ground among the mountain savages. Accordingly on Monday, April 11, we left Tai-wan-fu for the village of Poah-be, and were carried in native sedans ten miles across the plain. I hired a number of coolies to convey my instruments, as I had determined to photograph the objects of interest which we might fall in with *en route*. The plain, a highly cultivated one, was dotted with Chinese farms, and with hamlets overshadowed by groves of bamboo. The chief products here were rice, sweet potatoes, earth-nuts, and sugar-cane. Many of the women were out at work in the fields ; most of them had the compressed feet so much in vogue among the females of the Fukien province, and hence they seemed to limp about uneasily over the furrows. They generally wore pretty dresses of white calico, edged with pale blue. As for the men, they were bronzed and fat; and they wore a lazy, loutish appearance, seemingly leaving the women to do the bulk of the field-work. There were children to be seen too, but their attire consisted simply of a small charm hung on a string around the neck. As at Tai-wan-fu, we passed along some beautiful sylvan lanes, shaded by areca-palms and bamboos, and leading to settlements which were truly enchanting when viewed from a distance, but less attractive, and thoroughly Chinese, on a closer inspection. The near approach to one of these hamlets was always known by the conflicting odours of garlic and manure, mingled with the fragrance of some sweet-smelling flowers, of which the Chinese are very fond, and which quite overpower the soft perfume of the white wild-rose that grows in profusion in the hedges. In the wild flowers which bloom hereabouts we discover the delicate hues of our more temperate climes blending charmingly with the vivid primary colours of the tropical flora. It was pleasant, too, to listen to the songs of the field-lark, a bird common to certain districts of the mainland both in the north and south of China; and, so far as I can recollect, to some parts of Siam.

Halting at the first range of hills, we send back the chairs, and await the arrival of my boy Ahong and the coolies, who were far in the rear. Ahong, unaccustomed to walking, was already foot-sore. Against my advice he had put on straw sandals, and so blistered the soles of his feet that the remaining eight miles of our journey tried him severely. The heat was intense. Even now I feel hot, uncomfortable, and inclined to cast off my coat, when I think of it. The road, if our route could be dignified by such a name, was a broken track, over dry hills, constantly interrupted by blocks of hard clay, and by pitfalls six or eight feet deep. But these were trifles to what lay before us. Slowly we progressed, now wending our tortuous way along the verge of a clay chasm more than 200 feet deep, now diving down into the recesses of a huge clay-pit, where the flat surface was so heated with the sun that it almost blistered the hands when we touched its bare walls. The soil became the more broken the further we progressed inland; the pits, too, grew wider and deeper. At the bottom of some of these we actually found cultivated fields, and traces of the mountain torrents that force a subterraneous passage, during the wet season, through the soft clay formation beneath, and thus effect the drainage of the central range of mountains, while at the same time they render farming in this hill region an enterprise full of peril. For the squatter tills treacherous ground, and is liable to find his fields and his dwelling swept away by the sudden subsidence of the soil. But the Hak-kas, who cultivate this shifting clay, are prepared for such emergencies, and are quite accustomed to a hasty change of abode, cheerfully resuming their agricultural labours wherever they may happen to settle. At times, indeed, the sudden disappearance of their whole property may lead to very desirable results. They emigrate, perhaps, to a healthier or more settled neighbourhood, or else to one where the trees and *débris* brought down by the torrents will furnish them with fuel during the winter months. All this will, no doubt, seem strange to those who have only heard of houses being removed from one quarter of a town to another by means of powerful hydraulic engines. But I venture to suggest that what happens in Formosa is an illustration of hydraulic power on a much more extended scale. I need hardly say that the Imperial Government has not seen fit to send a geographer to lay down a map of this ever-changing region; and it will be a matter of difficulty, I should think, for the farmer, at the end of each wet season, to find out exactly where he and his neighbours have settled. Poah-be was reached by about 4 P.M. This place is the first settlement of a tribe of aborigines whom the Chinese call 'Pepohoan,' or 'foreigners of the plain.' These people have a lively and warm recollection of their Dutch masters. They still cherish traditions of their kind-hearted red-haired brothers, and for this reason they receive foreigners with a cordial welcome. Once, in the times of the Dutch, they lived down in those fertile plains which we had just been crossing; but they have long ago been driven back out of the richer land of their forefathers, by the advance of the ruthless Chinese. Higher up, in the mountain fastnesses, their hardy kinsmen have held their own, defying all the forces of the Imperial conqueror.

Let the Japanese make friends of those wild mountaineers, and the Chinese will find it a hard task to drive the intruders from the island. The natives came out in great numbers to meet and welcome Dr. Maxwell, whom they had not seen for a considerable time. They were a fine, simple-looking race, and had a frank sincerity of manner which was refreshing after a long experience of the cunning Chinese. These Pepohoans had acquired the Chinese arts of husbandry and house-building. Their buildings were even superior to those of the Chinese squatters, and the people themselves were better dressed. It struck me, as I have noticed elsewhere, that they resembled the Laotians of Siam both in features and costume, while their old language bore undoubted traces of Malayan origin. (*See* Appendix.)

There was a small Christian chapel at Poah-be,[1] built and supported by the natives themselves, the mission having only to pay the salary of a native helper. I visited several of the houses, and found them clean, well arranged, and comfortable. Their mode of construction is as follows :—A bamboo framework is first set up ; this is then covered with a lathing, or rather wattle-work, of reeds or split bamboo, and the whole is afterwards plastered over with the clay that abounds in the neighbourhood, and finished when dry with an outer coating of the white lime made out of the limestone rock which is plentiful in these hills. The dwellings usually form three sides of a square; but I will describe the interior accommodation in more detail further on in my narrative. Only two articles in any of the Pepohoan settlements bore tokens of ingenuity and mechanical skill; these were the butts of their matchlocks and a native rat-trap, which was very curious indeed. The rat is esteemed a great luxury among the mountaineers—so great that the invention of this trap must have been a most important

[1] One of over a dozen mission-stations established by the Missionaries connected with the Presbyterian Church of England. There are about 3,000 natives constant attendants at the chapels.

event in the history of their race; but the mechanical genius who discovered it seems to have accomplished nothing greater for the civilisation of his countrymen; resting for ever, after this crowning achievement of his skill, a contented rat-eating Pepohoan.

Friday, April 11.—We left Poah-be at 7 A.M. to-day to walk to Baksa, twelve miles off. It was a beautiful morning, and the scenery became gradually so interesting as to warrant the belief that we had now got clear of the broken shifting lands through which our yesterday's journey had extended. By about ten o'clock the heat became intense, and Ahong was fairly knocked up. We had to reduce our pace, too, on account of his sorely blistered feet, so that it was twelve o'clock before we reached Baksa valley. Here, again, the people rushed out to welcome us. Troops of pretty little children came trotting along the road, shouting 'Peng-gan,' 'Peace be with you,' while many a horny hand was stretched out from its toil to grasp the doctor's as we entered the village, or rather as we passed through the lanes, and beneath the palms that shaded the scattered dwellings in this Pepohoan paradise. I could now understand what the Portuguese meant when they named the island Formosa; and yet what we saw here was but the first foreshadowing of the wilder grandeur of the mountain scenery inland. A crescent of limestone hills sweeps round Baksa valley, presenting in many places a bare rocky front in striking contrast to the foliage which luxuriates elsewhere. Perhaps the bamboos were the most remarkable feature in the scene, for these plants here attain exceptional proportions, and are some of them more than 100 feet high. In the history of Tai-wan it is stated that there are 'thirteen varieties of Bamboos'[1] (a species of grass) known in Formosa, one being reported to attain to the enormous girth of two feet. I will here give a brief account of the many uses to which the bamboo is applied—a plant which figures extensively in the social economy of the people throughout the length and breadth of China. Were every other means of support withdrawn, except rice and bamboo, these two plants would, I believe, supply the necessaries for clothing, habitation, and food; indeed, the bamboo alone, as I propose to show, would bear the lion's share of the burden. No tending is needed for this hardy-natured plant, nor is it dainty in the choice of its locality; and, although it probably reaches its highest state of perfection in the rich valleys of Formosa, yet it grows with nearly equal vigour on the thin soil of rocky hill-sides. It is first used to hedge the dwelling around with an almost impenetrable barrier of prickly stems, and to cast a cool shade over the abodes with its lofty pale-green plumes. The houses themselves may be constructed entirely of its stems, and thatched with its dried leaves. Within, the couches and chairs are made of bamboo, and so is the table, except its deal top; so, too, are the water-cans, the drinking-jugs, and the rice-measures. Hanging from the roof are a number of prickly bamboo stems supporting dried pork, and such like provisions, and warding off rats with their *chevaux de frise*. In one corner we may see the proprietor's waterproof coat and hat, each made out of leaves of the plant, which overlap like the plumage of a bird. The agricultural implements are many of them made of hard bamboo stems; and, indeed, the fishing-

[1] Chinese *Notes and Queries*, ii. 135.

net, the baskets of divers shapes, the paper and the pens (never absent from the humblest Chinese abodes), the wine-cups, the water-ladles, the chop-sticks, and, finally, the tobacco-pipes, are all of bamboo. The man who dwells there is feasting on the tender shoots of the plant; and if you ask him he will tell you that his earliest impressions came to him through the basket-work of his bamboo cradle, and that his latest hope will be to lie beneath some bamboo brake, on a cool hill-side. The plant is also extensively used in the sacred offices of the Buddhist temples. The most ancient Buddhist classics were cut on strips of bamboo; the divination-sticks, and the case which contains them, are manufactured out of its stem; while the courts outside the temple are fanned and sheltered by its nodding plumes. There are a variety of different sorts of paper made from the bamboo, but the kind which struck me as showing a new property in the fibre of the plant was that commonly used by the Fukien gold-beaters in the production of gold-leaf, and thus occupying the place of the parchment employed for the same purpose in Europe. Fans and flutes are also made of bamboo; and even the looms on which the Chinese weave their silken fabrics are chiefly made out of the plant. Indeed, it is impossible to estimate its value to the Chinese. This much, however, I may unhesitatingly affirm, that so multifarious are the duties which the bamboo is made to discharge, and so wide-spread are the benefits which it confers upon the Chinese, as to render it above all others the most useful plant in the Empire.

We spent the night at the Baksa mission-station, and left early next morning to walk to Ka-san-po, a distance of twenty-six miles. The first hill we got to after quitting Baksa gave us some faint notion of the journey now before us. We had to climb a steep ridge, where the soil had been completely broken away on either side; and thus, along the sharp edge of a wedge, we made our way upwards to the summit of the hill. It was with no feelings of ease that I kept looking back upon our baggage-bearers (six strong Pepohoans from Baksa), who, had they slipped their footing, would have been precipitated several hundred feet on whatever side they chanced to fall. At last we reached the summit safely, and were rewarded with a view of a splendid valley surrounded by a circle of hills, while the central mountain ranges of the island could be descried towering heavenwards in the distance beyond. The little settlement of Kamana could just be made out at the eastern extremity of a long glen. Resting for a short time in a Pepohoan hut, where the people were glad to see us, and where we had a refreshing draught of spring-water, we then pushed on to Kamana, and were there met by a sturdy old native helper named Tong, a man of good Chinese education, who had formerly held a post in a yamen. He was a fine-looking fellow, and had suffered a good deal of persecution for having embraced the Christian faith. At about one o'clock, under the guidance of Tong, we left this station, and commenced another toilsome ascent beneath a blazing sun, and without a breath of wind to temper the intense heat. At length, after surmounting the first range, we fell in with a buffalo herd, and found an old man living in a rude shed in the centre of a parched wilderness. He received us kindly, and gladly shared with us his supply of water, which he held in a bamboo tube. Our arrival evidently afforded him great pleasure, and he was anxious we should remain for a smoke and a chat. Off again to climb another hill, or rather to scramble up deep fissures in one, over a broken stratum of clay and slate, exhaling a noxious smell, and reflecting the hot sun to such a degree that I felt extremely faint, and nearly gave in before we had scaled the height. The Doctor confessed that he had never experienced any fatigue like this, in all his previous travels. Once on the top, we flung ourselves down beneath the scant shade of some shrubs in a rocky clift, at the same time dislodging from the roots and stones numerous tribes of centipedes, each about as long as one's finger, and of a rich chocolate colour, with bright yellow feet. These centipedes inflict a fearful sting, but we were too much exhausted to get out of their way, and fortunately they got out of ours. More than once I thought I could feel these creatures making their way up my back, but it turned out to be nothing more than a cold stream of perspiration trickling down. A steep descent on the other side of this ridge brought us to our next halting-place, where a brook was reported to exist. A channel indeed was there, but the waters had dried up long ago. Here, while at breakfast, our crowning trouble overtook us. 'One of the bearers incautiously broke off the green stem of a plant, which, in return for the outrage, sent forth a perfectly putrid odour. It was some time before we discovered the cause of the nuisance, for the Pepohoan nose seemed to account it a luxury rather than otherwise. This plant was known to them as the 'foul dirt' shrub, and is one which the Chinese ought dearly to prize, for its very breath might be sufficient to manure a whole region. As the reader may imagine, we made no long stay in this spot; but resuming our journey, marched on up and down great pits similar to those encountered in our first day's travel, and containing some of them great boulders rounded, probably, and left in position, at the bottom of the pits, by the denudations of the mountain torrents.

We were now on one of the spurs that lie at the foot of the central range, and could enjoy a splendid view of a valley that stretched out in front of us, half cultivated and half in its pristine grandeur, while the mountain sierras rose up pile behind pile, Mount Morisson lifting its deep blue peak on high above them all. A river flowed far down beneath our feet, and we could hear the distant boom of its waters, as they rushed onward through dark ravines and over a rocky mountain bed. This river was now at its smallest, but was still a broad stream, and was spanned by a number of bamboo bridges, if such these rude structures might be called. Far away, at the northern end of the valley, the village of Pau-ah-liau could be descried peeping out amid a mass of foliage; and high above this settlement rose mountains wrapped in the gloom of primeval forests, the haunts of wild beasts and savage men. These mountain tribes just referred to exact a heavy black mail from their more civilised kinsmen in the valleys below; and not content with this, they will at times swoop down in troops of sixty or seventy to waylay travelling parties, whom they plunder and put to death, or else to make a raid on some village in their vicinity.

We had now reached the banks of the stream, and

had to cross it to gain the village; but the bridge here, which possessed the great merit—from an engineering point of view—of extreme simplicity, was about the most crazy, break-neck contrivance it has ever been my lot to see. The whole structure consisted of one or two poles of bamboo, stretched from bank to bank some twelve feet above the river, which was here quite deep enough to drown even the giant Chang. These poles rested on stone piers, jutting out beyond the banks, and made out of the boulders near at hand. To me this bridge seemed the very thing for a reckless man who might wish to tempt Providence, and yet just escape a watery grave. But the natives walked easily over it Blondin fashion, using their burdens to sustain their equilibrium; and so there was nothing for it but to cross, if we would reach our journey's end. The Doctor, who had seen these pieces of architecture before, managed with comparative ease: as for me, we had been walking in straw sandals, so I damped mine to make them more elastic, and then, throwing out my arms and squaring my feet, crossed like an acrobat, looking back with no small satisfaction when I had overcome the difficulty, and was safely landed on the other side. These elegant structures are the common property of the natives, and suffice for the purposes of trade and intercommunication in this benighted region. They are understood to be rebuilt, or kept in repair, by the man who happens to break them, should he survive the accident, or by the next comer should he not. Providence has supplied a bountiful stock of raw material for their construction in the surrounding vale, and along the river's bank. There we may see the boulders for new piers, and ratans growing in the thickets, wherewith, if need be, to bind the cross-poles to the piers; and there are bamboos everywhere.

About half a mile from Pau-ah-liau we passed beneath the spreading branches of the 'Png-chieu' tree, as the natives term it, whose roots spread along the ground in curious writhings and contortions, now forming an inviting chair, now a couch on which one might pass the hot nights with comfort; or elsewhere a small shrine connected with the fetishism of the village. These spirit-shrines were encountered at the roots of many of the finest trees, and consisted commonly of one basement stone, and four other slabs together forming three sides, and a roof. Within, in the centre, was a tiny stone altar, on which the offerings reposed. The trunk of this 'Png-chieu' tree was six feet in diameter, and the spread of its branches was ample enough to shade the inhabitants of the adjoining village. The news of our arrival had somehow preceded us, as it invariably did, but how we could never tell; and mysterious figures were seen darting out from the hedgerows and thickets to have a look at the 'red haired men,' as foreigners are politely termed.

Our path was along a pleasant shady road, on the margin of a stream that had been made use of for irrigation. On our left hand was a hedge adorned with numerous wild flowers—fuschias, roses, guavas, wild mint and convolvulus—besides a profusion of wild raspberry-bushes that had lately been laden with fruit as sweet as our own English raspberries, if we may judge from what little still remained. Again we had to cross a bamboo bridge, and thence to follow a foot-road by the edge of the rice-fields, where the young blades rose in vivid green above the water, just high enough to obscure the reflection of the mountains on its glassy surface. We now entered the village of Pau-ah-liau, and made straight for the house of an aged blind Pepohoan named Sin-chun. We were followed into his enclosure by troops of savage-looking women and children; the latter some of them ten years old, and without a rag to hide their youthful proportions. A number of the villagers had a warm recollection of a visit from the Doctor eighteen months before, and of how he had kindly ministered to their wants. Carefully did they examine our baggage and clothes, and finally awarded the palm of beauty to my checked flannel shirt. Here the men, women, and children were all provided with bamboo tobacco-pipes, of which they made a vigorous and unceasing use. I had not long to wait before a haggard old dame came up to where I stood, and offered me her pipe for a smoke. When I accepted the courtesy, she went on to ask for my cigar, from which she took one or two hearty pulls, and then her face disappeared in a compound series of wrinkles, denoting delight at the unusual piquancy of the weed. After this the cigar was passed from mouth to mouth through the crowd, and carefully returned to me when they had all had a pull. The villagers were most of them tall and well formed, with large brown eyes kindling at times with a savage lustre that told of a free untamed spirit, born amid the wild grandeur and solitude of these mountain lands. And yet the race, from all accounts, is a gentle and inoffensive one, in spite of a sort of haughty savage swagger not wanting in dignity and grace.

The women wear a profusion of dark brown or black hair, combed straight back from the forehead, and caught up and folded in behind the head. Then the long tresses are twisted into a sort of cable, into which a strip of red cloth is entwined, and the whole is then brought over the left ear, passed like a diadem across the brows, and firmly fixed up at the back of the head. The effect of this simple head-dress is very striking, and contrasts well with the rich olive skin of its wearer.

The Chinese say the women are extremely barbarous, because even the finest of them never paint. Time appears to deal hardly with them as they advance in years; toil and exposure rob them quickly of the attractions of their youth; but yet their hair is dressed neatly and carefully to the last, and they fight a stubborn battle against the encroaching hands of fate. The oldest crone in the lot would scorn to shield her weakness and infirmities from the enemy behind the earthworks of paint and powder, false fronts, or dye. The bronzed and furrowed cheek, and the grey locks of age, meet everywhere with respect, and would even command a safe passport through the territory of a hostile tribe.

The men now came trooping home in greater numbers from the fields; tall, erect fellows, wearing an air of perfect good-will, frankness, and honesty. In spite of their horny hands and poor clothing, there was a manly nobility in their demeanour, and a perfect gentleness, a heartiness, and a simple hospitality, which it was truly touching to observe.

In these respects there was a marked difference between the different villages. Thus where the Pepohoans had come into closer contact with the Chinese, they were better dressed but less friendly than in those villages where we encountered the aborigines alone. Sin-chun invited us into his cabin, and there I lay down on a mat to rest, and soon fell fast asleep. I awoke again with a start, as a gust of fetid air passed across the apartment. These natives, I must tell you, have a way of salting their turnips, and placing them in a jar of water, where they are kept till they decompose, after which they eat them as a relish to their rice. The truth was dinner was ready, and young Sin opened this domestic treasure, so that I got a full blast of the imprisoned gas as it escaped from the jar—a blast which sent me flying to my feet, and out to the open air to make my dinner there. As for the Doctor, he finished his repast within, while I enjoyed a hearty meal off a bowl of rice, two hard-boiled eggs, and a piece of fowl. While travelling I made it my rule, as far as possible, to live on the food that could be purchased most readily on the spot. When dinner was concluded Dr. Maxwell as usual commenced to attend to his patients; and a very numerous, though pretty healthy-looking, train they were. Some had fever; other cases were more or less grave; while not a few discovered pains and aches in different parts of the body which required to be treated with iodine. A feather was needed therefore to make a brush, and a fowl had accordingly to be secured. But fowls are more difficult to lay hold of than one would have supposed, and half the village was engaged in chasing first one fowl and then another before one could be caught and robbed of a plume. A few minutes afterwards a dozen bare legs, arms, and backs, had been painted and exposed to dry. Quinine also was eagerly sought for and distributed.

It was now 3 P.M., and we were still six miles from

Kasanpo. Pursuing our way by the river-side, we arrived at that village by five o'clock, and proceeded to the house of one Ah-toan, an old man with whom the doctor was acquainted. Ah-toan was not at home; but he soon appeared, driving his cattle before him into the pen. He, too, was very pleased to see us, and quickly made an apartment ready, in which we deposited our things. On the verandah behind his dwelling a narrow space had been screened off for bathing, and of this convenience we at once took advantage. Our arrival was the signal for the villagers to crowd in and have a look at us; but I could not make out why the male portion of the community appeared to treat our visit as a highly humorous incident, and why they had lost the erect and dignified bearing peculiar to their race. One old savage, more than six feet high, got hold of my pith hat, turned it round, looked into it and over it, and finally burst into a broad grin. I noticed, too, that he had abandoned all control over his facial muscles; and though he evidently meant to be civil, that he could not bring back the normal expression of sober gravity to his countenance; his features, in spite of him, would dissolve into a grin. At last I smelt sam-shu, and it transpired that the villagers had been thatching a neighbour's house, and, as is customary, had been entertained at a wine-feast. The Pepohoans, you must know, distil a very strong spirit from the sweet potatoe, which they cultivate as a staple food, like rice.

Tong after a time addressed the people on the foolishness of idolatry, and on the advantage of worshipping the one true God; he gained a few attentive hearers; but as for the drunken part of the community, they could make nothing of his sermon. I will now endeavour to describe our bedroom; but in the first place I must tell you that the Pepohoan huts are infested with rats, and the chamber we occupied did not escape their forays. This apartment measured about eight feet each way, one half of which area was taken up by a platform of bamboo raised about eighteen inches above the hard clay floor. This platform formed our bed; and the only other articles of furniture to be seen within were two billets of wood, which served the purpose of pillows. On this unyielding couch, then, I stretched myself till supper was ready. Our repast consisted of a fowl, which cost us half-a-crown, and which Ahong was now making ready in the next apartment. He was very tired, poor fellow; but he liked cooking, more especially when hog's lard was abundant. Nothing marks the savage more conspicuously than his utter unconcern about those minor social arrangements, without which civilised races would hardly find life endurable. Thus these Pepohoans, with the most eager anxiety to make us comfortable, yet managed to kindle a great fire of reeds, to boil our servants' rice, in such a position that the thick smoke poured in upon us in volumes as we lay at rest. No doubt it never occurred to them that smoke could be a nuisance at all. By way of a lamp we had a small cup of oil, in which floated a few shreds of burning pith; and by this flickering light I could see that the clay walls were blackened, and the rafters glazed, with sooty smoke. In a corner above my head were a bundle of green tobacco, one or two spears, a bow, a heap of arrows, a primitive matchlock, and lastly—an object which I had not hitherto noticed—a huge bin of unhusked rice at the side of the bed. I fain hoped that there the rats might find occupation during the night more profitable than worrying our slumbers.

Ahong informed me, in strict confidence, that the dexterity of the savages hereabouts in the use of the bow and poisoned arrows was no less wonderful than the cool way in which they boiled and ate their tender-hearted but tough-limbed Chinese foes. He besought me not to venture much further into the mountains, as the hill men never show themselves when they attack, but discharge their arrows high into the air, with such unerring precision that as they fall they pierce the skulls of their victims and cause instant death. I strongly advised Ahong to keep his head well protected. When he served up the fowl we found it as tough as any Chinaman could well be, even when boiled down for a cannibal's repast; and as for our tea-pot, it had contained sam-shu.

These Pepohoan dwellings, almost all of them, form three sides of a square, and enclose a yard in front, wherein produce is dried, and where the family conduct their 'at homes.' In the evening, at about nine o'clock, the natives assembled in force around a blazing log fire, which they kindled on this open space in front. The aged men and women, and the children, squatted round, smoking their pipes and talking, while a herd of long prick-eared curs sat intently watching the crackling embers. As the fire blazed up the flare edged the dark forms of the adjacent palms, and sported fitfully among the quivering leaves of the overhanging bamboo, while the strange figures gathered around the fire, now burst into strong relief against the dark background of the night, now vanished into impalpable shadows as the flames flashed up or sank before the varying breeze. Wood and reeds were piled on; the fire grew brighter and brighter, and the spirits of the party seemed to rise as the heat increased. At last the young men and women cleared a space, crossing arms and joining hands, till they formed a crescent, and commenced a plaintive native song, marking the rhythm the while in exquisite time, with a graceful tripping dance. First one man led off with a solo, and was followed by the band with a chorus of interrogation always ending with the exclamation Hai! To this the women responded with another chorus, and the time and words changed to a strophe in which each stanza ended with Sakieo! The movement became gradually faster, and the nimble feet of the dancers quickened as the measure increased, but still the time was marked with perfect precision. The graceful and intricate step set off the fine forms of the dancers to good effect in the weird light. Quicker and quicker grew the time, until at last it became furious; in place of 'Sakieo' the air was now rent with fierce savage yells, and the flitting forms could only be dimly seen amid a cloud of luminous dust, like wild phantoms hovering in space. The dance was kept up until a late hour, the hostess wisely supplying her guests with nothing more intoxicating than tea—a discretion due most probably to the presence of Europeans. Had the beverage been sam-shu, there is no knowing how the scene might have ended. As it was, I had never before, not even among Scotch Highlanders, witnessed such a wild display of animal spirits. We did not sleep much, as we found that rats were by no means the only vermin we had to entertain, and once or twice

I woke up to find the rats making short tracks across my body for the rice-bin.

Next morning we started for Lalung, about eleven miles distant, through some of the grandest scenery I have ever beheld. Old Atuan furnished us with an armed guide—a good-looking young fellow named 'Teng-Tsai.' The path was an unsafe one, leading as it did through the lower hunting-grounds belonging to tribes of savages higher up in the hills. Teng-Tsai called a friend, who joined our party with his match-lock, and both carried small priming-flasks of stag-horn suspended round their necks with strings of glass beads. They had also cord fusees coiled on bamboo rollers or bracelets round their left arms. These cords will keep alight for twenty-four hours, and when kindled the burning end is attached to forceps, which bring the light down into the powder-pan when the trigger is pulled. All the savages hereabouts use English powder for priming, when they can get it supplied them by the Chinese. As soon as our guides lost sight of the village, they lighted their fusees and enjoined us to keep together and make our way in silence. For the first half of our journey we were marching along the bed of a stream, but at length we ascended a narrow defile, where mighty rocks towered high above our heads, arched over in places by great forest-trees or giant ferns. A clear rill leapt from ledge to ledge, or rested now and again in some great stone bason, where with its glassy surface it mirrored the bright reflection of the ferns as they flung their fronds from the mossy rock to form a frame around the pool. Here we halted awhile to admire the intense loveliness of the mountain gorge, and to obtain a photograph of the scene, regretting all thc time that the picture on glass would, after all, give us but the bare light and shade, with none of the varied tints of the hoary bearded rocks, their mossy nooks and crannies, the colours of the pendant climbing plants, or the play of the bright sunshine through the canopy of leaves, and among the dark rocky masses beneath. Apart from the natural beauty of this spot, its rocks and plants would afford a rich field for any geologist or botanist who might find his way so far from the haunts of civilised man. An armed party of six friendly Pepohoans came upon us as we were enjoying a bath and a swim in a clear deep pool. They were out on a fishing excursion; and one old fellow was cleverly shooting his fish with an arrow, while the others were hunting for crabs among the rocks, twisting off their legs, and devouring them shell and all alive. The younger members of the party caught fish by beating the water with a bamboo rod, and thus stupifying their prey. A tedious climb over a mountain path, that wound its way through the forest, brought us at last to a change of scene.

Here the trees, many of them, were of gigantic proportions; their great lateral branches striking out at a considerable altitude like the yards of a ship, from which hung a multitude of the bare stems of parasite plants, like cables and rigging flying adrift before the breeze. We noted a number of fine specimens of the camphor-tree, the largest about four feet in diameter, and rising to a great height straight as an arrow, with a slight taper and devoid of branches, till it reached the free air above.

Besides there were interminable ratan plants,

passing in and out of the dense undergrowth; and in a comparatively open space we fell in with a splendid lily, of great size and in full flower, the entire plant standing about twelve feet from the root. Orchids, too, were there in abundance, filling the air with their perfume on every side. From the summit of this hill we got a view of the central mountain chain. In the foreground, like huge billows rolling in upon the shore, were a series of parallel ranges of forest-clad hills, like the one on which we stood. Lalung was still hidden from sight, in a valley six miles off. A vapoury haze obscured the distant landscape, transforming the mountains into broad masses of a deep blue, whose soft outlines gleamed beneath the rays of the now declining sun. A Pepohoan here joined our party; he had travelled over the mountains from the other side of the island, and was now homeward bound. From him we learnt the existence of a fine harbour on the eastern shore, and he added that the tribes granted him a free pass over their territory on the payment of three bullocks. It was about four o'clock when we entered Lalung; this village stands on the bank of a broad river, now reduced to narrow dimensions, and to be seen winding along some half a mile from its proper bank, which rose about sixty feet above the dry channel of the stream. But during the rains we were assured that the river swells to such a volume that it fills up this entire bed, and, as we have already seen, it is constantly forcing new passages for its overflowing waters through the lower hill lands near the western plain. This is evidently one of the great arteries of the drainage of the central mountains: and, if we take into account the vast altitude of those mountains, and the force of the torrents which make their way over the narrow plain, carrying with them, annually, immense quantities of *débris* that the sea continually throws back and deposits along the western shore, we shall probably get some insight into the way in which land is gradually being built up and re-

LALUNG VILLAGE, INTERIOR OF FORMOSA.

deemed from the ocean on the west, independently of the volcanic action still at work in certain quarters of the island. Thus probably we may account for the disappearance of the Taiwan harbour within the brief period of 200 years, as well as for the formation of Takow harbour further south. Perhaps no example can be found anywhere better than in Formosa of the power of water to transform the physical aspect of a country. In many places on that island no settled water-courses exist; and thus the torrents, in the fearful impetus of their headlong rush down the mountain steeps, attack weak positions in the rocks and soils, and form new passages for themselves.

On leaving the mountain top our course lay for an hour through the dry bed of a stream, cut through a black rock stratum, where we discovered traces of shale and coal. On reaching a small stream we found Mrs. Hong, who told us that her husband would put us up at the village. This lady was accompanied by a party of young savages, who carried tackle for fishing. Lalung village is only separated from the territory of the most purely savage aborigines by the stream which I have just described, and its inhabitants number about 1,000 souls. Hong we found from home; but he soon returned, and informed us that Boon, his eldest son, had lately lost his wife, and was off to his savage kinsmen in the mountains to secure another bride. He was expected to return that night, and would be accompanied by an escort from his partner's tribe. Here, in these Pepohoan villages, I found the only instance I encountered of China-men employing middle-men or brokers to deal with natives of the country. It seems that Pepohoans are very often used as go-betweens in the barter trade between the mountaineers and the Chinese; for the latter, though they are great and patient traders, yet as a rule possess but little of the bold spirit of adventure, aud entertain a wholesome dread of these highlanders. They are not without good grounds for their fears; for in one village at least, a missionary, who lately repaired thither, found the men adorning their huts with skulls of their Chinese foes; and the report goes that they are cannibals too. Strangely enough the weapons and ammunition used by the hill tribes to destroy wild animals, and Chinamen, are supplied by the Chinese themselves.

Family ties, between the wild hill tribes and the Pepohoans, are kept up by constant intermarriage. The wedding ceremony is a simple one. The father of the lady merely takes his daughter by the hand and passes her over to her lord, and then there is a drinking-revel to conclude the rites.[1] In the old Dutch accounts of the people it is said that the offer of a present by a suitor, and its acceptance by the lady, entitles the giver to be esteemed the legal husband, according to the rule '*Nuptias non concubitus sed consensus facit*:' and the marriage tie is with equal facility dissolved. Indeed it would almost seem as if the 'Free Lovers' of America had borrowed their creed of inconstancy, and their fickle practices, from the unchivalrous Formosan tribes.

Hong, having at length appeared, gave us a cordial welcome to his house, insisting on the sacrifice of a pig for the more perfect accomplishment of hospitable rites. The porker was therefore slaughtered before the door, and in the presence of a pack of half-starved hunting-dogs, that fought savagely over the drops of blood.

My boy Ahong set it down as his solemn belief that these people could not after all be classed as utter

[1] See for further information *Natives of the West Coast of Formosa*, translated from an old Dutch work by Rev. W. Lobscheid.

barbarians, for they clearly understood the use of roast hog. At this place I collected a number of old Pepohoan words, which appear in the vocabularies in the Appendix.

Next morning we resumed our journey under the guidance of Goona, the youngest son of our host. Goona was a pure young savage, full of laughter and frolic, wearing a crown of ferns on his head, and little else by way of clothing, so he could hardly have felt very hot. We were now descending a narrow path to the dry bed of the river, when our progress was arrested by a yellowish snake about seven feet long which shot out his head across our track. I struck him over the neck with a heavy bamboo staff which I had in my hand. On this the reptile rolled down the bank, and when we had completed the descent we found him again lodged beneath a boulder. Aided by one or two natives I managed to topple the mass over, and then our enemy made another dart forward, hissing, glaring with his fiery eyes, and quivering his forky tongue. I dealt another blow and dispatched him. I should have carried him off, but he was too big to be easily disposed of, so I left him to be devoured by the Pepohoans, who are said to be fond of snakes. I was anxious to cross the river, but was urged not to do so, as two men had been killed by a hostile tribe about a month before, just opposite where we stood.

I obtained some good types of the aboriginal tribes in this quarter, and managed also to photograph the scenery. About two o'clock we set out again to walk to Lakoli, which lay some twelve miles off. At one place we crossed a small stream of strongly alkaline water, and here on the banks some alkali, soda or potash, had crystallised in such quantities as to resemble a recent fall of snow. The banks of the main stream now towered more than 200 feet above the dry bed, and alternating strata of clay and boulders could be distinctly seen. Before us we had a panorama of surpassing grandeur. The mountains rose up range above range covered with dense forest, and bathed in the purple light of sunset, their gigantic forms softened, and beautified by the foliage of the ancient forests. The attractions of this spot were as varied as they were beautiful. At one place a mountain stream, leaping out of some dark chasm, tumbled in foam over the rocks, and was lost again in the forest; and everywhere around us we could see that the same Power who clothed the stupendous mountains with a mantle of evergreen verdure, embroidered by the sunset with purple and gold, had not left the minutest fissure in the rocks without some special grace of its own: there, too, in flowers, ferns, and mosses, we found a modest world of microscopic beauty.

The grandeur of this region during the wet season must baffle description. Then a thousand cataracts, veiled in vapour, and illumined with rainbow hues, leap from the mountain sides, roaring and tumbling in their downward course to the broad river.

Before us, as in a peaceful vale, we could see the settlement of Lakoli—a few rude dwellings, and a patch of tilled land, amid a jungle wilderness. In the fast-failing light we could just make out its hedges and areca-palms, its mango and langan-trees; but ere long the darkness closed in around, and left us groping our way forwards at the outskirt of the hamlet. We could hear the sounds of wild music, laughter, and dancing;

but there was no one to be seen until we fell in with the hut of one 'Kim-Siang,' an old acquaintance of Dr. Maxwell.

Here we met but a cool reception. The old man was laid up with the effects of rheumatism and opium-smoking, and we found a slave girl fanning him in an adjoining hut. His son, a fellow over six feet high, stood in front of the doorway of the cabin, and beside him was his wife, a woman from a friendly mountain tribe. Outside this abode hung festoons of deer-skulls and boar-heads that had been taken in the chase. When the father had finished his opium-pipe, he consented to allow us to occupy an outer shed for the night.

Anxious to procure food, and a vessel in which to boil down my nitrate of silver bath to dryness (photographers will know what is meant by the bath having struck work, and obstinately refusing to produce a picture), I made my way by torchlight to the hut of one 'La-liat,' an Amoy man, engaged here in barter traffic with the hill-tribes. We found little or no evidence of any goods in La-liat's abode. There was a table on the clay floor, and a taper flickering feebly in a cup of oil above it; and here, in this cheerless dwelling, a boisterous party had gathered themselves together, and were engaged in smoking and drinking. Our entrance was but little noticed, and less appreciated. They had nothing we wanted, not even a civil word. A drunken old woman staggered up with a teapot containing sam-shu, and offered to sell us the vessel, when she had first carefully exhausted its contents. Meanwhile La-liat, who had been sleeping on a sort of counter, woke up, recognised my friend, and agreed to trade. Strange to relate, in grateful remembrance of his former acquaintance with the Doctor, he supplied us with a dozen eggs and a brown jar, and then positively refused to accept payment, so that finally we had to force our money upon him. He also showed us raw camphor, skins, horns, boars' tusks, ratan, and other wares, which he had obtained from a party of savages who had come down from their hunting-grounds to Lakoli the day before. In return for these goods he had supplied them with beads, turkey-red cloth, knives, and gunpowder.

Our armed guide slept on a mat in the hut beside us, while Ahong and I were engaged till about 2 A.M. boiling down my bath in the Chinese pot. It was a tedious job. First Ahong slept as we sat before the fire; then I slept; then we both slept, and the fire went low, and had to be tended. I complained of my boy's sleeping, and immediately dozed off myself, and so on, until the whole liquid was evaporated. Once the alcoholic fumes, in passing off, caught fire; then I heard a terrible shriek, and started up to find the scared face of a savage old woman glaring close to mine. She must have been placed there to watch us, and she vanished instantly into the darkness whence she had appeared. Ahong, disturbed in his sleep, caught sight of the apparition, and declared that it was the—well, never mind what! But he did not rest quite so comfortably after that incident. I am not myself prepared to say what the old witch could have been, or how she vanished. She certainly looked haggard, hideous, and unearthly; and her flight, too, was as sudden and as noiseless as the puff of smoke which she jerked fiercely out from her short bamboo pipe.

Four hours rest, and we were up again by daylight, and ready for the road. After the night's doctoring, my nitrate-of-silver bath gave every satisfaction; only the water which I used to dilute it was so extremely alkaline that I had to employ a goodly supply of Chinese vinegar to turn it—slightly, to the acid side.

As I must needs quit Formosa with this chapter, it will be necessary to summarise my experiences from this point, and to condense my narrative within narrower limits.

On the summit of the first range, on our homeward route, above Lakoli, in place of setting up my instruments to photograph, I felt I would much rather have lain down and slept; but there was no time for that, as we had by the route we followed between twenty and thirty miles to walk before night, and a day's work of photographing to overtake besides.

Dr. Maxwell was not feeling well; he had, however, promised to be at Baksa next day to conduct the service in the chapel there, so we pushed on. At the foot of another range, on the brink of a clear cool stream, I secured two more photographs, and waited for a short time to admire a sedgy pool and to bathe our feet in its clear cool water. At our approach a myriad of tiny fish dived for shelter beneath the pebbles. The surface was alive with strange insects, that shot like comets into the reeds; while, perched on a broad leaf, sat a lusty toad, watching our movements with gentlemanly self-possession and gravity, and looking as if he fully expected an apology for being thus interrupted at his morning toilet. The remainder of the day's journey was almost an uninterrupted toil over hill and dale.

At noon we halted at a small village in front of a hut, where an old woman was selling fruit. Here a large party of Pepohoans—in clothing that might have been decent, had it covered their nakedness—assembled to see us eat; and it must have been a very barbarous spectacle to them, for they groaned audibly and uttered strange ejaculations when they beheld us furiously devouring hard-boiled eggs and tea; but the prevailing expression on the faces of this cheaply-dressed crowd was that of low-bred animal curiosity. The satisfaction, however, of the bystanders could hardly have been excelled by that which we ourselves derived from the repast. The Doctor, as was his custom, conversed with the people, and prescribed for some who were sick.

We came upon a large sheet of water at the place where we next halted, and there we swam about for some time. It was probably an imprudent thing, but it refreshed us for the moment. A few hours after this my friend became very ill, and had to lie down beneath the shade of some shrubs, in a place where there was not a drop of clear water to be procured for miles around. At his request, I gave him a dose of quinine and iron, and after an hour's rest we resumed our march. I took a picture of one of the deep dry clay-pits of this region, and had to proceed ten miles farther on before I could get a drop of water to wash the plate and finish the negative. It turned out one of my finest pictures nevertheless.

On the hill above Baksa we halted at a hut, and were there regaled with a cup of pure honey. Descending the ridge which I described at starting my foot slipped, but fortunately I saved myself from the fearful fall by clinging to the sharp edges of the rock, cutting my hands, however, badly in the accident. Need I say that when we reached the chapel at Baksa our rest that night was profound and refreshing. My friend, although feverish and ill, was still well enough to conduct the service next morning. All business at Baksa was suspended throughout that day, and there were more than three hundred apparently devout worshippers at the little mission chapel. There is a school attached to this edifice, and there children and even adults are taught to read and write in the Amoy dialect of the Chinese language.

One or two local airs had been adapted to our hymns, and there was something wild yet plaintive about them, like the sighing of the winds through their grand old forests, or the noise of the storms along their rocky coast. Apart from one or two such airs—simple ballads handed down from father to son—the Pepohoans have no music and no musical instruments, so far as I know. They are extremely primitive in their habits too, practising no art save the tilling of the soil, and that in its rudest form. But there is one great charm about these untutored tribes, and this consists in their artless good faith and honesty. During the entire journey my boxes were frequently left open and unprotected, and yet I never lost the value of a pin.

But I must now quit this island, remarkable no less for its beauty than for the hospitality of its simple inhabitants. I afterwards travelled overland to Takow, for the purpose of visiting the haunts of the savages farther south; but they were at war with the Chinese, and their territory could not be entered with safety:

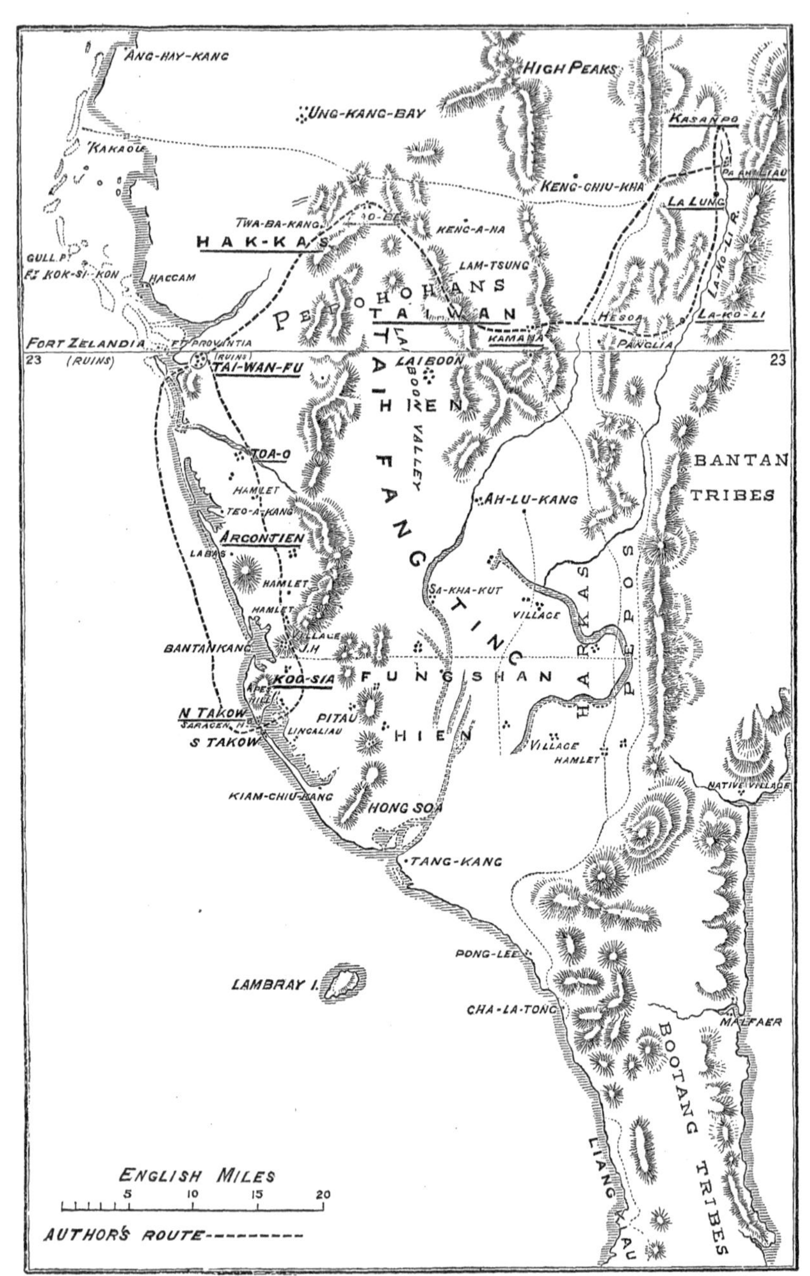

SOUTH-WESTERN FORMOSA.

CHAPTER XII.

The Japanese in Formosa—Cause of the Invasion—The River Min—Foochow Arsenal—Chinese Gun-boats—Foochow City and great Bridge—A City of the Dead—Its Inhabitants—Beggars—Thieves—Lepers—Ku-shan Monastery—The Praying Bull—The Hermit—Tea Plantation on Paeling Hills—Voyage up the Min—Shui-kow—An Up-country Farm—Captain Cheng and his Spouse—Yen-ping City—Sacrificing to the Dead—Shooting the Yen-ping Rapids—A Native Passenger-boat.

THE island kingdom of Japan is to all appearance destined to afford an unparalleled example of progress. She has indeed preferred, to quote Professor Tyndall's words, 'Commotion before stagnation, the leap of the torrent before the stillness of the swamp;' and we have just seen, in Formosa, how such leaping torrents in their impetuous courses cut out new channels in the mountain sides, spread fertility over the plains below, and even reclaim the land from the barren domain of the ocean with the *débris* which they sweep down.

There is vigorous life, and hope, and high promise for the future, in the busy movement that is carrying Japan from darkness and semi-barbarism into the realms of civilisation and light; and the impetus, if we mistake not, which she is gathering in her onward course, will clear away mighty obstacles, and check stagnation and decay in other quarters as well as her own.

The invasion of Formosa by Japanese troops is a fact full of deep significance; and more righteous grounds for such aggressive action it would be impossible for any government to possess. Scores of Japanese sailors, wrecked from time to time upon the Formosan coasts, have there been plundered and murdered by the savage tribes; and as these barbarities were perpetrated on Chinese soil, redress was applied for at Peking. The members of the Imperial Cabinet, in a moment of weakness—moments of not unfrequent occurrence in Chinese state history—appear to have conceded the right for the Japanese to proceed to Formosa and seek redress for themselves.

It would be extremely interesting to know what share the aborigines of Formosa have really taken in the cold-blooded massacres of castaways that have recently been reported from that island. It seems pretty clear that it was the Kalee tribes who put the crew of the 'Rover' to death: at the same time it is equally certain that the murder of the captain and sailors of the 'Macto' was perpetrated by Chinese villagers at Takow.

If we are thus to believe that pure motives of humanity gave rise to this invasion of Formosa by the Japanese, it would be only just to award to the Mikado and his ministers the highest meed of praise; but, perhaps, it ought to be borne in mind that the Japanese have not yet forgotten their ancient feuds against China, and still fall somewhat short of that almost unattainable pitch of national virtue, which would induce them to enter upon costly expeditions to redress outrages committed upon native crews. However the matter end, its results will, as I should anticipate, be advantageous. China may get off by paying the cost of the expedition—a proceeding which, while it humbled her national vanity, would stir her up to imitate and rival Japan, so as, if possible, to outstrip her in the march of progress, from the sheer necessity of self-preservation; and I have no hesitation in saying that China, petrified and stagnant as she is, and has been, for so many centuries, yet contains within herself all the material elements that will, one day, win her a proud pre-eminence among the nations of the earth.

Truth even now is busily at work loosening the earth about the ancient foundations of classical lore and superstition on which her venerable wall of fossil institutions is reared; and that wall, ere long, will be lowered stone by stone, or overthrown with some violent shock, till a way has been opened across it for the purer institutions of progressive government. Should war be the alternative, it will probably only hasten the work of regeneration.

I will now take leave of the island of Formosa, and cross again to the mainland of China, where, in the province of Fu-kien, I gathered some information relating to the progress made by the Chinese in the arts of natural defence, and the construction of implements of war.

The river Min, flowing through the heart of the Fu-kien province, is one of the main outlets for the drainage of the mountainous region where the celebrated Bohea hills stand, and is also the channel down which the produce of one of the richest tea districts in China is conveyed for exportation. The stream, however, although a broad one, is not navigable for large vessels beyond the town of Shui-Kow, which stands on its left bank at the foot of dangerous rapids one hundred miles from the coast.

The entrance to the Min by the south channel is nearly opposite to a group of islands known as the 'White Dogs.' There are, however, two other channels now in use; the most northerly between Sharp Peak Island and the mainland, and only available for vessels of light draught, while the middle channel, discovered quite recently, and to the south of Sharp Peak, has a breadth of about three-quarters of a mile, and is nearly three fathoms deep at low tide. The south channel is not quite so roomy, nor yet so direct, except for vessels trading south.

A lighthouse now being built on the 'White Dogs' will prove of great advantage to the port. The Kin-pai and Min-Ngan passes, through which the anchorage is gained, recalled the approaches to the Pearl River.

The harbour is about thirty miles from the mouth of the river, and is wide enough to contain the entire merchant fleet of China. This spot is called 'Pagoda Anchorage,' and takes that name from a small island crowned with an old pagoda, which forms a conspicuous object in the landscape. But for this purely Chinese edifice, one might readily suppose oneself transported suddenly to a scene on the river Clyde. There stand the houses of a small foreign settlement, and yonder are a dock, tall chimnies, and rows of workshops, whence the clang of steam-hammers and the hum of engines may be distinctly heard. Here, in fact, is the Foochow Arsenal, on a piece of level ground redeemed from an old swamp, and looking in the distance like an English manufacturing village.

But side by side with the residences on the hill, there is a crescent-shaped stone shrine of imposing proportions, designed to correct the Feng-shui, which has been seriously disturbed by the construction of an arsenal after a foreign type.

This arsenal, like all the others on Chinese soil, was raised simply because the native authorities deemed it expedient to remodel their military equipments with all possible speed, and then Feng-shui, or the Geomantic luck of the locality, was treated with but scant consideration. Feng-shui, indeed, had to yield to the stern necessity of the times, and was relegated to this very humble station on the hill-side, where the outraged terrestial dragon, and the no longer venerated tiger, may weep sympathetically over the evidences of a degenerate age. Thus we find that the most cherished superstitions of China are compelled to give way, so often as expediency may necessitate change.

The latest news from this quarter brings the startling announcement that since the landing of the Japanese troops telegraphic communication has actually been established between Foochow city and the coast: (the authorities also propose to lay a submarine cable, to connect Formosa with the mainland); and that the local authorities have inscribed notices on the telegraph posts that anyone who is caught doing damage to them will be severely punished. By steps like this the fanatic dread of the common people will readily be overcome; for they account their scholarly mandarins much better judges of Feng-shui and its influences than they themselves can pretend to be. But let us visit the Chinese foreign arsenal.

The first building we enter, when we land, reminds

us, by its lofty roof and general appearance, of a plain English railway-station. It is constructed of brick on a solid granite foundation, and is enclosed by a wall, which is also of granite, and which rises about five feet above the floor. Passing in through a spacious doorway we make our way along an iron avenue, lined on both sides with smith's forges, whose blast is supplied by steam. The engine which ministers to these forges has a driving-wheel of colossal proportions, and may also be seen quickening a row of steam-hammers, with forces mighty enough to forge a shaft for the biggest steamer afloat, or so delicate as to straighten a pin. Strange as it may appear, these giant tools, when first seen working, produced but little impression on their Chinese spectators. Whether it be that the celestials when brought face to face with any new wonder do not care to display vulgar emotion, or whether rather stolid apathy and indifference are national characteristics, it is difficult to decide; but I well remember a lady expressing her surprise to me, when she had landed in England with a Chinese nurse, who had never been in Europe before, to find the woman passing through London quite unmoved by all the marvels of that city, and stepping into a railway-carriage as if she had been accustomed to express trains all her life. She did, however, volunteer one remark, to the effect that it was 'too muchee fast pidjin, very good for Englishman, but too muchee bobbery for a Chinese gentleman.'

The next workshop we visit is as spacious as the preceding one, and contains the half formed skeleton of a mammoth engine for rolling out sheet iron and steel armour-plating for iron-clad ships. An iron driving-wheel, eighteen feet in diameter, is to be seen there propped up in position. We next cross a broad paved court, having a line of railway along one of its sides, used in conveying materials to the different workshops which run parallel to the rails and face the river. In these shops practical engineering and ship-building in its various branches are being carried on; and in one there is a sort of school, where mechanical drawing and modelling are taught by French masters. These instructors, all of them, remarked to me on the wonderful aptitude displayed by the Chinese in picking up a knowledge of the various mechanical appliances employed in the arsenal. Many of the men who are there working at the steam-lathes, and guiding the planing-machines, had two or three months before been ordinary field labourers; and yet there they are now turning shafts, and planing iron plates to specified dimensions, as accurately as if they had been trained for years to the trade.

In one apartment a powerful machine is punching rivet-holes in boiler-plates—holes which, any one of them, would keep a native blacksmith drilling for half a day, but which are here pierced in less than a second. In another department we found men at work making wooden patterns for iron castings, and others constructing models of steam-engines, to be used in educating the pupils of this great training-school.

There are indeed many admirable specimens of complicated work carried out solely from drawings; the whole betokening a very advanced degree of skill and knowledge on the part of the workmen. All these results have been achieved under the guidance of European foremen. For my own part, from what I have seen in these arsenals, I firmly believe that when the Chinese find it convenient to throw off their grossly superstitious notions regarding foreign inventions and appliances, they will excel in all that pertains to the exact sciences, and in their practical application to the construction of machinery. Chinamen, as a rule, are careful, painstaking, and exact in their own occupations. Hence the facility with which the mere tiller of the soil can be trained, in such an establishment as this arsenal, till he becomes competent to take charge of an engine, where a single error in the handling of a lever, or turn of a screw, might at any moment cost him his life. Pupils in the arsenal or training-school are boarded and placed under efficient foreign masters. They are there taught to read and understand foreign books, and thus to ascertain for themselves that science is the true Feng-shui of foreign progress. No expense is spared to render the institution efficient. The mandarins connected with the arsenal look with pardonable vanity at the steam gun-boats that have been built under their own eyes, and sent into commission from their own naval and ship-building yards. A gunboat had been launched from the patent slip a few days previous to our visit, and the sister vessel was already on the stocks.

Proceeding on board the former, we are received by the Chinese captain and his lieutenant with great courtesy, and conducted all over the ship. This a nautical friend present pronounced to be an honest, solid, masterly piece of work throughout. The woodwork of the cabin is simply varnished, and relieved with narrow gold mouldings. The officers' cabin and mess-room are finished in the same unpretending, and yet not inelegant style; and in the sailors' quarter we notice that each seaman is supplied with a strong teak bunker, to hold his effects, and to serve him also instead of a couch or chair.

This gun-vessel carries one huge Armstrong gun on her upper deck, and is to be fitted with the same weapons throughout. Her armament, therefore, will render her a formidable enemy to pirates, though not perhaps of much service in a combat with any European Power.

Our next visit is to a vessel in commission lying off the arsenal, and manned throughout, from captain to cabin-boy, by an entirely Chinese crew. Stepping on deck from the gangway, we are saluted in military style by a Ningpo marine, who informs us, in tolerable English, that we shall find the captain in his cabin. The dress of this marine is admirable, consisting of a black turban, blue blouse, pantaloons with red stripe, and a pair of neat and strongly made native shoes. A well-kept belt fastens in the blouse at the waist, and supports also a cartouche-box and side-arms.

An officer of marines next welcomes us on board, and says :—

'S'pose you likee, my can show you my drill pidjin,' an offer which we gladly accept. 'My hab got two squab, one too muchee new, other olo, can saby drill pidjin.' He means to say that he has two squad, one well trained, and the other raw recruits. It wants still fifteen minutes to drill time, so, at the captain's request, we will take a peep into his cabin.

In most respects this resembles that of some English gunboats; but on a small table, supported by graceful brackets, we note a strange assortment of foreign nautical instruments spread around a small idol. This idol was the only visible token of native superstition, and was used in conjunction with the barometer and thermometer to avoid coming storms, or to find out lucky days for sailing. Nevertheless, everything around us bears unmistakable evidence of progress. Having partaken of wine with our hospitable entertainer, we next return to the upper deck to see the marines at drill. The bugleman sounds to quarters, and the men, with Enfield rifles in their hands, fall, or rather tumble, into position, six or eight at a time. Then one, more dilatory than his fellows, pops his head out of a hatchway, in order to satisfy himself that his company could not be dispensed with, scrambles on deck as he drags himself into his blouse and pantaloons, and fixes his belt as he falls in. Some, too, have misplaced their rifles, but all have now fairly got into line, and all appear orderly enough until one unlucky fellow, feeling perhaps a sudden twinge of itch, drops his weapon to have a scratch. A comrade politely leaves the ranks to clear his throat over the side; and so the drill proceeds, its forms seemingly well understood by most of the men, but its object, so far as we could judge, almost entirely ignored. Thus there is a marked absence of the discipline we always associate with naval or military training. Possibly they may have learned something of this stricter discipline within the past two years, for they have lately had an able European instructor resident at the arsenal, though in charge, more particularly, of the rising generation of naval cadets attached to the school.

It had been reported that native workmen were making the chronometers and telescopes in use on board the gunboats; so, to ascertain for ourselves how much the Chinese can accomplish in this way, let us visit their optical and horological departments. There we certainly see the native mechanics grinding and polishing lenses ; but they are lenses of the simplest character—plano-convex, for the eye-pieces of telescopes—and we could not learn that they have any notion how to produce the achromatised object-glasses, which are by far the most important part of the instrument. In the same way, while they are capable of making some parts of the chronometer works, they do not yet understand its mechanism, nor have they appliances or knowledge to fit them to construct the chronometer throughout.

The opticians make ships' compasses, portions of sextants, and the brass work of other nautical instruments. How they acquired these arts it is difficult to make out, as their foreign teacher confessed to his complete ignorance of their language.

P. Giguel was the chief director of this establishment, and to him the Chinese are mainly indebted for its success. It was no small achievement to have trained, within a limited time, the little colony of Chinese labourers to such a degree of perfection as to enable them to produce, with their own toil, a small fleet of well-built gunboats that would not dishonour our own ship-building yards at home.

The Viceroy Tso, under whose auspices the arsenal was built, is also deserving of some credit, although he was not the first to see the need for a change in the construction of the warlike implements of his nation.

The monthly expenditure of the whole establishment is reported at about 17,000*l.* It appears that the authorities have recently discharged the foreign employés, though what may have been their reason for this step, which happened just before the Japanese invaded Formosa, it is impossible for me to say.

Foochow city, one of the great tea marts of China, stands about seven miles above the arsenal and the harbour where the vessels load tea. Of all the open

UPPER BRIDGE, FOOCHOW.

ports this is perhaps the most picturesque, and its stone bridge of 'ten thousand ages' proves that the ancient Chinese, had they so chosen, might have left monuments behind them more worthy of their civilisation and prowess than their great unwieldy wall—monuments which would have shed a gleam of truth across the obscure pages of their bygone history. This bridge was erected, it is said, about 900 years ago, and displays no pretensions to ornamentation except in its stone balustrade. It is indeed evident that its builders had convenience and durability alone in view; and the masses of solid granite then employed, still but little injured by the lapse of time, bear high testimony, in their colossal proportions, to the skill of the ancient engineers who raised them up out of the water, and placed them in position on the stone piers above. The bridge is fully a quarter of a mile in length, and the granite blocks which stretch from pier to pier are some of them forty feet long.

The foreign settlement is separated from Foochow city by the great bridge, and by a small island which here rises in the middle of the stream, The site was formerly that of an old Chinese burial-ground, and abundant disputes arose in consequence when plots had to be purchased for the erection of houses, the natives being loath to see the dwellings of living 'foreign devils' erected over the resting-places of their own hallowed dead. But money, which exercises as potent an influence here as elsewhere, procured a solution of the difficulties: even the spirits of the departed were to be consoled by timely offerings at their shrines; and so now, on these hills, the dust of the long-forgotten dead is trodden under foot by the hated foreign intruder, and mingles with the roses with which his garden is adorned. Even the tombs have, some of them, been turned to account. Living occupants have entered into joint tenancy with the silent inhabitants who repose beneath, and pigs or poultry may be seen enjoying the cool shade and shelter which the ample granite gravestone supplies. But I need not give any detailed description of the foreign residences at Foochow. The reader knows nearly all about them already, if he has ever chanced to dwell in a house of not quite modern date, such as is to be seen not unfrequently in Surrey, surrounded by an acre or two of garden ground. The furniture and accessories are as nearly European as they can be beneath an almost tropical sun. But as for the crowd of spacious offices away down near the river, I have no doubt that a whole volume might be written about them, and about the mysteries of the tea-trade carried on beneath their roofs. The residents form a very agreeable community. Petty feuds, of course, occur among them, as they have abundance of leisure on their hands when the tea season is over; but, as a rule, they employ their spare time much more wisely than in idle local squabbles, and seek healthful recreation among the mountains and glens of the province. The only regret I experienced, when I quitted Foochow, was that I could not prolong my stay there.

This notice of the graves in the foreigners' quarter may be supplemented by some account of the living tenants to be met with in a city of the dead close by; but before proceeding to describe the condition of these wretched beings, it may be as well to give the reader a notion of the condition of the poor in Foochow.

In China the beggar pursues his calling unmolested, and has even won for himself a protection and quasi-recognition at the hands of the civic authorities. The fact is, that the charitable institutions of the country cannot cope with a tenth part of the misery and destitution that prevails in popular localities. No poor law is known, and the only plan adopted to palliate the evil is to tolerate begging in public, and to place the lazaroni under the local jurisdiction of a responsible chief. In Foochow the city is divided into wards, and within the limits of each ward a head-man is appointed, able to trace his descent from a line of illustrious

THE KING OF THE BEGGARS.

beggar-chiefs who, like himself, exercised the right to keep the members of their order under their own management and control.

During my stay in Foochow I was introduced to one of these beggar kings; he was an inveterate opium-smoker, and consequently in reduced circumstances. I afterwards visited the house of another head-man, and was much struck with the many evidences of comfort and affluence with which he was surrounded. His eldest son received me at the entrance, and conducted me into a guest's chamber; and while I was seated there two ladies, dressed in silks and with a certain degree of refinement in their air, passed the door of the apartment in order to steal a glimpse at its inmate. These were the chief and the second wives of this Lord of the Lazaroni, who was himself unfortunately absent on business.

Beggar chieftains of this kind have it in their power to make an agreement with the business men of the streets in their respective wards, under which they levy a kind of poor-rate for the maintenance of themselves and their subjects. A composition thus entered into exempts the streets or shops whereon the chief has placed his mark from the harassing raids of his tattered troops. Woe betide the shopman who has the courage to refuse his dole to these beggars! The most loathsome and pertinacious specimens of the naked tribe will be dispatched to beset his shop. Thus, while walking along one of the best streets in the city, I myself saw a revolting, diseased, and filthy object carried on the shoulders of another member of the fraternity, who marched into a shop and deposited his burden on the polished counter, where the tradesman was serving customers with ornaments for shrines and food for the gods. The bearer, with cool audacity, proceeded to light his pipe and smoke, until he had been paid to remove the cripple. A still worse case was narrated to me by an eye-witness. A silk-mercer had refused to contribute his beggar's-rate, and accordingly received a domiciliary visit from a representative of the chief. This intruder had smeared his bare body with mud, and carried a bowl slung with cords, and filled with foul water to the very brim. Having taken up his stand in the shop he commenced to swing this bowl round his head without, indeed, spilling a drop of its contents, yet so that, had anyone attempted to arrest his arm, the water would have been distributed in a filthy shower over the silks piled upon the counter and shelves.

But there is still another and a worse class of beggars—outlaws who own allegiance to no prince or power on earth—and these were the men whom I visited and found dwelling in the charnel-houses in a city of the dead. Many of the little huts in this dismal spot were built with brick and roofed with tiles. They contained coffins and bodies placed there to await the favourable hour for interment, when the rites of Feng-shui might be duly performed, and the remains laid to rest in some well-situated site, where neither wind nor wave would disturb their sacred dust. But poverty, death, distress, or indeed a variety of causes, not unfrequently intervene to prevent the surviving relatives from ever choosing this happy site and bringing the final ceremonies to a consummation; and thus it comes to pass that the coffins lie forgotten and moulder into dust, and the tombs are invaded by the poor outcasts, who there seek shelter from the cold and rain, creeping gladly to slumber into the dark corners of a sepulchre, and then most happy when they most imitate the dead.

On my first visit to this place I recollect being attracted to an ominous-looking tomb by hearing some one moan there. It was growing dark, and I may have, perhaps, felt a little superstitious as I peeped in and beheld what seemed to be an old man clad in rags too scant to cover his bony frame. He was fanning a fire made up of withered branches, but he was not the only tenant; there was a coffin there, too, looming out from the darkness within, and I almost fancied he was the ghost of its owner. But no! there was no mistaking the moan of suffering humanity. The cold wind was chilling his thin blood, and racking his joints with pain. Administering some temporary relief, which made the old man smile like a grinning figure of Death, and passing on to a tomb where I could hear sounds of mirth, I found four inmates inside, the members of a firm of beggars. I visited them again next morning, and came upon the group at breakfast. The head-man—a lusty, lazy, half-naked lout—was standing in front of the entrance enjoying a post-prandial pipe, and he offered me a smoke with the air of a Chinese gentleman. After this he invited me in to inspect the interior, where his partners were busily engrossed with chopsticks and bowls of reeking scraps collected on the previous day. They were chatting noisily, too, forgetful of their cares, and of the coffins that surrounded them. One, the jester of the party, was seated astride a coffin, cracking his jokes over the skull of its occupant. The repast concluded, they had to adjust their counterfeits of disease and deformity, and to map out their pilgrimage for the day. One of the fellows made a good thing of it by acting the religious devotee, and driving an axe into his skull; another carried on a brisk trade in a loathsome skin disease; while a third was daily lame from birth; thus, with ingenuity that might have earned them more honest livelihoods, even in a land where it is difficult for the poor, however industrious, to subsist at all, they supported a miserable existence by artful dodges and imposture. The coffins, sprinkled with a little straw and rubbish, formed their seats and beds.

While at Foochow, after visiting the beggars, I thought I might as well see what the detectives are like. These men are commonly known as the 'Ma-qui' or 'Swift as horses,' and are attached to the yamens of the local authorities, receiving a small stipend out of the Government supplies, but obtaining the bulk of their earnings from persons who seek to recover stolen goods, or even from the thieves themselves.

The Ma-qui is supposed to know personally all the professional robbers of his district; and one wishing to recover his property from the thieves must make a liberal offer to the Ma-qui, at least one half the value of the articles lost: failing this, it is probable that he will never hear of his goods again, unless indeed direct and secret communication can be opened with the thief himself, who, as he will not in that case have to share his gains with the detective, can afford to take a smaller profit on his labour. But transactions of this kind are generally effected through the Ma-qui, who simply acts as a broker, and takes his percentage from both sides. Should the thieves refuse to yield up the property at the price he offers, they run the risk of being imprisoned and tortured. I photographed a thief who had just escaped from gaol; he had been an unprofitable burglar, a bad constituent of the Ma-qui, and was accordingly triced up by the thumbs until the cords had worn the flesh away and left nothing but the bare bones exposed. It was told of this detective, who might more appropriately be called the chief of the thieves, that he, one day, fell in with an old thief whom he had known and profited by in former times, but who was now respectably clad, and striving to lead an honest life. He at once had the man conveyed to prison, and there, in order to impress upon him the danger to which he exposed himself in falling into

AN UNFORTUNATE THIEF.—PUNISHMENT OF THE CANGUE.

honest ways, suspended him by the thumbs, stripped off his clothes, and discharged him with one arm put out of joint. When a thief is not in the profession, and cannot be discovered, the Ma-qui is liable to be whipped. He then whips his subordinates, and they in turn whip the thieves. Should this plan fail, it is reported that the police have been whipped, and that the stolen property cannot be found.

A word about leprosy, and the leper villages of the Chinese. This disease—not an uncommon one in China—may be seen in a variety of its loathsome forms in the public streets of almost every city, including our own colony at Hongkong; and at the latter

FOOCHOW LEPERS.

place, in the early morning, I have passed a dozen lepers together, begging in the open thoroughfares for bread. It is to be hoped that, by this time, such poor outcasts from society have been provided with some asylum wherein to hide the visible death that is rapidly eating up their frames. In Penang, too, there was formerly a spot where the lepers loved to congregate, on a patch of green turf beneath a wide-spreading green tree; and in the very same place, when the lepers were absent, I have seen native nurses and European children at play. This disease however is held not to be infectious by many Asiatics, as well as by a number of European physicians who have had to prescribe for sufferers; and, for my own part, I am inclined to adopt their view. It has also been proved that the malady, although to a certain extent hereditary, will at last die out of a family. Thus in the Canton leper village there are direct descendants of lepers, now alive, who are entirely free from the disease; and in the leper settlement at Foochow I was informed that the inhabitants were permitted to marry, and rear families; and the statement was evidently true, for we found there many parents surrounded by healthy children, some of whom, though they had reached maturity, were still free from the fearful blight that had fallen on the wretched community around.

The village to which I allude is a walled enclosure, standing about a mile beyond the east gate of the city; and on February 25, 1871, I set out with the Rev. Mr. Mahood, to pay a visit to this asylum. It was now about four in the afternoon; a drizzling rain had already set in, and a sudden darkness overcast the heavens as we entered the gate of the village. The dreariness of the weather, and the gloominess of the gathering clouds overhead, intensified the wretchedness of the scene; and we were soon surrounded by a crowd of men, women, and children, some too loathsome to bear description, and all clamouring for alms to buy food to sustain their miserable lives; nor did their importunity cease until the governor of the place, himself a leper, came out to keep his subjects in order.

It would appear that the original idea of the institution had been lost sight of, and that it is now made as much the means of extorting money from wealthy lepers as of conferring a boon upon the community by keeping the leprous shut up, and cut off from contact with the outer world. The poor among them, who are unable to pay for their own maintenance, are allowed a nominal annual sum by government, sufficient to support them probably one month out of twelve, and for the rest they are daily sent adrift into the public highways, and I believe, as in the case of ordinary beggars, certain shops and streets may unite together and purchase freedom from their most objectionable visits. This little settlement numbered something over 300 souls, and had once contained a theatre for the amusement of its inhabitants, but that edifice had long fallen into decay. The streets, however, looked wonderfully clean, and the houses, many of them, partook of the same charm. The inmates not unfrequently were engaged in occupations of divers kinds, but the bulk of the population were quite unable to work, as their fingers were either partly or entirely gone. The most surprising feature in the whole village was the wonderfully cheerful aspect of a considerable portion of its occupants; who, though cut off in a great measure from social intercourse with the outside world, yet manifested a tender and grateful attachment to the flowers which they reared with constant care round the doors and windows of their cabins—flowers which blossomed in return with ungrudged beauty and sweetness, breathing their simple perfume as lavishly in these sepulchres of the living, as in the proud gardens of the rich.

The streets of Foochow are so similar to the streets of all the other cities of Southern China as to require no description here. Foochow, too, has its parade-grounds, its yamens, its temples, and its pagodas; all of great importance to the citizens themselves, and of comparatively little interest to the stranger from outside; unless to one who wishes to make himself acquainted with an endless variety of dry details as to religion, Feng-shui, or local jurisdiction; none of which subjects could possibly be digested into a volume of such dimensions as mine. I will therefore only remark, as I quit the town, that the visitor must not fail to observe the oysters—oysters which are not only very good, but very remarkable, too, in their way. It may be said that a bamboo rod is not the 'native climb' of that highly-prized shell-fish; and yet, in the main thoroughfares at Foochow, one finds an endless array of fish-stalls, where oysters are served out to passing customers; and these oysters are grown in clusters on bamboo rods, stuck into the beds at the proper season, pulled up again when mature, and brought in this fashion to market. The Foochow oyster-shells, unlike our own, which are of nearly uniform mould, follow no law in this respect; but each oyster shapes its dwelling to suit its own tastes or requirements: thus the jagged and irregular bamboo clusters have no two shells alike.

There are a number of trades which are peculiar to this city, and among the most interesting is that of the lamp-maker. One lamp, of a very pretty though rather fragile kind, is made up of thin rods of glass set so closely together as almost to imitate basket-work.

The light shines through these rods with a very effective lustre; and though no lamps of the sort, so far as I know, have yet been introduced into this country, they would form very attractive novelties at a garden fête.

There are many charming resorts in the vicinity of Foochow, but to my mind 'Fang-Kuang-Yen-tien-chüan,' better known as the 'Yuan-fu' monastery, is the most fascinating of them all. It was my good fortune to visit that retreat as the guest of a foreign merchant who made up a party for a cruise on the Yuan-fu branch of the river Min. Two private yachts were manned and fitted for the trip; and in these, at midnight, we started from Foochow. The tide was on the ebb, and when we awoke next morning we found ourselves at anchor, with Pagoda Island still in view.

Intense cold, with drifting sleet, made the prospect ahead unpromising. The bold mountains, known to the natives as the 'Wu-hu' or 'five tiger' range, were wrapped in a thin veil of now gradually-lifting mist; but it was nearly mid-day before the last shred of vapour had withdrawn from the rugged overhanging crag which has been called the 'Lover's Leap.' Those five tigers are supposed to exercise some geomantic influences on Foochow city, which lies to the north of the range; and, in order to counteract this effect, a corresponding number of stone lions have been erected, and may yet be encountered, in one of the main streets of the town.

The mountains rise to a considerable altitude about this part of the river, and terminate in bold rocky cliffs; but beneath, wherever an available patch of soil is to be found, it has been terraced and cultivated up to the very face of the rocks. A walk along the bank, or a climb among the crags, is amply repaid by a thousand charming details of form and colour. There are ferns and flowers in multitudes; stately pines, and beetling precipices over which clustering bamboos wave their graceful plumes. Here a quaint rock, gray-headed with lichen, and bearded with ferns, looks like some giant reclining on the mossy bank; and there is a bank of turf, more rich than any cloak of velvet that I ever saw, and embroidered with a thousand gay wild flowers. In that dell yonder a slight effort of fancy, and a few glancing fire-flies, might introduce us to some fairy revel. It is a dim retreat, shaded by an archway of ferns. An old branch spans a fissure in the rock, and there imagination plants some grim-faced goblin, blowing music from his elfin horn on a summer's eve for a thousand dainty figures that dance upon the floor below. But the place felt damp and disagreeable, although it presented a pleasant scene.

Two days were thus spent amid a ceaseless diversity of grand river and mountain scenery; and on the third morning, at a short distance above the first rapid, we landed to make the journey to Yuan-fu monastery. My friends had brought their sedans and bearers with them; as for me, I hired one at the nearest village; my dog, as was his custom, at once scrambling inside, and stowing himself comfortably beneath the seat. The chair, being intended for mountain use, was small, so that I had to sit in a cramped and awkward posture. When ascending steep parts of the path the bearers purposely made the swinging motion so irksome that I had to get out and threaten to send them back, informing them further that, as I had no intention of staying outside and walking, they might as well stop their jolting and earn their hire.

This is an old dodge of the chair coolies. In all mountainous regions they pretend, as they climb some steep place, that the jolting cannot be avoided; but my threat had the desired effect of rendering the ascent easy as far as the chair could be used. At one spot there is a flight of 400 steps (I had the curiosity to count them as our progress was slow), and this brought us to the entrance of the ravine overlooked by the monastery, which was also perhaps the most romantic bit of scenery to be encountered there. Above these steps the path winds beneath a forest, and around a rich undergrowth of ferns and flowering shrubs, and finally seems suddenly to terminate in a cave. This cave in reality forms the passage through which the dell is approached. A small idol stood at the foot of the rocks, on the right of the entrance, and there was incense burning before its shrine.

On the stone walls of the natural tunnel, and on every striking rock, there were also a number of ancient incised inscriptions, out of which the following may be selected as a fair specimen of the whole: 'The scenery at this place is equal to that where the genii dwell.' Other inscriptions are nothing more than the names of pious visitors to the temple above. Passing through beneath the rock, which here rises in a gigantic precipice on the hill-side, we emerged from the darkness of the tortuous passage into, what looked like, a tropical dell of palms, and seemed, in a few steps, to have passed from a temperate latitude into some southern clime. But the broad leaves that spanned the ravine were nothing more than huge ferns. Bending back, and looking upwards through the foliage to catch a glimpse of the sky, I could see nothing save the bright colours of a curious building standing out against a dark cavern which overhung the ravine. As we ascended a narrow path cut in the face of the rocks, we obtained a full view of the monastery, perched upon a huge boulder above our heads, and overshadowed by a grove of stalactites which hung down like pointed ornaments from the vaults of some cathedral roof. Never had I seen, nor ever dreamt of seeing, any edifice so strange as this. There it stood, with its broad eaves, carved roofs, and ornamental balustrades, propped up on the face of a precipice 200 feet in height, and resting above this awful abyss, on nothing more durable than a slender-looking framework of wooden beams.

The outer edge of the limestone dome was fringed with drooping plants that stood out in bright patches of sunlight against the gloom of the cavern beneath. I remained in this monastery for some days, while my friends returned at once to Foochow. There were only three monks in residence here; one a mere boy full of fun, the second an able-bodied youth, and lastly, the abbot, who was old, infirm, and blind. I was accommodated with an apartment commanding a good view of the valley far beneath, and built out of thin pine planks, plastered over with lime. Inside this chamber were a pine table, a pine chair, and a pine bed, and on the latter the same unyielding wooden pillow which forms its usual cheap, and durable, appurtenance. As for the bedstead itself, it was a kind of square chocolate-coloured well of wood; and in this unluxurious contrivance I had to pass the nights, which here were extremely cold. My coolies slept in the apartment beneath, packed together like sardines, to keep themselves warm. Every evening, at about sunset, my friends, dressed in their yellow canonicals, went up into the temple to pray. One knelt to the right, the other to the left, of a small altar, and the third took up his place between the two; and then they serenaded their gods, to the monotonous accompaniment of the usual Buddhist instruments. The fervour of a long-winded prayer was much impaired in my eyes when I found that it was meaningless mummery to the young devotee who chanted it. After a time the latter got up and exercised himself, by striking a huge bell with a wooden mallet. Not content with this, he next attacked a monstrous but unoffending drum with equal vigour, saying some hard things about it under his breath the while; and thus ended this worship, the old monk striding out again into the court, and looking to me blinder than he could ever have known himself to be.

At dawn I was awoke by the repetition of the same noisy rites. The mornings were dark and chilly, and the opposite mountains looked like a mammoth figure, asleep in a very damp place, the heavy fleecy clouds resembling a covering that left half the recumbent body exposed. The black pines nodded and creaked dismally, and the bamboos bent till I thought they would break, in the blast that swept the valley.

On one of the altars I saw an image known as the 'Laughing Buddha,' the god of longevity; and before this jovial-looking idol, a sort of joss-stick time-piece had been set up. This time-piece consists of a series of thin fire-sticks, placed parallel to each other, over a flat clay bed contained in a box of bronze.

Each stick will burn for twelve hours, and a fresh one is ignited when the one already burning is about to expire. Thus the time of day, or night, might be ascertained at a glance. This fire, like the vestal fires of Rome, so the old monk assured me, had been smouldering uninterruptedly for untold years before he came to the place.

'Ku-Shan,' or 'Drum Mountain,' stands about seven miles below Foochow, and forms part of a range that there rises abruptly out of the level cultivated plain. The mountain enjoys a wide celebrity, as the great 'Ku-Shan' monastery is built in a valley near its summit, on a site said in ancient times to have been the haunt of poisonous snakes or dragons, able to diffuse pestilence, raise up storms, or blight the harvest crops.

One Ling-chiau, a sage, was entreated to put a stop to these ravages; so the good man, repairing to the pool in which the evil serpents dwelt, recited a ritual called the Hua-yen treatise, before which, like wise serpents, they took instant flight. It must indeed have been a powerful composition, for not even deadly snakes would risk a second recital; and the Emperor, hearing of the miracle, erected the Hua-yen monastery on the spot in the year 784.

The establishment, though repeatedly destroyed, has been constantly rebuilt on its original foundations, receiving considerable additions from time to time, until at the present day it accommodates 200 monks.

The ascent from the plain is a steep and tedious one, but many picturesque views of the surrounding country are to be obtained *en route*, and we reach the monastery itself at length, through a grove of ancient pine-trees, 2,500 feet above the level of the sea.

The entire establishment covers a large area, resembling, in this respect, the great Lamasary at Peking, and forming indeed by far the most prosperous and extensive Buddhist monastery I have seen in the south of China. Inside the main entrance sit four colossal images of the protectors of the Buddhist faith,

TWO OF THE GUARDIANS OF BUDDHA, KU-SHAN MONASTERY.

and two of these the reader may see reproduced in the accompanying illustration. Ku-Shan monastery, like almost all such edifices in China, is made up of three great detached buildings, set one behind the other, in a spacious paved courtyard; and, opening inwards from the walls which surround this enclosure, we may see the apartments of the monks. At this shrine a number of relics of Buddha are shown, and it is said that they annually draw crowds of weary pilgrims from afar. Sacred animals, too, are maintained in the grounds; and if there be any member of the brute creation that has shown more than usual instinct, it will find a welcome reception here. At the time of my visit to the place the most interesting of the sacred creatures was a praying bull. This bull, so the story goes, was being one day conveyed by its owner to the slaughter-house, when, bursting its bonds, it rushed off down the streets of the city, and never drew breath till it reached the Governor-General's yamen, at the moment when his Excellency was stepping into his sedan. Then, falling on its knees before the representative of the Imperial throne, this long-horned suppliant was heard to utter a short prayer for mercy. The governor, mute with amazement, could only motion to his retainers to remove the animal, and they forthwith conveyed it to the monastery, where it has ever since luxuriated in a sort of bovine paradise, with no Damoclean pole-axe to dread. A story afterwards got abroad that this venerated bull, when it charged the Governor's yamen, had really been tripped up by the steps there, but this can be nothing more than a scandalous invention got up by the impious, and we only notice the report to condemn it.

The 'Three Holy Ones,' the chief images of every Buddhist temple, were here as conspicuous as usual in the central shrine; each figure being in this instance more than thirty feet in height, and rising up behind the customary altar bespread with candelabra and votive offerings of various sorts.

I remained three days in this place, and occupied some of my leisure in visiting the rooms of the priests, one among them more frequently than the rest.

THE KU-SHAN HERMIT.

Having mounted the ladder by which access to this chamber was to be gained, we entered a bare apartment, lit by a small window above, and furnished with a deal table and a chair. Within I was always certain to discover some member of the order, improving himself by sitting, like an image, meditating on the precepts of his sect, and at long intervals tolling a bell suspended in a tower above.

Then again, away some distance from the central temple, in one of the many beautiful avenues on the mountain-side, was a water-bell, that could be heard tolling there, night and day; and just below the little shrine to which this bell was consecrated, a deep dark glen wound its way beneath the thick shade of a wood, and between rocky precipices that walled it in on either side. Against the foot of one of these rocks a small hut had been constructed. One day I ventured within it, and found a Buddhist image set up on a stony ledge inside. I was thinking it was about the finest thing of the sort I had seen for some time, when the head moved forward, the limbs unbent, and the idol descended from its perch—'*Verus incessu patuit Deus*'?. No, I can hardly venture to affirm so much of this bald-headed, yellow-robed god.

'Tsing, tsing, sir, good morning; what side you come?' was his greeting as he lighted on the ground. Less awe-stricken than might perhaps have been expected, I returned the enquiry, and asked: 'What side *you* come?' to which his response was quickly vouchsafed: 'Long time my got this side.' This, then, was the hermit, of whom report had said so much. It turned out that he had been an Amoy trader, and after years of strife with the world, had come to end his days, and repent of his sins, within this mossy dell. At the water-bell shrine there was a most unholy and very tall raw-boned priest, who, after we had inspected the miraculous water-wheel, and listened to the dreary tones of the bell, followed us everywhere up and down, demanding a present which his displeasing pertinacity determined us to withhold. Buddhists do not take life, otherwise this cadaverous-looking fellow who pestered us for money would gladly have sacrificed mine.

Among the other temples in the neighbourhood of Foochow one of the most striking is 'The Island Temple,' which covers the entire surface of a small islet about eight miles from the city. This shrine is dedicated to the 'Queen of Heaven,' a deity worshipped

THE ISLAND TEMPLE, RIVER MIN.

by the boating population on the river Min. A banyan-tree grows upon the islet, so as partly to shade the shrine; and it is supposed that the shrub depends solely for its nourishment upon the bounty of the goddess, for its roots are rivetted to all appearance in the solid stone.

The nearest tea-plantations, in this province, are in the Paeling Hills, about fifteen miles north of Foochow. These I visited in company as the guest of two of my

Foochow friends. We put up at a small temple on one of the farms, and made a three days' stay in the locality. Here some foreigners, who had visited the district before us, had imparted a very limited and confused acquaintance with the English tongue to the priest who presided at the shrine. It therefore startled us, when we approached the edifice, to be met by this ragged follower of Buddha, evidently proud to parade his knowledge of our language, with the salutation: 'Good morning, can do! you bet!' Can do what, we enquired; but alas! our friend's vocabulary was limited to this single phrase. He said he had forgotten all the rest, and perhaps he had no great need to bemoan his loss.

The clouds lay like a wet blanket on the hills throughout the whole of our stay. It was in vain each morning that we looked for a gleam of sunshine, as we watched the vapour lifting before the wind, and then falling into its old position once more. Nevertheless, we inspected the farms as well as the fog and rain would allow, and noticed the curious effects of the mist as it lay in pools in the valleys, or parted in fleecy windows, through which glimpses of the bright sunny plain and the villages far below might be descried. And yet at other times, as we looked back along the steep path, we could but just make out the heads and shoulders of our coolies, toiling through a wreath of cloud that wrapped their feet in mist, and struggling onward with their burdens up hill.

One of the plantations in these Paeling Hills was said to belong to a Cantonese comprador, employed in a foreign Hong. It was of considerable extent—a rare feature in these tea-growing regions, where the cultivation of the shrub is carried on piecemeal, after some such method as follows. The farms are usually small, seldom exceeding a few acres in size, and are rented by the poor from the landowners of the district. To these landowners the tenants undertake to dispose of their crops at a certain stipulated price. Thus the men who grow that tea which is a source of so much wealth to China very rarely possess any capital at all themselves; and, like millions of their labouring fellow-countrymen, they can earn but a hard-won sustenance out of the luxury which they thus produce. Those farmers who are so fortunate as to be able to rent their land without first mortgaging the crops are esteemed men of affluence. At the proper season—that is, usually in the beginning of April—the first picking of the leaves takes place. These leaves, when gathered, are dried partially in the sun, and then offered for sale in baskets, at a kind of fair, at which all the neighbourhood attends. The native buyers from the foreign ports—usually Cantonese—here enter upon a keen competition, and buy up as much as they can of the leaf. In the end the lots bought, from a variety of these small farms, are mixed together by the purchaser, and then subjected to the firing already described, up-country, in houses hired specially for that purpose.

Thousands of poor women and children are next employed in picking out stems and stalks; after which the leaves are winnowed, the cured portion is carried away, and the uncured left behind to be subjected again to the fire. When the firing process is completed, the tea is sifted, and separated into two or three different parcels, or 'chops' as they are called, the quality of each parcel varying with the quantity prepared at a time. Thus the first and highest 'chops' consist of the smallest and best-twisted leaves; the second is somewhat inferior; while the third is made of the stalks, dust, and siftings. This last, which is perfectly innocuous and wholesome, is used in this country to mix with the better sorts of teas, and thus to produce the cheap good teas of commerce.

These parcels or chops are next packed into chests of about 90 lbs., half-chests of 40 or 45 lbs., and boxes of 21 lbs., lined each of them with lead, and thus forwarded to the open ports for sale. Most of the Bohea teas are brought down to Foochow by the river Min—a voyage, as we shall presently see, requiring no ordinary nerve and skill. The cargoes, as a rule, begin to arrive at about the end of April; but at the time I speak of (1871) the market, for two or three seasons past, had not been opened till some time in June. The year before, the mandarins gave native dealers credit for the duties on the leaf, and thus aided them to hold back their teas until scarcity should force the market into rates highly favourable to China. The Europeans do not seem to succeed in banding together like the Chinese to secure the tea crop on profitable terms. The probable advantage to be gained by being first in the field presents a temptation too great for the impetuous foreign merchant to resist. But although the Chinese sellers enjoy many facilities, such as borrowing money from the banks in Foochow against the chops which they hold, they have to pay high rates of interest, and the up-country competition among themselves, too, is strong; so that they are not unfamiliar with losses—and heavy ones, too, sometimes. On the whole, however, by dint of caution and commercial combination, they have made their trade steadily remunerative and sure—a fact which may readily be gathered from the great wealth of the Chinese tea merchants, both at Foochow and elsewhere

But let us now proceed up-country, and gather some notion of the difficulties which beset the transit of this precious herb. I made an excursion for 200 miles up the Min, as far as Yin-ping city, in the company of Mr. Justice Doolittle, whose valuable book on the 'Social Life of the Chinese' is the result of years of painstaking labour and careful observation among the people of this district. Armed with the requisite passports, we started for Shui-kow, at mid-day on December 2, in a yacht kindly placed at my disposal by one of the English merchants at Foochow.

Boating on a Chinese river, and with a Chinese crew, is always a trying experience to the temper of a European, except where the men have been bound by contract to perform their work for a fixed price and within a given period of time. If this precaution has been neglected, the notion takes possession of the boatmen that foreigners are by nature wealthy, and that as a duty to themselves—who are always, both by birth and by necessity, extremely poor—they must make the most of the rare opportunity which good fortune has cast in their way. Inspired by considerations such as these, the men set themselves to enjoy a good deal more than their usual scanty leisure, a good deal more food, a longer spell of the opium-pipe, and deeper drains out of the samshu-flask. Hence, in one's diary, such jottings as the following by no means unfrequently recur: 'The men have been amusing themselves all day long running the boat on to sandbanks, and eating rice.' 'Tracking-line entangled again with that of another boat; two crews quarrelling for half an hour, another half hour spent in apologies, and a third in disentangling the lines.'

I halted to take a view at a place called 'Pak-taou' (white-head). Here a poor pedlar, marching along the bank, his wares slung over his shoulder, became so engrossed in watching my operations that he failed to observe two buffaloes coming up from the opposite direction. These buffaloes took fright at my camera, charged along the path, and sent the pedlar spinning heels over head down the bank. But he was a pedlar of no ordinary mould; he gathered up his bundle, shouldered it once more, and came back to finish his observations on the spot from which he had been so suddenly dislodged.

Sunday we spent quietly at a place called 'Teuk-kai,' or Bamboo Crags. Here I had a walk ashore with my boy Ahong, and stopped for awhile to rest on a green mossy bank, whence our boat could dimly be made out through a sheet of mist, that rose above the river, like the steam from a cauldron's mouth. This vapour crept onwards up the mountain in a number of grotesque shapes, here and there forming beautiful vignettes out of the clumps of giant pines, and in a moment blotting out the picture again as it rolled waywardly along the woody steeps. These mists were a phenomena of daily occurrence, caused, I suppose, by the difference of temperature between the water and the air. We next passed over a lovely bit of country, through olive and orange plantations, where the trees bent down beneath their fruit, and the air seemed laden with perpetual fragrance. In one orchard we fell in with a watchman ensconced in a snug little straw hut containing a bamboo table, a tea-pot, two chairs, and a fine cat and kittens. The old man—he was very old, he could not tell us how old, but he had been watching the place, he said, for more than half a century—showed us the way to the farm, conducting us

A TRAVELLING BLACKSMITH AT A FARM-HOUSE.

through fields of sugar-cane to the group of picturesque well-built brick houses of which the settlement was composed. That portion of this homestead allotted to the proprietor's family we found to be very strongly walled round, and near at hand, in a small out-house, the family physician had his home. This gentleman,

Akum by name (who was watching a travelling blacksmith at work), received us with what I took to be a friendly spirit; but the expression of his face was a difficult thing to interpret, for his eyes were defective, and his otherwise passable nose had lost both bridge and point; hence, while one eye beamed with a kindly warmth, the other kept strict guard over the broken bridge. We entered his shop, and the people came out to have a look at me. Many of them had never set eyes on a foreigner before, and I was evidently an object of curious interest to a group of really pretty women and chubby children. The instant I moved they all rushed into the stronghold, and could there be seen peering out from all sorts of holes and corners. I made the old man a small present, and he gave me some fine oranges in return.

When we had left this place, and had sat down on a hill-side to talk over old times and former scenes of travel, Ahong confessed to me, among other matters, that he had no particular religious views at all. He had, at one time, been a Christian in Singapore, but had got bullied out of his change of faith by his friends. In a general way he thought it a good thing to have plenty of pork while alive; then to be laid in a comfortable coffin, and buried in a dry place; and hereafter to have one's spirit fed and clothed continuously by surviving sons. I spoke to him about Christianity, and about the folly of worshipping idols, when every flower and insect around told so plainly of the great unseen God, but I doubt whether I produced much impression upon his tough Chinese heart.

Next day we reached Shui-kow, and found it built on the slopes of the hills, on the left bank of the river.

SHUI-KOW

This town was unlike any which I had seen on the plains. There was something new in its piles of buildings, towering story above story, and in its picturesque situations; and here, too, I found that a water system had been elaborated out of a complex

CHINESE PLOUGH, FUKIEN PROVINCE.

series of bamboo pipes and gutters, which passed from house to house, and brought constant supplies of water from a spring more than a mile away, in the hills.

At Shui-kow I hired a 'rapid-boat' to take us

on to Yen-ping-fu. Our captain was Cheng-Show, or rather his wife, a lady who had a great deal to say both for him and herself too; who stood no more than four feet high, and yet talked about half as much again as any other woman twice her size. Of a truth she was the wonder of her sex, the great female phenomenon of the modern Chinese age! Thus, when we ascended the first rapid, there was Mrs. Cheng to be seen well to the fore, at one moment nursing her baby; at another, the child had been tossed into a basket, and the mother was fending her boat with a long pole from destruction on the rocks. Then to her brat again, or to cooking, cleaning or husband-baiting; to each and every pursuit she was found equal, as fancy prompted or necessity compelled. Ours was a small boat, like all the others, carrying a high bridge, and a rudder in the shape of a long oar which swung on a pivot aft. This oar was nearly as long as the boat itself, and its effect when used was to make the vessel turn at once in its own length. The craft is built entirely of pine; is as strong as it is light; and admirably adapted in every respect for the navigation of the perilous rapids which begin to show themselves about half a mile above Shui-kow. All these rapids are full of rugged rocks, rising some of thèm above the stream, and some lurking more dangerously below. We anchored for the night close to a military station, if two or three shanties, and the half-dozen miserable looking soldiers armed with matchlocks who occupied them, could be honoured with so dignified a name.

Next morning, as usual, there was a thick fog upon the river. This prevented our seeing more than two or three feet around the boat, and put a stop to all traffic till within an hour of noon. Our halting-place that evening was the village of Ching-ku-kwan; and there Mr. Doolittle and myself went ashore to inspect a Snake Temple. There was no image of the snake to be seen in this shrine; but the tablet of the snake king was there, set up for worship in a holy place; and we learned that, during the seventh month, a living snake becomes the object of adoration. Next day Mrs. Cheng and her husband had a little conjugal disagreement. The lady stamped her tiny feet on the re-echoing deck, and ramped, and raged like a fury, threatening to cut her throat rather than touch an oar of that boat again. As for Captain Cheng, he sat meekly smoking his pipe, a true example of marital equanimity, waiting till the storm should be over-past. Half an hour later his wife was working away as busily as ever. Each night the boat is arched over, waggon-fashion, with a telescopic arrangement of bamboo matting, forty feet long, ten feet wide, and four feet high, which covers the entire deck. My friend and I occupied a small space at the bow. Ahong, the cook, and fourteen boatmen, were stretched out amidships, a small space at the stern being curtained off for the captain and his spouse. The representatives of three generations of the Cheng family are to be found living on board the craft. First the grandfather. He does almost nothing except smoke; and his pipe, a bamboo-cane with a knob at the end of it, he cherishes with wonderful affection. On his head is a relic of antiquity as venerable as himself—the tattered framework of a greasy-looking felt hat; while as for his thickly-padded jacket, it is reported that he removes that garment from his person about once a week, in order to destroy the small colonists that disturb his repose. For upwards of half a century he had been learning to swallow the smoke of his pipe, but with only partial success. Once or twice I fancied that he had fairly choked himself, and was about to expire; but he came to himself again by-and-bye, and was seen puffing more vigorously than before.

As soon as the roofs were drawn over for the night, smoking commenced; the entire crew, Mrs. Cheng and all, setting to work in business-like fashion; and, as there was no outlet for the fumes, the atmosphere can be imagined much more easily than it could be endured. On the following day we passed a newly-wrecked boat, which had struck a sunken rock and then gone down. We also encountered a second boat dashing down the same rapid with a fatal way on her. She was bearing straight for the breakers away from the main channel; the helmsman could not alter her course, and so she, too, struck and settled down, but not before the crew had had time to scramble out on the rocks, and make the wreck fast with a cable.

At one little village, where we went ashore, a number of small-footed women were washing clothes in the stream. At our approach they fled with startling celerity, scaling the rocks, and finding foothold where only cloven-hoofed goats might have been supposed to make their way.

The river at this point presents a variety of most attractive scenes. Between the many rapids great masses of rock rose up in bold headlands, covered above with waving plumes of tall flowering grasses, and draped with a profusion of foliage that reached right down to the shore, and was there reflected in the placid pools. Beyond the banks we see hills, dales, and giant rocks mingled together in grand disorder, clothed with dark pines and other trees, and wearing rich autumnal tints.

As for the rapids, their tumultuous cataracts alternate with great basins of smooth water slipping glassily onward from shoal to shoal. In some rapids the channel was so thickly bestrewn with rocks as to be concealed from view at but a very short distance off; while in the great Yen-ping rapid my ears were deafened by the roar of the boiling torrent, and my sight bewildered by the wide expanse of leaping and foaming water. Here, as we ascended, the ancient mariner Cheng flung his pipe down in a moment of peril; shouted out to the trackers on shore; and, snatching up a pole, planted it on a sunken rock to ease the strain that threatened to snap the cable by which we were being tracked from the bank, and send us to destruction on the rocks. It was an instant of intense excitement and danger; the power of the rushing water seemed to baffle the efforts of the crew, till all hands were at the poles, and with one combined effort we moved slowly up the current; the old man prostrating himself, and preparing a burnt offering of paper in honour of the sailors' protecting goddess.

On Sunday we reached Yen-ping, in time for service at the Methodist Mission Chapel in that place. Yen-ping-fu stands on a hill, and faces the main stream at a point where it is fed by two nearly equal tributaries, the one flowing from the Bohea Hills, and the other from a source further to the south-east. The town contains a population of about thirty thousand souls, and does a considerable trade in paper, lackered ware, baskets, and tea. The foot of the hill was encircled by a high wall, from within which rose an inclined plane of roofs, broken here and there by groves of trees and temples, but still almost appearing one solid slope of tiled steps, over which an Alpine tourist might scramble to the outermost wall above, whose top could be seen in a faint line sweeping round the heights that closed in the city from behind. Beyond this hill, which looked as if it had been made for the town that covers it, a high range of mountains rose up in a deep purple belt, like a great protecting barrier.

The Mission-house, in the main thoroughfare, was a miserable place enough, and we learnt that no one would let a decent house to Christians. The native missionary, when we entered the chapel, was conducting the morning service in the midst of an attentive congregation. He resided here with his family, and looked happy and contented: although, as I have said, his abode was a poor one, built and partitioned off with bamboo-laths and plaster, so thin that one could have pushed one's finger through the walls; while the roof was festooned with cobwebs, and admitted more daylight and air than was either necessary or agreeable. The interior beneath, however, wore a clean and even cheerful look. The back of this dwelling, like many others, was perched upon the city wall; and there was a path running beneath the fortifications, along which I picked my way with caution, and yet narrowly escaped being tripped up by a herd of pigs, as they rushed to banquet upon some filthy refuse dropping down from a house above.

Yen-ping was a Chinese city, very much so, indeed, and yet one could breathe pure mountain air on its upper wall, and encounter some very pretty sights.

On one occasion, when taking a view from a steep hill on the other side of the river, and while making my way up to a level space, I slipped my footing and caught hold of some grass that stood twelve or fifteen feet high there. The blades of this grass are furnished with an array of sharp teeth, that ripped my hands up like a saw; but at the same time it saved me a rapid descent of about two hundred feet, and a final plunge of a clear hundred more into the river below. Near this place, in a small village, we found the two widows and family of a deceased mandarin sending a complete retinue to the spirit of their departed lord. A pile of huge paper-models of houses and furniture, boats and sedans, ladies-in-waiting and gentlemen-pages, were brought down to the banks of the river and there burned before the wailing widows. One of these ladies seemed to me to weep much more bitterly than the other, but this might only be a fancy of mine. These effigies are supposed to be transformed by fire into the spiritual reality of the things which they represent. Many of the articles were covered with tin-foil, and when the sacrifice was over a seedy-looking trader bought the ashes, that he might sift them and secure the tin that had refused to put on an ethereal shape.

Many of the men hereabouts appeared deformed, but the deformity was due to the small charcoal furnaces which they carried concealed beneath the dress, and used to keep their bodies warm. As there are no fire-places in the houses, these portable furnaces prove very convenient substitutes. At first, when I saw so many humps about, I supposed that some special disease must be common in the place, or else that the sufferers had gathered themselves together from different parts of the empire to test the efficacy of some curative spring, like those hot wells near Foochow, where I have seen crowds of feeble and infirm folk bathing in the healing vapours. But the little copper furnaces encased in basket-work supplied a less melancholy explanation of the mystery.

When I watched the coolness, pluck, and daring, with which these poor river navigators will shoot the rapids of the river Min, risking their lives in every voyage—in a country where there are no insurances, except such as the guilds may chance to afford, and where no higher reward is to be gained than a hand-to-mouth subsistence on the most wretched fare—I began to get a truer insight into the manly and hardy qualities latent in this mis-governed Chinese race.

In some of these watery steeps the channel winds and writhes from right to left, and forms acute angles among the rocks at every two or three boats' lengths. Once, when we descended, our frail craft tearing down these bends at a fearful speed, I thought for a moment that our fate was sealed, for it seemed impossible that the helmsman could ever bring the vessel round in time to clear a huge rock which rose up right ahead. There he stood on the bridge, calm and erect, with an iron grasp on the long rudder, impassive until we were just plunging on to the rock; and then, as I prepared to leap for life, he threw his whole weight on to the oar, and brought the boat round with a sweep that cleared the danger by the breadth of a hair. Thus we shot onwards, down! down! down! like a feather tossed to and fro by the caprice of the irresistible waves.

As we passed down stream we saw a great number

of men fishing with cormorants. These fishermen poled themselves about on bamboo-rafts, and on each raft was a basket, and two or three cormorants trained to dive and bring up fish for their owners. As I intended to take some pictures on the way down to Foochow, my friend, who was pressed for time, determined to find his way home in a native passenger-boat that was about to leave Shui-kow. So after dinner I accompanied him on board, not without a last vain effort, as he was but in feeble health, to persuade him to complete the voyage in the yacht or house-boat in which we had come. A Chinese passenger-boat makes a pretty swift trip, and may be very suitable for natives, but it does not quite come up to our European notions of comfort. Thus the steerage accommodation consists of a long low cabin, in which one can scarcely kneel upright; and within this narrow space we found about fifty persons stowed away. Many were pedlars carrying their wares along with them for sale; and the air of this packing-box was strongly tainted with garlic, tobacco, samshu, opium, and a variety of other Chinese perfumes, which issued from the mass of humanity that writhed and tumbled about, in fruitless efforts to discover places for repose. When they were a little settled, we had literally to grope our way over a reeking platform of half-naked limbs and bodies, and amid a torrent of cursing and vile abuse, in order to reach the state cabin, where my stout friend, after sundry efforts, succeeded in depositing himself at last. This cabin measured about four feet by three. The door was shut, and there he was, in a sort of locker with one or two openings to admit the air, or rather the stench and din, of the unwashed noisy crowd in the steerage. So we parted, to meet again and recount our adventures in Foochow.

As I walked through the streets of Shui-kow on my way back to the boat, I lost my dog 'Spot,' who had been my constant companion; but recollecting a door in a wall that had been suddenly opened and shut, I felt certain my pet had been there caught up and taken in, as his white silken hair was much admired by the Chinese. Back I trudged to the door; and as, when I whistled, I seemed to hear a whining response, I commenced a vigorous assault on the entrance. My knocking soon collected a crowd, to whom my difficulties were explained; when, after a knock and a push more dangerous than the rest, my dog was quietly handed over the wall to me, and we turned our backs upon the place to descend to Foochow, and to photograph the points of interest on the route.

CHAPTER XIII.

Steam Traffic in the China Sea—In the Wake of a Typhoon—Shanghai —Notes of its Early History—Japanese Raids—Shanghai Foreign Settlement—Paul Sü, or 'Sü-kwang-ki'—Shanghai City—Ningpo—Native Soldiers—Snowy Valley—The Mountains—Azaleas—The Monastery of the Snowy Crevice—The Thousand Fathom Precipice—Buddhist Monks—The Yangtsze Kiang—Hankow—The Upper Yangtsze—Ichang—The Gorges—The Great Tsing-tan Rapid—Mystic Mountain Lights—A Dangerous Disaster—Kwei-fu—Our Return—Kiukiang—Nanking; its Arsenal—The Death of Tsing-kwo-fan—Chinese Superstition.

THE opening of the Suez Canal has probably wrought as great a change in the China trade as in the commerce of the Malayan Archipelago; and nowhere is this change more marked than in the carrying traffic from port to port along the coasts of China. Old lumbering junks, lorchas, and even square-rigged sailing ships, are gradually disappearing before the splendidly-equipped steamers of the local companies that ply regularly between the different stations from Hongkong to Newchwang; and then innumerable vessels, owned, not a few of them, by private firms, as well as by public companies, frequently find lucrative employment, when the tea and silk seasons have not yet begun, either in running between the treaty ports, or in making short voyages to the rice-markets of Indo-China.

It was my good fortune to make a coasting trip to

Shanghai in a fine steamer belonging to a private line, engaged in the tea trade during the greater portion of the year, but at that time making a cruise northward till the Hankow tea-market should open, and hence touching *en route* at one or two of the places to which the reader has already been introduced. Our captain was a quiet, homely man, who prided himself on his ship, his officers, and crew, and on the sumptuous fare of his table. He had traded on the coast of China for many years, had been wrecked several times, had fought for his life with pirates, and battled with typhoons as pitiless as they. He was a genius, too, in his way. Thus he had invented several new nautical instruments, too advanced for the present age, and had even designed a safety-ship, that would ride out the fiercest storm. But this vessel, like the instruments, had not yet been constructed and put to the test. He had also a new theory of storms, based on personal experience and actual observation. It would be necessary, however, for the man who would verify those important conclusions, not only to trust himself to the mighty deep during the worst of weather, but to sail boldly into the heart of the tempest, that he might there, with his anemometer, measure the force of the wind, and try his barometer upon the rarity of the air. As we neared Shanghai the glass indicated either that a typhoon was approaching, or else that we were just upon its verge. The latter conclusion was the true one. It turned out that we had followed in the wake of a hurricane, and thus our experience afforded a good example of the limited area to which the circle of these typhoons are frequently confined. We had encountered nothing save calms and light winds throughout our passage;

and yet, when we entered Shanghai river, we found many ships disabled, some of them swept clear to the deck—masts, spars, and rigging, having all gone over the side. Here we had to wait twelve hours till a licensed pilot came on board; and when that individual did at last make his appearance, he gravely remarked that he was only a fifteen-foot man, but that he could make it all right with another pilot of superior depth, to take us up. What he meant to convey to us was that his license only allowed him to pilot vessels drawing fifteen feet. An unfortunate accident occurred as we were steaming up the Wong-poo to the wharf at Shanghai. The Chinese have a superstitious belief that bad luck will attend their voyage, if they fail, at starting, to cross the bows of a vessel as she sails across their track; and so, as we steamed on with a full head of steam, we perceived a native trading-boat making frantic efforts with sails and sculls to pass under our bows. The whistle was plied, but in vain. On they pulled to their own certain destruction; and the ear-piercing shriek of the engine must have sounded to some of the victims like a wail that foretold their death. The engines could not be backed amid such a crowd of shipping, and I was gazing helplessly over our bulwarks when we came crashing through the dry timbers of the fated craft. There was a yell of despair, and the wreck was next seen drifting down the stream. A number of the crew had been projected by the shock some distance into the water; others clung to their property until it was submerged; but very fortunately none of them perished, as a number of boats had seen the incident, and had put off to their assistance at once.

Shanghai has always been able to hold its own as the great Chinese emporium of foreign trade. It was therefore with feelings of profound interest, that I, for the first time, beheld the splendid foreign settlement that now stands there on the banks of the Wong-poo, at a spot which about thirty years ago was a mere swamp, dotted with a few fisher huts, and inhabited by a miserable semi-aquatic sort of Chinese population. In 1831 Dr. Gutzlaff, who visited the place for the first time in a junk, describes it as the centre of a great native trade, and tells us that from this port, 'more than a thousand small vessels go up to the north several times annually, exporting silk and other Kiangnan manufactures,' and besides, that an extensive traffic was carried on by Fukien men with the Indian Archipelago. But we may venture much further back in the history of the town. Several centuries ago, even before the Wong-poo river became a navigable stream at all, there was a great mart established in this locality on the banks of the present Soo-chow Creek, twenty-five miles distant from the harbour in which we have just anchored.[1] The topographical history of the district is full of records telling of the physical changes to which the vast alluvial plain where Shanghai stands has from time to time been subjected. Streams have been silted up, new channels have spontaneously opened ; and yet, amid constant difficulties and never-ceasing alterations, the ever-important trade of the place has been maintained within the same narrow area, where the annual floods of the Yang-tsze-kiang deposit their alluvium on the margin of the ocean, and raise new land up out of its bed.

[1] See the *Shanghai Hein Chi.*

The political, as well as the commercial and physical history of this region, is no less full of interest. In process of time the old Wu-sung-kiang became innavigable; and during the thirteenth century, a settlement was founded on the present site of Shanghai, to which trade was rapidly transferred by the closing of the old waterway: finally, in A.D. 1544, the settlement was converted into a walled city, as a defence against the repeated attacks of the Japanese. These Japanese raids, which date from A.D. 1361, when the Ming dynasty had just come to the throne, were not confined solely to this quarter, but distributed generally over the maritime provinces in the north. The Japanese, time after time, proved more than a match for their less warlike foes; but the latter always managed, in the long run, to prevent the daring invaders from obtaining a permanent foothold upon their coveted shores. These Chinese successes were sometimes secured by intrigue and diplomacy, or by fair promises and bribes; the slow-moving, crushing ponderosities of Chinese warfare, being only resorted to when all else had failed.

To illustrate these two methods of repelling an invading force, I will relate the following story. In 1543 when the Japanese had spoiled, and laid waste, no small extent of the country around Shanghai, the latter, seeing that she was too feeble to fight against her enemies with success, had recourse to intrigue. Accordingly, the Governor-General of the province invited the Japanese leaders, 'Thsu-hai,' 'Chen-tung,' 'Mayeh,' and 'Wang-chen' to come over to the side of the Chinese; promising them the rewards of high rank, and untold treasure, if such valiant leaders would but join the Imperial standard. Tempted by the offer, they presented themselves to arrange conditions, and were forthwith seized, dispatched to Peking, and there put to an ignominious death. On another occasion it is reported that the Japanese came down upon their enemy with a fleet of 300 vessels; and after carrying all before them, and plundering to their hearts' content, they departed laden with their spoil; the Chinese troops pursuing them valiantly out of the country, and making an imposing hostile demonstration on the shore, as they unfurled the sails of their ships. It will be gathered from such facts as these, which are taken from the native topographical history of Shanghai, that if the Formosa difficulty be not settled peacefully, it will by no means be the first occasion on which Japan has crossed swords with China. In ancient times the Japanese had the best of it; but ere long the wealth, and superior resources of the Chinese drove their foes back, and taught them to confine their warlike spirits within the narrow limits of their own islands. Probably a similar result, arising from a similar cause, may be expected of these two old enemies should they now, once again, go to war; the civilised world looking on the while, and watching the varying issues of the conflict to its uncertain close. But Japanese raids on Shanghai would be less likely to succeed now-a-days, when we consider the world-wide interests that centre in the small foreign settlement there, protected by the flags of the most powerful and civilised nations in the world. It is a place where there are close on a score of different nationalities, ruled over by a municipal body, whose members are chosen from among the resident community, irrespective of nation, caste, or creed.

As to the settlement itself, those of my readers who have not visited China will feel interested in a brief description of its present appearance. The approach by the river almost looks like that of any busy prosperous European seaport. There one finds ships of all nations; and, anchored in mid-channel, or making their way to their moorings, a long line of ocean steamers; while steam-launches, bearing mails and despatches, dart in and out among the crowd of native craft that are seen around, with their brown sails spread out to the breeze, like winged insects skimming the glassy surface of the stream. Everywhere around there are signs of ceaseless activity and busy life. Far away as the eye can reach into the dim distance, not an inch of vacant space on the broad river can be discovered; and yet, looming out from a forest of masts and spars, and from a dark cloud of smoke, we see the hull of a great steamer crowding up to join the throng that wait to bear their precious burdens down the tortuous channels to the sea. At the wharves, there are ships loading or discharging cargo; and amid the din of voices and the throbbing of engines we can hear the songs of the sailors, the rattle of chains, and the dull splash of anchors as they drop into the turbid water. Advancing further up the river, we pass rows of storehouses, foundries, dockyards and sheds. Next to these, the substantial buildings on the American concession; and then a full view opens before us of the public garden, and the imposing array of European offices, which front the river, on the English concession ground. What surprised me most about this settlement was the absence of anything temporary or unfinished in the style of its buildings, such as might remind one that the place was, after all, nothing more than a trading depôt, planted on hostile and inhospitable shores, and sustained in its position in spite of the envy which its appearance excited among the rulers of the land. What pangs of regret and remorse must be awakened among these proud unenlightened men when, in their moments of honest reflection, they cast their eyes upon this 'Model Settlement,' and perceive that a handful of outer barbarians have, within the space of thirty years, done more with the little quagmire that was grudgingly allotted to them, than they themselves, with their highest efforts, have achieved anywhere in their own wide Empire, during all the untold centuries of its fame.

As I have said already, there is a finish about the whole settlement, a splendour and sumptuousness about its buildings, its wide roads, and breathing spaces, its spacious wharves, and elegant warehouses, that stand as a solemn rebuke to the niggardliness and grinding despotism which, within the narrow limits of the greatest walled cities of China, have penned hundreds of thousands of struggling beings in the most temporary abodes; there to carry on a ceaseless strife for existence, breathing the fetid air of narrow polluted alleys, exposed to the constant risk of fearful conflagration, and the grim horrors of pestilence or famine. Good men and true I know to exist among the officials of China; and they, seeing all this, and feeling conscious of the freedom and higher life which European communities enjoy, would gladly strike off the fetters that have broken the spirit of their countrymen, and would lift them up, if they but knew how, from their low estate to taste the purer air of that freedom, for which the waves of rebellion that have swept across the pages of their history tell us that they have never ceased to pine.

Perhaps the Tien-wang, better known as the Taiping chief, or 'Heavenly King,' had some such vision, when he first started on his career; ere his mind gave way before the intoxication of easily-achieved success, and he became the drivelling fanatic that at length sank unwept to his doom within his gory palace at Nanking.

Sü-kwang-ki, or 'Paul Sü,' celebrated as the pupil of Mathew Ricci, the great Jesuit missionary of the sixteenth century, appears to have been a man who mourned over the condition of his country. He was a native of Shanghai, a scholar of great renown; and he not only aided Ricci in his translation of a number of the books of Euclid, but left behind him many valuable original works; notably one on agriculture, which is still highly prized. But although admitted by the Emperor 'Kia-tsing' and his successor to be a man of singular ability and foresight, his wise councils were disregarded, and he himself was repeatedly treated with suspicion, due to the intrigues of jealous rivals. Accordingly his counsel was set aside, and his measures for the preservation and defence of the last Chinese dynasty were systematically neglected. But to this day he occupies a shrine in one of the temples of Shanghai; and there his fellow-townsmen pay him reverent worship as a sort of divinely-inspired sage.

I can only say a word in passing about the present trade of Shanghai. Most of my readers are aware that in spite of a host of troubles (not the least of which was the Taiping rebellion, or rather I believe the attack upon the city by the short-sword or dagger rebels) it has continued to advance steadily, and has always maintained its position as the greatest emporium of China. It must be, at the same time, borne in mind that this commercial success is, in some measure at least, attributable to the semi-European customs administration which was inaugurated at this city in 1843, and which now extends its ramifications to all the open ports of the Empire

There are doubtless certain commercial grievances (such as the Lekin tax, and the inland transit dues) which still demand redress, or adjustment, at the hands of the central government; but it cannot be denied that the remodelling of the customs administration was the commencement of a new mercantile era, and has proved a great boon, not to the nations of Europe only, but also to the Chinese themselves.

Some of my readers will naturally enquire whence the labour came which transformed this dismal swamp into what I have just described; and built houses there fit for any capital of Europe, and infinitely superior to some of the edifices that adorn our own greatest ports. One might think that structures such as these must have been reared by skilled workmen from Europe; but a very short residence in Shanghai suffices to undeceive us. Then we mark the avidity with which the native builders, carpenters, and mechanics of every sort, compete with each other to win the remunerative employment which those buildings afford; and the facility with which they pick up the extended knowledge needful to enable them to carry out their contracts, and to impart to their work that elegance and perfection which the cultivated tastes of the foreign architect demand. But it is not to these buildings alone that we must look to discover the hidden resources of Chinese toil. Visit the dockyards and foundries, and there, too, watch the Chinese craftsmen, the shipwrights, engineers, carpenters, painters, and decorators, busily at work under European foremen, who bear the highest testimony to the capabilities of their men. Pass on next to the Kiang-nan arsenal, outside the city walls, and there you will find perhaps the highest development of Chinese technical industry, in the manufacture of rifles and field-guns, and the construction of ships of war.

The native walled city of Shanghai stands to the south of the foreign settlement, and is separated from it by the French concession ground, and by a canal which here sweeps round, and forms, with Soo-chow Creek and the river, a water boundary for the entire English ground. The latter, on its western side, supports a Chinese population of over 50,000 souls; but inside the walls of the Chinese city, in an area measuring little over a mile long by three-fourths of a mile in breadth, and in a densely crowded suburb on the water's edge close by, about 130,000 inhabitants reside.

Like all other Chinese towns, Shanghai has its tutelary deity, upon whom the Emperor, as brother of the Sun, has conferred an honorary title. This guardian of the fortunes of Shanghai stands in the 'Cheng-hwang-Miau' or 'Temple of the City God,' in the northern quarter of the town; and though he, and his shrine, have from time to time been rudely overthrown, both, after each disaster, have been reverently restored; and now he may be seen looking out upon wide pleasure-grounds—in a more or less dilapidated state, it is true—but still now and again regaled with theatrical performances, and leading, for an idol, a not altogether unenjoyable life. In the same spot are two drum-towers, superintended by a number of inferior deities, and used more especially to spread the alarm of fire, or to notify the approach of a foe. Then there is the Confucian temple; besides a host of other Buddhist and Taoist sacred edifices, occupying the best spaces of ground within a city where the miserable population have too often scarcely breathing space. The foreign settlement supports three hospitals for the benefit of the natives; but, as I have already noticed, many more such benevolent institutions are needed to relieve the be-drugged, be-sotted, and unfortunate sick among the vast population of the land.

Our route now lies away among the azalea-clad mountains in the province of Che-Kiang. But before re-embarking we must have a parting glance at the streets of the 'Model Settlement.'

There are no cabs; but the residents, many of them, possess private carriages. The substitute for the cab here is the wheelbarrow—a very undignified sort of conveyance, but nevertheless comfortable enough when one has once grown accustomed to its use. It is pleasant to see the Chinese domestics and their families; or native ladies dressed in silks, their glossy hair held in by a broad black velvet band with a spray of pearls in front, being propelled along the bund in their hand-carts: but they are not used among Europeans, excepting after dark. Ahong procured me two of these wheel-barrows from the nearest stand, and thus, with my two boys, my baggage, and 'Spot,' I set out for the Ning-po steamer. There is not much risk of accidents in a steady-going vehicle such as this. The coolie who propels it is neither skittish nor given to shying, and the pace he puts on is never dangerous.

The main roads, and the streets which branch in all directions from them, are wide ; and ample provision has thus been made for a traffic which tends constantly to increase ; they are level too, and smooth as a billiard-table, so that there at least one escapes the risk of

THE SHANGHAI WHEELBARROW.

broken limbs, or a slush-and-water grave in the pitfalls and mud-pools which disfigure the imperial highways of China.

The steamer sheers off from the wharf, and cautiously drops down through the shipping and out of the river, where she plunges merrily on the waves. A passenger on board gave us a strange account of the ancient port of Ningpo.

He said he had not been there for some years; but that the last time he was there he experienced difficulty in finding anybody about. 'Trade had deserted the place, and it seemed to be running to dry rot. I anchored below the settlement, and rowed up in a small boat, to see if I could find my consignee; at length, coming upon two semi-European, antiquated houses, with a few feet of clear ground in front of them, I went ashore; but still there was not a soul to be seen, until at last a miserable European emerged out of one of the houses, dressed in the garb of a bygone age. As soon as this strange being set eyes on me he gave a frantic shout of joy, and said, "My dear fellow, whoever you are, I am delighted to see you. You are the only European who has been here for many a day. I had almost forgotten my mother tongue; have you such a thing as a dollar?" "Yes," I said, "I am so fortunate as to possess one or two." "Let me see one, then, friend. Oh! let me see one!" He gazed upon it ardently for some time, and then said, "Ha! I have not seen one of these coins for a very long period." "Can you," I said, "direct me to Mr. Moulds', my consignee?" "That's my name, and I have been here for half a century; but come to the office." The approach to the office presented the vegetable kingdom in full swing; a grassy path and trees invading the quiet domain of business. The doors had been taken down, or had fallen off their hinges, and were now standing against the wall, gracefully festooned with creepers. What looked a mossy carpet was moss or fungus on the floor; and the chairs had velvet covers of green mould. A silken drapery of spiders' webs hung in the corners of the room, and in one there was

. . . . "Well," I said to my ancient friend, "you are fond of nature, a botanist perhaps? What a splendid herbarium you have in the corner there, what beautiful ferns!" "Do not jest, dear sir," said my consignee; "that you must know is my iron safe. It has not been used for some time, and really the growth of fungus and vegetable matter in this region is troublesome; but when business revives we won't let grass grow at our heels, no we won't!"'

I thought it probable that the picture was slightly overdrawn, and that the ancient merchant described might possibly be a miserable survivor of the early Portuguese who were established on the river Yang at the beginning of the sixteenth century, and were finally massacred by the natives in revenge for their barbarous conduct, according to the Chinese account.

These Portuguese were said about that time to have joined with the Japanese in several of their raids on the maritime provinces of China; and it will be remembered that, some sixteen years ago, there was another massacre of Portuguese and Manilla men at this very same town. They were then in some way implicated in the piracies of daily occurrence in the China Sea at that time, and the general feeling was that the retribution was not altogether undeserved. Another disaster befel Ningpo in 1861, when it fell into the hands of the Taipings; remaining in their possession for about six months, when it was retaken for the Imperialists by the English and French war vessels, and since that time, like many other Chinese cities, has been labouring on peacefully in a languid effort to regain what it lost at the hands of the rebels and the Imperial troops.

It was daylight when we steamed up the Yang river; and the harsh outlines of the islands, and of Chin-hai promontory close by, were mellowed in the morning light. A great fleet of fishing-boats bound seaward contributed to enliven the scene; and there were Fukien timber-junks, too, laden till they looked like floating wood-yards, and labouring on their way up stream.

One feature full of novelty was the endless array of ice-houses lining the banks of the river for miles, and presenting the appearance of an encampment of troops. These ice-houses, or ice-pits, are thatched over with straw; and the ice is used to preserve fresh fish during the summer months.

There is a small foreign community on the banks of the Yang, making up in all about eighty residents of different nationalities, including the missionary body. The native city is a walled enclosure, somewhat larger than that at Shanghai, and with nearly double its population; but as for the foreign trade of the place, it has never been very important, in spite of the proximity of Hang-chow-fu, the capital of the province, which the great Venetian, when he passed through it, described as an Eastern Paradise.

Among the chief attractions of Ningpo are the Fukien guild-hall, the 'Tien-how-kung,' as it is called, or 'Temple of the Queen of Heaven;' one of the finest buildings of the kind in China. Indeed it is only the temples, the yamens, and the houses of the rich—the latter, outside the official ranks, few and far between when one considers the vastness of the population—that possess any noteworthy architectural features in the country. The comfortable, elegant, and tasteful abodes of the middle classes, which adorn the suburbs round our cities at home, are conspicuous by their absence in the 'Flowery Land.'

In the Fukien guild-hall we find a really splendid specimen of Chinese temple architecture. The principal building of this commercial shrine is supported by a series of exquisitely sculptured monolithic pillars, each representing the dragon of native mythology; while the upper roof furnishes a very perfect example of the complex Chinese system of open ornamental bracketing, on which the heavy superincumbent weight is sustained.

In this town, too, I met the remnant of that 'ever-victorious army' which achieved so many triumphs. Now, 'after much turmoil,' these warriors rest from their labours, and form the Ning-po city guard; a small compact body of disciplined native troops, under two English officers, well drilled, well cared for, and well paid. This, I fear, is more than can be said of all, or even a large portion, of the Chinese forces now under arms. At any rate they are not all well, and but few of them regularly, paid. Notwithstanding this the condition of the Chinese soldiers is better than it has been in former years; and I believe that, were the Imperial Government obliged to make an effort, they could turn out an army infinitely better equipped, and far more formidable, than is generally supposed; although, at the same time, any force the Chinese might thus muster would be wofully deficient in the discipline, organisation and science, required in coping with the machine-like masses that are placed upon the modern battle-fields of Europe.

These are the impressions I gathered from actual

observation of large bodies of men encamped and under review in China. I think that a Chinaman who has received an English education, of a not very high-class sort, might try to put a letter together in pure English with just about as much success as his government, with the knowledge they at present possess of the science of modern warfare, to send a thoroughly efficient army to face our troops. I cannot, indeed, march a regiment of Chinese before my reader for review, but of their shortcomings in European literary composition I will give an actual sample.

An Englishman had occasion to send a note to his doctor's native assistant, and here, in facsimile, is the reply:—

'Dear Sir,—I not know this things Dr. —— no came Thursday More better you ask he supose you what Fashtion thing can tell me know I can send to you.

'Yours truly
'HANG SIN.'

Now in the foregoing we have a very fine specimen of the sort of results achieved by Chinamen who flatter themselves that they can write English perfectly. They have learnt the letters, and something of the syntax and grammar, but not enough to be of value to them; and so it is with the Chinese soldier of to-day. He possesses the right weapons, but he lacks the full knowledge essential to make use of them effectively, and the perfect discipline which alone can unite him to his fellows on the field, as an important unit in a compact and well-organised mass.

On April 4th I left Ningpo for Snowy Valley, in a

native boat which I hired to take me up stream to Kong-kai. It was close on midnight when we started from Ningpo wharf, and we hoped to reach Kong-kai village by about 9 or 10 A.M. next day. But we had made no allowance for the leisure-loving character of the natives of Ningpo. There is, above the city, a floating bridge across the river; and the first thing we had to do was to wait until men could be found to draw up the central pontoon, so as to permit our boat to pass through. When this business was settled, the boatmen suddenly discovered that the tide was against them, and were about to anchor and go to sleep. I thereupon ordered them to pull me back to the city, and after a good deal of trouble and delay they were got to push forward. Not long after I fell asleep, and when I next awoke I found myself plunging down an inclined plane. Starting up, I noticed that we had reached a weir, and that our boat had been hauled up by a windlass and was now being dropped over to the higher level on the other side. In the end we reached Kong-kai within the allotted time. My party consisted of my two China boys and four Ningpo coolies engaged to transport my baggage to the hills. Our path lay across fields of bean and rape, now in full bloom, and exhaling a delightful fragrance, which contrasted strikingly with the morning whiffs from the manure-bestrewed fields, which commonly salute the wanderer in China. Everything hereabouts shone with freshness and beauty, and it was evident that we must have landed in a real paradise of cultivation.

There lay the village in front of us, nestling cosily amid the trees! and, as we marched along, I pictured to myself a quiet rustic hamlet, such as we encounter in our English counties—pretty cottages where rose and honeysuckle climb the rustic walls, or peep in at open doorways ; children, flushed with the bloom of health, prattling over their play; and sturdy villagers pursuing their useful daily toil.

But notwithstanding the natural beauty of the situation, Kong-kai was disappointing. No perfume of rose or honeysuckle greeted us as we approached ; no rustic cots, no healthy, blooming children; not even the fondly-expected sturdy villager, were among what was here to be seen. The place looked as if it had been stricken with blight. The houses along its main alley were huddled together, jostling and elbowing each other for space and breathing room, and leaning forward upon the broken and muddy pavement in various stages of decay; while, as for their occupants, they were little better. Not a few could be recognised as the pale shrivelled victims of the opium-pipe, and the majority seemed sickly and dirty. As I stood at this little hamlet, on its old bridge, a striking contrast presented itself to my gaze. Towards the hills, through a drapery of pale green foliage that shaded the old wall, you might discern the river, flowing between its reedy shallows, reflecting the waving plumes of bamboo that bent over its banks, and the purple of the distant mountains; you might mark the water meandering through the far-off fields until it was lost in the dim hot air of the plain; and, nearer at hand, some heavy-laden raft of earthenware gliding lazily down stream, the owner resting on a jar, basking in the sun, and smoking the pipe of contentment and repose. To the left, again, in the direction of Kong-kai, a small temple rose up from beneath the shade of an ancient tree, and hard by it were the squalid villagers trooping out to have a look at my strange apparatus. One group had scaled the treacherous height of a dung-heap, which, faint with its own odour, had sunk against the gateway of the shrine. The tutelary idol within could have been but a worthless and disreputable god, else how could he have allowed his mud-begrimed worshippers to fall into so unprosperous a condition?

At this place we procured mountain-chairs for an eighteen miles' journey to the monastery of Tien-tang. The chair-bearers looked a worn and feeble set, but as I walked a good deal they were not over-fatigued. We were now fairly on our way across the plain, glad once more to be free of the foul atmosphere of the village. One or two of the hamlets which we passed on the road were much more attractive than Kong-kai; and, indeed, the people seemed to improve in condition the further we advanced inland. Near the hills the women and children adorn their raven tresses with the bright flower of the azalea—a plant found in great profusion in the highlands of the locality. The halting-places were little wayside temples; and in one of these I met two old women, the priestesses of the shrine. Most haggard, ill-favoured crones, were they; and it was with grave forebodings that I allowed them to prepare my repast. As they leant over a fire of reeds in the dim light of an inner court, with hideous idols glaring around, I should not have been surprised to have seen them vanish in the smoke. I half suspected that I was being made the victim of some spell or incantation, when I observed one of these beldames stretch forth her withered hand and pluck a leaf from some strange plant which grew near the altar, dropping the herb mysteriously inside the cup, as she handed me some tea. I certainly sipped the decoction eyeing the old priestess the while ; but nothing came of it. Probably she divined the drift of my thoughts, for her oaken face shrunk up into a weird grin.

The bearers rested as often as they possibly could, and spent their money and their leisure in gambling among themselves, or with wayside hawkers. Some of the small temples hereabouts differed from any which I had seen in China, having their outer porches adorned with two or three well-modelled life-size figures in the costume which appeared to be that of the ancient lictors of the Ming dynasty. But the idols within were invariably the same, the ordinary Triad of the Buddhist mythology. Each shady nook about these shrines was the resort, and at times the sleeping-place, of wayfarers ; and there, too, vendors of fruit and other provisions had set up their stalls, ready either to sell the traveller his daily food, or to gamble with him for it, if he preferred that plan. The wandering minstrel and the story-teller were not absent from the scene, beguiling the mid-day repast with quaint ballads or with some tale from the rich stores which the folklore of the country has to supply. At one of these halting-places, while the coolies were tossing dice with an aged hawker, a Chinese pedlar laid down his burden for a rest. He had been carrying two baskets slung on a pole, and from these there issued such an incessant pattering, and ceaseless chirping, that my curiosity induced me to open one of them and have a look inside. There I found about a hundred fluffy little ducklings, all of an age, flapping their rudimentary wings, and opening their capacious mouths, clamorous for food.

They were of our friend's own hatching, and but one or two days old; yet in that short space of time they had developed the instinct of self-preservation as strongly as their owner, who, poorly-clad and hungry-looking himself, was taking them to market for sale.

Hatching poultry by artificial heat has reached great perfection in China. My dog 'Spot' manifested a strong interest in these callow nestlings; his eyes filled with tears, his tail dropped pensively, and he uttered a touching whine of regret, as I sternly commanded him to withdraw his scrutiny from the baskets and their contents. 'Spot' was a singularly thoughtful dog; whenever I slept he used to awake me next morning, by jumping up and quietly poking me in the ribs, with his cold black nose; and when I was fairly astir he would next rouse the boys to the preparation of breakfast. He was full of humour, too, and waggishness of tail, withal; but to the presence of strange Chinamen he retained unconquerable objections. When I was eating he felt it his duty to be close at hand, carrying on a sort of dumb conversation the while, one ear up, the other down, and responding to my enquiries with sundry blinkings of the eyes, and grave movements of an expressive tail. When all was over, and he, too, had had his share of food, he would wind himself up for the day by pursuing his tail round and round, and then finally dart off in advance to take a survey of the road. He was a dog, too, endowed with a sort of national pride, and could never be brought to associate with, or even take notice of, Chinese curs.

The plain which we were now crossing was dotted with little grave-mounds crowned with towering shrubs. And here and there a farm-house could be seen peeping out amid the groves, or a haystack clinging round the trunk of a tree, and propped six feet clear above the ground.

The ascent to the monastery of the 'Snowy Crevice' afforded a succession of the finest views to be met with in the province of Cheh-kiang. The azaleas, for which this place is celebrated, were now in full bloom, mantling the hills and valleys with rosy hues, and throwing out their blossoms, in clusters of surprising brilliancy, against the deep green foliage which bound the edges of the path. The mountains themselves were tossed in wild disorder; here swelling into richly-wooded knolls, or rising in giant cliffs and beetling crags; there sweeping down into dark rocky ravines, or sylvan valleys, where we could hear the carolling of birds, or the faint murmuring of a mountain rill. But it was not till we had almost reached the monastery, that we came upon the grandest scene. Here, as we looked back from an altitude of 1,500 feet, the eye wandered over an endless multitude of hills. A single cloud rested on a distant summit, as if to watch the windings of a stream which ran, wrapped in the glory of the waning sun, like a belt of gold, dividing the valleys, and girdling the far-off mountain sides.

As the day declined the hills seemed to melt and merge into the fiery clouds; deep shadows shot across the path, swallowing up the woody chasms, and warning us that night was near at hand. Darkness had already set in before we arrived at our destination. 'Spot' had proceeded on, and his appearance had brought out a venerable bonze, who almost without question, suspended the evening reckoning of his sins on his rosary, and lit us to our quarters in a large block of buildings behind. The apartment assigned to us was a plastered, white-washed chamber, built out of pine wood, and containing a magnificent hardwood bed, one of the finest, and certainly the hardest (excepting one or two made of downright brick), that I came across in my travels. After intimating that foreign wine was much better than any of his country's liquors, our old guide took his leave. We were not long, however, in finding our way to the kitchen for ourselves, and there the boys kindled a fire, while I had a smoke with the monks. Among these recluses was a fine-looking jovial fellow, like a friar of the olden time, one of those who understood, not the culture of the grape only, but the use of its wine as well; less remarkable, perhaps, than he ought to have been, for the rigid austerities of his order, and rather an affecter of that milder discipline which tolerates occasional excesses, such as are not altogether unfamiliar to some members of the Buddhist fraternity in Cathay.

The monastery of the 'Snowy Crevice' reposes, far from the haunts of men and the tumult of cities, in a broad, fertile valley, part of the imperial patrimony upon which its members subsist. It has, of course, a miraculous history; and, like many similar establishments, is popularly supposed to be extremely ancient. Probably it was erected in pre-historic times. One of the stories connected with the place is, that in 1264 A.D. the Emperor Li-tang dreamed a dream about the temple, and named it accordingly 'The famous Hall of Dreams.' This formed one of the most important events in its annals, for the dream was followed by substantial gifts. There is another legend which tells us of an anchorite, and of an Emperor who essayed in vain to slay the Holy Man. At last the monarch fell down and worshipped the priest, for he had never before come across a being whom he could not slay. This Emperor was distinguished for his wise rule, and had just put a million of the common sort of his subjects to death; but he was, at that time, athirst for some victim of rarer eminence, and sanctity, than any of those whom he had already brought to their end. He died at last a pious priest, and left some suitable gifts behind him, too.

Something like this is not unknown even at the present time. There are monks, I am told, in those places, who have passed their lives in crime, and who find it expedient to retire to these choice retreats (making them places of refuge like the temples of the ancient Jews and Greeks) to die pleasantly chanting 'Omita-Foh!'

Such holy ones, rescued from the grasp of justice and the jaws of the pit, take good care, nevertheless, to live as long as they can. Many of the Buddhists are doubtless good and true men, if judged by the laws of their own faith; and the majority of them, whom I came across, I found hospitable and kind to strangers. They seldom failed, however, to let me know if the presents I chanced to give them were not quite equal to those which other visitors had bestowed.

Early next morning a mute and aged monk conducted me to view the 'Thousand-fathom Precipice.' A heavy cloud was hanging like a pall over the scene as I followed the guide along a mountain path; and the trees above and in front of us loomed out like dark spectres, groping with their long arms through the

THE DREAM. (*Chinese Drawing*)

mist. My companion was apparently in haste, and as he flitted in his flowing robes along the road in front, he seemed like a phantom figure projected on the cloud.

At length we reached a summit that stood out bold and clear, though still wet with the vapoury rain; and there, in a small rest-house perched upon one of the rocks, we sat down to listen to the roar of the fall and the foaming torrent beneath.

The monk next led me to where, clinging to a tree, I could lean over the edge of the precipice and get a look right down into the abyss; but there was nothing to be made out save a sea of mist, through which the deafening roar of the waters could be heard as they leapt from rock to rock in their descent to the valley more than 1,000 feet below. While giving way to the reverie which the moving scene evoked, I was suddenly recalled to myself by a vulture that shot out from the face of the rock, and caught a tiny bird as it hovered above the cloud. Impressed with what I had just seen, and with the anticipations of that which I had still to see, I found my way back to the monastery, where breakfast was already prepared.

The sun then gradually shone out, and by its aid we descended to the foot of the fall through a steep shady path, and secured some pictures of the scenery. The cataract takes a leap of about 500 feet, and then gushes downwards over the clefts and edges like the graceful folds of a bridal veil; while the variously coloured rocks are covered with ferns and flowering shrubs. By climbing over huge boulders and beneath bamboo groves, I managed to reach the stone basin below. Here the spray was lit up with countless rainbow hues ; and the ferns that leant their broad leaves, as it were, to catch the burden of the fall, had their never-ceasing toil rewarded by showers of sparkling gems.

It was interesting to watch the monks at their refections ; and this we contrived to do without being noticed ourselves. We found them always scrupulously particular in observing those rules of Buddhism by which the duties of cleanliness are enforced. The following are some of the laws which regulate diet[1] :—

'The dinner of a priest consists of seven measures of rice mixed with flour, the tenth of a cubit of pastry, and nearly the same weight of bread. To eat more is cupidity, to eat less is parsimony; to eat vegetables of any kind besides these dishes is not permitted.'

The last injunction is by no means commonly followed in China :—

'Then the priest shall offer to the good and bad spirits, and repeat five prayers. He must not speak about his dinner, nor steal food like a dog, nor scratch his head, nor breathe in his neighbour's face, nor speak with his mouth full, nor laugh, nor joke, nor smack in eating ; and if he should happen to find an insect in his food he must conceal it so as not to create doubt in the minds of others.'

There are a host of other very good rules laid down for his guidance ; but their general tendency is to make a monk's dinner the most solemn and most unsocial event of his in other respects too dreary day. When we look through the Buddhist laws and precepts, we find them so minute and so wide-reaching, that

[1] *Laws and Regulations of the Priesthood of Buddha, in China.* Trans. by C. F. Newmann.

SUNG-ING-DAY FALL, SNOWY VALLEY

they hedge the priest completely round, shutting him out from the gratification of his most natural desires, and rendering it indeed uncertain whether any perfectly devout and faithful Buddhists can possibly exist in China.

It is an undoubted fact that some of the monks indulge in secret potations; and there are others who smoke opium and gamble; while their covetousness, their meanness, and as a rule the extreme dirtiness of their dress and habits, are patent to every observer. Even in the monastery of the 'Snowy Crevice,' amid the grandest and most ennobling scenery, we still discovered practices of the outer world which had not been wholly cast aside; and some of the members of the order who, though honest enough, had still a greedy hankering after earthly pelf, and were disfigured with a few other weaknesses which they took no pains to conceal.

Within three minutes' walk from my quarters I discovered a natural shower-bath, with a convenient stone basin in which I bathed every morning; and if we followed the stream for about a mile further up we came upon a second great fall, known in the neighbourhood as the Sung-ng-day, and approached by a bridge of a single arch concealed by a profusion of creeping plants. The water at this fall descends into a deep narrow chasm, while groups of dull dark pines look sombrely over the brink of the precipice into the dark abyss below.

Far beneath, the river may still be seen winding along a rough and broken bed: the peaceful cultivated hills above, and the rugged foreground, together presenting a contrast as striking as it is rare.

The return voyage, to Ningpo and Shanghai, I must pass by unrecorded, that I may hurry forward to describe my journey up the Yang-tsze river to Sze-chuan.

Having dined with a literary friend in Shanghai, I returned to the hotel towards midnight January 13, 1872, and there found my boys with everything in readiness, and a gang of coolies waiting to bear our baggage on board the 'Fusiyama,' which was getting up steam for Hankow. It was a bitter night, and the scene was as dark and gloomy as the wind was cold. The lamps blinked and shivered as the blast swept by, and a thousand lanterns of ships and steamers, gleaming dimly in the distance, shot long shafts of broken light down the chill black river beneath. The ships' bells tinkled the midnight hour, and then the Chinese watchmen woke from their first slumbers to beat their bamboo clappers. The bund was deserted; only some stray woman would now and again emerge from the darkness, and then be swallowed up once more, like a sinful victim in the jaws of night.

We soon passed on to the 'Fusiyama' across the floating landing-stage alongside of which she was moored. She was a fine steamer, although by no means the finest among the S. S. N. Co's. fleet. There were many passengers on board, bound for the open ports on the Yang-tsze. One, an American, seemed to be a man of great versatility of talent. He informed us that in his own country he had followed a number of different occupations. 'If a man fails in one calling,' he remarked, 'that is the very best reason why he should try his hand at something else, until he discovers the drift of his genius.' Accordingly he had himself started first of all with a friend and ran a saw-mill: but that concern ran down one morning. He tried to wind it up, but 'it wouldn't go no how!' Left then without a 'red cent,' he took to railways; got to be conductor of a train, and went through three smashes, 'and the best of it was it warn't no fault of mine.' 'The last was a big thing; it mashed up twenty-five passengers, and the cars ran into each other like tubes; so I hauled out of that, and took to mining, and made a pretty good thing; then here I am, to try my fortune in trade.'

Reserving what I may have to say about Nanking and the ports on the lower Yang-tsze, I will transport the reader at once, about 600 miles higher up to Hankow, the furthest point on the Yangtsze river to which steam navigation has been carried. Hankow holds an important position, at the confluence of the rivers Han and Yang-tsze. The ancient name of the Han river was the Mien, and its course, as well as the point at which it joins the Yang-tsze, have been subjected to frequent change. It was only in the last decade of the fifteenth century that the river created its present channel, and at the same time the advantageous site to which Hankow owes no little portion of her prosperity. The early trade of the district was confined to Hanyang, a place described as a flourishing port at the remote period treated of in the 'History of the Three States.' Hanyang is now taken up chiefly with official residences, though its suburbs are still the resort of a considerable native trade.

Hankow flourished under the rule of the Mings, and does not seem to have suffered greatly during the disasters which attended their fall. It was then known as the great mart, in fact the commercial centre of the Empire; and was the resort of traders from the furthest north, and from the southernmost provinces Kiang-su and Yunan. Most of the provinces indeed were represented there by guilds, whose halls are still famous for their size and decoration. During Kien-loong's time the prosperity of Hankow continued to advance until the disastrous epoch of the Taiping rebellion. Then the decay was as rapid as the ruin was complete; and finally, in 1855, the whole city was burned to the ground.

After the Taipings had been expelled from Hupeh, Hankow rose once more out of its ashes, and in 1861 the final arrangements for a concession of land to the British Crown were carried into effect. The hoisting of the English colours was followed at once by a splendid settlement, erected on a very unfortunate site. The land was bought up in small lots at 2,500 taels each, and enormous sums were squandered, to no purpose, before it was discovered that the spot chosen for a foreign settlement was exposed to constant inundations of the most destructive kind. Thus, in the year before my arrival, the flood, which is always looked forward to as the event of the season, bestowed its fertilising favours with no grudging hand; and indeed there was no foretelling to what height the waters, which had already swept away entire suburbs from the cities higher up stream, might deluge the vicinity of Hankow. Well, first of all, it rose slowly until it had submerged its banks; thence it made excursions along the outlying streets; crept up like a silent foe till it had breasted the fortifications; and finally made the captured settlement over to a sort of watery sack. The inhabitants retreated to their garret fastnesses, while pigs, poultry, and even cattle, were sheltered in boats, or found refuge in the bedrooms, on the upper floors. At any rate, it was a convenience to 'Paterfamilias' to have his milch-cow next door to his nursery, and chanticleer perched upon a friendly bed-post to screech the approach of day. But when the novelty of these domestic arrangements had worn off, and when the richly-papered walls began to weep through a lacework of fungus, and the limbs of the polished furniture to show symptoms of dissolution; when the silken hangings grew mildewed and pale, and the boundary walls tottered and sunk with a dull splash into the red stream, the dire insecurity of the position, and the dread of impending disaster, pressed heavily upon the despondent inhabitants. But, with a truly philosophic spirit, they made the best of events. The halls and staircases became really admirable docks and landing-stages, where visitors might disembark, and a dining or drawing-room made a much better plunge-bath than one could have imagined. Bachelors, too, while they indulged in a morning swim, could call at the bank, to enquire the rate of exchange, or dive to their breakfast beneath the doorway of some hospitable friend. At length the water reached its height; and then, to the relief of all, began slowly to recede. It is apprehended that but for a back wall (erected originally by the Chinese Government at a cost of 80,000*l.* as a protection against organised raids from the banditti of the plain), which acted as a breakwater, the entire settlement might have been swept into the Yang-tsze by the strong reflux currents from the Han.

The business at Hankow has never come near the

anticipations of the Europeans who flocked thither when the place was opened; but nevertheless, as the centre of the districts which produce the Congou teas, it must always secure a very important share of foreign commerce. The total value of the trade in foreign shipping was reported to be about 14,000,000*l.* in 1871, while in 1873 it appears to have fallen off; but this was owing to a sort of commercial stagnation which has been felt all over China.

The Taotai of Hankow, Ti-ming-chih, who furnished me with a passport for the upper Yang-tsze, and whom I had twice the pleasure of meeting, had been born in the province of Kiangsu, and commenced his official career at the age of thirty by an appointment to a modest clerkship. From this his abilities advanced him step by step, until he attained his present position, where he has earned a high reputation by his just, mild, and intelligent rule.

Woochang city, on the opposite bank of the river, presents a picturesque appearance, due partly to the elevated ground on which it stands, and partly to its celebrated tower, which tradition reports to have been first set up there 1,300 years ago. This tower was overthrown by the followers of the 'Heavenly King' during the Taiping rebellion, and has only been rebuilt and finished within the last four years. It is quite unlike the ordinary Chinese pagoda, and from its peculiar design runs no risk of ever being mistaken for any other monument.

During the journey to the upper Yang-tsze, which I now propose to describe, I had two American gentlemen for my companions. Two native boats were secured, and we engaged them to carry us to Ichang.

Into the smaller of these craft we stowed the cook and servants, reserving the larger one for our baggage and ourselves. Our boat was divided into three compartments with well-carved bulkheads between. The fore-cabin was taken up by a boy to wait on us, and by our newly-appointed Chinese secretary 'Chang' (who was in no way related to the giant of that name). This secretary was a small compact man, full of Chinese lore and self-satisfied complacency. The 'central state room' was our own, while Captain Wang and his wife found shelter in the after-cabin. Besides this there was an ample hold, which contained our baggage, our provisions, and our crew.

We left Hankow about mid-day on January 29, 1872; but as there was no wind, we had to pole our way through thousands of native boats, and anchor for the night at Ta-tuen-shan, only ten miles above the town. A hard frost set in during the evening, and it seemed quite impossible to keep the intense cold out of our quarters.

To make matters worse, the skipper and his spouse smoked stale tobacco half through the night, and the fumes came through the bulkhead and filled my sleeping-bunk. Next day we set to work with paper and paste to cure both evils by patching up every crevice, and by fixing up a stove which had been lent us by friends for the voyage. These preparations were a source of disquietude to Mrs. Wang, who turned out to be a tartar more desperate even than the lady of the Min.

The boatmen were a miserably poor lot. They neither changed their clothes nor washed their bodies during the entire trip; and 'Why should they?' said Chang the secretary; they could only change their garments with one another. They have but a single suit apiece, and that too, some of them, only on loan for the winter months. Their clothes were padded with cotton, and formed their habiliments by day and their bedding by night. Poor souls, how they crept together, and huddled into the hold! and what an odour rose from their retreat in the morning, for they had smoked themselves to sleep with tobacco, or those of them who could afford it, with opium. It was always a difficult matter to get them up and out on deck to face the cold. I confess I never cared to be the first to lift the hatch. But the voice of Mrs. Wang is equal to the occasion. She shakes those sluggards from their rest with her strident tones; she stamps in her cabin, and 'slings slang' at them, like the foulest missiles. At last, at about seven o'clock, they may be seen unwillingly turning to and hauling up the anchor not more slow-moving than themselves. As it happened, we had a fair wind; the sails were set, and we bounded on briskly up the chocolate-coloured stream between banks that stood up high above us and were furrowed with the lines of age.

We made a good day's run, but the iron stove seemed to be a failure, or at any rate our coal would not burn. It took us half a day of hard work to turn 'Farmer's Bend,' although one might easily walk across the neck of land which divides the two extremities of the curve in a single quarter of an hour. A canal cut across here would be a great saving in the river navigation. We noticed many timber rafts from the Tung-Ting lake, looking like floating villages, and indeed they are neither more nor less than hamlets. Each on its floating substructure of timber supported two rows of huts, and in these dwelt the little colonies of Chinamen who had invested their time, labour, and small capital in the trade. When the rafts reach Hankow, these huts are lifted off and placed on the river's bank; the owners residing inside them till all their wood has been disposed of. If ever steamers are seen even thus far up the Yangtsze river (46 miles above Hankow), experienced pilots would be required; especially at this season, when the water is at its lowest; and it might perhaps be necessary even, to survey the stream annually, for its channel tends constantly to shift. At Paitsow, where we anchored for the night, we found men manufacturing bamboo cables. They had no rope-walks, but only high temporary-looking scaffoldings, with some men above and others below, making and twisting the thick strands.

Next morning the skipper's wife, and the crew, got through a good deal of bad language between them before we made a start. The conversation was a shrill-toned one, and alternated between Mrs. Wang in her cabin at one end of the boat, and the crew in the hold at the other. The latter objected to turn out until their captain was at his post. This difficulty the gentle wife settled ultimately, by kicking her husband out of bed on to the deck, hurling torrents of abuse at his unhappy head, and supplementing those delicate attentions by a plentiful supply of cooking utensils.

Let the reader imagine himself afloat in such a vessel as I have described, with such a crew, on a river red like the soil through which it flows, and from half a mile to a league in breadth; let him conceive himself ascending the stream between low level monotonous clay walls; he will then have a picture of our craft and our surroundings for many days as we pursued our voyage upward to the Gorges.

We breakfasted and dined, anchored and slept, surveying the river as well as we could, and here and there marking out sundry sandbanks and other barriers to commerce, formed since the one and only chart of the river had been made.

We had chosen our opportunity well. There can

OUR NATIVE BOAT

be no better time for examining the features of a river than when it is at its lowest, and the Yang-tsze was now running far below its banks, which in summer are completely submerged. But our careful soundings, our notes of bearings, and our chart-projecting, need find no record here. Their very sameness grew wearisome at last; but, as for our secretary, he would have been quite willing to sail on until he had digested the whole of the ancient classics, drinking our wine, and smoking our cheroots as frequently as they were offered. He had marvellous raiment, Chang! A padded robe of classic cut, with sleeves reaching down to his knees, and a collar that stood up like a fortress around his spare neck. When in a corner, seated at study, he looked like a huge bolster surmounted by a tiny cap. He would remain in this posture for hours, with his eyes closed, and audibly rehearsing whole books of classic lore; but he had also a good deal of accurate information about the country, and was extremely polite in his manner, and willing to make himself useful.

It was a mistake having two boats; their unequal sailing powers caused grievous delays—delays which the servants and cook readily turned to account in explaining all sorts of shortcomings, and which contributed greatly to the leisure and enjoyment of the crews, who were paid by the day.

On the 23rd we passed the point where the 'Ta-Kiang'—or great river—is joined by the stream from the 'Tung-Ting' lake. At this place there were abundant evidences of considerable trade in the fleets of boats we continually passed. The river, in some of the long reaches hereabouts, would be dangerous for steam navigation, at any rate during the months when the banks are submerged. Hence suitable landmarks would have to be erected, as not a single tree, shrub or knoll, can at such times be seen for many miles around. All the shoals at this (the winter) season are well defined, and, with the exception of two reefs of rocks which stand well clear of the water, consist of soft mud and sand,

and occur just at the bends, where anyone accustomed to river navigation would expect to find them. Whereever the current struck upon the clay, a good channel was almost invariably to be found.

On the 24th we ascended a small rapid which ran about five knots, and were detained by a snow-storm for about six hours. The little hamlets we passed, or anchored at, day after day, were temporary miserable-looking settlements, conveying the idea of a thinly-peopled country; and the inhabitants wore the poverty-stricken look only too common in other parts of China. We have walked over the country, and along the banks, for nearly half a day without encountering a single individual.

At many places the river had undermined the banks, and these were falling in in great blocks eight or ten feet wide; and there was one point where we noticed that the stream was cutting out the heart of an old settlement, for there were old foundations of houses exposed, and many coffins protruding from the bank.

On the 27th we reached Shang-chai-wan, and remarked that the banks in front of an old pagoda there had been carefully faced up with stones. Thus a useful sort of landmark was well protected from the inroads of the stream, while the houses were left to be swept away as the bank fell in.

This village indicated some slight degree of prosperity, and presented a pretty winter's scene. A row of leafless trees stretched out their white arms against the leaden sky. The roofs of the houses and the sloping banks were covered with snow, while the red light of reed fires gleamed through the open doorways, and sparkled in the oyster-shell windows. There was no one astir, not a footprint stained the pure white mantle in which the soil was wrapt; only on one level patch the leaves of a winter crop shot up in rows, and formed a pale green pattern on a snowy ground. A little further on was the town of 'Shang-chai-wan,' where our boys went ashore and spent half a day in a vain search for coal. Then the crew had to be hunted up all over the place, and one by one the men dropped in, each with as much samshu as he could hold inside him, or else stupified with opium. Capt. Wang we found in a filthy alley, enjoying the nectar of a grog-shop, amid a group of natives and half-a-dozen enormous pigs, that seemed to be listening with a lively interest to the conversation about foreigners and their ways. The natives were civil enough. Few of them had ever set eyes upon a genuine white man before, and all made numerous good-natured enquiries about our relations, and our clothes; one old man even suggested that our faces and hands had only acquired a pale colour through the use of some wonderful cosmetic, and that our bodies were black as sin. I bared my arm to refute this calumny, and its white skin was touched by many a rough finger, and awoke universal admiration. Not knowing exactly what our barbarous views of decency might be, we were kindly recommended by an unwashed, but polished member of the community, not to gratify vulgar curiosity by stripping entirely, as we had already completely satisfied the more intelligent members of the crowd.

The reader can easily gather, from such incidents as these, what depraved notions some of the Chinese must entertain about ourselves, and our customs. They always seem to feel that we have a great deal to learn;

the merest coolie, if he be a kindly-disposed person, will readily place his knowledge at our service, and put us in the way of picking up something of a purer Chinese civilisation. I have in my possession one of the valuable works upon which this popular belief is fed. It is a sort of ethnological treatise, written down to the limited comprehension of facts, and to the inordinate craving for fable, which characterise the lower classes among this highly superstitious nation. The author gravely describes races of men who, like ourselves, live on the outer edges of the world, that is outside the benign influence of Chinese rule. Some are very hairy men, clothed with leaves; others hop about on one leg; while others again are adorned with the claws of birds. There is one very singular tribe indeed. These have only a single huge eye in the forehead, while the women carry a multitude of breasts. There are men, too, with big holes through their bodies above the region of the heart, so that they may be spitted like herrings, or carried about on poles; and lastly, there is one community more gifted still, for they can fly through the air with wings.

An old man at Shang-chai-wan came down the bank to our boats to sell sweets. His hands, feet, and head seemed to be sticking through an ancient bedquilt, rendered waterproof by a glossy coating of dirt. We sent some of his wares to the natives as a parting gift.

It was at this place, too, that our writer Chang, who said he was suffering from cold, dispatched one of the boatmen ashore to buy a bottle of samshu. The trust which he displayed in the integrity of the messenger was no less marvellous than touching. 'I do not know how much there is here,' said he, as he placed his purse in the boatman's hands; 'but take what you require, and put back the rest.' Just before, however, I had noticed the crafty rogue carefully count the cash in this very purse, which, as it turned out, contained no more than exactly sufficient for the purchase.

On the 29th, when passing a customs station, we were pursued and overtaken by a fiery official, who came on board, received a cigar and a glass of wine, and went away greatly impressed with our respectability. We also sailed by a large cotton-junk lying wrecked on the bank, and a second one which had run aground where the water was deeper, and whose owners were now living in a mud hole, waiting till the river should rise high enough to float their craft. 'Three blank uninteresting days, with a few temporary huts at long intervals,' is the next entry in my journal.

At Shi-show-hien we bought a quantity of fish; among them was one described by Captain Blakiston, which carries a sword above its wide toothless mouth. This sword it is said to use for boring into the soft mud to dislodge the tiny fish, which thereupon rush for shelter down its dark capacious throat. The stomach of the specimen we purchased contained one or two of these half-digested mud-fish. Its colour, from the spine half way down to the belly, was dark blue or slate; the belly was white; the tail and fins were white and red. Length from point of sword to tip of tail 4 feet 2 inches; length of sword 14 inches.

Shi-show-hien was formerly held by the rebels. Here they built a fortress, whose ruins may still be seen. We were now within sight of the hill ranges in the province of Hunan, and on one hill, close at hand, stood a temple called the 'Ti-tai-shan,' which forms a striking land-mark for river navigation. Above this point many islands and shoals occurred, and the channel, too, grew shallow and intricate, again showing the need for frequent surveys, as the condition of the bed at one season is no guide to what we might find it in the succeeding year. The changes which have taken place since our Admiralty chart was laid down renders that map comparatively useless, both for this and other parts of the river, at any rate when the waters are low.

At a large village where we made a halt, some ten miles below the town of Shasze, we fell in with a hawker, and purchased some of his wares. For these, when the payment was to be made, he demanded about three times their value. At first we declined to pay the amount, but the independent old impostor came on board and would not budge. A crowd collected, and the respectable members decided in our favour, advising us to drop Shylock overboard, or bear him in captivity away. With a determination worthy of some nobler cause, our feeble oppressor agreed to suffer death rather than forego his advantage. So we paid him the money, in order to keep the peace, whereat the old villain laughed heartily when he got ashore, and firmly expressed his opinion that, after all, we were nothing more than foolish foreign devils. This manifestation of ill-feeling was in itself sufficient to denote that we were drawing near a big town.

'Shasze' stands on the left bank of the Yang-tsze river, which is here more than a mile and a half broad with a deep roomy channel, and we may gather from the crowd of native shipping that lie anchored off the town, or close to its fine stone embankment, that we have reached an important centre of trade.

This embankment terminates, at its upper end, in a sort of bulwark, crowned with the finest pagoda to be found anywhere along this river. Immense labour has been bestowed in fortifying this site against the undermining influence of the current; and the town is placed at such an angle on the stream, that the action of the water always keeps a clear channel, close to its strong stone-retaining wall. Stone is freely used in this part of the upper Yang-tsze, and is readily obtainable in unlimited supplies in the gorges above the town. At Shasze, landing-stages for steamers might be made at almost any part of the bank, while there are splendid sites for a foreign settlement on the hills across the stream.

Coal abounds in Hunan and Szechuan, and yet we found it difficult to procure. In the former province, it is worked at two places only, Tsang-yang-hien and Pa-tung-hien, and there to an extremely limited degree; but in Szechuan there is a good deal more coal-mining going on. The coal is of good quality, in every way suitable for steam purposes—at least, the samples which we collected were first-rate.

After passing one or two small towns, where the people were better dressed and more prosperous-looking than we had found them lower down stream, we arrived on February 3 at the town of 'Kiang-kow.' Here the men struck work, as they wished to go ashore for what they called rice, but which Chang interpreted as *wine*. We offered to supply them with rice; but that they would not accept, demanding an advance of money, and leave of absence to spend it. This we stedfastly refused to concede, and threatened to cut off their captain's pay unless he brought his men to terms. The mutineers next hauled in the sails, and sat themselves down for a smoke; but in about an hour, seeing no prospect of our yielding, the skipper consulted his sweet spouse, and then forthwith ordered the men to turn to, under penalty of letting the wife of his bosom loose on them. This prospect produced such a powerful effect on the men that they instantly resumed their work.

We were now fairly entering the mountainous region, and quitting the great alluvial plain that stretches hundreds of miles southward to the sea. We could just see the 'Mountains of the Seven Gates,' towering in dark masses above the horizon, as the evening closed in upon us and we cast anchor for the night. Our skipper determined to serve us out for our obstinacy. He assured us that the place was infested with pirates, and that it would be necessary to keep an armed watch all night. Perhaps he feared his men, who were certainly a dare-devil looking set.

I kept the first watch, and employed myself in writing letters, with my revolver close at hand. Once or twice, there appeared to be a noise about the cabin window, as of some one trying to open it; but when I looked out into the night there were no signs of life on the river, nor any sounds to be heard save only the heavy breathing of the boatmen in the hold beneath. At length, shortly after midnight, voices were audible close to the boat, and seemingly coming nearer. I grasped my revolver, determined to sell my life dearly, and once more crept cautiously to the window, prepared for the worst. I concealed the light, and looked abroad; and then my companion, who had himself been the author of the alarm, arrived to relieve me in the watch.

We noticed men fishing with trained otters on this part of the river. There were a number of boats, and each boat was furnished with an otter tied to a cord. The animal was thrust into the water and remained there until it had secured a fish ; then it was hauled up and the fisherman, placing his foot upon its tail, stamped vigorously until it had dropped its finny prey. We passed two prosperous-looking little towns, Po-yang and Chi-kiang, and on the morning of February 5 were sailing beneath bold rocky bluffs, backed by a chaos of fantastic mountain peaks. Here, on the highest pinnacle, a Buddhist monastery was perched not far from the brink of the river, and nearer heaven than any other object in the landscape. It was fronted by a precipice of 600 feet, and looked quite inaccessible at its altitude of more than 1,200 feet above the stream. But after all, to scale this stony height, and to rear a shrine amid the clouds, although a wonderful achievement in its way, sinks into insignificance when compared with the task of self-subjection daily set before each inmate of the cloister, who, even in such a retreat as this, removed as far as it well can be from the haunts of men, finds the lusts of the flesh and the pride of life too strong to be effectually subdued. Many of the Buddhist monastic establishments in China, as we have already seen, are planted in most romantic and lovely spots ; and in the one now before us we found no exception to the rule. It was set in the midst of a region where Nature showed herself in her sublimest moods ; where, even when we passed, the dark clouds, tossed and riven by the winter's wind, were pierced by fitful gleams of sunshine that gilded the sacred rock when all around was wrapped in gloom. But in summer the scene must be more impressive still. Then sometimes, the wild raging of the tempest echoes through the deep ravines, the vapoury heavens are rent upon the black crags, and a thousand cascades leap and flash in the lightning as they descend impetuously to swell the wild torrents of the Yang-tsze. Onward, ever onward, roll the waters of this mighty stream, now fertilising, now laying waste. Time after time have man's hands striven to limit and confine its course, but his efforts end abortively, his greatest works are silently levelled by the invading floods. Who, then, can wonder if the Buddhist recluse, perched upon this rocky pinnacle, and looking down upon the great river at one time smiling in the sunshine and dotted with many a sail, at another bearing on its turbid breast the wreck of cities, should be deeply impressed with the mutability of human affairs, and stimulated to seek that absolute repose which can only come, as his sacred books teach him, by disencumbering himself of all human affections?

On the same day, at noon, or a little after, we anchored before Ichang. This city is one of considerable commercial importance, and, as it stands at the entrance of the Gorges, it would be the highest point to which steam navigation could be carried until these rocky defiles, which extend for upwards of 100 miles beyond it, shall have been thoroughly surveyed, and some obstacles removed, which render the navigation there by far the most dangerous on the rivers of China. That Ichang will ultimately be opened to foreign trade is tolerably certain. My only surprise is that this has not been done already; but while the Chinese themselves are disinclined to open new ports, those foreigners who have vested interests in Hankow probably look with anything but satisfaction, on the threatened rivalry of Ichang. However, if the opening of that mart is desirable, and this can hardly be doubted, Hankow interests can never stand in the way, nor will Chinese opposition succeed, unless some very good reason can be shown for excluding foreign commerce from the upper waters of the Yang-tsze.

For information as to the trade of Ichang I must refer the reader to the 'Report of the Delegates of the Shanghai Chamber of Commerce,' published in 1869. At present, foreign goods, in limited quantities, are distributed from this port through the surrounding provinces, while the rich plains of Hupeh, besides the usual cereal crops—beans, millet, rice, and rape—produce yellow silk, tung-oil, and opium; the latter in small quantities, although it is raised more plentifully in Szechuan and Yunnan.

The town of Ichang sweeps in a crescent-shape round a bend on the left bank of the river, and is divided into two halves by a canal. The one half occupies high land, while the other is on lower ground, and comprises a large suburb which suffered severely in the flood of 1870, but has since been rebuilt. There are two or three unoccupied sites well adapted for a foreign settlement. Building materials are also to be had in great variety and abundance; while coal, which can hardly yet be said to be an article of trade, is very plentiful in the neighbourhood. As to the steam navigation of the river up to this point, I have no hesitation in saying that small boats of light draught could reach

Ichang without difficulty, even at this season, when the water is at its lowest; while, during summer, the steamers which ply on the lower river would find no obstacles greater than those they already surmount between Shanghai and Hankow.

In the afternoon we were the spectators of a naval review. Six small gun-boats, each mounting a six-pound gun at the bow, were drawn up in line and fired their cannon at irregular intervals. I say irregular, because some of the artillery refused to go off at all; and when the sham fight was all over, we could hear them discharging themselves during the night. The boats were small, and had each about forty rowers on board. When the review was over, the admiral landed and rode off on a gaily-caparisoned pony, followed by his retainers.

At Ichang we had to hire a large rapid boat to make the ascent of the Gorges, and we left our sailing vessels to await our return. Before we started a cock was sacrificed to the river goddess; its blood and feathers were sprinkled on the bow, while a libation was poured upon the water. We had a crew of twenty-four men at the sweeps, who worked to the tune of a shrill piping song, or rather yell, and under their exertions it was not long before Ichang had been passed and the mouth of the first gorge was before us. Here the river narrows from half a mile to a few hundred yards across, and pours through the rocky defile with a velocity that makes it difficult to enter.

The hills rose on each side from 500 to 2,500 feet in height, presenting two irregular stone walls to the river, each worn and furrowed with the floods of ages, and showing some well-defined water-markings seventy feet above the winter stream, up which we were now toiling on our way. Thus, then, we had before us an unmistakable register of the height to which the Yang-tsze had risen in the seasons of former floods.

The further we entered the gorges the more desolate and dark became the scene, the narrow barren defile presenting a striking contrast to the wide cultivated plains, through which we had been making our way from the sea, for more than 1,000 miles.

The only inhabitants of this region appeared to be a few fishermen, who prosecuted their avocation among the rocks, while their rude huts could be seen perched high in inaccessible-looking nooks and crannies among the mountains above. Huts, indeed, they could hardly be called; at least, those of them which we visited were either natural caves, or holes scooped out beneath the sheltering rocks, and closed in with what resembled the front of an ordinary straw-thatched cottage.

These smoke-begrimed abodes called to my mind the ancient cave-dwellings which sheltered our forefathers at Wemyss Bay, in Scotland. The interiors were dark and gloomy, the clay floors cold, and covered with fishbones and refuse, while a dull light, glimmering from a taper in a recess in the rocks, revealed at once the grim features of a small idol and the few and simple articles of furniture that made up the property of the inmates. A residence of this sort, with all it contains, might be fitted up at an original cost of probably one pound sterling, and yet it was in such places that we found the frugality and industry of the Chinese most conspicuously displayed; for, outside the caves, wherever there was a little soil on the face of the rocks, it had been scraped together and planted with vegetables, which were made to contribute to the domestic economy of the inhabitants. This was, indeed, taking bread out of a stone! Further on we found a number of men engaged in quarrying the stone, and in forming river embankments. The stream in many places hereabouts had undermined the limestone formation of the rocks,

SZECHUAN BOAT, UPPER YANG-TSZE.

so that the softer portions had been washed away, and a series of grotesque flint pillars were left, supporting the upper strata which towered above our heads in precipices of a thousand feet. In other places the rocks looked like the high walls and ramparts of a fortress, or the battlements and towers of a citadel. The inhabitants of this sterile region must have a hard struggle for existence, but they are a hardy and independent race, scorning the mendicant tricks of their more abject fellow-countrymen in the plains. Thus I only fell in with a single beggar in these mountain passes, although many of the people were very poor and miserable. Our men slept on deck in the open air, and I was always afraid lest I should find some of them dead in the morning, for the cold was intense during the night. But they huddled themselves together beneath the awning of matting, and thus managed to keep the night air from freezing their blood. Near the upper end of the gorge the huts were of a better class, the soil improved, and small orchards came into sight, displaying a profusion of plum-blossoms even at this season of the year.

On February 8 we were compelled to spend half a day at a place called Kwang-loong-Miau, that the crew might celebrate the Chinese New Year. The festival was conducted at the village shrine, which stood on a picturesque spot surrounded with pine and backed by a mountain 2,000 feet high. Chang had here a dispute with the boatmen, who, as he protested, had sullied his honourable name. He complained of their riotous, drunken conduct; but I soon found that our venerated interpreter was himself not without sin, and was indeed unable to stand erect. He suggested that the chief offenders ought to be taken before the nearest magistrate, and, if need be, beheaded in order to sober them

In truth, they made a great uproar during the night, firing crackers, quarrelling, and gambling; but next morning they were once more ready for work, though some had sold a portion of what little they had in the shape of clothing, to give the new year a fair start, and looked all the more savage for the change. They soon got heated, as we had cleared the first gorge and were now ascending a rapid. It was the first, but by no means the least dangerous. The bulk of the men were on the bank, attached to a tracking-line. Off they sped, yelling like fiends above the roar of the water; while the boy, to add to the din, lustily beat a gong, and the cook a small drum, for the purpose of stirring the men to put forth their full strength. At about the centre of the rapid there was a dead halt, just as if the boat had stuck fast on a reef, though the trackers were straining to their utmost with hands and feet planted firmly on the rocks. The skipper stamped, danced, and bellowed to his crew; and they, responding with a wild shout, a desperate tug, and a strain, at last launched our boat into the smooth water above. The danger of this rapid consists not so much in its force as in the narrowness of the channel, and in the multitude of rocks, sunken as well as above water, on which the boat, were the tracking line to part, would certainly drift, and there be dashed to pieces.

In the second, or Lukan Gorge, the mountains rise to a greater altitude, projecting in some places over the chasm, as if they longed to join and exclude the light from the already darkened river. There were numerous strange perpendicular markings in these rocks, like borings for the purpose of mining. These had apparently been made by a sort of natural sand-drill. Small hard pebbles, imprisoned in the recesses of soft rock, with the aid of sand and water, have in time pierced these deep vertical shafts; and the attrition of the water on the face of the rocks has at last brought the tunnelled apertures to light.

At the next rapid, Shan-tow-pien, we noticed the wrecks of two Szechuan trading-boats, making in all nine which we had come across since we started from Ichang. It was snowing heavily, as we made our way over the rocks to the village which came down close to the water's edge; and towards dark we found ourselves in front of a small cabin made out of the *débris* of a wrecked boat. The owner of the wreck, an aged man, resided within it, and had been residing there for some days past. He looked cold and wretched; but he would have nothing to say to us, and haughtily rejected our proffered help.

We had now reached the great rapid of the Upper Yang-tsze, which occurs at the mouth of the Mitan Gorge. Here, while I was engaged in photographing the scene, I fell in with a mandarin, who asked many questions about my honourable name and title, my country, my kinsmen, and, as he had never set eyes on a photographic instrument before, he wanted to see the result of my work. When the picture was shown to him, he enquired by what possible means a drawing could be so perfectly completed in so short a space of time; and then, without waiting for an answer, and casting an anxious glance at me to make sure I had neither horns, hoofs, nor tail visible, he hurried off to the village with the conviction perhaps that my art was an uncanny one, and that my diabolical insignia were only craftily concealed. Accordingly, on taking my next view at the same village, I was surrounded by a crowd of sullen spectators, who, though it was explained that I was only securing a picture, favoured me with sundry tokens of their dread in the shape of sods and stones. Chang tried his eloquence on the people, but with little effect. We packed up as quickly as we could, and marched down the bank to cross over

THE GREAT RAPID, MITAN GORGE.

to the other side, where my companions were preparing for the ascent of the rapid. No doubt these villagers, some of them, had heard the popular fiction that pictures such as mine were made out of the eyes of Chinese babes. I narrowly escaped a stroke from an oar as I took refuge in a boat ; but the blow was warded off with a force that nearly sent its author spinning headlong into the stream.

This rapid is one of the grandest spectacles in the whole panorama of the river. The water presents a smooth surface as it emerges from the pass ; then suddenly seems to bend like a polished cylinder of glass ; falls eight or ten feet, and finally curves upwards in a glorious crest of foam as it surges away in wild tumult down the gorge. At this season sundry rocks enhance the peril of shooting this rapid. On our way down we persuaded Chang to come into the boat with us ; but as the vessel plunged and groaned in an agony of straining timbers, he became perfectly sick with panic fear. It was, indeed, hardly to be wondered at. The pilot we employed at this time was a tall bony man, with dark piercing eyes, a huge black moustache, and a mouth full of foxy fangs. He and his assistant guided the boat to what seemed to be the worst part of the rapid, and then launched her into the raging waters broadside on. After the first plunge she swept round bow foremost, tossing and writhing until I thought she would go to pieces and disappear. Meanwhile the pilot, flinging his arms on high, yelled and danced like a fiend about the deck, conveying the notion that the craft was doomed, although in reality he was only guiding his men at the helm. But the boat, regardless of oaths, oars, and rudder, sped forward with a fearful impetus, bearing right down for the rocks, dodged them at the last moment, when the pilot had been seized with a fit of frantic despair, and then with a groan of relief, darted into the comparatively smooth water far below. The pilot's buffoonery is probably part of his game. It pays when at last he presents himself for his legitimate fee, and for the trifle extra which he expects for saving our lives at the risk of his own. That there is great danger in shooting this rapid may be gathered from a survey of the wrecks that strew the shore, from the life-boats in constant attendance, or from the fact that the Chinese unload their boats at the head of the rapid, and have their cargo and themselves transported overland to the smooth waters below.

This 'Tsing-tan' rapid, then, is the greatest obstacle to the steam navigation of the Upper Yang-tsze. We had to hire fifty trackers from the village to aid our men in hauling the boat up the stream, which here ran about eight knots an hour; but I see no reason why the kind of steamer Captain Blakiston has suggested should not navigate this, and indeed any of the other rapids on the river, the steam power to be capable of being detached and made available either for towing the vessel up, or for retarding her swift and hazardous descent. Were the river once opened to trade, daring and scientific skill would be forthcoming to accomplish the end in view.

The mountains of this gorge are on the same stupendous scale as those of the Lukan passage below. On the 11th we reached a small walled town called Kwei, with not a single craft nor a human being near it to betoken trade of any kind. Yes! I forgot, there *was* one man, a beggar, on the bank; but even he was about to leave the place. Here we halted for the night, and in the morning visited some coal mines at a place called Patung, where the limestone strata, in which the coal is formed, stand up in nearly perpen-

THE MI-TAN GORGE, UPPER YANGTSZE

dicular walls against the edge of the river. Adits had been carried into the face of the rock, but they were all of them on an exceedingly small scale, simple burrowings without any depth. No shafts were sunk, and no ventilation was attempted. Coal abounds, and, even with such rude appliances as the miners possess, is turned out in considerable quantities; but the quality is not so good as some we got further up the gorge. The miner, when at work, carries a lamp stuck in his cap, much the same as those in use with us before Sir H. Davy's invention. The coal was shunted from the mouth of the pit down a groove cut in the face of the cliffs, and when conveyed any distance is transported in kreels on the backs of the women.

There were several mining villages at this place, and there every household is employed entirely in the trade, the children making fuel by mixing the coal with water and clay, and then casting it in moulds into blocks which weigh one catty (1 lb. $\frac{1}{3}$rd) a-piece. The miners who are occupied in this work earn about seven shillings a week, and their hours of labour are from seven o'clock in the morning to about 4 P.M.

Baron von Richthofen has assured us that there is plenty of coal in Hunan and Hupeh, and that the coal-field of Szechuan is also of enormous area. He adds that at the present rate of consumption the world could draw its supplies from Southern Shensi alone for several thousand years; and yet, in the very places referred to, it is not uncommon to find the Chinese storing up wood and millet-stalks for their firing in winter, while coal in untold quantities lies ready for use beneath their feet. These vast coal-fields will constitute the basis of China's future greatness, when steam shall have been called in to aid in the development of her enormous mineral wealth.

Wu-shan Gorge, which we reached on the morning of the 18th, is more than twenty miles long, and we entered this great defile at about ten o'clock. The river was perfectly placid, and the view which met our gaze at the mouth of the gorge was one of the finest we had hitherto encountered. The mountains rose in confused masses to a great altitude; the most distant peak, at the extremity of the passage, resembling a cut sapphire, with snow-lines that sparkled in the sun like the gleams of light on the facets of a gem, while the cliffs and precipices gradually deepened in outline until they reached the bold lights and shadows of the rocky foreground.

The officers of a gun-boat stationed at the boundary which parts the provinces of Hupeh and Szechuan, warned us to beware of pirates, and they had good reason for so doing. We came to anchor at a place where the rocks towering overhead wrapped the scene in pitchy darkness; and it was nearly 10 P.M. when our skipper sent to say we had better have our arms ready, as pirates were prowling about. One boat had just passed noiselessly up alongside, and its occupants were talking in whispers. We hailed them, but they made no reply; so we then fired over their heads. Our fire was responded to by a flash and a report from some men on the bank, not far off. After this we kept a watch all night, and at about two in the morning were all roused again to challenge a boat's crew that was noiselessly stealing down on our quarters. A second time we were forced to fire, and the sharp ping of the rifle-ball on the rocks had the effect of deterring further

A MINING VILLAGE, HUNAN PROVINCE

advances from our invisible foe. The disturbers of our repose must have been thoroughly acquainted with this part of the river, for even by day it is somewhat dark, and at night it is so utterly without light that no trading-boat would venture an inch from her rock-bound moorings. On another night, in this gorge, I

NATIVES OF SZECHUAN.

was summoned by my boy, who appeared in the cabin with a face of blank terror, and told me that he had just seen a group of luminous spirits that were haunting the pass. It was evident that something unusual had occurred, as I had never seen the boy in such a state of clammy fear before ; so we followed him on to the deck, and, looking up the precipice about eight hundred feet above our heads, we then saw three lights on the face of the rock performing a series of the most extraordinary evolutions. My old attendant declared, the cold perspiration trickling down his face the while, that he could make out sylph-like forms waving the lights to warn wayfarers off from the edge of the abyss :—

> 'This seraph band, each waved his hand,
> It was a heavenly sight:
> They stood as signals to the land,
> Each one a lovely light.'

The true explanation of the phenomenon lay in the fact, perhaps, that in this very gorge there are hapless beings, convicts immured in prison-cells cut in the face of the rocks, into which they are dropped by their gaolers from above, and from which they can never hope to escape unless to seek destruction by a plunge into the river below. Here, too, we find inhabitants of a widely different stamp, a number of the philosophic followers of Laou-tsoo, who pass their lives as hermits in these dark solitudes. In one cave we came across the remains of a Taouist philosopher of this sort ; a recluse who expired, so my boy informed me, at the ripe age of 200 years. Several of the boatmen averred that they knew him to have been more than a century old. His relics lay in the centre of the cave, covered over with a cairn of stones and sods, which had been thrown up by passing mountaineers.

February 15.—To-day we met with a disaster as we were ascending a rapid. The boat was caught by a blast of wind, and this, aided by a strong eddy, was just sending her over when the skipper's mate, the most active youth on board, sprang forward and cut the tracking line. The trackers, unexpectedly relieved of the great strain, were sent sprawling over the rocks; while, as for the boat, she righted at once, spun round and round, and then drifted down the rapid, till at last she settled on a spit of sand half a mile below the scene of the accident. So far the result was satisfactory; but then we were on one side of the stream and our crew on the other. As there was a village near at hand, we at once repaired thither to engage a boat to convey our men across; but not a soul would stir unless we paid them beforehand nearly as much as would buy another village, such as it was. We offered them what the boatmen considered a fair hire, but this they stedfastly refused; until at last we jumped into one of their boats, and threatened to use it ourselves. Seeing this, they thought better of it, apologised, and struck a fair bargain. We came to, for that night, above the Wu-shan Gorge. Before us, on the left bank, lay the walled town of Wu-shan, surrounded by low hills and richly-tilled valleys; and here we noticed the outlet of a small river that joins the Yang-tsze, and down which salt is brought in great quantities from mines at a place called Ta-ning.

Opium, silk, and tea, are among the chief products of this district, and it is also singularly rich in fruits of various sorts. We bought the most delicious oranges I ever tasted in China for a shilling a hundred. Next day we made a strenuous though futile effort to reach Kwei-chow-fu; but we could make no headway in the face of a storm that swept in fearful blasts down the gorge, and filled the air with a fine blinding sand, most irritating to the eyes. We therefore left Szechuan on the 16th, after having ascended a distance of between twelve and thirteen hundred miles above Shanghai. The return voyage was comparatively easy, and eighteen days after leaving Szechuan we again set foot on the foreign settlement at Hankow. Here our friends received us with a hearty welcome, and plied us with the most minute enquiries as to the state of the river, and the exact appearance of the proposed new treaty-port at Ichang. Several even supposed that we must have been looking out for land in the new settlement, and had perhaps negotiated some secret investments in likely sites—a course of action which, as things have turned out, would on the whole have proved a rather premature and ruinous speculation.

At Hankow I rejoined some of my oldest friends in China, and they greeted me, after my voyage, almost as one risen from the dead. It was not without a pang of sincere regret at parting from them that I stepped on board the steamer.

I stopped at Kiukiang on the downward trip, and spent two or three days in the settlement. The native city, although it holds an important position near the mouth of the Po-yung lake, and thus communicates with the network of canals and streams that form the trade routes into the vast green-tea fields of Kiangsi and Ngan-Hwei, has nevertheless failed to attain a high commercial position; nor has the foreign settlement either done much yet towards monopolising the traffic of the richly productive districts by which it is surrounded. The city suffered a severe blow at the hands of the rebels, who left it a ruined waste in 1861;

and even at the time of my visit it had not regained its former prosperity. Nevertheless, the streets were again struggling up by degrees out of the wreck and *debris* which had been left behind by the benign followers of the 'Heavenly King.'

Kiukiang will probably rise into much greater commercial importance when the Po-yung lake shall have been thrown open to steam navigation. One or two excursions which I made into the surrounding districts enabled me to form a very favourable estimate of the fertility of the soil, and the prosperity of its cultivators. The region, however, seemed thinly populated, and this fact alone is sufficient to account for the absence of the poverty and misery which fall to the lot of the toiling millions in many quarters of the land.

At a place called Tai-ping-kung, about ten miles inland from Kiukiang, I found the ruins of an ancient shrine, presenting most remarkable architectural features. All that remained of a once extensive edifice were two towers pierced with windows, which looked something like the pointed gothic apertures of a mediæval European building. The walls of a small joss-house adjoining were built partly of finely sculptured stones: and the whole ruin, indeed, was unlike anything I had before seen in China. It seemed more European than Chinese, and possibly may point to Ricci's Jesuit mission to that part of the province in 1590. It is, however, said to have once been one of the greatest Buddhist establishments in Cathay. On the way back from this old shrine I passed over classic ground, where the rocks are inscribed with the praises of Chu-fu-tze, a celebrated Confucian commentator and philosopher who lived in the twelfth century.

Even the spot where he dwelt as a hermit is still pointed out, and his tomb may be seen on a mound there, shaded by venerable cypress and pine-trees. He is depreciated now-a-days by the modern school of Chinese doctors as somewhat unsound in his doctrine, and as having been influenced by the philosophy of the Buddhists.

The next point at which I touched was Nanking, the ancient capital of China, where there is no foreign settlement, nor any port open for trade. It was dark when, with my boys, and baggage, and two Chinese officers of the Governor-General's household, I descended from the steamer 'Hirado' into a native boat, and landed on the muddy bank beneath the outer walls of this famous city. We had to spend the night in a small shed which had been provided for the convenience of passengers making use of the river steamers. The place was crowded with an orderly company of natives, who very kindly made room for me to repose myself on a table; but it was in vain that I courted sleep, for the air was obscured by clouds of tobacco-smoke, and conversation was kept up with an incessant clamour all night through. As it happened, the talk was of the deepest interest; Tseng-kuo-fan, the great Chinese general who had fought side by side with Li-hung-chang and Colonel Gordon in the suppression of the Taiping rebellion, had just expired at his palace in Nanking. Many present said that he had perished by his own hand, or had succumbed to an overdose of gold-leaf; whereas the truth was, as I afterwards discovered, that he had died in a fit of apoplexy, the second with which he had been attacked. His death was a great disappointment to me, as my chief motive in visiting Nanking had been to see the celebrated leader, and, if possible, obtain his likeness for my larger work. I carried with me an introduction to him from Li-hung-chang, the Governor-General of Pei-chil-li, and this note I duly presented to his son, who sent me a reply expressing the deep regret of the family that they should have missed the opportunity of obtaining a portrait. But a general officer subsequently remarked that after all it was, perhaps, as well for me that I had not arrived in time to take the picture, as most assuredly the speaker himself, and others as well as he, would have accused me of causing the untimely death. It is a wide-spread Chinese belief, from which men of the highest intelligence are by no means free, that, in taking a photograph, a certain portion of the vital principle is extracted from the body of the sitter, and that thus his decease within a limited period is rendered an absolute certainty.

The reader will gather from this that I was frequently looked upon as a forerunner of death, as a sort of Nemesis, in fact; and I have seen unfortunates, stricken with superstitious dread, fall down on bended knees and beseech me not to take their likeness or their life with the fatal lens of my camera. But all this might have occurred in our own country not many years ago, where a photograph would have been esteemed a work of the devil, or to catch the sunlit image with the dark eye of science would have been likened to the ancient miracle of our Lord when he gave sight to the blind.

Tseng-kuo-fan was one of the foremost statesmen of his time. He was a member of the Grand Secretariat, and was created a noble of the second class after the expulsion of the rebels from Nanking. He was then at the zenith of his power, and it was even said that his wide-spread influence was dreaded by the court at Peking. In 1868 he became Governor-General of Pei-chil-li, and was removed from that office after the Tientsin massacre, and for the third time appointed Governor-General of the two Kiang.

The view of Nanking was a disappointing one. It is simply a vast area enclosed within a high wall which makes a circuit of twenty-two miles, and is therefore the largest city in the kingdom. Near at hand are several heights crowned with temples, and such-like sacred buildings, while a number of yamens and religious edifices may be seen dotting the great open spaces where cultivation is carried on. But the city itself, as usual, is crowded into the narrowest limits capable of supporting half a million struggling sons of Han.

There were still many dreary acres of demolished streets with not a single occupant, but in other quarters the work of restoration was being actively carried on. This great 'Southern Capital' must probably have been at one time what Le Comte stated, 'a splendid city surrounded by walls one within the other,' the outermost 'sixteen long leagues round.' Such may have been its condition some fourteen hundred years ago, when it first became the Imperial head-quarters, or perhaps even so late as the fourteenth century, when Hung-Woo, the first Ming Emperor, is reported to have restored it to its pristine glory. But the place had already fallen sadly off at the advent of the Tien-wang, who conferred upon it the questionable honour of making it the capital of a Chinese dynasty once more.

It was said to have been at the recommendation of a very humble follower, an old sailor, that the 'Heavenly King,' as he styled himself, decided on making Nanking the seat of his celestial government; but in other matters this self-made potentate was not so easily persuaded. Why should he have been? He believed implicitly that he was a second son of God sent down to redeem China.

When the Imperialists were marshalling their forces around the great Ming tomb, and when his old soldiers and faithful adherents were starving in the streets, he gave orders that they should be fed on dew and sing a new song till the hour of deliverance came. Calmly he sat within his palace looking with disdain upon the gathering forces that ere long were to strike the fatal blow. The city had not yet fallen into the hands of his foes when his faith and fortitude forsook him, and he ended his days by his own hand.

It is a tedious journey round the city moat to the southern gate. Many boats were to be met winding their way along this canal, or else drawn up into groups and forming little market-places every here and there. Sometimes we fell in with a wretched petty settlement on the banks, that looked like the scum and refuse that had been tossed over the city wall; and at one small bridge beneath which we passed it was told me that there, after the fall of Nanking, the canal had been dammed up by the rebel heads. Outside the southern gate there is a large suburb. Why it should have been planted there, when there is so much vacant space within the walls, is difficult to tell. Many of its dwellings are nothing more than rude huts erected over ground strewn with the graves and bones of Taipings and Imperialists mingled together in kindred dust. Here, too, I found the old porcelain tower of Nanking (once one of the seven wonders of the world, but now levelled to the earth), and a number of small speculators driving a trade in its porcelain bricks. But most of the bricks of this tower, and of the 'Monastery of Gratitude' to which it belonged, were used in constructing the Nanking arsenal close by: and of the two edifices I should say that the latter, planted as it has been by the foremost son of Han (Li-hung-chang) in the very heart of the 'Central Flowery Land,' will be held to be far the more wonderful structure, except by those who may have a special prejudice in favour of porcelain pagodas. Here, then, the old Buddhist tower and the monastery, with its monotonous chants, have been replaced by a temple dedicated to the Chinese Vulcan and Mars, whose altars are furnaces, whose worshippers are melters of iron, and from whose shrines come the never-ceasing rattle of machinery and the reports of rifles that are being tested for service.

This arsenal, built as I have said, under the auspices of Li-hung-chang, was the first of its kind in China, and is conducted on the most advanced scientific principles under the superintendence of Dr. Macartney. It is, indeed, a startling innovation on the old style of things. If the Chinese first taught us the use of guns (they are said to have employed them in 1232 at the siege of Khai-fung-fu), we are certainly repaying the obligation with interest by instructing them how our deadliest weapons are to be made. In this arsenal many hundreds of tons of guns and ammunition are manufactured every year, and I have no doubt its products have already proved of great service in the prompt suppression of the Mahometan outbreak in the provinces of Kiangsu and Shensi. Here the Chinese can turn out heavy guns for battery-trains, or field-artillery, howitzers, gatling-guns, torpedoes, rockets, shot, shells, cartridges and caps. The rocket factory stands on an open plot of ground some distance from the main building; and this is the place appropriated to the filling of rockets and shells with their explosive contents. With respect to these arsenals and their high state of efficiency, I have one further remark to offer; and that is, that were the strict foreign management under which they have matured to be withdrawn, they could not at present be carried on so as to be of really effectual service. Probably the same amount of money would be spent on their maintenance, but it would be subjected, in all likelihood, to a process of official filtration which would admit of nothing more than the purchase of inferior materials, and the employment of labourers so underpaid, that they would have no heart to bestow honest work on the implements of whose construction now they are so justly proud. An experiment of this sort was once tried, to humour an officer who boasted himself able to produce everything in the shape of modern warlike inventions as perfectly as any foreigner in the Empire. But the attempt was not repeated, as the shells he manufactured turned out much more deadly projectiles in the hands of his own men than they could ever have proved in the ranks of an enemy. They were badly cast with coarse iron, and their dangerous imperfections were filled up with black-leaded clay. So my humble opinion is, that before the Chinese can hope to take a position among the civilised Powers of the world, they must acquire something of simple honesty, and unlearn much of the science of deception by which they study to enrich themselves, while making ready to conquer their foes. It may happen that Li-hung-chang, the Chinaman who has now most power in the Empire, will in time teach his subordinates something of the value of this simple quality of honest dealing.

'Kin-Shan,' or 'Golden Island;' 'Silver Island;' and the mouth of the Grand Canal, were the last objects of interest I saw on the Yang-tsze river. The Grand Canal may be set down as the greatest public work of the race who wasted years of needless labour in constructing the great wall to shut out the barbarous hordes who, after all, are now masters of the Empire. But this huge artificial waterway is now useless in many places, and utterly broken down; although it might have proved of incalculable service in draining off the great waters of the Yellow River, which have from time to time spread their desolating floods over the vast productive plains of the interior.

CHAPTER XIV.

Chefoo—The Foreign Settlement—The Yellow River—Silk—Its Production—Taku Forts—The Peiho River—Chinese Progress—Floods in Pei-chil-li—Their Effects—Tientsin—The Sisters' Chapel—Condition of the People—A Midnight Storm—Tung-chow—Peking—The Tartar and Chinese Divisions of the Metropolis—Its Roads, Shops, and People—The Foreign Hotel—Temple and Domestic Architecture—The Tsungli Yamen—Prince Kung, and the High Officers of the Empire—Literary Championship—The Confucian Temple—The Observatory—Ancient Chinese Instruments—Yang's House—Habits of the Ladies—Peking Enamelling—Yuen-Ming-Yuen—Remarkable Cenotaph—A Chinese Army—Li-hung-chang—The Inn of 'Patriotic Perfection'—The Great Wall—The Ming Tombs.

Of late years Chefoo has become the favourite watering-place for foreigners resident at Peking or Shanghai, for there bracing air and sea-bathing may be enjoyed during the hottest months of summer.

The beach on which the European hotel is built skirts the foot of a low range of grassy hills, and reminded me, in its semicircular sweep and general aspect, of Brodic Bay in Arran, on the west coast of Scotland. I have a lively recollection of Chefoo Bay; of its stretch which at the time appeared interminable; and of the soft yielding sand over which, with a friend remarkable alike for his good-nature, weight, and agility, I had to run from the steamer to forestall the other passengers and secure the best apartment for an invalid lady from Shanghai. The thermometer at the time was standing at about one hundred degrees in the shade, so that after completing our task we were in a condition to enjoy to the full the cool breeze that swept through the verandah of the hotel. It was an unpretending but charming retreat, and none the less so on account of the many comforts which the enterprising proprietor had in store for his guests.

Chefoo foreign settlement lies on the opposite side of the bay, and is about the least inviting place of the kind on the coast. But still we must not forget that it enjoys the honour of standing on the ground of the most classic province in the Empire, where the engineering labours of the celebrated Yu were in part performed. Confucius, too, was a native of the Shan-tung province, and so indeed was Mensius his successor. While Pythagoras was pursuing his philosophical researches at Crotona, Confucius was compiling the classical lore that has since been to China what the compass is to the mariner at sea. But this ancient guide to national prosperity, social, political, and religious, when relied on by those who now-a-days control the helm of the Empire, is as untrustworthy as the compass in a man-of-war, where the steersman makes no allowance for the influences of the iron plates and steel guns with which science has surrounded his needle. And yet fain would the wisest Confucianists of the 'Central Flowery Land' still rivet their fond gaze on their ancient books; fain would they guide their steps by the rushlight of a dim science and philosophy, lit by sages of a thousand years ago; and that though truth, like the sun in noonday splendour, is shining on the nations around.

The foreign trade of Chefoo is small, though not unimportant. Whether it be that the natives affect more the simple robes of their ancient sages than the less costly cotton fabrics of Manchester, or whether the constantly recurring floods of the 'Hwang-ho' or 'Yellow River' have so impoverished the inland districts as to materially damage trade, is a difficult point to determine. At any rate the commercial relations of Chefoo with the outer world are by no means so extensive as they might, and undoubtedly would be, were foreigners and their wares once freely admitted into the interior, and European science made use of for keeping the old waterways open, draining the plains, and thus protecting the people from the grievous inundations that annually lay waste their lands.

Since the Yellow River has changed its course and now flows to the north of the Shan-tung mountains, a great portion of the Grand Canal has been rendered useless. In many places the banks have been carried away, and an eye-witness has described the scene in the following words:—'For dreariness and desolation no scene can exceed that which the Yellow River here presents; everything, natural and artificial, is at the mercy of the muddy dun-coloured waters as they sweep on their course towards the sea.'[1]

But we shall see, as we pass through Pei-chil-li, how these floods actually affect the people. Thus while a considerable extent of country suffers from the withdrawal of the great river from its old channel, parts of Shan-tung and Pei-chil-li come in for a superabundant share of its waters. Notwithstanding this there are some portions of the former province which are as productive as any soil in the world, and where the nature of the climate is favour-

[1] *Journal of the Royal Geographical Society*, xl. 5.

able to the culture of a wide range of products. These include millet, wheat, barley, rice, tobacco, and beans—the latter, in the shape of 'bean cake,' forming a valuable article of exportation. Besides the foregoing a certain sort of dark-coloured silk fabric, known as 'Pongee' silk, is produced in Shan-tung, and exported in steadily increasing quantities from Chefoo. This silk is obtained from a wild black worm that feeds on a different kind of leaf from the mulberry. Rearing silkworms in China is an exceedingly delicate process, and one which one might almost have supposed unsuited to the natives, for the little worm is most exacting in its habits. It has even been stated that it will refuse either to feed or to work before strangers; and the Chinese aver that it cannot endure the presence of foreigners or the sounds of barbaric tongues. If in this respect it resembles its masters, it differs from them widely in its abhorrence of uncleanly odours, and indeed in a polluted atmosphere will sicken and starve itself to death. For this reason the Chinese, from the time when the worm emerges from the egg to the moment when it perishes in its own silken robe, must suffer great inconvenience by the compulsory absence of all those strong smells wherein so many of them take an unaffected delight. No wonder, then, if the close of the silk season, when the dainty little toiler has woven its shroud and met its doom, should be one of great rejoicing.

Like the culture of tea, silk—which confers an enormous revenue on China and has now become a luxury indispensable to the world—is the most modest industry imaginable. Let us cast a glance on the various progressive steps through which the staple passes till it is ready for the looms of China or Lyons.

The eggs are hatched about the middle of April, and the best season to obtain them for exportation is in March or the beginning of April. The young worms, when hatched, are placed on bamboo frames and fed on mulberry-leaves cut up into small shreds. As the worms increase in size they are transferred to a larger number of frames, and are fed with leaves not so finely shred; and so the process continues until, in their last stage, the leaves are given to them entire. The price of leaves runs from four shillings and sixpence to eight shillings a picul (133 lbs.).

After hatching, the worms continue eating during five days, and then sleep for the first time for two days. When they awake again their appetite is not quite so good, and they usually eat for four days only and sleep again for two days more. Then they eat for the third time for four days and repose for two. This eating and sleeping is usually repeated four times, and then, having gained full strength, they proceed to spin their cocoons. The task of spinning occupies from four to seven days more; and when this business is completed three days are spent in stripping off the cocoon, and some seven days later each small cultivator brings his silken harvest to the local market and disposes of it to native traders, who make it up into bales.

Leaving popular superstitious influences out of account, the quality of the silk is first of all affected by the breed of the worms that spin it, then by the quality of the leaves and the mode of feeding. As I have already remarked, the silk-worm is injured by noise, by the presence and especially by the handling of strangers, and by noxious smells. They must be fed, too, at regular hours, and the temperature of the apartment must not be too high.

The greatest defect in Chinese silk is due to the primitive mode of reeling which the natives adopt, and if they could only be induced to use foreign reeling machines its value might be raised 40 or 50 per cent. The rude way in which silk is at present reeled imparts damaging irregularities to the thread. Shanghai is the great silk mart, and there, about June 1, the first season's silk is usually brought down. It is never the growers who bring the silk to the foreign market. These growers are invariably small farmers, who either purchase the leaves, or have a few mulberry bushes planted in some odd corner of their tilled lands, and the rearing of the worm and the production of silk by no means monopolise the whole of their time. It is only a spring occupation for the women and younger members of their families. Chinese merchants or brokers proceed to the country markets, and there collect the produce until they have secured enough to make up a parcel for the Shanghai or Chefoo markets, where it is bought up by foreigners for exportation.

I paid two visits to Chefoo, and must have experienced the extremes of temperature. On the first occasion the heat was intense, but on my return the cold was so severe that my boy Ahong had his ears and nose frost-bitten. We had proceeded to a hill-top to obtain a picture of Chefoo, but the north-west wind, blowing from the icy steppes of Mongolia, was like to freeze the blood in our veins. Having, however, succeeded in taking a photograph, I sent to a neighbouring hut for a bottle of water to wash the negative;

but no sooner had I withdrawn the plate from the shelter of the dark tent, and poured the water over it, than the liquid froze on its surface and hung in icicles around its edge. Ahong was standing nearly knee-deep in snow, with his face buried in his coat sleeves; and as for the bottle, the water within had frozen into a solid lump. In spite of these difficulties we adjourned to a friendly hut, where we thawed the plate over a charcoal fire and washed it with hot water. Circulation had been arrested at the point of Ahong's nose and also round his ears, so that sores broke out soon after, and for the space of a month or more kept him in lively recollection of Chefoo.

The next place of importance at which we touched on our route north was Taku, at the mouth of the Peiho. The Taku forts are mud strongholds, which have been often and well described. At the time of my visit these forts had been under repair; still they were not yet properly garrisoned, nor were their guns all mounted. I passed along a stone pavement which leads from the river across the inner extremity of the mud slough. It was here, in 1859, that so many of our men were shot down in the unsuccessful attempt to storm the southern fort. We carried the place without much difficulty a twelvemonth afterwards. The only entrance into this fort is across a wide ditch from behind. As for me, I passed inside it without a word being asked; for, indeed, there were only one or two coolies loitering about the enclosure. The walls are of great thickness, and built, as formerly, of mud and millet-stalks—a composition well adapted to resist shot. Within were two batteries of over fifty guns a-piece, one above the other, and commanding the entrance to the stream. Some of them, however, were rusty, badly mounted on their carriages, and altogether sadly in want of repair. Lastly, I noticed two large American smooth-bores lying half buried in mud in front of the officers' quarters. On the whole the place wore the look of a deserted mud-quarry rather than a fortress. But I have been informed that a great change has since come over the scene—that these fortresses, one on each side of the Peiho, are now armed with Krupp guns and properly garrisoned; so that thus the defence

TAKU FORTS.

of the capital has been secured, after a scheme planned out and decided upon long before the Formosa difficulty cropped up. I myself saw a battery of Krupp guns landed at Tientsin before I left that place of dark memories; and, indeed, there can be no question that the Chinese are busily arming themselves with modern weapons, laying up stores of destructive projectiles and ammunition, and addressing themselves with earnestness to the task of guarding their own shores from invasion. It may be—nay, it must be—that there is a purpose in all this. The Chinese Government have not been blind all these years to what has been going on in Japan, to say nothing of the visions they may entertain of possible encounters with more formidable foes. They undoubtedly still retain the notion that they have an absolute right to do what they like with their own country and in it; and they are probably only preparing themselves to assert or defend this right when a suitable opportunity presents itself. Prince Kung, in his despatch about the Woosung bar at Shanghai, has declined to dredge a channel to facilitate trade, and looks upon the sand-bank as a barrier set there by Divine Providence to aid the Chinese in the defence of the country and its approaches. He further points out that each nation has a right to guard and protect its own territory by the means it alone deems best. It is perhaps very natural to suppose that China was made exclusively for the support of Chinamen, and that no other race has a right to question this divine arrangement, or to seek by the simple dredging of a sand-bar to thwart the plans of a kind Providence, who is thus closing up the river-courses against the commerce which furnishes millions of Chinese with means to feed and clothe themselves that formerly they could never have obtained.

In this narrow policy there is not the faintest recognition of that divine progress which, by a thousand telegraphs, railways, and industries, is tending more and more to bind the nations of the earth together in one universal kinmanship, where, by free intercourse and liberal enlightened government, peoples of every nation, kindred, and tongue, will be rendered mutually dependent on each other.

Perhaps the mandarins in charge of the hydrography of Pei-chil-li will also say that the waters which have perpetually laid waste the province wherein the Imperial city stands have been sent there by divine superintendence, to prevent the advance of an enemy on their great metropolis. And yet few enemies could work more disasters in annual raids over the fertile plains of Shan-tung and Pei-chil-li than do those turbid waters which the Yellow River, with an awful certainty, spreads far and wide through these provinces from year to year. In spite of this, by the exercise of a little foresight and honesty, the great Hwang-ho, which in former days was only a messenger of peace and plenty, might be kept flowing on within its natural channel.

The inundations were predicted just as they happened years before the swollen river burst its barriers at Lung-men-Kan, and might have been easily prevented by keeping clear 'what has always been an artificial channel.'[1] The business was put off, however, from one year to another, until at last the red flood burst upon the plains, and transformed a fruitful smiling country into lakes, lagoons, and pestilential marshes.

As we steamed up the Peiho there were many places where not a trace of the river's banks was to be discovered, and the further we ascended the more apparent became the fearful ravages of the flood. The millet-crop was rotting under water, and whole hamlets had in many places been swept away. The village dwellings, like the Taku forts, were for the most part con-

[1] *Journal of the Royal Geographical Society*, xl. 19.

structed of millet-stalks and mud; but however well calculated to resist the shots of an ordinary foe, these frail abodes, one by one, had silently dissolved before the invading waters, leaving nothing behind them but something that looked like grave-mounds, the melancholy landmarks of each new work of desolation. We could see the wretched villagers squatting on the tops of their hillocks, sheltered by scraps of thatch or matting which they had rescued from the flood. All who had the means were removing to Tientsin, where the authorities were said to be doing their utmost to relieve the sufferers. Singularly enough I overheard a Chinaman say that he considered the flood a punishment for the Tientsin massacre, which had occurred just a year before.

It is quite impossible to estimate the misery that such disasters bring upon the toiling poor of the province, who are thus bereft of food, shelter, and fuel; and that, too, when the winter is just at hand. The scene on all sides presented one sheet of water, only broken by the wrecks of villages, and by islands of mud, where herds of cattle were packed and perishing for want of pasture. Men, women, and children, were to be seen fishing in the shallows of their harvest-fields. Fish were abundant; and this was fortunate, as the people had little else to subsist on. How they got through the hot days and cold nights, and how many of them survived their hardships only to be subjected to them in the succeeding year, it is impossible to say. We could tell from the bodies drifting seaward that Death was busy among them, relieving the sick and satisfying the hungry in his own sad final way.

The Chinese, like all peoples both ancient and

modern, have a superstitious dread of disturbing the resting-places of their dead. For many miles around Tientsin the country is one vast burial-ground, and it was pitiful to notice the efforts the living were making to lash the coffins of their dead to trees or to posts which they had driven into the mud. But numbers of the huge clumsy coffins were to be seen floating adrift, with no living relation to care for their silent occupants.

The water was so deep that in many places the tortuous river's channel had been abandoned, and native craft were sailing overland, so to speak, direct for the city.

Our steamer, the 'Sin-nan-sing,' had great difficulty in turning the sharp bends of the river; her bow would stick in the mud of one bank, and her screw in the other; but at length Tientsin was reached, and there we found the water five or six feet deep at the back of the foreign settlement, and the Peking road submerged. The club, too, was surrounded, and could only be reached by boat, and boating excursions could also be made to the celebrated treaty joss-house.

The foreigners were looking forward to the prospect of soon being shut in by a sea of ice. Here, on the bank of the river, was a British hotel called 'The Astor House,' its modest proportions almost concealed by the huge sign-board in front. This establishment was constructed of mud, and on one side of it a window had fallen out, while on the other the wall had fallen in. I had a look at this unpromising exterior, and some conversation with its proprietor. The latter was an Englishman, and he lamented to me over the wreck of his property. There were still two apartments in front, one containing a billiard-table and the other a bar; but a couple of mud bed-rooms had dissolved, and could be seen in solution through a broken wall. The stabling in the rear, also, out of sheer depression at losing its occupants, had taken a header into the water and disappeared. We next passed out of doors to examine the ravages of the flood in sundry outhouses, which had also settled down; but the dreary prospect was obscured by a cloud of musquitoes, the pests of the place during the summer months. In the bar-room I found a Scotchman connected with the Tientsin Powder Factory, saying some very hard things about the peculiar views of a Chinese tailor to whom he had entrusted some 'vara guid braid claith to mak a pair of breeks.' It appeared that the tailor had found it necessary, on account of family concerns, to remove from Tientsin to another district, and had taken the cloth with him without going through the ceremony of leaving his card.

I slept on board the steamer, and started for Peking on August 29. Before setting out I engaged a Tientsin man named Tao, or 'Virtue,' at the rate of nine dollars a month; but this sum was a trifle compared with what he intended to make out of me, as in every transaction, whether it was simply to change a dollar into cash or to buy provisions, he made a profitable bargain for himself. My own southern men could have managed better, although they were ignorant of the northern dialect, and could only make known their wants in writing. Systematic pilfering, however, I soon discovered to be the common attribute of servants in the north.

We engaged a boat to convey us to Tung-chow,

the nearest point by water to Peking. This boat carried a wooden house in the centre, which could be shut up all round at night, so as to keep the cold out; and it was just large enough to accommodate my party and baggage. The space within it was divided into two compartments, and in the after one stood a clay cooking-galley, around which the boys were stowed. Our crew consisted of a father, Wong-Tsing, and his two sons Wong-su and Wong-soon. We had to make our way up through the city of Tientsin along a narrow ever-changing channel between thousands of native trading-boats. Many of these, to all outward appearance, were in the last stages of dry rot, although, according to the strange notions of the Chinese, they would be esteemed in every respect seaworthy as long as they could hold together. The only sound pieces of wood about them were slung over the side, to prevent the iron-spiked poles of passing boatmen from destroying the crazy old hulls.

It was not without a free use of such poles, and the vilest epithets in the language, that we got clear of the floating Babel at last. The left bank, hereabouts, was covered with mounds of salt, piled up beneath the mat sheds which the salt monopolist had erected to protect his precious store.

Here, too, were junks laden with cargoes of cotton and cotton fabrics, which the Chinese merchants were about to convey to the markets of the interior. These native merchants have their own agents in Shanghai, who send up cotton, piece goods, opium, and other foreign products, in the steamers which ply between that port and Tientsin.

The river at this point was about 200 yards wide,

and on the right bank Tao pointed out the black bare walls of the Sisters' Chapel, that had been burned twelve months before. There, too, we could see the ruins of the hospital, where the Sisters of Mercy had consecrated their lives to the ministration of the sick, and to rescuing outcast children; for which good works they had here been brutally murdered by an ignorant and superstitious mob. There was still a heap of ashes in front of the edifice, and the long breach in its wall through which the murderers dragged their hapless victims to their doom. The breach had indeed been plastered up with mud, a fitting type of the unsatisfactory way in which the Chinese sought to atone for an outrage which was perpetrated almost within sight of the Governor-General's yamen.

From this point, too, we could descry, at the upper end of the reach, the imposing ruins of the Roman Catholic cathedral, the only striking object in the city of Tientsin; and the reflection was forced upon me, from what I know of native superstition, that that noble pile of building, standing as it did so much above what the Chinese themselves hold most sacred in their yamens and shrines, must in itself have stirred up a bitter feeling against foreigners. This feeling was without doubt greatly intensified by horrible stories most ingeniously spread abroad by the literary members of society, describing how foreigners manufacture medicines from the eyes and hearts of Chinese children, or even of adults. In the latter case it is to procure silver that these practices are alleged to be carried on; and this we may gather from the accompanying passage out of a native work which was in brisk circulation when the massacre took place. 'The reason for extracting the eyes is this. From one hundred pounds of Chinese lead can be extracted eight pounds of silver, and the remaining ninety-two pounds of lead can be sold at the original cost. But the only way to obtain this silver is by compounding the lead with the eyes of Chinamen. The eyes of foreigners are of no use, hence they do not take out the eyes of their own people.' Further on it says: 'The people of France without exception follow the false and corrupt Tien-chu religion. They have devilish arts by which they transform men into beasts,' &c.

This pamphlet is full of matter unfit for quotation, and concludes with an appeal to the people to rise and exterminate the hated strangers :—

'Therefore, these contemptible beings having aroused our righteous wrath, we, heartily adhering to the kingdom of our sovereign, would not only give vent to a little of the hate that will not allow us to stand under the same heaven with them, but would make an eternal end of the distress of being obliged to have them ever near us. . . . If the temporising policy is adopted, this non-human species will again increase.'[1] The author goes on, without mincing matters, to urge the utter extermination of foreigners, and the preservation of the virtuous followers of Confucius. When we consider that this pamphlet had a wide, though, as it was pretended, a secret circulation; and above all, when we reflect on the utter ignorance and superstition, and the savage fierceness, of the half-starved classes whom it professed to caution and enlighten, and on whom the calm, moderate, and subtle style of some of

[1] *Death-blow to Corrupt Doctrines.*

its worst passages must have produced a fearful effect, we cannot wonder at the result. So far as I can judge, too, the future looks dark and foreboding; nor will matters mend while Roman Catholic missionaries persist in offering violence to Chinese prejudices by raising their churches far above the level of the highest roofs of the Imperial Palace itself, and by exercising a sort of semi-political protection over their converts.

Tao believed implicitly in the strange stories which he had heard about the priests, and about the poor Sisters who had been so cruelly put to death. The ruins now were being carefully guarded by a fleet of native gun-boats; but there were none of them at hand when succour was really needed, nor did they reach the spot until long after the deed had been accomplished.

I could not refrain from offering some remarks to my new man about the miserable mud huts in which his countrymen dwelt. Whereupon, with a vanity not uncommon in his race—although it surprised me at the time—he pointed out what he held to be the advantages of occupying such abodes. His argument ran something like this:—The materials, mud and millet-stalks, can be had all over the plain at every man's doorway cheaply; for the lifting, indeed; whereas wood and stone are too dear for poor people to procure. Then, again, with such materials every man can be his own architect and mason; and finally, when floods and rain dissolve the tenement, it sinks down quietly, forming a mound on which the furniture and domestic utensils may repose, and on which the family may sit till the waters have subsided, and they are able to set too again, and raise up their broken walls.

The river here is spanned by one or two pontoon

bridges, which had to be opened to let us pass through. These bridges form great impediments to the traffic, both on land and by water; for the pontoon is never pulled up to make a passage until about a dozen junks and boats have collected, and their owners, who by that time have been long waiting for the event, are clamouring and fighting amongst themselves to get first through. While the boats are passing through, the land traffic is of course interrupted, and crowds of foot passengers and vehicles are pressing forward on each side of the aperture to await the replacement of the pontoon. One or two of them, unable to make their way back, were driven over into the water, and rescued by boat-hooks as we passed. The narrow wooden pavement of the bridge was made still narrower by a throng of shops and stalls, lepers, beggars, and jugglers.

The country on both sides of the stream presented a poor aspect, and seemed to be anything but thickly populated. Many of the houses, in the mud villages which we passed, were overgrown with grass and weeds to such an extent that they hardly looked like human abodes; while the finest, or rather the least objectionable, specimens of the domestic architecture of the district, though to all appearance built of solid brick, proved not to be really so constructed. Thus there were some of them where builders were at work, and then the walls were seen to consist only of two thin layers of bricks filled in with mud; but should the mud by some leak in the roof become moist, it settles gradually down. Simultaneously the brick barrier begins to bulge out, and increases in size slowly, until at last it bursts and discharges the mud, whose presence it can no longer confine. Other houses of a much more ingenious kind were made of a sort of honeycomb of brick filled in with clay. This might form a cheap style of wall for the erection of our magnificent modern London terraces, where the houses are, I believe, built in continuous blocks, simply to prevent them from being blown down like nine-pins. But these honey-combed brick walls were really very ingenious, whereas our metropolitan masonry is quite the opposite.

As the land rose towards the hills, which sweep like a crescent around the north of Peking, we emerged from the flooded plains into a less desolate region, where the people were not so destitute of the common necessaries of life, and where the banks were lined with ripe fields of millet. Our boatmen, like the dwellers on land, lived on the flour of this useful cereal, which they season with salt-fish and garlic. The flour is made into bread, or rather cooked and pulled out into strings of hot tough elastic dough. This the people consumed in great quantities at meal-times, and always appeared to recover from its effects, although to me it seemed just about as digestible as worsted balls, rolls of flannel, or india-rubber cables.

Here we encountered many ponies, mules, and donkeys in use; the mules being of an exceedingly fine breed, and having, many of them, zebra stripes—across the legs. As for the donkeys, they were thoroughly domesticated, and followed their masters to and fro like dogs.

The huts improved in appearance as we neared Tung-chow, and the villagers, too, were more robust-looking, although even the best of these, in spite of their willow-shaded dwellings and their harvest-fields, betrayed evidences of a hard-struggling hand-to-mouth existence.

I shall never forget a sunset which I witnessed in this district, and which even produced an impression on my material-minded Chinese followers. So much was this the case that the Wong family insisted on a halt, and my boys cooked my dinner with native garlic —a graceful compliment to the charms of the locality, though disgusting to my own less educated tastes. There was an unnatural heat, and an oppressive stillness in the air. The sky was aflame with saffron-coloured light, while on the banks the millet, with its thousand plumes, stood out like a rich entablature of gold, supported by the glowing shafts that the sun sent deep down into the placid stream. As day declined the distant hills passed from a bright sapphire into a dull leaden hue; broad shadows were flung across the plain, while a dark ominous cloud, like some strange spirit of the night, caught the last gleam of sunshine as it slowly unfolded its wings across the west. Wong, the skipper, silently cast out another anchor, and his sons moored the craft stem and stern to the bank. It was useless urging him to proceed. He said: 'No man living would tempt him to move: the strange sky and the oppressive stillness boded no good;' and so he sat and smoked, while his sons made all secure. The insect world, too, seemed to chirp and twitter uneasily, as if dreading some impending storm; the birds escaped into shelter; and soon a deep silence, only broken at intervals by the whispering of the wind among the millet, took entire possession of the scene. Wong smoked more than usual, and kept watch. It was well he did. Placing my revolver beneath my pillow, and the matches close to the candle, I was soon fast asleep, and must have been slumbering till about midnight, when I was rudely roused by a sudden shock that sent me heels over head across the narrow cabin floor. I was still endeavouring to extricate myself from the miscellaneous property heaped around me, when the boat seemed to be lifted right out of the water, then struck a second time, and almost capsized. We were caught in a storm. I could hear the wind growling and gathering its fury for another blast, as I forced the cabin door to learn the worst. The boatmen were out on the bank looking to the moorings; but they informed me that the worst was over.

Meanwhile, Ahong and the others, as soon as they could extricate themselves from the wreck of the cooking galley, were out too. But the worst was not over. Like a remorseful flood of tears after a fit of passion, the rain poured down in torrents, deluging everything; so that even the matches were thoroughly soaked and useless before I could manage to lay my hands upon them. My clothes and cotton mattress were in the same sorry condition; but somehow, when the rain abated, and I had made myself as comfortable as circumstances would permit, I fell asleep again, and woke at daylight to find my boys busy drying their property, that they might appear clothed and in their right mind at Tung-chow.

It was not till the afternoon of the fourth day that we reached this place, though we made but another halt, to visit a village fair, where we saw a poor conjuror perform tricks for a few cash that would make his fortune on a London stage. And yet his greatest trick of all was transforming three copper cash into gold coin. His arms were quite bare, and, having taken his cash in the palm of his hand, he permitted me to close the fingers over them. Then, passing a wand above the clenched fist, he opened it again, and feasted the greedy eyes of his rustic admirers on what looked extremely like glittering gold. He also killed a small boy whom he had with him by plunging a knife into his body. The youth became suddenly pale, seemed to expire, then jumping up again removed the knife with one hand while he solicited patronage with the other. There was one feat which this conjuror performed with wonderful dexterity. He placed a square cloth flat upon the ground, and taking it by the centre between his forefinger and thumb with one hand, he waved the wand with the other; and, gradually raising the cloth, disclosed a huge vase brimful of pure water beneath it.

At Tung-chow our boat was boarded by at least a dozen coolies eager to carry our baggage. One of them incautiously lifted a trunk, and was making off with it, when he was suddenly relieved of the burden by Tao and hurled pell-mell into the water. This summary procedure on the part of my Tientsin man almost cost him his much-venerated tail, for it had nearly been torn out at the roots by the infuriated coolies before I could come to the rescue. Here we engaged carts for the journey to the metropolis. These carts are the imperial-highway substitutes for our railways, cabs, and omnibuses, but they have no springs. Notwithstanding this they might be comfortable enough if so constructed as to allow the passenger to sit down, and used only on a perfectly level road. Tao had himself carefully packed into his conveyance with straw, but as for me, not liking the look of the vehicles, I determined to walk at least a part of the way.

There may be passages in what I have still to relate which may seem strange to a European reader, and I may be allowed perhaps, therefore, here to remind him that I am describing only what I actually saw and experienced. Soon we were entering Tung-chow, the carts plunging and lumbering behind us over what at one time had been a massively constructed Mongolian causeway. Gallantly the carters struggled on beneath an ancient archway, when suddenly the thoroughfare was found jammed by a heavily laden cart drawn by a team of mules and donkeys, that had stuck fast among the broken blocks of stone. Straightway the air re-echoed with the execrations of a hundred carters who found their progress obstructed, and it was a full half-hour before we managed to pass. I should think that the distinguished members of the Peking Board of Works can hardly have ventured so far as Tung-chow on their tours of inspection. A few moderate-sized stone walls thrown across the street there could scarcely prove more serious impediments to the traffic than the existing dilapidated pavement. As for the town and its inhabitants, we had ample leisure to inspect them before the carts had struggled clear of their streets. The shop-fronts were of richly carved wood, quite different from what one sees in the south, but seemingly stained with the accumulated dust of ages. The townsfolk, too, looked dry and dusty, as if they as well as their shops belonged to some bygone era, and had been suddenly unearthed to resume their tasks with senses partially impaired by disuse.

Even outside Tung-chow the roads were knee-deep

in mud, in consequence of the heavy rain which had fallen during the previous night, so that I had no further choice, and perforce took refuge in the cart. My driver smelt of samshu and garlic; and placed such implicit trust in his mule that, once fairly on the road, he fell asleep on the shaft, and had to be reminded frequently, by a shove off his perch, that he might as well do something to extricate his jaded beast and its burden from the pitfalls and mud-pools of the way. A long *détour*, taken to avoid an impassable portion of the stone highways, brought us at last once more upon the track, and then I wisely determined to resume walking, as I thought it as well to have one or two bones in my framework unbroken, to be relied on in case of need.

At length we made a halt at an inn. These inns supply food for man and beast, and occur at frequent intervals along that road, reminding one in some respects of those similar old-fashioned wayside resting-places which are now dying out rapidly in our own land.

Outside this inn ran a long low wall, whitewashed, and inscribed in huge black characters with the sign or motto, 'Perpetual felicity achieved.'

Along the entire front of this establishment a narrow dwarf-table had been set up, and groups of travellers seated round it discussed reeking bowls of soup or tea, and the latest news from the capital. Their cattle they had already made over to the care of hangers-on at the inn.

Tao and my Hainan men had gone on ahead, but I stopped here and partook of a dinner *à la Chinoise*, which was served up to me in a bedroom. This apartment was a filthy place, and contained nothing on earth save a table and a chair, and a bed, or kang, made of bricks. As for the table, it was covered with a surface formation of dirt into which I could cut like cheese. But I must say that the dinner here supplied me was the best I ever tasted at a Chinese inn. The viands were stewed mutton cut up into small pieces, rice, an omelette, grapes, and tea. The room had recently been used as a stable; and its window, filled in with a small wooden frame and originally covered with paper, was now festooned with dark dirty spiders' webs. Another long *détour* at length brought us to the Chi-ho gate of the Tartar metropolis.

Before we enter I will run over some of the more general characteristics of the city at which we have now arrived. It stands, as we have already seen, on a plain sloping down to the sea, and is indeed made up of two towns—a Tartar or Manchu quarter, and a Chinese settlement—joined together by a wall more than twenty miles round.

At the time of the Manchu conquest these two divisions were parted from each other by a second, inner, wall; the true natives of the soil, at least those of them supposed to be friendly to the new dynasty, being confined within a narrow space to the south; while the Tartar army was encamped around the Imperial palace in the northern city, which covers a square space of double the area of the Chinese town.

In so far as the features I have just described are concerned, Peking is the same to-day as it was a trifle over 200 years ago, when the descendant of Kublai Khan mounted the Imperial throne. There are still in the Tartar city the same high walls pierced with nine double gateways; the same towers and moats and fortified positions; and within, the palace is still surrounded by the permanent Manchu garrison, like that which was established in most of the provincial capitals of China.

The army was originally divided into four corps, distinguished by the white, red, yellow, and blue banners under which they respectively fought. Four bordered banners of the same colours were subsequently added, and eight corps of Mongols, and an equal number of Chinese adherents, were created at a later date.

Each corps of Manchu bannermen possesses, or rather is supposed to possess, its ground as originally allotted to it within the Imperial city; and before the cottage doorways one may still see square paper lamps, whose colours denote the banners to which their proprietors respectively belong. But time has changed the stern rules under which the Chinese were confined to their own quarter. Their superior industry, and their slowly but surely accumulating wealth, have gradually made them masters of the Tartar warriors, and of their allotments within the sacred city. In fact, Chinese thrift and commercial energy have conquered the descendants of the doughty Manchus who drove the Mings from the throne.

It can hardly be credited by the stranger who visits this Chinese centre of the universe, that the miserable beings whom he sees clad in sheep-skins out of the Imperial bounty, and acting as watchmen to the prosperous Chinese, are in reality the remnants of those noble nomads who were at one time a terror to Western Europe, and at a later date the conquerors of the 'Central Flowery Land.'

The old walls of the great city are truly wonderful monuments of human industry. Their base is sixty feet wide, their breadth at the top about forty feet, and their height also averages forty feet. But alas! time and the modern arts of warfare have rendered them practically nothing more than interesting relics of a bygone age. A wooden stockade would now-a-days be about as effective a protection to the Imperial throne within. They seem to be well defended, however. Casting our eyes up to the great tower above the gate-way, we can see that it bristles with guns; yet the little field-glass of modern science reveals to us after all only a mock artillery, painted muzzles on painted boards, threatening sham terrors through the countless embrasures.

A few rusty dismantled cannon lie here and there beneath the gateway, but everything looks out of repair. The moats have become long shallow lagoons, and yonder a train of 100 camels is wading calmly through one into the city. The Government probably know all this, and have wisely turned their attention to the defence of the coast line and frontiers; in the hope perhaps that a foreign foe will never again be able to flounder over the broken highways, and bring warfare to the palace door. A vain delusion truly, unless China is prepared to take to heart the sad lessons of modern battle-fields, and to keep pace with the ever-progressive science that is at work in our European arsenals. How can she do this? She may squander wealth—distilled out of the blood, sinews, and sweat of long-suffering labour—upon fleets and armaments; but where will she find the genius to use her weapons to advantage? In the event of a collision with a foreign

Power, what good end would the hasty purchase of iron-clads and arms secure? If—as a distinguished Chinese scholar the other day remarked—it takes 1,200 years for the Chinese to introduce successfully a new tone into their language, how long, I would ask, must it be before they would even make it in the first place thoroughly understood, throughout the length and breadth of the Empire, that in order to sustain an efficient army the soldiers must be paid—paid regularly, and on a scale sufficient to prevent their becoming a greater terror to their own peaceful countrymen than they would ever be probably to their foes. As for the new weapons which they are manufacturing for themselves, we will hope that the rulers may never become so utterly blinded as to place these in the hands of untrained troops, to defend the ancient policy of exclusiveness so fatal to progress in China.

But let us hasten our steps, and enter the gate to behold this great metropolis. A mighty crowd is pressing on towards the dark archway, and we betake ourselves again to our carts, feeling sure that our passports will be examined by the guards on duty at the portal. But after all we pass through unnoticed in the wake of a train of camels laden with fuel from the coal-mines not far off. There is a great noise and confusion. Two streams, made up of carts, camels, mules, donkeys, and citizens, have met beneath the arch, and are struggling out of the darkness at either end. Within, there is a wide thoroughfare, by far the widest I encountered in any Chinese city, and as roomy as the great roads of London. All the main streets of Peking can boast of this advantage; but the cartway runs down the centre of the road, and is only broad

ONE OF THE INNER GATES OF PEKING

enough to allow two vehicles to pass abreast. The causeway in the middle is kept in repair by material which coolies ladle out of the deep trenches or mud-holes to be seen on either side of it. Citizens using this part of the highway after dark are occasionally drowned in these sloughs. Thus one old woman met her end in this way when I was in Peking, so that I never felt altogether safe when riding through the streets at night; while in the morning, when the dutiful servants of the Board of Works were flourishing their ladles, one had to face the insalubrious odours of the putrid mud; and at mid-day again, more especially if the weather was dry, the dust was so thick that when I washed my beard I could have supplied a valuable contribution towards the repairs of the road.

Notwithstanding all this, if there are no dust-clouds to obstruct the sight, the Peking streets are highly picturesque and interesting. Along each side of the central highway an interminable line of booths and stalls has been set up, and there almost everything under the Chinese sun is to be obtained. Then outside these stalls, again, there are the footpaths, and beyond them we come upon the shops, which form the boundaries of the actual road. It is a complicated picture, and I only hope that the reader may not lose himself, as I have done more than once, amid the maze of streets.

The shops had a great fascination for me. In both cities they are almost always owned by Chinese, for the Tartars, even if they have money, are too proud to trade; and if they have none, as is most frequently the case, they possess neither the energy nor the ingenuity to make a start. The Chinese, on the other hand, will many of them trade on nothing; and some seem capable of living on nothing too, until, by patience and thrift, if they have ever had the ghost of a chance, they manage to attain prosperity.

The shops in Peking, both outside and within doors, are very attractive objects. Many of their fronts are elaborately carved, and painted and gilded so beautifully that they look as if they ought to be set under glass cases; while as for the interiors, these are fitted up and finished with an equally scrupulous care, the owners ready for business inside, clothed in their silks, and looking a prosperous, supremely-contented tribe. I could discover evidences of a liberal distribution of the wealth of the official classes in all those shops which in any way supplied their wants, or ministered to their expensive and luxurious tastes.

On the other hand, fearful signs of squalor and misery were apparent everywhere in the unwelcome and uncared-for poor: all the more apparent, perhaps, when brought face to face with the tokens of wealth and refinement.

I have not space to relate a tenth of what I beheld or experienced in this great capital: how its naked beggars were found in the winter mornings dead at its gates; how a cart might be met going its rounds to pick up the bodies of infants too young to require the sacred rites of sepulture; how the destitute were to be seen crowding into a sort of casual ward already full, and craving permission to stand inside its walls, so as to obtain shelter from the wintry blast that would freeze their hearts before the dawn. There are acres of hovels at Peking in which the Imperial bannermen herd, and filth seems to be deposited like tribute before the very palace gates ; indeed, there is hardly a spot in the capital that does not make one long for a single glimpse of that Chinese paradise we had pictured to ourselves in our youth ; for the bright sky, the tea-fields, orange-groves, and hedges of jasmine, and for the lotus-lakes filling the air with their perfume. Once or twice in China I had almost realised this dream ; but the perfection of the scene was always marred by something defective about the people themselves, or their habits.

Next to the shops, the footpaths in front of them are perhaps most curious to a foreigner. In these paths, after a shower of rain, many pools occur—pools which it is impossible to cross except by wading, unless one cares to imitate an old Pekingese lady, who carried two bricks with her wherever she went, to pave her way over the puddles. But watery hollows are not the only obstacles to traffic. As in the Commercial Road in London crowds congregate in front of the tents and stalls of the hawkers, while the shop-keepers spread out their wares for sale so as to monopolise at least two-thirds of the pavement, so also in Peking, in yet greater numbers and variety, the buyers and sellers occupy every dry spot. Sometimes one can only get through the press by brushing against the dry dusty hides of a train of camels as they are being unladen before a coal-shed ; and one must take care, should any of them be lying down, not to tread on their huge soft feet, for they can inflict a savage bite. In another spot it may become necessary to wait until some skittish mule, tethered in front of a shop, has been removed by its leisurely master, who is smoking a pipe with the shopman inside. Once, as I threaded my way along, I had to climb a pile of wooden planks to reach the path beyond, and finding that a clear view could be obtained from the top, of a fine shop on the other side of the road, I had my camera set up and proceeded to take a photograph. But in two or three minutes, before the picture could be secured, there was a sudden transformation of the scene. Every available spot of ground was taken up by eager but good-natured spectators ; traffic was suspended : and just as I was about to expose the plate some ingenious youth displaced the plank on which I stood, and brought me down in a rapid, undignified descent, immensely entertaining to the crowd.

Some of the booths close to the foot-way are built of mud or brick, and would indeed become permanent structures but that their occupants may be ordered at any moment to clear them away, so as to make room for the progress of the Emperor. For I must tell you that whenever the Sovereign is carried abroad, outside his own palace walls, the roads must be cleared, and even cleaned, that his sacred eyes may not be offended with a glimpse at the true condition of his splendid capital. After he has passed by, booths, tents, and stalls are re-erected, and commerce and confusion resume their sway. As matters stand, these road-side obstructions are really a great boon to the people. Anything can be bought at the stalls, and their owners are neither slow nor silent in advertising the fact. At one a butcher and a baker combine their crafts. The former sells his mutton cut to suit the taste of his customers, while at the same time he disposes of all the bones and refuse to the cook, who manufactures savoury pies before a hungry crowd of lookers-on. Twirling his rolling-pin on his board, he shrieks out in a shrill key a list of the delicacies he has prepared, while a chorus of dogs around respond in unfeignedly sympathetic howls.

Jewels, too, of no mean value, are on sale here as well, and there are peep-shows, jugglers, lottery-men, ballad-singers, and story-tellers ; the latter accompanying their recitations with the strummings of a lute, while their audience sits round a long table and listens with rapt attention to the dramatic renderings of their poets. The story-teller, however, has many competitors to contend against, and of all his rivals the old-clothes-men are perhaps the most formidable tribe. These old-clothes-men enjoy a wide celebrity for their humorous stories, and will run off with a rhyme to suit the garments as they offer them to the highest bidder. Each coat is thus invested with a miraculous history, which gives it at once a priceless value. If it be fur, its heat-producing powers are eloquently described. 'It was this fur which, during the year of the great frost, saved the head of that illustrious family Chang. The cold was so intense that the people were mute. When they spoke their words froze, and hung from their lips. Men's ears congealed, and were devoid of feeling, so that when they shook their heads they fell off. Men froze to the street and died by thousands ; but as for Chang of honoured memory, he put on this coat, and it brought summer to his blood. How much say you for it ?' &c. The foregoing is a rendering of the language actually used by one of these sellers of unredeemed pledges.

I saw two or three men who were driving a trade in magic pictures and foreign stereoscopic photographs, some in not the most refined style of art: and as for the peep-shows, well, the less one says about them the better; they certainly would not be tolerated in any public thoroughfare in Europe. The original Punch and Judy also, is to be encountered in the Peking streets; puppets worked by the hands of a hidden operator, on just the same plan as with us. At night, too, I have frequently seen a most ingenious shadow pantomime contrived by projecting small moveable figures on to a thin screen, under a brilliant light from behind.

Capital clay images may be purchased at some of the stalls; but in no part of China has this art of making coloured clay figures reached such perfection as at Tientsin.

At that place tiny figures are sold for a mere song which are by far the cleverest things of the kind I ever saw. These are not only most perfect representations of Chinese men and women, but many of them hit off humorous characteristics with the most wonderfully artistic fidelity.

If I go rambling on in this way over the city, we shall never reach the hotel, nor receive that welcome which was so warmly accorded to me by Monsieur Thomas, the proprietor. Thomas was not the cleanest man in the world, but he was extremely polite, which was something. There was, however, about his costume a painful lack of buttons, and its appearance might perhaps have been improved by the addition of a waistcoat, and by the absence of the grease that seemed to have been struggling up to reach his hair, but had not arrived at its destination. His hands, and even his face, in prospect of our coming, had been hastily though imperfectly washed. But then he was a cook, a good cook, too; and he remarked, when I flattered him on this head, that there was nothing like a little *eau-de-vie* to enable an artist to put the finishing touches on a *chef-d'œuvre* either of cookery or painting. Had he confessed to a great deal of that stimulant, he would have been much nearer the truth.

My bedroom was not a comfortable one. How could it be?—it was chiefly built of mud. The mud floor, indeed, was matted over, but the white-washed walls felt sticky, and so did the bed and curtains; a close, nasty smell, too, pervaded the whole apartment, and on looking into a closet I discovered a quantity of mouldy, foreign apparel. This, as I found out next morning, had been left there as plague-stricken by a gentleman who, some days previously, had nearly died of small-pox in this very room. Fortunately, I escaped an attack of the malady.

I paid a visit to the Corean Legation in the Tartar quarter of the city. It is customary for the King of Corea to send an annual embassy of tribute-bearers to Peking. The first detachment of the embassy had just arrived before I quitted the capital. There were but a few members present at the Legation at the time of my visit, and the apartments in which they dwelt were so scrupulously clean that I almost wished that I had left my dirty shoes at the doorway, in my fear of soiling the white straw mats. I was also most favourably impressed with the spotless purity of their garments, which were almost entirely of white. It was with great difficulty, however, that the accompanying illustration was secured, but it was on that account all the more prized, as it is about all I can offer the reader in connection with this isolated and interesting race.

After my return from the Ming tombs, H. B. M.'s Minister kindly invited me to stay at the Legation ; but I had promised Thomas to remain in his house, and

COREAN.

although unfortunate in some respects, he proved thoroughly honest, and did his best to make me comfortable.

I bought a Mongolian pony, to save me time in exploring the city, and a saddle and bridle were kindly lent to me by a friend; but the brute was a large-boned, large-headed animal, with a great round belly, over which, for want of a crupper, the saddle-girths were always sliding. It had, too, an enormous appetite, at least, so said the groom whom I employed. The

CHINESE HORSE-SHOEING, PEKING.

first night it consumed its bed, and when I examined it in the morning it seemed to be hungry still; for it had barked the tree to which it was tethered, and had besides this devoured about five shillings' worth of millet-bran, and so forth. I soon found out that I was being fleeced by the stable-boy, who had a pony of his own in the next house, and had determined to feed it at my expense.

The Pekingese have a strange mode of shoeing their horses. They pull three feet together with cords, and leave the hoof that is to be shod free. Then they sling the animal bodily up between two posts, after the manner shown in the engraving.

In the plan of the city of Peking there is every evidence of careful design, and this has been carried out minutely, from the central buildings of the palace to the outermost wall of fortification. The ground-plan of the Imperial buildings is in most respects identical with the ground-plans of the great temples and tombs of the country. So much alike are they, even in the style and arrangement of their edifices, that a palace, with scarcely any alteration, might be at once converted into a Buddhist temple. Thus we find that the Great Yung-ho-Kung Lamasary of the Mongols, in the north-east quarter of the city, was at one time the residence of the son and successor of Kang-hi. The chiefs halls of the Imperial palace—if we may judge from the glimpse one gets of their lofty roofs when one stands on the city wall—are three in number, extending from the Chien-men to Prospect Hill, and in every instance are approached by a triple gateway. The like order prevails at the Ming tombs. There one finds an equal number of halls, with a triple doorway in front of each; while the temple and domestic architecture throughout the north of China is based upon the same plan. In the latter case there are three courts, divided from each other by halls, the apartments of the domestics being ranged about the outer courts, while the innermost of the three is devoted to family use.

It is interesting to observe the evidences which crop up everywhere, showing the universal sacredness of the numbers three and nine. Thus at Peking, the gates with which the outer wall of the Tartar city is pierced form together a multiple of three, and the sacred person of the Emperor can only be approached, even by his highest officers, after three times three prostrations. The Temple of Heaven, too, in the Chinese city, with its triple roof, the triple terraces of its marble altars, and the rest of its mystic symbolism throughout, points either to three or to its multiples.

The Rev. Joseph Edkins was, I believe, the first to draw attention to the symbolical architecture of the Temple of Heaven, and to the importance which the Chinese themselves attach to the southern open altar as the most sacred of all Chinese religious structures. There, at the winter solstice, the Emperor himself makes burnt offerings, just as the patriarchs did of old, to the supreme Lord of Heaven. In the city of Foo-chow, on the southern side of the walled enclosure, are two hills, one known as Wu-shih-shan, and the other as Kui-shen-shan, or 'the Hill of the Nine Genii.' On the top of the former there is an open altar—a simple erection of rude unhewn stone, approached first by a flight of eighteen steps, and finally by three steps, cut into the face of the rock. This altar is reputed to be very ancient, and to it the Governor-General of the province repairs at certain seasons of the year as the representative of the Emperor, and there offers up burnt sacrifices to heaven. In this granite table, covered with a simple square stone vessel filled with ashes, we have the sacrificial altar in what is probably its most ancient Chinese form. The southern altar at

Peking bears a wonderful resemblance to Mount Meru, the centre of the Buddhist universe, round which all the heavenly bodies are supposed to move; and there we find the tablets of sun, moon, and stars arranged around the second terrace of the altar, according to the Chinese system of astronomy.

The city of Peking, or rather the Tartar portion of it, is laid out with an almost perfect symmetry. The sacred purple city stands nearly in the centre, and there are three main streets, which run from north to south. One of these streets leads direct to the palace gates, and the other two are nearly equi-distant from it on either side; while myriads of minor thoroughfares and lanes intersect one another in the spaces between, but are always either parallel with or at right angles to the three main roads. Viewed from any stand-point on the outer wall, the whole scene is disappointing. With the exception of the palace buildings, the Buddhist shrines, the Temple of Heaven, the Roman Catholic cathedral, and the official yamens, the houses never rise above the low modest uniform level prescribed for them by law. Much, too, that is ruinous and dilapidated presents itself to the gaze. Here and there we see open spaces, and green trees that shade the buildings of the rich; but again the eye wearies of its wanderings over hundreds of acres of tiles and walls, all of one stereotyped pattern, and cannot help noticing that the isolation of the Chinese begins with the family unit at home. There stands the sacred dwelling of the mighty Emperor, walled round and round; his person protected from the gaze of the outer world by countless courts and 'halls of sacred harmony;' and one can note the same exclusiveness carried out in all the dwellings of his people. Each residence is enclosed in a wall of its own, and a single outer entrance gives access to courts and reception-rooms, beyond which the most favoured guest may not intrude to violate by his mere presence the sanctity of the domicile. There are, of course, tens of thousands of houses and hovels where this arrangement cannot be observed; but where the people, nevertheless, manage to sustain a sort of dignified isolation by investing themselves with an air of self-importance, which the very street beggars never wholly lay aside. These, if they be Manchus, are proud at any rate of their sheepskin coats; or if they be not, then the more fugitive covering of mud, which is all that hides their nakedness, is still carried with a sort of stolid solemnity which would be ludicrous were it not for their misfortunes.

I had the good fortune while in the metropolis to be introduced to Prince Kung and the other distinguished members of the Chinese Government; and they wisely availed themselves of my presence to have their portraits taken at the Tsungli-yamen, or Chinese Foreign Office. Prince Kung, as most of my readers are aware, is a younger brother of the late Emperor Hien-fung, and consequently uncle to the reigning monarch Tung-che. He holds several high appointments, military as well as civil, and in particular he is a member of the Supreme Council—a department of the State which most nearly resembles the Cabinet in our own constitution. He is, too, a man esteemed by all who know him, quick in apprehension, comparatively liberal in his views, and regarded by some as the head of that small party of politicians who favour progress in China.

The creation of the Tsungli-yamen, or Foreign Board, was one of the important results which followed the ratification of the Treaty of Tientsin. Up to that time all foreign diplomatic correspondence had been carried on through the Colonial Office, where the great Powers were practically placed on a level with the Central Asian dependencies of the Empire. This yamen stands next to the Imperial College, where a staff of foreign professors is now employed in instructing Chinese students in European languages, literature, and science. Accompanied by one of these professors, who kindly undertook to be my interpreter, I found myself one morning entering a low narrow doorway through a dead wall. After making our way along a number of courts, studded with rockeries, flowers, and ponds ; and after passing down dingy corridors in dismal disrepair, we at length stood beneath the shade of an old tree, and in front of the picturesque, but purely Chinese-looking, audience-chamber, wherein the interests of vast numbers of the human race are from time to time discussed. We had barely time to glance at the painted pillars, the curved roofs, and carved windows, when a venerable noble issued from behind a bamboo screen that concealed a narrow doorway, and accorded us a quiet courteous welcome.

The Prince himself had not arrived ; but Wen-siang, Paou-keun, and Shen-kwe-fen, members all of them of the Grand Council, were already in attendance. Wen-siang is well known in diplomatic circles as a statesman endowed with intellectual powers of the highest order, and as one of the foremost ministers of his age. It is said of him, that in reply to the urgent representations of a foreigner who was clamouring for Chinese progress, he delivered himself of the following prophecy, which has not yet, however, been fulfilled:—'Give China time, and her progress will be both rapid and overwhelming in its results; so much so, that those who were foremost with the plea for progress will be sighing for the good old times.' This transformation may be looming in the far-off distance, like some unknown star whose light is travelling through the immeasurable regions of space, but has not yet reached our own sphere. China has had her ages of flint and bronze; and her vast mineral resources tell us that she is yet destined to enter upon all that is implied in an age of coal and iron.

Wen-siang and Paou-keun are Manchus, while Shen-kwe-fen is one of the Chinese members of the Grand Council of State.

Cheng-lin, Tung-sean, and Maou-cheng-he, ministers of the Foreign Board, were also present. Tung-sean is the author of many valuable works. One of these, on the hydrography of northern China, was in the press at the time of my visit; and, as the reader will have gathered from my account of the inundations, his treatise is likely to be of great value, provided that its suggestions for draining the country and restoring the broken embankments can, or rather will, be carried out. The ministers wore simple robes of variously-coloured satin, open in front and caught in by a band at the waist; collars of pale blue silk tapering down from the neck to the shoulders, and thick-soled black satin boots. This costume was extremely picturesque, and, what is of far greater importance, the ministers, most of them, were as fine-looking men as ever our own Cabinet can boast. All of them had that air of quiet dignified repose which only comes of constant intercourse with highly-cultured minds.

The arrival of Prince Kung on the scene cut short our general conversation. The Prince for a few minutes kept me in a pleasant talk, enquiring about my travels and about photography, and manifesting considerable interest in the process of taking a likeness. He is a man of middle stature, and of a rather slender frame; his appearance, indeed, did not impress me so favourably as did that of the other members of the Cabinet; yet he had what phrenologists would describe as a splendid head. His eyes were penetrating, and his face when in repose wore an expression of sullen resolution. As I looked upon him I wondered whether he felt the fearful burden of the responsibility which he shared with the ministers around in guiding the destinies of so many millions of the human race; or whether he and his distinguished colleagues were able to look with complacency upon the present state of the Empire and its people.

These men have had many and great difficulties to contend against in their time. Foreign war, civil insurrection, famine, floods, and the rapacity of their officials in different quarters of the land, have done much to weaken the prestige and power of the great central Government; and her authority now can never be properly felt and acknowledged in the more distant portions of China, until each remotest province of that vast kingdom shall have been united to Peking by the iron grasp of railways and by a network of telegraphic nerves.

Perhaps the most grave and distinguished-looking member of the group now before me was Maou-cheng-he. This man's scholarly attainments had won him the highest post of literary fame, and formerly he had been chief judge of the metropolitan literary examinations.

Extraordinary is the honour which the Chinese attach to literary championship, and to the achievement of the Chong-ün or Han-lin degree which is conferred by the Peking examiners. At the triennial examination of 1871 a man from Shun-kak district, in the Kwang-tung province, carried off the Chong-ün. His family name was Leung. Now this literary distinction had been obtained by a Kwang-tung scholar some half-a-century before, and he was the first who achieved that success during a period of 200 years. Thus the new victory of their own candidate was hailed by the men of Kwang-tung as a great historical event. It was reported, however, that Mr. Leung had after all obtained the honour by a lucky 'fluke.' As one of a triad of chosen scholars of the Empire, he produced the composition which was to decide his claims. There were nine essays in all, and these, when they had been submitted to the Han-lin examiners, were sent by them to the Empress Dowager (the Emperor being under age) to have their own award formally confirmed. The work of greatest merit was placed uppermost; but the old lady, who had an imperial will of her own, felt anxious to thwart the decision of the learned pundits; and, as chance would have it, the sunlight fell upon the chosen manuscript, and she discovered a flaw, a thinness in the paper, indicating a place in the composition where one character had been erased and another substituted. The Empress rated the examiners for allowing such slovenly work to pass, and proclaimed Leung the victor.

The superstitious Cantonese declared that it was a divine choice, that the sunbeam was a messenger sent by Heaven to point out the blemish in the essay at first selected for the prize.

Mr. Leung reached Canton in May 1872, and was received there by the local authorities with the highest possible honours. All the families who bore the name of Leung (and who also had means to afford it) paid the Chong-ün enormous sums of money to be permitted to come and worship at his ancestral hall. By this means they established a spurious claim to relationship, and as soon as the ceremony was over were allowed to place tablets above the entrances of their own halls inscribed with the title Chong-ün.

An uncle of the successful senior wrangler, uniting an exalted sense of his duty to his family with a laudable desire to repair his own fortune, forestalled the happy Chong-ün, and acted as his deputy before his arrival, in visiting sundry halls. For such honourable service this obliging relative at times received a thousand dollars, and his nephew, for the sake of the family name, had to sanction the steps thus prematurely adopted to spread his fame abroad.

To show the great esteem in which such a man is held by the Chinese, I may add that a brother of Mr. Leung rented a house in Canton, and its owner hearing that he was the brother of the famous Chong-ün made him a free gift of the tenement.

After partaking of tea with one or two of the members of the Cabinet, and after some general talk on topics of common interest, we rose and quitted the yamen.

I must leave many of the temples and other objects of interest in Peking undescribed, as my aim at present is rather to convey a general impression of the condition of the country and of its people, as we find them now-a-days, than to enter into minute details. I can therefore only cast a passing glance at a few places of public importance. The Confucian temple covers a wide area, and like all palaces, shrines, and even houses, is completely walled around. The main gateway which leads into the sacred enclosure is presented in the accompanying picture. This gateway is approached, as were the ancient shrines of Greece and Rome, through an avenue of venerable cypress trees; and the whole establishment forms perhaps the most imposing specimen of purely Chinese architecture to be found among the ornaments of the capital. The triple approach, and the balustrading, are of sculptured marble; while the pillars and other portions of the gateway are of more perishable materials—wood, glazed earthenware, and brick. On either side are groves of marble tablets, bearing the names of the successful Hanlin scholars for many centuries back; and that one to the left, supported upon the back of a tortoise, was set up here when Marco Polo was in China.

Within this gate stand the celebrated stone drums, inscribed with stanzas cut nearly 2,000 years ago in the most primitive form of Chinese writing. Thus these drums prove the antiquity at once of the poetry and of the character in which that has been engraved. These inscriptions have been translated by Dr. S. W. Bushell, the gentleman who has also recently discovered the site of the famous city of Shang-tu, referred to by Coleridge as Xanadu, and spoken of by Marco Polo as the northern capital of the Yuen dynasty. The great hall within simply contains the tablet of China's chief sage and those of twenty-two of his most distinguished followers.

The spirits of the departed great are supposed to

PEKING OBSERVATORY. JESUIT INSTRUMENTS.

reside in their tablets, and hence annually, at the vernal and autumnal equinoxes, sheep and oxen fall in sacrifice in front of this honoured shrine of literature.

Close to the Confucian temple stands the Kwo-tze-keen, or National University; and there, ranged around

GREAT GATEWAY, TEMPLE OF CONFUCIUS

the Pi-yung-kung, or Hall of the Classics, are 200 tablets of stone, inscribed with the complete text of the nine sacred books.

The Observatory has been set up on the wall on the eastern side of the Tartar city. Here, in addition to the colossal astronomical instruments erected by the Jesuit missionaries in the seventeeth century, we find two other instruments in a court below, which the Chinese made for themselves towards the close of the thirteenth century, when the Yuen dynasty was on the throne. Possibly some elements of European science may have been brought to bear on the construction of even these instruments; although the characters and divisions engraved on their splendid bronze circles point only to the Chinese method of dividing the year, and to the state of Chinese astronomy at the time. Yet Marco Polo must have been in the north of China at about the period of their manufacture; or, at any rate, John de Carvino was there, for he, under Pope Clement V., became bishop of Cambalu (Peking) about 1290 A.D., and perhaps, with his numerous staff of priests, he introduced some knowledge of Western art. Mr. Wylie (than whom there is probably no better authority) was with me when I examined these instruments, and is of opinion that they are Chinese, and that they were produced by Ko-show-king, one of the most famous astronomers of China. One of them is an astrolaba, furnished beneath with a splendid sundial, which has long since lost its gnomon. The whole, indeed, consists of three astrolabæ, one partly moveable and partly fixed in the plane of the ecliptic; the second turning on a centre as a meridian circle; and the third the azimuth circle.

The other instrument is an armillary sphere, supported by chained dragons, of most beautiful workmanship and design. This instrument is a marvellous specimen of the perfection to which the Chinese must, even then, have brought the art of casting in bronze.

The horizon is inscribed with the twelve cyclical characters, into which the Chinese divide the day and night. Outside the ring these characters appear again,

ANCIENT CHINESE ASTRONOMICAL INSTRUMENT.

paired with eight characters of the denary cycle, and four names of the eight diagrams of the book of changes, denoting the points of the compass; while the inside of the ring bears the names of the twelve States into which China, in ancient times, was portioned out. An equatorial circle, a double-ring ecliptic, an equinoctial colure, and a double-ring colure, are adjusted with the horizon ring. The equator is engraved with constellations of unknown antiquity; while the ecliptic is marked off into twenty-four equal spaces, corresponding to the divisions of the year. All the circles are divided into 365¼ degrees, for the days of the year; while each degree is subdivided into 100 parts, as for everything less than a degree the centenary scale prevailed at that period. I take these instruments to be of great interest, as indicating the state of astronomical science in China at about the end of the thirteenth century.

While in Peking I made the acquaintance of many educated and intelligent natives, one of whom accompanied an English physician and myself on an excursion to the ruins of the Summer Palace. With another gentleman, Mr. Yang, I became considerably intimate; and in this way enjoyed some opportunity of seeing the dwellings and domestic life of the upper classes in the capital. Both my friends were devoted to photography; but Yang, not content with his triumphs in that branch of science, frequently carried his researches and experiments to a pitch that caused the members of his multitudinous household no less inconvenience than alarm. Yang was a fine sample of the modern Chinese savant—fat, good-natured, and contented; but much inclined to take short cuts to scientific knowledge, and to esteem his own incomplete and hap-hazard achievements the results of marvellously perfect intelligence. His house, like most others in China, was approached through a lane hedged in by high brick walls on either side, so that there was nothing to be seen of it from without save the small doorway and a low brick partition about six feet beyond the threshold—the latter intended to prevent the ingress of the spirits of the dead. Within there was the usual array of courts and halls, reached by narrow vine-shaded corridors; but each court was tastefully laid out with rockeries, flowers, fish-ponds, bridges, and pavilions, as may be gathered from the accompanying illustrations. Really the place was very picturesque, and admirably suited to the disposition of a people affecting seclusion and the pleasures of family life; and who (so far as the women are concerned) know little or nothing of the world in which they live beyond what they gather within the walls of their own abode.

Here I was, then, admitted at last into the sacred precincts of the mysterious Chinese dwelling. Its proprietor was an amateur, not merely of photography, but of chemistry and electricity, too; and he had a laboratory fitted up in the ladies' quarter. In one corner of this laboratory stood a black carved bedstead, curtained with silk, and pillowed with wood; while a carved bench, also of black wood, supported a heterogeneous collection of instruments, chemical, electrical, and photographic, besides Chinese and European books.

The walls were garnished with enlarged photographs of Yang's family and friends. In a small outer court care had been taken to supply a fowl-house with a steam saw-mill, with which the owner had achieved wonders in the short space of a single day.

The machine, indeed, had never enjoyed but that one chance of distinguishing itself; for the Pekingese, disturbed by the whirr of the engines, scaled the walls with ladders, clustered on to the roofs, and compelled the startled proprietor to abandon his undertaking.

CHINESE GENTLEMAN'S GARDEN

There, then, stood the motionless mill, with one or two dejected fowls perched upon its cylinder—a monster whom long familiarity had taught even the poultry to despise. I saw the ladies several times while I was teaching my friend how to concoct nitrate of silver and other photographic chemicals. Some of these women were handsome, and all were dressed in rich satins; but the following information, which I received from an English lady (Mrs. Edkins), who is much and deservedly esteemed for her good works among the natives, will give further insight into the daily life of the Pekingese ladies.

Many Chinese ladies spend a great portion of their time in gossiping, smoking, and gambling—very unlady-like occupations, my fair readers will exclaim; nevertheless, these accomplishments, taken either singly or collectively, require years of assiduous training before they can be practised with that perfection which prevails in polite circles in China. Gambling, it is to be regretted, is by far the most favourite pastime, and it is perhaps but cold comfort to reflect that this vice is not monopolised by the ladies of Cathay, but that it is their lords who set them the example. They never dream of playing except for money; and when they have no visitors of their own rank to gamble with, they call up the domestics and play with them.

Poorer women meet at some gaming den, and there manage to squander large sums of money; thus affording their devoted husbands at the end of the year, when debts must be discharged which they are unable to pay, an excuse for committing suicide.

The married lady rises early, and first sees that tea is prepared for her husband, as well as some hot water for his morning wash. The same attention is also exacted by the mother-in-law; for she is always present, like the guardian angel of her son. As a rule, however, the mother-in-law is not held to be an angel by the wife, who, during the lifetime of her husband's mother, has to be a very drudge in the house. It may be unkind to relate it, but the truth must be told: the ladies, in the morning, fly about with shoes down at heel—that is, the Tartars do, who have not small feet—dressed *en déshabille,* and shouting out their orders to the domestic slaves. In short, a general uproar prevails in many Chinese households until everything for the elaborate toilet has been procured.

Each lady has generally one or two maids, besides a small slave-girl who waits on these maids, and trims and lights her mistress' pipe. The dressing of a lady's hair occupies her attendants from one to two hours; then a white paste is prepared, and daubed over her face and neck; and this, when dry, is smoothed and polished once. Afterwards a blush of rose-powder is applied to the cheeks and eyelids, the surplus rouge remaining on the lady's palm, as a rose-pink on the hand is greatly esteemed. Next they dye the nails red with the blossom of a certain flower; and finally they dress for the day. Many of them have chignons and false hair; but no hair-dyes are used, for raven hair is common, and golden tresses are not in repute.

Numbers of ladies pass a portion of their time in embroidering shoes, purses, handkerchiefs, and such like gear; while before marriage, nearly all their days are occupied in preparations for the dreary event of wedding one whom probably they never yet have seen, and for whom they can never care. Women of educa-

CANTONESE BOATWOMAN.

NINGPO WOMAN.

PEPOHOAN.

TARTAR.

tion—there are, alas! but a few—occasionally hire educated widows in needy circumstances to read novels or plays to them. Women capable of reading in this way can make a very comfortable living. Story-tellers and ballad-singers are also employed to entertain them in the courts of their houses.

The evenings they generally spend in their court-yards, smoking and watching the amusements of the

TARTAR LADIES.

children; and on these occasions conjurors, Punch-and-Judy men, and ventriloquists, are much in demand. The families retire early to rest, the ladies never caring to spoil their eyes by working under the light of a lamp. Opium-smoking is freely indulged in by many women in China.

The romance of love is not unknown in the land,

although few marriages are ever celebrated where the contracting parties have formed an attachment, or even seen each other, before their wedding-day.

On leaving Yang's dwelling, I had always to make my way across a flooded court, where a steam mining-pump had once been set going, and had deluged the premises before it could be stopped. My friend, when I took my departure, was daily expecting the complete apparatus for a small gas-work, to supply his house with gas—a feat which I believe he successfully accomplished without blowing up his abode.

Pekingese Enamelling.—There are but one or two shops in Peking where the art of enamelling is carried on. The oldest enamelled vases were made during the Ta-ming dynasty, about three centuries ago; but these are said to be inferior to what were produced about 200 years later, when Kien-lung was on the throne. Within the last quarter of a century the art has been revived. One of the best shops for such work stood not far from the French Legation, and was—strangely enough—kept by a Manchu named Kwan.

The first part of the process consists in forming a copper vase of the desired form, partly beaten into shape, and partly soldered. The design for the enamelled flowers and figures is then traced on to the copper by a native artist, and afterwards all the lines engraved are replaced by strips of copper, soldered hard on to the vase, and rather thicker than the depth of the enamel which they are destined to contain. The materials used for soldering are borax and silver, which require a higher temperature for fusion than the enamel itself. The design is now filled in with the various coloured enamels, reduced to a state of powder

MAKING ENAMEL, PEKING

and made into a paste by the admixture of water. The enamel powders are said to be prepared by a secret process, known only to one man in Peking, who sells them in a solid form, like slabs of different-coloured glass. The delicate operation of filling in the coloured powders is chiefly carried on by boys, who manage to blend the colours with wonderful perfection. After the design has been filled in, the vase is next subjected to a heat that fuses the enamel. Imperfections are then filled up, and the whole is fused again. This operation is repeated three times, and then the vase is ready to be filed, ground, and polished. The grinding and polishing are conducted on a rude lathe, and when completed the vase is gilt. Some of the largest and finest vases sell for thousands of taels, and are much prized by the Chinese, as well as among foreigners.

On October 18 I set out with two friends for the Summer Palace at Yuen-ming-Yuen, about eight miles to the north-west of Peking. One of our party, Mr. Wang, to whom I have already referred, was connected with the Peking Board of Works. This gentleman used his official cart and was followed by a mounted retainer, while Dr. Dudgeon and I rode ponies. On the way, near the Imperial palace, we fell in with a procession of sixty-four men bearing a huge sedan, wherein sat fourteen friends of Wang, his colleagues at the Board of Works. These gentlemen were testing the strength of the chair which they had prepared to convey the remains of an Imperial princess to sepulture. Something, this, on the principle of placing a railway director in front of every train! A great vase filled to the brim with water had been set up in the centre of the sedan, in order to train the bearers to maintain an accurate level. Whether the tea and refreshments, and the general hilarity of the party, had anything to do with this official investigation I am at a loss to determine, but at any rate the duties of the Board, apart from their extreme usefulness, appeared to be far from disagreeable. Further on the road I had a race with a cavalry officer, and I managed to get ahead of him, but not until the saddle of my trusty steed was nearly over its shoulders.

By four o'clock we had reached the grounds of the palace, and there we found a wilderness of ruin and devastation which it was piteous to behold. Marble slabs and sculptured ornaments that had graced one of the finest scenes in China now lay scattered everywhere among the *débris* and weeds. But there were some of the monuments which had defied the hand of the invaders, or been spared, let us hope, on account of their beauty. Among these is a marble bridge on seventeen arches, which spans a lotus lake. This was still in perfect preservation; and in the far distance, too, the great temple on Wan-show-shan could be seen sparkling intact in the sunlight. At the base of this pile were a multitude of splendid statues, pagodas, and other ornaments, overthrown during the fearful raid of the allies. Enough yet remained, however, to give some faint notion of the untold wealth and labour that must have been lavished on this Imperial retreat.

The Summer Palace lay in ruins within its boundary walls, just as it was looted and left. It is a pity that redress for a breach of treaty obligations was not sought by some less destructive mode than this; by some really glorious achievement, which would have impressed the Chinese with exalted ideas of our civilisa-

WAN-SHOW-SHAN

tion as much as it terrified them with the awfulness of our power. If, for example, the capital had been held long enough to show what improvements a wise and liberal administration could, even in a short time, accomplish in the condition of the people and the country; then, after a suitable indemnity had been paid for the lesson which we had been forced to convey, we might have withdrawn with dignity and left no deep-rooted rankling hatred behind. This hatred will probably manifest itself ere long, not in the petty annoyances to which foreign travellers or traders have now to submit, but in one desperate concentrated effort to drive the foreigner from Chinese soil.

Wang made not a single allusion to the wreck around him. He admired, indeed, what little was left of the former splendour of the palace; but it was impossible to fathom his real sentiments, for a Chinaman, when interrogated, will never disclose what he thinks.

At the monastery of Wo-foh-sze, or 'the Sleeping Buddha,' we found a resting-place for the night. The old Lama here was complaining of bad times. There was not enough land, he said, to support the establishment, and that though every monk enjoyed a yearly grant of twelve taels (equal to about 3*l.* 10*s.* of our money) from the Peking Board of Rites. But of late years there have been but few of the members of the Imperial family to bury—a ceremony for which this establishment receives a fee of some 300 taels.

A remarkably beautiful place was Wo-foh-sze; and the quarters of the monks there, though furnished with the usual simplicity, were wonderfully clean and well kept.

There are many institutions and objects of interest

in Peking, but to describe even the most prominent among them would require a volume by itself.

The most remarkable, and perhaps the finest, monument in all China is the marble cenotaph erected over the robes and relics of the Banjin Lama of Thibet. This edifice stands in the grounds of the Hwang-She monastery, about a mile beyond the north wall of Peking. When on my way to inspect it I witnessed a review of some of the northern army on the Anting plain. Many thousands of troops, infantry as well as cavalry, were in the field, and at a distance they made a warlike and imposing show; but nearer examination always seems to me to alter one's conceptions of the greatness of human institutions, and more especially so where Chinese are concerned. Thus a close view of one of their river gun-boats revealed to me that a stand of rifles which occupied a prominent place on its deck were all constructed of wood; and the ancient foes of China have more than once in the same way advanced with caution to surprise a tented camp, and discovered that the tents were but white-washed clay mounds in undisturbed possession of the field. Thus also on the Anting plain, beneath the flaunting banners, we found the men armed with the old matchlocks or with bows and arrows; and carrying huge basket-work shields painted with the faces of ogres to strike terror into the hearts of a foe. For all that, evidences of military reform were not altogether wanting. Thus there were modern field-pieces, modern rifles, fair target practice, and, above all, desperate efforts to maintain discipline and order. At the same time I could not help thinking of Le-hung-chang (to whom I had the honour of being introduced at Tientsin), the founder of the first arsenal on a foreign type in China, and the companion in arms of Colonel Gordon and Tseng-kwo-fan. Personally Le is the picture of a military leader, tall, resolute, and calm, a man of iron will, and altogether the finest specimen of his race whom I ever fell in with. He probably at the present moment is influencing the progress and destinies of his countrymen more than any living son of Han. Perhaps he entertains an exaggerated belief in the capabilities of his nation; but at the same time he is deeply conscious of the power of Western kingdoms, and ardently desires to fathom the secrets of their superiority. On one occasion, when filled with honest admiration of the beauty and genius displayed in a piece of foreign mechanism, he exclaimed, 'How wonderful! how comes it that such inventions and discoveries are always foreign? It must be something different in the constitution of our minds that causes us to remain as we were.' But after all perhaps he may have intended to compliment his auditors rather than to give genuine expression to his opinions. He probably knows that for untold centuries there has been little or no opportunity for the development of genius in China. The light of truth has been sought for only in the dark pages of past history; and the Chinese, in their efforts to attain to the perfection of their mythical kings and of the maxims embodied in their classics, have set up an inquisition which perforce suppresses originality and uproots invention like a noxious weed.

We are now at the grand cenotaph; but, after all, what is there in its massive proportions, its grotesque sculptures, its golden crown, and its shady groves of cypress and pine that will for a moment compare in interest with the daily life and aspirations of the meanest coolie who comes here to gaze with reverend awe and to place his simple votive offering before the temple shrine! The story of this building is a short one. The broad white marble base which gleams in the sunlight covers the relics of a Mongol Lama who was esteemed an incarnate Buddha. Yonder is the vacant throne in the Hwang-Shi, or 'Central Hall,' whereon this human deity sat in state with his face to the East. In another apartment we see the bed on which his holiness expired; poisoned, as is said, by a jealous Emperor towards the end of the eighteenth century, the Imperial murderer treating his victim with the most stately courtesy to the last, and even worshipping and glorifying him in public while his sacrifice was being secretly prepared.

Mr. Wylie, of the London Bible Society, who was journeying into the Northern Provinces, accompanied me to the great wall; and Mr. Welmer, a Russian gentleman, also joined our party. Outside the Anting plain we halted at an inn called 'The Gem of Prosperity,' and, praise be to the Board of Works! we there found men repairing the roads. At Ma-teen there was a sheep-market, and Mongols disposing of their flocks. It is strange to note the strong nomadic tendencies of this race. In the Mongol quarter at Peking I have seen them actually place their beasts of burden inside the apartments of the house they hired, and pitch their own tent in the court outside. The condition of the sheep testified to the richness of the Mongolian pastures; while the shepherds, clad in sheep-skin coats, were a hardy, raw-boned looking race. At Sha-ho village, in the inn of 'Patriotic Perfection,' we made a second halt. Here in our chamber we found this maxim written up on a board: 'All who seek wealth by the only pure principles will find it.' Judging by this doctrine our host must have been a sad ruffian, for the poverty of his surroundings bore witness that he, for his part, must have sought after riches in some very questionable channel. We spent the night at Suy-Shan Inn, Nankow. It was truly a wretched place: the 'grand chamber' measured about eight feet across, and was supplied with the usual brick bed, having an oven underneath it. In a room of this sort the fire is usually lit at night and is made up of charcoal, so that persons sleeping there are apt to be poisoned by the fumes. Such a calamity indeed, at times, will occur. In other respects those who are used to a brick bed and a billet of wood for a pillow may sleep comfortably enough; unless by chance the bricks become red-hot, and then one is apt to be done brown. We left Nankow at six o'clock in the morning, and followed the old Mongol road formed by blocks of porphyry and marble. Through the pass our conveyances were litters slung between two mules, one in front the other behind. Although there is here a great traffic between Thibet, Mongolia, Russia, and China, the road in many places was all but impassable, not to say extremely dangerous, skirting as it does precipitous rocks where the slip of a hoof on the part of either mule might end in a fatal accident. We were constantly falling in with long trains of camels, mules, and donkeys, all heavily laden, some with brick-tea for the Mongolian and Russian markets, while others bore produce to the capital from the outer dependencies of China. At Kew-yung-kwan, an inner spur of the great wall sweeps across the pass;

and here, too, is the old arch to which I have already referred, and which has been rendered famous by Mr. Wylie's successful labours in translating the Buddhist prayer inscribed in six different languages on its inner wall. On this arch, too, we find bas-reliefs representing the Kings of the Devas in Buddhist mythology. The structure is supposed to have been erected during the Yuen dynasty, and is said originally to have carried a pagoda on its summit: but this was afterwards taken down by the Mings, to propitiate the Mongol tribes. I have on another page drawn attention to the Indian mythological figures with which this arch is adorned, and Mr. Wylie's notice of the inscription will be found in the 'Journal of the Royal Asiatic Society,' vol. v., part 1, pp. 14, *seq.*

It is necessary to be careful in bargaining with the men who take one up this pass, for they will impose on foreigners in every possible way. Thus, when about to struggle through the rough parts of the roughest road in the world, they will ask for a guide a-piece to pilot them over each rock and boulder that has to be crossed. It always happens that these guides are themselves most extortionate characters, and as the way grows more difficult some fresh demand is certain to be put forward. Our friend, Mr. Welmer, had arranged everything with our men before we left Peking, but still they made most pertinacious efforts to extort more money from us.

At the great wall I reluctantly parted from Mr. Wylie, who is one of the most distinguished and modest travellers it has been my good fortune to meet.

The wall has been often described, but I confess that it disappointed me. It is simply a gigantic useless stone fence, climbing the hills and dipping down into the valleys. At the point I visited it has been frequently repaired, and only attained to its present massive proportions during the Ming dynasty. That piece of it which we see in the Nankow pass at Pan-ta-ling is not so old by several centuries as the outer wall, which was built by 'Tsin-she-whang,' B.C. 213.[1] In its route of over 1,000 miles there are some portions of the wall which, from neglect, have now fallen into decay; but it was never much more than a clay mound even in its best parts, faced with sun-dried bricks, and in the passes, as at Pan-ta-ling, with stone. It now only stands as a colossal monument of misdirected human labour, and of the genius which the Chinese have ever displayed in raising costly barriers to shut out barbarians from the 'Central Flowery Land.' In vain were all these toilsome precautions! The danger that was threatening them within the country they all the while failed to guard against, and from this very cause at last the native dynasty had to succumb before an alien race.

To understand this we must remember that a rebel wrested the throne from the last Chinese Emperor, and that, when this usurper had been in turn dethroned, the Manchus, taking advantage of the existing disorder, came in and conquered China.

On my return journey I fell in with a gang of convicts, heavily chained, and sent adrift to seek a precarious living in the pass. There they spent their existence, shut out from the villages and shunned by all. One, who had charge of the rest, rode an ass. Half the hair had been rubbed off this poor brute's

[1] See *Journeys in North China*, Rev. Dr. Williamson, ii. 390.

back by the irons of its rider, and even with it respectable donkeys, as they passed in trains, would hold no intercourse. Many of the traders we met were fine-looking men, and few went by us without bestowing a kindly salutation.

At Nankow I put up again at the inn, and there found a native merchant in possession of the best room. He politely offered to vacate it in my favour; but this I, of course, refused to allow, contenting myself with an apartment where Ahong, having first obtained the unwilling consent of the landlord, set to with a half-naked slave to reduce the table and chair until they disclosed the wood of which they were made. There were also many spider-webs; but we left these undisturbed, for their bloated occupants were feasting on the flies with which the room was infested. The merchant had a train of fourteen mules, an elegant sedan, and a troop of muleteers, who were carousing in the next apartment. A merry time they had of it! One of them was still gesticulating like a Chinese stage-warrior as I dropped off to sleep.

In the morning I was awakened by the clang of a smith's anvil, and found that the smith was one of the many travelling workmen who abound in Cathay. He was making knives and reaping-hooks, and had contrived a simple forge by attaching a tube to his air-pump, passing this beneath the ground, and then bringing up the end, so as to play through the fire which lay in a hollow in the soil.

There was also a Mohammedan inn at Nankow, and there the host and his attendants were remarkable for their Indian physiognomies. At the same place, too, I found a guide, who had distinguished himself by showing former visitors through the pass. This individual had fallen heir to a pair of enormous foreign boots, which he kept on his feet by pads and swathes of cloth. He had, besides, obtained a number of certificates from his patrons, which, almost without exception, described him as a great ruffian. These certificates he presented for my inspection, with an evident air of pride. He also said that his sympathies were not Chinese, and, pointing to his boots, declared that he was a foreigner like myself.

From Nankow I proceeded on to the Ming tombs. For the information of those among my readers who may be still unacquainted with the great burial-ground where thirteen Emperors of the Ming dynasty were interred, I will give a brief summary of my experiences in that place.

It will be remembered that Nanking, the ancient capital, where the founder of the Ming dynasty established his court, contains the first mausoleum of those Kings—a mausoleum in almost every particular resembling the tombs of the same line in the valley thirty miles north of Peking. These tombs lie at the foot of a semi-circle of hills, which has something like a three miles' radius.

The temple of Ching-tsoo, who reigned with the national designation of Yung-lo, from 1403 till his death in 1424, is by far the finest of these Imperial resting-places. It is approached through an avenue of colossal animals and warriors sculptured in stone, and although some of the figures are in attitudes of perfect repose, well becoming in the guardians of the illustrious dead, yet when we view them as the finest specimens of sculpture which China has to show, we must acknowledge that her ancient art falls far short of our own modern standard. I doubt, however, whether Chinese artists of the present day could produce anything, I do not say better, but even so good as these Ming statues. The great tomb may be set down in most respects as a counterpart of the architecture which prevails in the temples, the palaces, and even the dwellings in China. I was pleased to find that Mr. Simpson, in his interesting account of his tour round the world, has also noticed this similarity. It must of necessity be so, as the Chinese look upon such a tomb as this as the palace of the spirit of Yung-lo. The animals and warriors form his retinue, while offerings to his soul are annually made at the shrine in the great sacrificial hall. In the same way with their gods: the temples are the palaces wherein the deities reside, and indeed the word 'kung,'[1] used to designate Taouist temples, signifies 'a palace.'

The Emperors of the present dynasty, who drove the Mings from their dominions, still offer sacrifices at the tombs of those sovereigns; and this they do, it may be, out of mere state policy, or perhaps because the spirits of the departed monarchs are supposed to exercise an influence over the Imperial throne.

Although Chinese buildings, in their general plan, present many points of similarity, differences nevertheless exist in the number of their courts, and in the details of the various kinds of edifices. Thus the magisterial yamen has usually four courts; the first three, with the apartments attached to them, comprising the various offices required for administrative purposes; while the fourth, with its buildings, is sacred to the

[1] *The Religious Condition of the Chinese*, Edkins, p. 42.

mandarin and his family. But it is impossible to treat, at the conclusion of a chapter, of a subject which would worthily fill a volume ; nor can I do more than bestow this passing glance at the Valley of Tombs, which marks the resting-place of the last Chinese dynasty.

In conclusion, I venture to hope that—so far as my years of travel and personal observation suffice—I have given the reader some insight into the present condition of the inhabitants of the vast Chinese Empire. The picture at best is a sad one; and though a ray of sunshine may brighten it here and there, yet, after all, the darkness that broods over the land becomes but the more palpable under this straggling fitful light. Poverty and ignorance we have among us in England ; but no poverty so wretched, no ignorance so intense, as are found among the millions of China.

APPENDIX.

THE ABORIGINAL DIALECTS OF FORMOSA.

THERE appears to be no trace of the existence of a written language among the aborigines of Formosa, unless indeed we take into account the use which the semi-civilised tribes have made of Roman and Chinese written characters.

The use of the former was taught by the Dutch over two centuries ago, when they occupied the island. Some singular specimens of Romanised Malay documents are still treasured up among the tribes, although they are quite ignorant of their value, as they are now unable to translate them. These papers are chiefly title-deeds to property, or simple business agreements between man and man.

The Chinese, since the time of the Dutch occupation, have impressed upon the Pepohoan, or 'strangers of the plain,' their own language both written and oral. It was therefore only from the oldest members of the Baksa Pepohoan tribe that I could obtain the words set down in the Vocabulary. At Baksa the native language has been superseded by the Chinese colloquial dialect.

The Shekhoan is the great northern tribe of half-civilised aborigines. They still retain their original tongue, although the crafty Chinese invaders are making rapid inroads on their fertile valleys, and civilising them out of the lands, if not out of the language of their fathers.

In the savage mountain tribes of Formosa—separated as they are from each other by impenetrable forests, rocky barriers, impetuous torrents, and deep ravines, as well as by ceaseless warfare—we have an example of the change which, in time, may be effected in a language by the breaking up of a race into tribes which for at least two hundred years have been from necessity, for the most part, isolated from each other, and where oral tradition afforded the only means of retaining a knowledge of their original tongue. We find that the numerals of the language, which were probably the sounds most constantly in use, have suffered least change, and the number five has retained its original sound. This may be from the fact that among primitive tribes, who have no written numerals, the five fingers of the hand are invariably used to solve their simple problems in arithmetic; so notably, indeed, is this the case, that in many dialects five and hand are synonymous: the hand in that way becoming a sort of—if I may use the expression—rude hieroglyphic signifying five. In the same way eye, or Mata, is a simple, easily remembered sound; and as it designates the organ of sight—something that has its sign in each human face, that is in constant use, and constantly appealed to to satisfy the savage, as well as the most cultivated instincts—it too has been retained, in nearly its pure sound, in the various dialects. Thus I might go on selecting the words that appear to me to have retained their primitive sounds, simply because they find their visible symbols in the objects which surround the simple abodes of the aborigines.

But the reader, by referring to the Vocabularies, will be enabled to form his own conclusions, and to trace out the affinities, or the opposite, that exist between the Formosan dialects, and also the close family likeness which they bear to the Polynesian languages. (See Polynesian Vocabularies in Crawford's 'Indian Archipelago,' vol. iii., and the words noted on Table III.)

Fresh evidence of the existence of races on the New Guinea coast who speak the Polynesian dialects has been afforded by the Rev. W. W. Gill, who made three visits to the island in 1872.[1] Thus, he tells us that the word for eye with two separate tribes is Mata, for ear Taringa and Taia, and for hands Ima-ima and Rima-rima. These words are all to be found in the Formosan dialects, and indeed might have been taken from them. As for the numerals in use among the

[1] *Proceedings of the Royal Geographical Society*, xviii. 45.

aboirgines of Formosa, they would afford but doubtful evidence of the Polynesian origin of the tribes were they not supported by the more direct testimony which the various dialects supply.

SHORT VOCABULARIES OF THE DIALECTS SPOKEN BY THE ABORIGINES OF FORMOSA.

TABLE I.

	Names of Tribes					
English	Pachien	Sibucoon	Tibolal	Banga	Bantanlang	Singapore Malay
Man	Lalusa	Lamoosa	—	Sarellai	Aoolai	Orang
Woman	Atlain	Maou-spingth	—	Abaia	Abaia	Prampaun
Head	Bangoo	Bangoo	Sapchi	Kapallu	Kapallu	Kapala
Hair	—	—	—	Ussioi	—	Rambut
Tooth	—	—	Nganon	—	—	Gigit
Neck	Guon-gorath	—	—	Oorohu	Oorohu	Leher
Ear	Charunga	—	—	Charinga	Charinga	Talinga
Mouth	Mussoo	Nipoon	—	Didisi	Muto-mytoo	Mulut
Nose	Ngoon-goro	Muttus	Nguchu	Coomonu	Ongoho	Idung
Eye	Ooraitla	Mata	Muchen	Macha	Macha	Mata
Heart	Takaru	Kanum	—	Kasso	Tookuho	Janteng
Hand	Ramucho	Tarima	Ramucha	Arema	—	Tangan
Foot	Sapatl	Ktlapa	Sapchi	Tsapku	Amoo	Kaki
Thigh	Bannen	Pinassan	Tangigya	Danoosa	Laloohe	Pauh
Leg	—	—	—	Tiboo-sabossa	—	Betis
Knee	Anasatoo	Khap	—	Pookuro	Sakaho	Lŭtut
Leopard	Lakotl	—	—	Likalao	Rikoslao	Animau Kambang
Bear	Chumatu	—	—	Choomatu	Choomai	Bruang
Deer	Putooru	—	—	Silappu	Caliche	Rusa
Wild hog	Aroomthi	—	—	—	Babooy	Babi-outan
Monkey	—	—	—	—	Mararooko	Monyet
Wild goat	Okin	—	—	—	Kehe	Kambing-outan
Fowl	Turhook	—	—	Turkook	Turkook	Ayam
House	—	—	—	Dami	Dami	Ruma
Chief	—	Titan-garchu	—	Tital-abahi	Tallai	Rajah
Bamboo	Baswera	—	—	—	Taroo-lahiroi	Bulah
Cassia	—	—	—	Tara-inai	—	Kŭlit Manas
Tea	—	—	—	Lang-lang	—	Daun Teh
Cooking pan	Kusang	—	—	—	Palangu	Kwali-Masak
Pumpkin	—	—	—	Tangu-tangu	—	Lăbŭ Fringgi
Fragrant	—	—	—	—	Anaremu	Wangie
Rice	—	—	—	—	Chiluco	Bras
Rice boiled	Oaro	—	—	Curao	Ba-ooro	Nasi
Fire	Apooth	Sapooth	Pooju	Apoolu	Apooy	Api
Water	Satloom	Manum	Choomai	Achilai	Achilai	Ayer
Ring	Tujana	Paklis	—	Tarra	Mata-na	Chin-chin
Ear-ring	—	—	—	Chin-gari	Ang-choy	Krabu
Bracelet	Pitoka	Push-tonna	—	Uliule	Issaise	Galang
Pipe	Katsap	Kaconan	—	Ang-choy	Ang-choy	Pipa
Gun	Taklito	Pavak-sapum	—	Guang	Guangu	Sanapang
Skin jacket	Nicaroota	Shiddi	—	Amalin	Carridha	Bajo-kulet
Cap	Sarapun	Tamoking	—	Tara-pung	Torra-pungu	Topie
Letter	—	—	—	Senna	Uraome	Surat
Smoke	Worlbooro	Khosalt	—	Uburon	—	Asap
By-and-bye	Chuden	—	—	—	Churana	Lagi-sabuntar
Warm	Machechu	—	—	Mechechi	Mechechi	Panas
Cold	Matilku	—	—	Matilku	Malilku	Sajuk
Rain	—	—	—	—	Maisang	Ugan

Note.—The Formosa vocabularies, with the exception of the Baksa Pepohoan, were supplied by Dr. Maxwell and the Rev. Mr. Ritchie, Formosa. The Baksa vocabulary was taken down by the author when among the Pepohoans.

TABLE II.

	Names of Tribes			Names of Tribes	
English	Shekhoan	Malay	English	Shekhoan	Malay
Man	Mamalung	Orang	Thou or ye	Isu	Inkang
Woman	Mameoss	Prampaun	Good	Riak	Biak
Child	Lakehan	Anak	Bad	Satdeal	Jăhat
Son	{ Lakehan Mamalung }	Ano	Sun Moon	Liddock Illas	Mata-hari Bulan
Daughter or girl	Mamaop	—	Star	Bintool	Bintang
Father	Aba	Bapa	Heaven	Babu-kanas	Surga
Mother	Inna	Ma	High	Baban	Tingi
Elder brother	Abusan	Abang	Mountain	Binaiss	Bukit
Younger brother	Soaip	Adik	Sea	Anass	Laut
Sister	Mamaop	—	Free	Katxaney	Mardika
Head	Poonat	Kăpala	Great	Matalah	Besar
Hair	Bakus	Rambut	Small	Tateng	Kechil
Mouth	Lahar	Mulut	Day	Lahan	Hari
Eyes	Darik	Mata	Night	Hinien	Malum
Nose	Mooding	Idung	One	Ida	Satu
Arm	Limat	—	Two	Doosah	Dua
Leg	Karan	—	Three	Tooro	Tiga
Live	Meirad	Idup	Four	Supat	Ampat
Die	Polekat	Mati	Five	Hassub	Lima
Eat	Makan	Mukanan	Six	Boodah	Anăm
Eat rice	Makan-somai	Makan-nasi	Seven	Bi-doosut	Tugu
Drink	Mudauch	Menam	Eight	Bi-tooro	Da-lapan
Drink wine	{ Mudauch inunsat }	Menam-angur	Nine Ten	Bi-supat Isid.	Simbilan Sa-puluh
I or me	Iakok	Aku			

TABLE III.

	Names of Tribes			Names of Tribes	
English	Tribe at Pilam	Malay	English	Tribe at Pilam	Malay
Man	Atinbe	Orang	Cold	Litak	Sajuk
Male	Mainaen	Jantan	Sea	A-nik	Laut
Female	Babaian	Batena	Earth	Darak	Tana or darat
Father	Amoko	Bapa	Fire	Apui	Api
Mother	Abu	Ma	Mountain	Adenan	Bukit
Son	Alak	Anak	Rice	Rumai	Bras
Daughter	Abavi	Anak dara	Good	Inava	Biak
Head	Tungrow	Kapala	Bad	Kaotish	Jahat
Eye	Mata	Mata	Darkness	Aruning	Galap
Nose	Atingran	Idung	Strike light	Pulalauit	Dapat-api
Mouth	Indan	Mulut	North	Loud	Utara
Face	Tungur	Muka	South	Daiah	Salalan
Ear	Tungila	Talinga	East	Ameh	Tmur
Hand	A-lima	Tangan	West	Timur	Barat
Body	A-liduk	Badan	One	Itu	Satu
Feet	Lapar	Kaki	Twe	Lusa	Dua
Heart	Ne-rung-arung	Jantong	Three	Taloh	Tiga
House	A-ruma	Ruma	Four	Sepat	Ampat
Garden	A-uma	Cabun	Five	Lima	Lima
Vegetables	A-ropan	Siuer	Six	Onam	Anam
Village	A-tikal	Campong	Seven	Pitu	Tugu
Wood	Kiau	Kiau	Eight	Aloo	Da-lupan
Water	A-tuei	Ayer	Nine	Siva	Sambilan
Heat	Beaus	Panas	Ten	Pelapsang	Sa-puluh

TABLE IV.

English	Names of Tribes.		English	Names of Tribes	
	Baksa Pepohoan	Malay		Baksa Pepohoan	Malay
Man	Kaguling-ma	Orang	Heat	Ma-kinku	Panas
Male	Ama	Jantan	Cold	Ma-hunmoon	Sajuk
Female	Enina	Batina	Rain	Mudan	Ugim
Son	Alak	Anak	Stone	Batu	Batu
Daughter	Yugant nina	Anak-dara	Wood	Kiau	Kiau
Child	Yugant	Anik	Iron	Mani	Bisi
Father	Ima	Bapa	Flower	Eseep	Bunga
Mother	Ina	Ma	Fruit	Toto	Bua
Elder brother	Jaka	Abang	Earth	Ni	Tana
Younger brother	Ebe	Adik	Water	Jalum	Ayer
Elder sister	Jaka	—	Wind	Bali	Angin
Younger sister	Ebe	—	Smoke	Atu	Asap
Husband and wife	Maka-kaja	—	Clean	Ma-kupti	Brisi
			Dirty	Ma-luksung	Cotor
Head	Mongong	Kapala	Black	Ma-edum	Etam
Body	Bwan	Badan	White	Ma-puli	Puti
Belly	Ebuk	Prut	Red	Ma-epong	Mera
Beard	Ngih	Jangut	Rice	Dak	Bras
Tooth	Wali	Gigi	Rice cooked	Rudak	Bras-masa
Mouth	Mutut	Mulut	River	Mutu	Sungi
Throat	Luak	Lhaer	Sky	Towin	Langit
Hair	Bukaun	Rambut	Sea	Baung	Laut
Hand	Lima	Tangan	To blow	Ayu	Teop
Foot	Lapan	Kaki	To push	Dudung	Kaki
Finger-nails	Ku-rung-kung	Kooku	Banana	Bunbun	Pisang
Eye	Mata	Mata	Cocoa-nut	Agubung	Kalapa
Ear	Tangela	Talinga	Mango	Mangut	Mampalam
Nose	Togunut	Idung	Orange	Busilam	Lemo
Death	Ilapati	Mati	Potatoe	Tamami	Obie
Life	Maonga	Idup	Bad	Masari	Jahat
Fire	Apoi	Api	Good	Magani	Biak
Tobacco	Tabacow	Timbacu	Disease	Maalam	Sackit
Pipe	Timbakang	Pepo	To kill	Lumpo	Kasa-mati or Bono
Stand	Netuku	Burderi			
Walk	Daran	Jalan	Sun	Wali	Mata-hari
Sing	Mururou	Ngnia	Moon	Buran	Bulan

COMPARATIVE TABLE OF THE LANGUAGES OF FORMOSA, THE PHILIPPINES, SINGAPORE, NEW ZEALAND, ETC.

TABLE V.

English	Paichien Formosa	Sibucoon Formosa	Tibolah Formosa	Banga Formosa	Bantanlang Formosa	Samobi Formosa	Baksa Pepo-hoan Formosa	Philippine Jagulo[2]	Philippine Bisaya[2]	New Zealand[3]	Des Habitans De Tikopa[4]	Des Papous De Waigiou	Tonga	Maw	Des Harfours[4] De Manado Célebes	Malay of Singapore
One	Saou	Tashang	Chum	Denga	Denga	Itsa	Saat	Isa	Usa	Tahi	Tassa	Saï	Taha	Tahi	Essa	Satu
Two	Soo	Lusha	Lusa	Noosa	Noosa	Lusa	Duha	Dalaua	Duha	Rua	Roua	Douï	Oua	Doua	Roua	Dua
Three	Torò	Taoo	Tooloo	Torò	Torò	Toroo	Turò	Tallo	Tatò	Toro	Torou	Kior	Tolou	Todou	Talou	Tiga
Four	Pati	P'at	Supat	Patù	Patù	Sipat	Da-pat	Apat	Upat	Wa	Fa	Fiak	Fa	Wa	Apat	Ampat
Five	Rimà	Timà	Limà	Limà	Limà	Limà	Da-rima	Limà	Limà	Rima	Lima	Rim	Nima	Dima	Lima	Lima
Six	Neum	Noom	Nauma	Neuma	Neum	Unum	Danum	Anim	Uniam	Ono	Ono	Onem	Ono	Ono	Anam	Anam
Seven	Pitò	Pitò	Pitò	Pitò	Pitò	Pitò	Dapitò	Pitò	Pitò	Witu	Fitou	Fik	Fitou	Witou	Piton	Tugo
Eight	Mivaroo	Awoo	Mevaroo	Mevaroo	Mevaroo	Aloo	Kuipat	Ualò	Ualò	Waru	Warou	War	Valou	Wadou	Walou	Da-lapan
Nine	Siwà	Sivà	Chuga	Bangatò	Bangatu	Sivà	—	Siam	Siam	Iwa	Siva	Sion	Hiva	Iwa	Sio	Sambilan
Ten	Koomath	Basau	Matl	Poorookoo	Poorooku	Porò	Kating	Sampu	Napulo	Nga-huru	Anhafouro	Somfour	Oulou	Nga Oudon	Poulou	Sa-puluh
Hand[1]	—	—	—	—	—	—	Lima	—	—	—	—	—	—	—	—	—

[1] I have added the word Lima, or Hand, in the Baksa dialect, in which it also means five. ('In many Negro languages Lima also means hand.' See the late Mr. Crawford's *Dissertation on the Malay Language*, &c., p. 236.

[2] *Essays Ethnological and Linguistic*, by the late James Kennedy, p. 74.

[3] *Du Dialecte de Tahiti, de celui des iles Marquises, et en général, de la Langue Polynésienne*, Table, p. 101.

[4] *Voyage de L'Astrolabe*, par M. D'Urville. Paris, 1834.

DIURNAL LEPIDOPTERA OF SIAM,

COLLECTED BY THE AUTHOR AND NAMED BY H. W. BATES, ESQ. F.L.S. &c.

Fam. DANAIDÆ.

Ideopsis Daos (Boisduval). One example.
Danais Meleneus (Cramer). Several examples.
Danais Aglea (Cramer). Apparently common.
Danais Similis (Lin.). Equally common with D. Aglea.
Danais Plexippus (Lin.). Two examples.
Euplœa Superba (Herbst). One pair.
Euplœa Eunice (Godart). One example.
Euplœa Midamus (Lin.). Many examples.

Fam. SATYRIDÆ.

Cyllo Leda (Lin.). Several specimens.
Mycalesis Mineus (Lin.). Several specimens.

Fam. NYMPHALIDÆ.

Melanitis Undularis (Drury). Several specimens, with varieties.
Cethosia Cyane (Drury). Two examples.
Terinos Clarissa (Boisd.). One example.
Cirrhochroa Thais (Fab.). One example.
Messaras Erymanthis (Drury). Several examples.
Atella Phalanta (Drury). Several examples.
Precis Ida (Cramer). One pair.
Diadema Bolina (Lin., Cram.). Several examples, of both sexes.
Athyma Leucothoë (Lin.). Two examples.
Adolias Monina (F.). Several specimens.
Minetra Sylvia (Cram.). Two examples.

Fam. PIERINÆ.

Pontia Nina (F.).
Terias Hecabe (L.). Several examples, with varieties.
Pieris Nerissa (Fab.).
Tachyris Lyncida (Cram.). Several examples.
Tachyris Paulina (Cram.). One example.
Eronia Valeria (Cram.). Several examples.

Fam. PAPILIONIDÆ.

Ornithoptera Rhadamanthus (Boisd.). Var. Thomsonii.

The single male example which Mr. Thomson collected in Siam differs from those of the Philippine Islands, by the longer and more falcate form of the anterior wings, and by the clear yellow colour of the hind wings, on which there is a dusky mark only round the three marginal spots near the anal angle. The yellowish gray streaks of the anterior wings are confined to the margins of the branches of the median nervure.

This local form, or subspecies, is distinguished from the North Indian form of O. Rhadamanthus by the distinct red collar, and by the yellow abdomen (of the male) marked only with a dusky patch in the middle of each dorsal segment; there is also a pinkish-red spot on each side of the base of the abdomen.

In a genus like Ornithoptera, offering so strong a tendency to the formation of local forms throughout the areas of distribution of the species, it is necessary that such forms should receive distinguishing names. Such has been the practice of most entomologists, and on this account the present Siamese form may bear the subspecific name of O. Thomsonii.

Papilio Macareus (Godt.). One example.
Papilio Diphilus (Esper). Many examples.
Papilio Erithonius (Cramer). Several examples.
Papilio Pammon (Lin.). Several examples.
Papilio Helenus (Lin.). Two examples.
Papilio Memnon (Lin.). Several examples.
Papilio Antiphates (Cram.). One example.
Papilio Agamemnon (Lin.). Several examples.
Papilio Sarpedon (Lin.). Several examples.

VALUABLE WORKS OF TRAVEL

PUBLISHED BY

HARPER & BROTHERS, New York.

☞ Harper & Brothers *will send any of the following works by mail, postage prepaid, to any part of the United States, on receipt of the price.*

DR. LIVINGSONE'S LAST JOURNALS. The Last Journals of David Livingstone, in Central Africa, from 1865 to his Death. Continued by a Narrative of his Last Moments and Sufferings, obtained from his Faithful Servants Chuma and Susi. By Horace Waller, F.R.G.S., Rector of Twywell, Northampton. With Maps and Illustrations. 8vo, Cloth, $5 00.

SCHWEINFURTH'S HEART OF AFRICA. The Heart of Africa; or, Three Years' Travels and Adventures in the Unexplored Regions of the Centre of Africa. From 1868 to 1871. By Dr. Georg Schweinfurth. Translated by Ellen E. Frewer. With an Introduction by Winwood Reade. Illustrated by about 130 Woodcuts from Drawings made by the Author, and with Two Maps. 2 vols., 8vo, Cloth, $8 00.

STANLEY'S COOMASSIE AND MAGDALA. Coomassie and Magdala: a Story of Two British Campaigns in Africa. By Henry M. Stanley. With Maps and Illustrations. 8vo, Cloth, $3 50.

CAPTAIN TYSON'S ARCTIC ADVENTURES. Arctic Experiences: containing Captain George E. Tyson's Wonderful Drift on the Ice-Floe, a History of the Polaris Expedition, the Cruise of the Tigress, and Rescue of the Polaris Survivors. To which is added a General Arctic Chronology. Edited by E. Vale Blake. With Map and numerous Illustrations. 8vo, Cloth, $4 00.

MACGAHAN'S CAMPAIGNING ON THE OXUS. Campaigning on the Oxus and the Fall of Khiva. By J. A. MacGahan. With Map and Illustrations. Crown 8vo, Cloth, $3 50.

MYERS'S REMAINS OF LOST EMPIRES. Remains of Lost Empires: Sketches of the Ruins of Palmyra, Nineveh, Babylon, and Persepolis, with some Notes on India and the Cashmerian Himalayas. By P. V. N. Myers, A.M, Illustrations. 8vo, Cloth, $3 50.

SIR SAMUEL BAKER'S ISMAILÏA. Ismailïa: A Narrative of the Expedition to Central Africa for the Suppression of the Slave Trade. Organized by Ismail, Khedive of Egypt. By Sir Samuel W. Baker, Pasha, M.A., F.R.S., F.R.G.S. With Maps, Portraits, and upward of Fifty full-page Illustrations by Zwecker and Durand. 8vo, Cloth, $5 00.

VINCENT'S LAND OF THE WHITE ELEPHANT. The Land of the White Elephant: Sights and Scenes in Southeastern Asia. A Personal Narrative of Travel and Adventure in Farther India, embracing the Countries of Burma, Siam, Cambodia, and Cochin-China (1871–2). By Frank Vincent, Jr. With Map, Plans, and numerous Illustrations. Crown 8vo, Cloth, $3 50.

PIKE'S SUB-TROPICAL RAMBLES. Sub-Tropical Rambles in the Land of the Aphanapteryx. By Nicholas Pike, U. S. Consul, Port Louis, Mauritius. Profusely Illustrated from the Author's own Sketches; containing also Maps and valuable Meteorological Charts. Crown 8vo, Cloth, $3 50.

TRISTRAM'S LAND OF MOAB. The Land of Moab: The Result of Travels and Discoveries on the East Side of the Dead Sea and the Jordan. By H. B. Tristram, M.A., LL.D., F.R.S. With a Chapter on the Persian Palace of Mashita, by Jas Ferguson, F.R.S., and Illustrations. Crown 8vo, Cloth, $2 50.

THE DESERT OF THE EXODUS. Journeys on Foot in the Wilderness of the Forty Years' Wanderings; undertaken in connection with the Ordnance Survey of Sinai and the Palestine Exploration Fund. By E. H. Palmer, M.A., Lord Almoner's Professor of Arabic, and Fellow of St. John's College, Cambridge. With Maps and numerous Illustrations from Photographs and Drawings taken on the spot by the Sinai Survey Expedition and C. F. Tyrwhitt Drake. Crown 8vo, Cloth, $3 00.

NORDHOFF'S CALIFORNIA. California: for Health, Pleasure, and Residence. A Book for Travellers and Settlers. Illustrated. 8vo, Paper, $2 00; Cloth, $2 50.

NORDHOFF'S NORTHERN CALIFORNIA, OREGON, AND THE SANDWICH ISLANDS. Northern California, Oregon, and the Sandwich Islands. By Charles Nordhoff. Profusely Illustrated. 8vo, Cloth, $2 50.

SANTO DOMINGO, Past and Present, with a Glance at Hayti. By Samuel Hazard. Maps and Illustrations. Crown 8vo, Cloth, $3 50.

AROUND THE WORLD. By Edward D. G. Prime, D.D. With numerous Illustrations. Crown 8vo, Cloth, $3 00.

BURTON'S LAKE REGIONS OF CENTRAL AFRICA. The Lake Regions of Central Africa. A Picture of Exploration. By RICHARD F. BURTON, Captain H. M.'s Indian Army, Fellow and Gold Medalist of the Royal Geographical Society. With Maps and Engravings on Wood. 8vo, Cloth, $3 50.

BURTON'S CITY OF THE SAINTS. The City of the Saints; and Across the Rocky Mountains to California. By Captain RICHARD F. BURTON, Fellow and Gold Medalist of the Royal Geographical Societies of France and England, H. M.'s Consul in West Africa. With Maps and numerous Illustrations. 8vo, Cloth, $3 50.

BELLOWS'S TRAVELS. The Old World in its New Face: Impressions of Europe in 1867, 1868. By HENRY W. BELLOWS. 2 vols., 12mo, Cloth, $3 50.

CURTIS'S THE HOWADJI IN SYRIA. By GEORGE WILLIAM CURTIS. 12mo, Cloth, $1 50.

CURTIS'S NILE NOTES OF A HOWADJI. By GEORGE WILLIAM CURTIS. 12mo, Cloth, $1 50.

CUMMING'S HUNTER'S LIFE IN AFRICA. Five Years of a Hunter's Life in the far Interior of South Africa. With Notices of the Native Tribes, and Anecdotes of the Chase of the Lion, Elephant, Hippopotamus, Giraffe, Rhinoceros, &c. With Illustrations. By R. GORDON CUMMING. 2 vols., 12mo, Cloth, $3 00.

DAVIS'S CARTHAGE. Carthage and her Remains: being an Account of the Excavations and Researches on the Site of the Phœnician Metropolis in Africa and other Adjacent Places. Conducted under the Auspices of Her Majesty's Government. By Dr. N. DAVIS, F.R.G.S. Profusely Illustrated with Maps, Woodcuts, Chromo-Lithographs, &c. 8vo, Cloth, $4 00.

DILKE'S GREATER BRITAIN. Greater Britain: a Record of Travel in English-speaking Countries during 1866 and 1867. By CHARLES WENTWORTH DILKE. With Maps and Illustrations. 12mo, Cloth, $1 00.

DOOLITTLE'S CHINA. Social Life of the Chinese; with some Account of their Religious, Governmental, Educational, and Business Customs and Opinions. With special but not exclusive Reference to Fuhchau. By Rev. JUSTUS DOOLITTLE, Fourteen Years Member of the Fuhchau Mission of the American Board. Illustrated with more than 150 characteristic Engravings on Wood. 2 vols., 12mo, Cloth, $5 00.

DU CHAILLU'S AFRICA. Explorations and Adventures in Equatorial Africa; with Accounts of the Manners and Customs of the People, and of the Chase of the Gorilla, the Crocodile, Leopard, Elephant, Hippopotamus, and other Animals. By PAUL B. DU CHAILLU, Corresponding Member of the American Ethnological Society, of the Geographical and Statistical Society of New York, and of the Boston Society of Natural History. With numerous Illustrations. 8vo, Cloth, $5 00.

DU CHAILLU'S ASHANGO LAND. A Journey to Ashango Land, and Further Penetration into Equatorial Africa. By PAUL B. DU CHAILLU. New Edition. Handsomely Illustrated. 8vo, Cloth, $5 00.

EWBANK'S BRAZIL. Life in Brazil; or, a Journal of a Visit to the Land of the Cocoa and the Palm. With an Appendix, containing Illustrations of Ancient and South American Arts, in recently discovered Implements and Products of Domestic Industry, and Works in Stone, Pottery, Gold, Silver, Bronze, &c. By THOMAS EWBANK. With over 100 Illustrations. 8vo, Cloth, $3 00.

ELLIS'S MADAGASCAR. Three Visits to Madagascar, during the Years 1853, 1854, 1856. Including a Journey to the Capital, with Notices of the Natural History of the Country, and of the Present Civilization of the People. By the Rev. WILLIAM ELLIS, F.H.S. Illustrated by a Map and Woodcuts from Photographs, &c. 8vo, Cloth, $3 50.

HALL'S ARCTIC RESEARCHES. Arctic Researches and Life among the Esquimaux: being the Narrative of an Expedition in Search of Sir John Franklin, in the Years 1860, 1861, and 1862. By CHARLES FRANCIS HALL. With Maps and 100 Illustrations. 8vo, Cloth, Beveled, $5 00.

ANDERSSON'S OKAVANGO RIVER. The Okavango River: a Narrative of Travel, Exploration, and Adventure. By CHARLES JOHN ANDERSSON. With Steel Portrait of the Author, numerous Woodcuts, and a Map showing the Regions explored by Andersson, Cumming, Livingstone, and Du Chaillu. 8vo, Cloth, $3 25.

ANDERSSON'S LAKE NGAMI. Lake Ngami; or, Explorations and Discoveries during Four Years' Wanderings in the Wilds of Southwestern Africa. By CHARLES JOHN ANDERSSON. With numerous Illustrations, representing Sporting Adventures, Subjects of Natural History, Devices for Destroying Wild Animals, &c. 12mo, Cloth, $1 75.

ATKINSON'S AMOOR REGIONS. Travels in the Regions of the Upper and Lower Amoor, and the Russian Acquisitions on the Confines of India and China. With Adventures among the Mountain Kirghis; and the Manjours, Manyargs, Toungous, Touzempts, Goldi, and Gelyaks; the Hunting and Pastoral Tribes. By THOMAS WITLAM ATKINSON, F.G.S., F.R.G.S. With a Map and numerous Illustrations. 8vo, Cloth, $3 50.

LIVINGSTONE'S SOUTH AFRICA. Missionary Travels and Researches in South Africa; including a Sketch of Sixteen Years' Residence in the Interior of Africa, and a Journey from the Cape of Good Hope to Loando on the West Coast; thence across the Continent, down the River Zambesi, to the Eastern Ocean. By DAVID LIVINGSTONE, LL.D., D.C.L. With Portrait, Maps by Arrowsmith, and numerous Illustrations. 8vo, Cloth, $4 50.

LIVINGSTONE'S EXPEDITION TO THE ZAMBESI. Narrative of an Expedition to the Zambesi and its Tributaries; and of the Discovery of the Lakes Shirwa and Nyassa. 1858–1864. By DAVID and CHARLES LIVINGSTONE. With Map and Illustrations. 8vo, Cloth, $5 00.

LAYARD'S NINEVEH. A Popular Account of the Discoveries at Nineveh. By AUSTEN HENRY LAYARD. Abridged by him from his larger Work. With numerous Wood Engravings. 12mo, Cloth, $1 75.

LAYARD'S FRESH DISCOVERIES AT NINEVEH. Fresh Discoveries at Nineveh and Babylon; with Travels in Armenia, Kurdistan, and the Desert. Being the Result of a Second Expedition undertaken for the Trustees of the British Museum. By AUSTEN HENRY LAYARD, M.P. With all the Maps and Engravings in the English Edition. 8vo, Cloth, $4 00.

MARCY'S ARMY LIFE ON THE BORDER. Thirty Years of Army Life on the Border. Comprising Descriptions of the Indian Nomads of the Plains; Explorations of New Territory; a Trip across the Rocky Mountains in the Winter; Descriptions of the Habits of Different Animals found in the West, and the Methods of Hunting them; with Incidents in the Lives of different Frontier Men, &c., &c. By Brevet Brig.-General R. B. MARCY, U. S. A. 8vo, Cloth, Beveled Edges, $3 00.

MOWRY'S ARIZONA AND SONORA. Arizona and Sonora. The Geography, History, and Resources of the Silver Region of North America. By SYLVESTER MOWRY, of Arizona, Graduate of the U. S. Military Academy at West Point, late Lieutenant Third Artillery, U. S. A., Corresponding Member of the American Institute, late U. S. Boundary Commissioner, &c., &c. 12mo, Cloth, $1 50.

MACGREGOR'S ROB ROY ON THE JORDAN. The Rob Roy on the Jordan, Nile, Red Sea, and Gennesareth, &c. A Canoe Cruise in Palestine and Egypt, and the Waters of Damascus. By J. MACGREGOR, M.A. With Maps and Illustrations. Crown 8vo, Cloth, $2 50.

NEVIUS'S CHINA. China and the Chinese: a General Description of the Country and its Inhabitants; its Civilization and Form of Government; its Religious and Social Institutions; its Intercourse with other Nations; and its Present Condition and Prospects. By the Rev. JOHN L. NEVIUS, Ten Years a Missionary in China. With a Map and Illustrations. 12mo, Cloth, $1 75.

NEWMAN'S FROM DAN TO BEERSHEBA. From Dan to Beersheba; or, the Land of Promise as it now appears. Including a Description of the Boundaries, Topography, Agriculture, Antiquities, Cities, and Present Inhabitants of that Wonderful Land. With Illustrations of the Remarkable Accuracy of the Sacred Writers in their Allusions to their Native Country. By Rev. J. P. NEWMAN, D.D. Maps and Engravings. 12mo, Cloth, $1 75.

OLIPHANT'S CHINA AND JAPAN. Narrative of the Earl of Elgin's Mission to China and Japan, in the Years 1857, '58, '59. By LAURENCE OLIPHANT, Private Secretary to Lord Elgin. Illustrations. 8vo, Cloth, $3 50.

ORTON'S ANDES AND THE AMAZON. The Andes and the Amazon; or, Across the Continent of South America. By JAMES ORTON, M.A., Professor of Natural History in Vassar College, Poughkeepsie, N. Y., and Corresponding Member of the Academy of Natural Sciences, Philadelphia. With a New Map of Equatorial America and numerous Illustrations. Crown 8vo, Cloth, $2 00.

PAGE'S LA PLATA. La Plata, the Argentine Confederation, and Paraguay. Being a Narrative of the Exploration of the Tributaries of the River La Plata and Adjacent Countries during the Years 1853, '54, '55, and '56, under the Orders of the United States Government. New Edition, containing Farther Explorations in La Plata during 1859 and 1860. By THOMAS J. PAGE, U. S. N., Commander of the Expeditions. With Map and numerous Engravings. 8vo, Cloth, $5 00.

PRIME'S (S. I.) TRAVELS IN EUROPE AND THE EAST. Travels in Europe and the East. A Year in England, Scotland, Ireland, Wales, France, Belgium, Holland, Germany, Austria, Italy, Greece, Turkey, Syria, Palestine, and Egypt. By Rev. SAMUEL IRENÆUS PRIME, D.D. Engravings. 2 vols., large 12mo, Cloth, $3 00.

READE'S SAVAGE AFRICA. Western Africa: being the Narrative of a Tour in Equatorial, Southwestern, and Northwestern Africa; with Notes on the Habits of the Gorilla; on the Existence of Unicorns and Tailed Men; on the Slave Trade; on the Origin, Character, and Capabilities of the Negro, and on the Future Civilization of Western Africa. By W. WINWOOD READE, Fellow of the Geographical and Anthropological Society of London, and Corresponding Member of the Geographical Society of Paris. With Illustrations and a Map. 8vo, Cloth, $4 00.

HOLTON'S NEW GRANADA. Twenty Months in the Andes. By I. F. HOLTON. Illustrations and Maps. 8vo, Cloth, $3 00.

REINDEER, DOGS, AND SNOW-SHOES. A Journal of Siberian Travel and Explorations made in the Years 1865–'67. By RICHARD J. BUSH, late of the Russo-American Telegraph Expedition. Illustrated. Crown 8vo, Cloth, $3 00.

PRIME'S (W. C.) BOAT-LIFE IN EGYPT. Boat-Life in Egypt and Nubia. By WILLIAM C. PRIME. Illustrations. 12mo, Cloth, $2 00.

PRIME'S (W. C.) TENT-LIFE IN THE HOLY LAND. By WILLIAM C. PRIME. Illustrations. 12mo, Cloth, $2 00.

SQUIER'S CENTRAL AMERICA. The States of Central America: their Geography, Topography, Climate, Population, Resources, Productions, Commerce, Political Organization, Aborigines, &c., &c. Comprising Chapters on Honduras, San Salvador, Nicaragua, Costa Rica, Guatemala, Belize, the Bay Islands, the Mosquito Shore, and the Honduras Inter-Oceanic Railway. By E. G. SQUIER, formerly Chargé d'Affairs of the United States to the Republics of Central America. With numerous Original Maps and Illustrations. 8vo, Cloth, $4 00.

SQUIER'S NICARAGUA. Nicaragua: its People, Scenery, Monuments, Resources, Condition, and Proposed Canal. With One Hundred Maps and Illustrations. By E. G. SQUIER. 8vo, Cloth, $4 00.

SQUIER'S WAIKNA. Waikna; or, Adventures on the Mosquito Shore. By E. G. SQUIER. With a Map and upward of Sixty Illustrations. 12mo, Cloth, $1 50.

SPEKE'S AFRICA. Journal of the Discovery of the Source of the Nile. By Captain JOHN HANNING SPEKE, Captain H. M.'s Indian Army, Fellow and Gold Medalist of the Royal Geographical Society, Hon. Corresponding Member and Gold Medalist of the French Geographical Society, &c. With Maps and Portraits and numerous Illustrations, chiefly from Drawings by Captain Grant. 8vo, Cloth, $4 00.

STEPHENS'S TRAVELS IN CENTRAL AMERICA. Travels in Central America, Chiapas, and Yucatan. By J. L. STEPHENS. With a Map and 88 Engravings. 2 vols., 8vo, Cloth, $6 00.

STEPHENS'S TRAVELS IN YUCATAN. Incidents of Travel in Yucatan. By J. L. STEPHENS. 120 Engravings, from Drawings by F. Catherwood. 2 vols., 8vo, Cloth, $6 00.

STEPHENS'S TRAVELS IN EGYPT. Travels in Egypt, Arabia Petræa, and the Holy Land. By J. L. STEPHENS. Engravings. 2 vols., 12mo, Cloth, $3 00.

STEPHENS'S TRAVELS IN GREECE. Travels in Greece, Turkey, Russia, and Poland. By J. L. STEPHENS. Engravings. 2 vols., 12mo, Cloth, $3 00.

THOMSON'S LAND AND BOOK. The Land and the Book; or, Biblical Illustrations drawn from the Manners and Customs, the Scenes and the Scenery of the Holy Land. By W. M. THOMSON, D.D., Twenty-five Years a Missionary of the A.B.C.F.M. in Syria and Palestine. With Two elaborate Maps of Palestine, an accurate Plan of Jerusalem, and *Several Hundred Engravings*, representing the Scenery, Topography, and Productions of the Holy Land, and the Costumes, Manners, and Habits of the People. Two large 12mo Volumes, Cloth, $5 00.

VÁMBÉRY'S CENTRAL ASIA. Travels in Central Asia: being the Account of a Journey from Teheran across the Turkoman Desert, on the Eastern Shore of the Caspian, to Khiva, Bokhara, and Samarcand, performed in the Year 1863. By ARMINIUS VÁMBÉRY, Member of the Hungarian Academy of Pesth, by whom he was sent on this Scientific Mission. With Map and Woodcuts. 8vo, Cloth, $4 50.

VIRGINIA ILLUSTRATED: containing a Visit to the Virginian Canaan, and the Adventures of Porte Crayon and his Cousins. Illustrated from Drawings by PORTE CRAYON. 8vo, Cloth, $3 50.

WALLACE'S MALAY ARCHIPELAGO. The Malay Archipelago: the Land of the Orang-Utan and the Bird of Paradise. A Narrative of Travel, 1854–'62. With Studies of Man and Nature. By ALFRED RUSSEL WALLACE. With Maps and numerous Illustrations. Crown 8vo, Cloth, $2 50.

ATKINSON'S SIBERIA. Oriental and Western Siberia: a Narrative of Seven Years' Explorations and Adventures in Siberia, Mongolia, the Kirghis Steppes, Chinese Tartary, and Part of Central Asia. By THOMAS WITLAM ATKINSON. With a Map and numerous Illustrations. 8vo, Cloth, $3 50.

BARTH'S NORTH AND CENTRAL AFRICA. Travels and Discoveries in North and Central Africa. Being a Journal of an Expedition undertaken under the Auspices of H. B. M.'s Government, in the Years 1849–1855. By HENRY BARTH, Ph.D., D.C.L. Illustrated. 3 vols., 8vo, Cloth, $12 00.

BALDWIN'S AFRICAN HUNTING. African Hunting, from Natal to the Zambesi, including Lake Ngami, the Kalahari Desert, &c., from 1852 to 1860. By WILLIAM CHARLES BALDWIN, Esq., F.R.G.S. With Map, Fifty Illustrations by Wolf and Zwecker, and a Portrait. 12mo, Cloth, $1 50.

KINGSLEY'S WEST INDIES. At Last: A Christmas in the West Indies. By CHARLES KINGSLEY, Author of "Alton Locke," "Yeast," &c., &c. Illustrated. 12mo, Cloth, $1 50.

www.ingramcontent.com/pod-product-compliance
Lightning Source LLC
LaVergne TN
LVHW021102110826
845150LV00001B/150

* 9 7 8 1 4 2 5 5 6 5 6 4 0 *